EXETER MEDIEVAL TEXTS AND STUDIES

General Editors: Marion Glasscoe and M.J. Swanton

'My Compleinte' and Other Poems
Thomas Hoccleve

edited by Roger Ellis

Thomas Hoccleve (1368–1426) was one of Chaucer's first disciples and is represented in this book by a selection of his works. They have been newly edited from his own copies and fully annotated. The book includes a full Introduction and marginal glosses and presents a complete modern edition of the *Series*, as well as some of Hoccleve's earlier poems. It provides students and other readers new to his work with a clear indication of his range and achievement as original writer and translator. It also offers those more familiar with his work a fuller account than has hitherto been available of the manuscripts of Hoccleve's own texts and, when he was translating from Latin or French, of the manuscripts of his sources.

Some of the themes and topics explored, with Hoccleve's light and witty touch, include women (for them or against them); money (always short of it); isolation and suffering (causes various, but always painful); the pains of hell and the joys of heaven; the serendipitous nature of literary production; the writer as translator, reporter, or even as gossip.

Roger Ellis is a senior lecturer in English at the University of Cardiff.

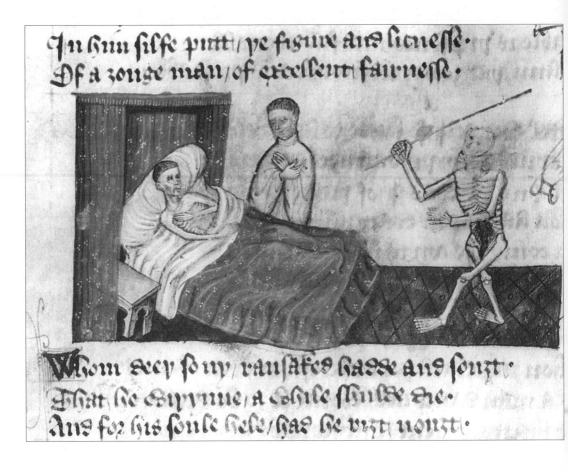

Death and a dying man (Oxford Bodleian Library MS Selden supra 53, f. 118r), reproduced here and on the cover by kind permission of the Bodleian Library.

'My Compleinte' and Other Poems

THOMAS HOCCLEVE

edited by

ROGER ELLIS

UNIVERSITY
of
EXETER
PRESS

First published in 2001 by
University of Exeter Press
Reed Hall, Streatham Drive
Exeter EX4 4QR
UK
www.ex.ac.uk/uep/

British Library Cataloguing in Publication Data
A catalogue record for this book is available
from the British Library.

Paperback ISBN 0 85989 701 X
Hardback ISBN 0 85989 700 1

Typeset in 11pt Plantin Light
by XL Publishing Services, Tiverton

Printed in Great Britain by Short Run Press Ltd, Exeter

Contents

Note to the Reader

Readers new to late medieval poetry will find useful the glosses set in the margins beside the text of the poems; these glosses explain individual words and phrases which may give difficulty. Such readers may also find it helpful to refer to the 'Note on Hoccleve's language' on p. 50.

Textual notes set at the end of each poem help to contextualize some of the ideas expressed in Hoccleve's verse. These notes are also designed to provide more detailed explanation of individual phrases than is possible in the marginal glosses; and to provide detailed instances of general points raised by the Introduction.

Finally, additional commentary and notes, set as individual appendices at the end of the book, explore the different manuscript traditions of Hoccleve's poems, and, where relevant, their sources. They also provide a detailed list of textual variants.

Acknowledgements

At a time when this volume was barely projected, scholars with much more of a stake in the Hoccleve industry than I had, like James Simpson, were generous in support and helped to persuade the publishers (originally Dent Everyman: at length, thanks to the interest of the editors of the *Exeter Medieval Texts* series, University of Exeter Press) that this was a venture worth supporting. It is a pleasure to thank them now for their support. I am also grateful to Diane Speed for helpful information about the Anglo-Latin *Gesta Romanorum*, to John Burrow for drawing my attention to a number of works cited in the bibliography (though I regret that his critical edition of the first two sections of the *Series* for EETS came out too late for me to make more than incidental use of it), and to Catherine Batt, whose detailed and helpful comments on the introduction have made it, I hope, more approachable. Publication of the volume was made possible by a grant from the Modern Humanities Research Association, whose interest in the volume it is a pleasure as well as a duty to acknowledge. I also want to thank my current students for working with me on the book while it was still in typescript and giving me the chance for some last-minute fine tuning. Lastly, I wish to thank the copy-editors and proof-readers at the Press, whose attention to detail has been exemplary.

Permissions to consult and quote from, or otherwise refer to, unpublished manuscript materials in their possession were generously and promptly given by:

The Master and Fellows of Gonville and Caius College, Cambridge

The Master and Fellows, Trinity College, Cambridge

The Syndics of Cambridge University Library

The City Archivist, Coventry City Archives

The University Library, University of Durham

The Trustees of the National Library of Scotland

Lord Salisbury, Hatfield House

The Dean and Chapter of Lichfield Cathedral

The Department of Manuscripts, the British Library

The State Library of Victoria (Melbourne, Australia)

Spencer Collection, The New York Public Library (Astor, Lenox and Tilden Foundations)

Bodleian Library, University of Oxford

The President and Scholars, Corpus Christi College, Oxford

The Master and Fellows of University College, Oxford

The Huntington Library, San Marino, California

Assistant Head of Public Services, the Beinecke Rare Book and Manuscript Library, Yale University.

Sigla of Manuscripts and Other Abbreviations

Sigla of Manuscripts

For comment on asterisked MSS, see references in the Index of MSS in Griffiths and Pearsall 1989.

Ad1	London British Library Additional 9066 (ME *Gesta*, ed. Herrtage)
Ad2	London British Library Additional 22937 (Deguileville's *Pèlerinage*)
Ad3	London British Library Additional 34193 (Hoccleve's 'Conpleynte paramont')
Ad4	London British Library Additional 38120 (Deguileville's *Pèlerinage*)
Ad5	London British Library Additional 44949 (Anglo-Norman 'balade')
Ad6	*London British Library Additional 37049 (ME version of Suso)
B	Oxford Bodleian Library Bodley 221 (Hoccleve's *Series*)
B2	*Oxford Bodleian Library Bodley 638 (Hoccleve's 'Epistre')
B3	Oxford Bodleian Library Bodley 770 (Hoccleve's 'Conpleynte paramont')
B4	Oxford Bodleian Library Bodley 789 (ME version of Suso)
Ba	National Library of Scotland, Advocates' MS 1.1.6 (Bannatyne MS) (Hoccleve's 'Epistre')
C	Coventry City Archives PA 325 (Hoccleve's *Series*)
Ca	Cambridge St John's College G. 5 (Anglo-Norman 'balade')
Ch	*Oxford Christ Church 152 (Hoccleve's 'Item de Beata Virgine', ed. Beatty)
Co	Oxford, Corpus Christi College 237 (Hoccleve's 'Conpleynte paramont')
D	*Durham University Library Cosin V.iii.9 (Hoccleve's *Series*, holograph except for ll. 1-652)
D1	*Oxford Bodleian Library Digby 181 (Hoccleve's 'Epistre')
D2	*Oxford Bodleian Library Digby 185 (Hoccleve's *Gesta* narratives)
D3	Durham, University Library Cosin V.ii.13 (Hoccleve's 'Epistre')
D4	Oxford Bodleian Library Douce 142 (Anglo-Latin *Gesta Romanorum*)
D5	Oxford Bodleian Library Douce 310 (Anglo-Latin *Gesta Romanorum*)
D6	Oxford Bodleian Library Douce 322 (chapter on dying from *The Seven Poyntes* and compilation entitled *Orilogium Sapientie*)
E	Oxford Bodleian Library Eng.poet.d.4 (Hoccleve's *Gesta* narratives)
Eg	*London British Library Egerton 615 (Hoccleve's 'Conpleynte paramont')
F	*Oxford Bodleian Library Fairfax 16 (Hoccleve's 'Epistre')
G	Cambridge Gonville and Caius College 124/61 (Hoccleve's 'Conpleynte paramont')

*H	the agreement of non-holograph MS copies of Hoccleve's works
H	Hatfield House MS Cecil 270 (Hoccleve's 'Conpleynte paramont')
H1	San Marino Huntington Library MS 111 (Hoccleve holograph)
H2	*San Marino Huntington Library MS 744 (Hoccleve holograph)
Ha1	London British Library Harley 172 (Hoccleve's Suso)
Ha2	London British Library Harley 2270 (Anglo-Latin *Gesta Romanorum*)
Ha3	London British Library Harley 5259 (Anglo-Latin *Gesta Romanorum*)
Ha4	London British Library Harley 5369 (Anglo-Latin *Gesta Romanorum*)
Ha5	*London British Library Harley 7333 (ME *Gesta Romanorum*, ed. Herrtage)
L	Oxford Bodleian Library Laud Misc. 735 (Hoccleve's *Series*)
Li	Lichfield Cathedral Library 16
M	Melbourne, Victoria State Library 096/G94 (Hoccleve's 'Conpleynte paramont')
N	*New York, Public Library MS Spencer 19 (Hoccleve's 'Conpleynte paramont')
R	*London British Library Royal 17 D vi (Hoccleve's Suso and *Gesta* narratives)
R2	London British Library Royal 20 B iii (Anglo-Norman 'balade')
S	*Oxford Bodleian Library Selden Supra 53 (Hoccleve's *Series*)
S2	*Oxford Bodleian Library Selden B.24 (Hoccleve's 'Epistre')
Sl	London British Library Sloane 4029 (Anglo-Latin *Gesta Romanorum*)
T	*Oxford Bodleian Tanner 346 (Hoccleve's 'Epistre')
Th	Chaucer's Works, edited by Thynne 1532 (and, virtually unaltered, 1541, 1562) (edition of Hoccleve's 'Epistre')
Tr1	*Cambridge Trinity College R.3.20 (Hoccleve's 'Epistre')
Tr2	*Cambridge Trinity College R.3.21 (Hoccleve's 'Item de Beata Virgine')
U	*Cambridge University Library Ff.i.6 (Hoccleve's 'Epistre')
U2	Cambridge University Library Kk.i.7 (Hoccleve's 'Conpleynte paramont')
Un	Oxford University College 181 (Hoccleve's 'Conpleynte paramont')
Y	New Haven Yale University 493 (Hoccleve's *Series*)

Other Abbreviations

Apoc.	(New Testament) Apocalypse (or Revelation) of St John
Cantic.	(Old Testament) Song of Songs
ClT	Chaucer's *Clerk's Tale*
1 Cor.	(New Testament) 1 Corinthians
CT	*The Canterbury Tales*
Deut.	(Old Testament) Deuteronomy
Eccles.	(Old Testament) Ecclesiastes
Ecclus.	(Apocrypha) Ecclesiasticus
EETS	Early English Text Society
ES	Extra Series

Exod.	(Old Testament) Exodus
Ezek.	(Old Testament) Ezekiel
Fr.	the French of Hoccleve's sources, where appropriate
FrkT	Chaucer's *Franklin's Tale*
Gen.	(Old Testament) Genesis
Is.	(Old Testament) Isaiah
Jer.	(Old Testament) Jeremiah
Lam.	(Old Testament) Lamentations
LGW	Chaucer's *Legend of Good Women*
MÆv	*Medium Ævum*
Matt.	(New Testament) Matthew
MED	The Middle English Dictionary
MerchT	Chaucer's *Merchant's Tale*
MkT	Chaucer's *Monk's Tale*
MLT	Chaucer's *Man of Law's Tale*
NPT	Chaucer's *Nun's Priest's Tale*
OED	The Oxford English Dictionary
OS	Original Series
Pet.	(New Testament) Peter
PF	Chaucer's *Parlement of Foules*
PG	Patrologia Graeca
Phil.	(New Testament) Philippians
PL	Patrologia Latina
PMLA	*Publications of the Modern Language Association*
ProlWBT	Chaucer's *Prologue to the Wife of Bath's Tale*
Prov.	(Old Testament) Proverbs
Ps.	(Old Testament) Psalms
Regement	Hoccleve's *Regement of Princes* (Furnivall 1897)
SAC	*Studies in the Age of Chaucer*
Sam.	(Old Testament) the two Books of Samuel
SCH	*Studies in Church History*
WBT	Chaucer's *Wife of Bath's Tale*

Introduction

This volume includes a selection of the works of Thomas Hoccleve (*c*.1367–1426), one of the most attractive, but also, until recently, one of the more neglected, figures of late Middle English literature.

I   Foreword

The volume started life as an edition of the *Series* (as it is called), Hoccleve's major contribution to the genre of the framed narrative collection. Even after I added a number of minor poems, in response to requests for a volume which could better introduce the poetry of Hoccleve to students, the *Series* remained, in length and interest, the chief text of the volume.* Consequently, though the other poems have their own interpretative notes, they figure much less prominently in the Introduction, and are discussed here, for the most part, only in relation to the questions more generally raised by the *Series*.

Readers coming to Hoccleve for the first time may find some of the material in the Introduction and Notes, as well as in the Appendices, not immediately amenable to their literary interests. They may feel daunted by the many Latin quotations, many of them provided by Hoccleve himself, which I have transcribed from the margins of the manuscript copies of his work. We are well used to marginal notes as an aid to interpretation in editions of medieval texts (witness, indeed, the textual glosses I provide for the texts of this edition). Marginalia were also extensively used in the Middle Ages to gloss authoritative Latin works. So, in principle, Hoccleve's marginalia provide a valuable interpretative tool. I say 'in principle' because authors frequently use notes not just to gloss their own texts but also to make claims about their own status, and sometimes even to satirize the whole drive to provide an authoritative interpretation of those texts. (Think, for example, of the glosses provided by T.S. Eliot for his *Waste Land*,

---

*   In the Introduction and the Notes to the present work, Roman numerals (I–VI) before line numbers refer to the minor poems edited here in addition to the *Series*; Roman VII followed by Arabic numerals refers to the main sections of the *Series*.

or Coleridge for his *Rime of the Ancient Mariner*; nearer Chaucer's own time, think of the wonderful way in which Boccaccio plays with the conventions of textual glosses in the margins of his *Teseida*.) The glosses, then, are not a straight-forward key to the interpretation of Hoccleve's texts; but they are well worth persevering with.

Beginning readers may also feel that, at least in the middle sections of the Introduction, the attention I give to minute differences of detail between Hoccleve's own copies of his own work, and those of later scribes, obscures the very literary ground on which they themselves need to build. Readers who perse-vere with those sections of the Introduction (III–V) will find that material treated there, in passing, is often developed more fully in the later, more straightfor-wardly literary, sections (VIII–IX). This might suggest to them that, if they preferred, they could, in Chaucer's phrase, 'turne over the leef', and focus simply on the later parts of the Introduction, as also on those notes addressing specif-ically literary matters.

I urge them *not* to do so. The poems edited here all survive in copies made by Hoccleve himself (i.e. holographs), and have been edited here from those copies. Nevertheless, as the Introduction argues, material in the other, non-holograph, copies often derives from earlier drafts by Hoccleve that have not survived. Consequently, as with Langland's various versions of *Piers Plowman* or Chaucer's two attempts at the Prologue to *The Legend of Good Women*, study of all the manuscript evidence offers a fuller view of Hoccleve's poetic processes than would otherwise be possible. If medieval writers regularly rework their texts, and those who copy their texts do the same, the medieval text is always, in the fullest sense possible, work in progress. (This understanding of the unavoidable provisionality attaching to the production of a text in the Middle Ages has echoes, of course, much nearer our own time, in post-modern literary experiments and theorizings.)

And this fact carries two further consequences of great importance for the study of medieval literature. First, except in purely formal terms, it proves almost impossible to distinguish the roles of author and scribe in the production of a medieval text. As Minnis has shown, St Bonaventura offered a model of literary activity under four headings of increasing sophistication: first, the scribe, the one who copies another person's text without adding anything; then the compiler, the person who combines existing texts and adds no original material; then, the commentator, who adds original material, by way of commentary, to the original text; lastly, the author, who shifts the balance between original and derivative material decisively in favour of the former.[1] Like Chaucer, and for much the same reasons, Hoccleve carefully claims for himself only the humblest literary role, akin to that of the scribe. To see Hoccleve *and* the copyists of his work in action is, however, to see this claim exposed as the fiction it is. In the same way, the totality of scribal involvement in Hoccleve's work critiques any simple-minded understanding of literature which privileges one literary function, the work of the author, over another, the work of the copyist.

Second, medieval literature is also work in progress across, as well as within, languages. So much medieval literature is translated from texts in other European vernaculars that the translator, as a function of the text, can be mapped onto the Bonaventuran grid, and the translator can be seen variously exercising all of St Bonaventura's roles all the way from that of scribe, when s/he translates as close to word-for-word as possible, to that of author, when a completely new work results from the act of translation. (Thinking only of writing in Latin, St Bonaventura did not feel the need to include translation in his list of scribal activities, though other writers do offer definitions of translation, and translation was the subject of lively debate, throughout the Middle Ages.[2]) Given a long-standing prejudice against translated works and in favour of original writing, as I note later in the Introduction, we need to keep clearly in view the very positive attitudes in practice to translation generally current in the Middle Ages.

Central to all of these processes, it can readily be inferred, is the question of interpretation. Whether acting as scribe, as author, or as translator, the writer is always interpreting, and interpreting for a fictional or actual reader, the texts on which s/he is working. (And the *Series* provides yet further interpretative aids for the reader in the shape of a Friend who can debate with the poet about the purposes and effects of literary activity.) The medieval text, then, exists as a point of reference in an evolving field which includes medieval, and modern, writers and readers.

I should not wish the foregoing remarks to suggest to the beginning reader that Hoccleve is hard work. Quite the opposite. The *Series* comes across to the reader as directly as anything Chaucer wrote. Even though it cannot match the range of voices and topics in Chaucer's major narrative collection, and wants the latter's organizing idea of pilgrimage as analogue for story-telling and a justification for excess, it does not suffer from comparison with *The Canterbury Tales*. In the *Series*, and in other quasi-autobiographical poems like the 'Male Regle', Hoccleve is as immediately approachable as a poetic persona as Chaucer. Indeed, Hoccleve's 'character'—by which I mean the complex relation between the persona of the narrator and his total environment, literary, political and social—becomes not only the formal occasion but also the informing principle of much of his poetry. It helps to know how much this character depends on existing literary models, especially the works of Chaucer. Consequently, the Introduction, and the Notes, regularly consider Hoccleve's debts to, and reworkings of, Chaucerian material. Nevertheless, Hoccleve's distinctive, and attractively lop-sided, slant on those models can be savoured without explicit knowledge of them.

I further argue in the closing pages of this Introduction for Hoccleve as a playfully comic and wittily conceived writer. (If he owes his sense of comedy in part to Chaucer, Hoccleve nevertheless goes further than Chaucer in his feeling for and use of the conceit.) Since I have always enjoyed—as, it is clear, medieval readers enjoyed—the broad-brush strokes of anti-feminist comedy, which colours three sections of the *Series*, I have deliberately included in the anthology Hoccleve's major exercise in (anti-)anti-feminism, the 'Epistre de Cupide'. I have also included, as his most impressive religious piece, a translation from Deguileville's *Pèlerinage*, which allows the reader to savour an understanding of wit, as intellectual dexterity, that links Hoccleve to other religious writers like Langland and, in the seventeenth century, the metaphysical poets.

Hoccleve's interest for students of medieval literature, then, is considerable. The Chaucerian link is readily established: Hoccleve knew Chaucer personally, as he acknowledges in his major work, *The Regement of Princes* (c.1411–12);[3] he may even have written some of the link passages in *The Canterbury Tales*.[4] Scribes copied his work into anthologies of Chaucerian literature, and sometimes ascribed his works to Chaucer; for example, one manuscript copy of *The Canterbury Tales* assigns to the Plowman-pilgrim Hoccleve's narrative of a miracle of the Virgin ('item de beata Virgine', no. V in this anthology); the scribe of the Bannatyne manuscript and the sixteenth-century editor Thynne both thought Chaucer had written Hoccleve's 'Epistre de Cupide' [Letter of Cupid].[5] Such mistakes are easy to understand. The *Series* clearly recalls *The Canterbury Tales* and Chaucer's earlier experiment with a framed narrative collection, *The Legend of Good Women*, or even *The House of Fame*.[6] Like Chaucer, too, Hoccleve contributed to an on-going literary culture which depended on, and looked for the patronage of, the greatest people in the land, including, most strikingly, King Henry V and his immediate family.

Also like Chaucer, and in common with many other writers at the close of the Middle Ages, Hoccleve is engagingly self-conscious about his own status as writer, in ways that anticipate the English Renaissance and hark back to the Italian Renaissance in the previous century. And Hoccleve shares with Chaucer a preoccupation with the accurate transmission and interpretation of a writer's own texts. For Hoccleve this resulted, excitingly, in three holograph copies of his minor poems. Moreover, one of his minor works, the 'ars vtillissima [*sic*] sciendi mori' [Most useful art of learning to die], has survived in two holograph versions, and so gives us the chance to see a poet at work revising his text. Additionally, two of the holograph manuscripts may originally have formed part of a single collection, something resembling a Collected Shorter Poems. . . [and] represent a novelty in the record of [medieval] English poetry: a single-author collection of poems gathered, ordered and copied by the poet himself.[7]

Hoccleve's work has further interest for the reader, in its explicit engagement with the immediate personal circumstances of the poet and the wider social context of his work. Here the contrast with the work of Chaucer is striking. Hoccleve spent his working life as a London-based civil servant, a clerk at the Office of the Privy Seal, and was as ready as Chaucer was reluctant to make his own story the subject of his poetry. From his pages we learn of a mis-spent youth, of a marriage which put paid to chances of ecclesiastical advancement, of constant financial worries, and (c.1414) of a nervous breakdown which exposed the poet to gossip even after he had recovered. We also learn, from Hoccleve's regular reference in his work to his noble readers, of his hopes for their patronage. That he makes so much more of his courtly connections in his poetry than Chaucer did suggests his greater personal insecurity: certainly his lower position in the social pecking order.

Conventional much of this material may be. The convention of soliloquy, for instance, which gives so much point to Hoccleve's writing, especially the first item in the *Series* ('My Compleinte'), has precedent in the *Confessions* of St Augustine and the *Meditations* of St Anselm. Again, the convention of dialogue-as-(self)-discovery, so prominent a feature of the Prologue to the *Regement* and the second item of the *Series* (the 'Dialogue'), as indeed of the whole narrative frame of the *Series*, has precedent in the *Consolatio Philosophiae* of Boethius (d. 524), and, closer to Hoccleve's own time, in the *Horologium Sapientiae* (? 1334) of Henry Suso, of which Hoccleve himself translated a chapter (the already-noted 'ars vtillissima'). Consequently, some critics have argued against reading any Hoccleve text as a simple reflection of the poet's own life. The opposing school of thought argues that poets always write conventionally; that convention is the condition of personal expression; and that, by and large, where Hoccleve's assertions about himself can be checked, they are accurate.[8] Hoccleve's self-presentation witnesses to a growing interest in the discovery and representation of the individual in the later Middle Ages. His writing therefore becomes another place where we can chart the move from the Middle Ages to the Renaissance.

We must not forget, though, the light touch with which Hoccleve lays himself bare to our scrutiny. If soliloquy is fundamentally serious, a mark of the divided self, dialogue is in principle comic, and there is plenty of comedy in Hoccleve's writing, both when he engages in dialogue with a fictional friend in the frame of the *Series*, and when, like Chaucer's Clerk, he enters into debate with fictional readers and actual authors of the works he is translating.

But there is more. Hoccleve was ready, as Chaucer was not, to refer directly in his poetry to the troubled and dangerous times in which he lived. Hence he writes both about developments in what would become known as the Hundred Years War with France (*Regement* 5286–397, *Series* VII.2.566–76, 610–16), and about the challenges posed nearer home, to both Church and state, by the growth of the Lollard heresy and its spread of Wycliffite ideas, and also by reaction to the deposition of Richard II, and the usurpation of the former's crown by Henry IV, in 1399.[9] His public support for conservative religious and political positions was an almost inevitable consequence of his involvement in the machinery of a government which, under Henry IV and still more under Henry V, had identified the Church's interests with its own.[10] This gives a characteristic flavour to his work which may not at first find favour with a modern reader. For example, Hoccleve praises Henry V for bringing the deposed King Richard's bones to Westminster for proper burial in 1413. He does not consider the political implications of Henry's decision: rather, he uses them to comment on the King's religious spirit, and to urge him to remain the champion of orthodoxy against the Lollards.[11] But, as recent studies are showing, it is possible to read Hoccleve less straightforwardly: at the very least, his personal situation interacts eccentrically with his desire to function, like his contemporary Lydgate, as an apologist for religious orthodoxy and social conservatism. However we approach the evidence, Hoccleve's writing does not completely succeed in its attempts to paper over its own cracks.

II   Previous editions; the scope of the present edition

It is regrettable, then, that the texts on which the poet's growing reputation depends are so difficult to get hold of. They have been available, complete, only in the Early English Text Society (EETS) editions of Furnivall (1892, 1897) and Gollancz (1925). Mitchell and Doyle reissued the first and third of these volumes, with corrections, in a single EETS volume, as *The Minor Poems* (1970). More recently (1968), the major work in the first Furnivall volume, the *Series*, appeared in a dissertation by Pryor. None of these editions carries much information in the way of explanatory footnotes. To be sure, Furnivall included a selection of variant readings from the non-holograph copies of some of the works, and he edited one work, the 'Epistre de Cupide', from a non-holograph copy, but without offering any account of the relation of the manuscripts to each other.

Recent editions of selections by O'Donoghue (1982) and Seymour (1981) have provided more in the way of commentary; in particular, Seymour's notes include important general comments about the complex situation of Hoccleve texts which survive in both holograph and non-holograph copies. But since both editions were aiming to introduce the whole of Hoccleve's work to readers, they were forced to include extracts from both the *Regement* and the *Series*, which gave no very satisfactory idea of either work. More recently, in 1990, Fenster and Erler edited, with a fuller commentary, Hoccleve's 'Epistre de Cupide', alongside the text he was translating, Christine de Pizan's *Epistre au dieu d'amours* (1399) [Epistle of the God of Love]. While acknowledging the existence of the other copies of Hoccleve's translation, however, Fenster and Erler used only the holograph version of the 'Epistre' for their edition. Still more recently, we have had Burrow's (1999) edition of the first two items in the *Series* for EETS. This very scholarly work provides much important information about the relation of the non-holograph copies to one another and to the Hoccleve holograph, and uses Hoccleve's scribal practices elsewhere in the holographs to reconstruct his text where his own copy of it has been lost (the whole of the first item of the *Series* and ll. 1–252 of the second survive in the holograph only in a sixteenth-century copy). But, in so restricting its field of vision, Burrow's work cannot give beginning readers any very clear or easy sense of the scope or significance of the whole work. There is, then, a case to be made—and the Introduction will be making it—for an edition which includes complete texts and also considers, where relevant, all the surviving copies.

Of course, the decision to include only complete texts in this volume, and the consequent exclusion of the *Regement*, mean that this selection is also partial as an introduction to Hoccleve. Of the several poetic genres which Hoccleve attempted, the one to which the *Regement* formally belongs, of advice to princes about the best way to govern themselves and their subjects—a genre of pressing relevance in the turbulent early years of the century, as Ferster's recent study has shown—is present in this anthology only back-handedly, and by implication, when Hoccleve tells us in the 'Dialoge' (VII.2.561–5) that he has decided *not* to attempt the translation of a manual on the art of warfare for King Henry V's brother, Humphrey Duke of Gloucester, since the latter knows much more about that art than Hoccleve could teach him. Another major theme, also occurring in the *Regement* and prominent in a number of poems addressed to, or connected with, royalty, is also present here only incidentally: that is, the need for the King to take firm action against the spread of heresy. In other words, this volume does not make much of the specifically political and historical dimension of Hoccleve's work. For that matter, were I now starting afresh on this project, I should be looking to include Hoccleve's letter to the Wycliffite rebel

Oldcastle, for its explicit evocation of the dangerous times in which Hoccleve was writing; as also Hoccleve's wonderfully funny roundel in mock-praise of an ugly mistress (a tradition still active when Shakespeare wrote his sonnet 130 and Donne his 'The Anagram'). But if this anthology encourages the reader to go beyond its confines to the other works of Hoccleve, and in particular *The Regement of Princes*, it will, I think, have served its turn.

And it *does* represent fairly directly a thread which regularly informs Hoccleve's address to the prince, and which figures in much of Hoccleve's minor work: that is, the poet's preoccupation with his own dire financial straits, and hope of being rewarded, if not for his good advice, then for his displays of wit. These preoccupations surface in the wittily semi-autobiographical 'Male Regle' (no. II) addressed to the head of the Exchequer, Lord Furnival, and 'Balade et chanceon' (no. III) addressed to the Under-Treasurer of the Exchequer, Henry Somer.[12]

In another respect, too, the present selection gives a good indication of the range of Hoccleve's work. It includes some of Hoccleve's more striking religious compositions: the 'Conpleynte paramont' (no. I), an allegorized lament by the Virgin Mary at the foot of the Cross; a prayer to the crucified Christ and the Virgin Mary (no. IV); the earlier-noted miracle of the Blessed Virgin; two moralized allegories (nos. VII.3, 5) from that huge repository of medieval romance, the *Gesta Romanorum* [Deeds of the Roman Emperors], the first a loose analogue to Chaucer's *Man of Law's Tale*, the second the story of the moral education of the prodigal youngest son of a Roman Emperor; the previously-noted translation from Suso about preparing for one's own death (no. VII.4). It cannot be denied that religious literature is an acquired taste these days: still more, literature about preparing for one's death. At the same time, as I hope these pages will show, literary expressions of religious beliefs are a taste worth acquiring.

The modern reader may also need to overcome initial resistance, as earlier implied, to another feature of the texts which, yet again, they share with Chaucer's work: several of them are translations or include translated material. We have already noted Hoccleve's translations of work by major writers (Suso and Christine de Pizan), and from the anonymous but equally important *Gesta Romanorum*. Hoccleve's 'Conpleynte paramont' is also a translation, this time from the influential *Pèlerinage de l'âme* [Pilgrimage of the soul] (*c.*1358) by Guillaume de Deguileville. Medieval writers like Chaucer and Hoccleve appear to defer to our prejudice in favour of original works when they describe translation as little more than the copying of a text from one language into another. In the Prologue to *The Legend of Good Women*, for instance, Chaucer defends his translations of Boccaccio's *Il Filostrato*, and of *Le roman de la rose* by Guillaume de Lorris and Jean de Meun, on the grounds that the translator has no creative input in his translation and cannot be held responsible for any offence caused (*Legend* G-Prol. 340–52).[13] By this light, Chaucer as translator was functioning exactly like the Chaucerian narrator of *The Canterbury Tales*, a humble scribe who must faithfully report the bawdy tales told during the Canterbury pilgrimage if he does not wish to 'falsen' his matter (*CT* I.725–42, 3170–5). In his 'Dialoge', Hoccleve takes up a similar line to defend himself against the charge of anti-feminism in his translation of Christine's *Epistre*. He borrows terms from the translation debate in *The Canterbury Tales* ('reherce', 'reportour');[14] he also recalls the general situation of the *Legend*, in order to defend his translation of Christine's *Epistre* against misreading:

therof was I noon auctour.	*author*
I nas in þat cas but a reportour	
Of folkes tales. As they seide, I wroot.	
I nat affermed it on hem, God woot.	*against*
Whoso þat shal reherce a mannes sawe	*recite; words*
As þat he seith moot he seyn and nat varie,	*the one. . . the other*
For, and he do, he dooth ageyn the lawe	*if*
Of trouthe. He may tho wordes nat contrarie. . .	*those; oppose*
Whan I it spak I spak conpleynyngly.	*in the style of a complaint*
I to hem thoghte no repreef ne shame. . . .	*wished them; reproof*
The book concludith for hem, is no nay. . .	*undoubtedly*
(VII.2.759–67, 772–3, 779).	

I shall have more to say about this passage later, but it would be a mistake to take it too seriously. In a culture which prized Latin learning as much as medieval culture did, and restricted the label of author to established and usually long-dead writers, vernacular writers trying to carve out a space for themselves could not do much more, publicly, than to adopt, like Chaucer and Hoccleve, the humbler roles of scribe/*reportour* and compiler, or the slightly more elevated role of commentator.[15] But in so describing themselves, Chaucer and Hoccleve were also, indirectly, advertising their work and laying claim to the same status that their predecessors enjoyed. Consequently, we do well to remember that for Hoccleve, as for Chaucer before him, the distinction between translated and original writing—between the 'enditour' and the 'translatour', as Hoccleve himself puts it, in his 'Inuocacio ad Patrem'—is not regularly observed in practice.[16] Like Chaucer before him, Hoccleve is able to make much in his work of the confusion of literary roles available to him. Here, too, Hoccleve makes common cause with modern theorists of literature and translation who are attempting to undermine what Frantzen has criticized as 'desire for origins', and Eagleton 'the fetish of the primary text'.[17]

III   The holographs

Our account of Hoccleve's minor poetry needs to begin with the reiteration of an obvious point. Most of the minor poems survive only in the holograph manuscripts made near the end of Hoccleve's life. Hoccleve produced the first of them, Durham University Library Cosin V.III.9, hereafter D, sometime in the period 1419–21; a marginal note to VII.2.543, to be discussed in more detail later, shows that he was still working on the manuscript as late as April 1422. This holograph contains one work, the *Series*, which also survives, in whole or in part, in ten later manuscript copies. The *Series* is a framed narrative collection which, as edited by Furnivall from the holograph, includes the following items: 'My Compleinte', 'A Dialoge', the first of the moralized *Gesta* narratives, the translation from Suso's *Horologium*, and the second moralized *Gesta* narrative. Completing the Suso translation is another brief translation of material from a reading for All Saints' Day. Mills has recently called this work 'Joys of Heaven', after its subject-matter,[18] but whether or not we should regard it as a separate item in the holograph is not certain, and a better title might be that offered by Bale (1559: 537) and followed by Pits and the annotators of D and Y, 'De caelesti Jerusalem' [concerning the heavenly Jerusalem].

Pryor speculates that Hoccleve composed the *Series* in two stages, first as a shorter collection for the Duke of Gloucester, without the second *Gesta* narrative, and then, with the second *Gesta* narrative added, as an enlarged collection for the Countess of Westmoreland, an aunt by marriage of the Duke.[19] Whether or not this is so, it is clear, as we shall see, that Hoccleve produced at least two versions of the second item in the *Series*, the 'Dialoge': he may then have produced this second version, along with the rest of the *Series*, for the Countess of Westmoreland, for whom he ends the work in D, though not in the non-holograph copies of the work, with a verse dedication. As we shall see, other texts in the *Series* have also undergone revision, perhaps when Hoccleve was preparing the *Series* for submission to the Countess. Since the 'Dialoge' includes complimentary reference to the Duke of Gloucester, it is possible that Hoccleve originally intended that work, and the *Series* as a whole, for him.[20]

The *Series* owes its shape, in part, to the structure of the poet's earlier work, the *Regement*. In the Prologue to the *Regement*, a solitary narrator meets by chance with, and is helped by, a beggar. Similarly, the first two items of the *Series* show a solitary narrator unable to escape from memories of mental disorder and social rejection—he writes them up compulsively, and they become the first item of the collection ('My Compleinte')—and then, as a result of his meeting with a friend ('A Dialoge'), enabled to break free from them and start writing for a wider audience once more. Between the second half of the *Regement* and the remaining items of the *Series* there is also a parallel of sorts. In the former, Hoccleve gives advice to the future Henry V, in part through exemplary narratives. In the latter, narratives of a formally edifying cast also figure prominently. And, of course, as earlier noted (n. 7 above), the *Regement* was regularly linked with the *Series* in non-holograph copies. By contrast with the public agenda of the *Regement*, though, the *Series* has a primarily domestic and personal frame of reference.

D predates by at least a few months, possibly more, Hoccleve's production of the other holographs, California Huntington Library HM 111 and 744, hereafter H1 and H2. We can date these by references, in the titles of several of the poems copied into them, to the death of Henry V,[21] which means that the copies must have been written after the King's death on 31 August 1422.

H2 begins with hymns to God, Christ, the Holy Spirit and the Virgin, and continues with the previously-noted miracle of the Virgin (no. V), but follows this religious beginning with comedy, Hoccleve's version of Christine's *Epistre* (no. VI) and three comic 'chaunceons', then with an interspersed 'Balade' in praise of Henry V, and lastly with an offering of a very different colour, a 'lesson of heuynesse', the second holograph copy of Hoccleve's Suso translation. This collection gives a good indication of the overall range of Hoccleve's verse, and seems to have no clearer principle of organization than might be suggested by the voice-over introduction to 'Monty Python's Flying Circus' ('and now for something completely different'): the logic, say, of fragment VII of *The Canterbury Tales*.

Hoccleve structured H1 more clearly about the, generally, noble readers who commissioned his work—for example, the Countess of Hereford, Henry V's aunt, who commissioned the Deguileville translation—or to whom the poet directed poems of praise and petition, and, in the case of a poem to the Lollard rebel Sir John Oldcastle, admonition. Yet here too he also addressed poems to the Virgin Mary with no clear reason discoverable for their inclusion.[22]

Equally striking about both H1 and H2 is the fact that Hoccleve composed many of the poems included in them some years earlier: the Deguileville translation before 1413, the date when a translation of the complete *Pèlerinage* was completed; the translation from Christine de Pizan in 1402 (VI.476); the 'Male Regle' in 1405–6.[23] Consequently, we have to allow for the fact that when he made these later copies of his own works he was acting as editor of them. Possibly too, when non-holograph copies of a Hoccleve text exist, they witness to an earlier stage in the composition and transmission of the works: so their evidence may give a fuller picture of Hoccleve's literary activity than we should be able to discover just from the holographs. In any case, even where their readings are scribal rather than authorial, they can usefully show how early readers interpreted Hoccleve's poetry. Where, therefore, more than one copy survives of any of the texts edited here, I have considered the evidence of all of them, even though, like earlier editors, I have edited from the holographs and emended only where necessary.[24]

IV   On Hoccleve's scribes

On the face of it, the study of textual relationships does not look a very promising introduction to a volume of poetry. But it is necessary to remind ourselves that the status—the very idea—of a text in a pre-print culture is much more fluid, and more obviously fluid, than that of a printed text. (I say 'obviously' because even printed texts like the novels of Hardy or the plays of Shakespeare do not enjoy as absolute and fixed an identity as we might think.) Consequently, we need to see a Hoccleve poem not so much as a finished product, even when the author has produced the copy himself, but more as a snapshot of an on-going literary process: a point in the complex field of literary relationships constituted by the totality of scribal and readerly activity connected with the work which, for the sake of convenience, we call a poem.[25] And when the Hoccleve text is itself translated from another text, we have to reckon with the further intersection of (interference from) another complex field of literary relationships. We need therefore to attend to the total manuscript situation of both Hoccleve's source texts and his translations in order to speak with certainty about the poetry of Hoccleve.

When a translated work survives only in a single holograph copy, and its original likewise only in a single copy, we have no option but to take the two texts at face value. We are not so fortunate with Hoccleve's translations, most of which survive in several copies. Fortunately, fewer than a dozen copies survive of each of Hoccleve's 'Conpleynte paramont', 'Epistre', and *Series*, and consequently the task of mapping those texts, though laborious, is not impossible. Nor is it impossibly difficult to map the manuscript traditions of the texts from which Hoccleve translated the 'Balade' for Robert Chichele (IV) and the 'Epistre' (VI): the former survives in one complete and two partial copies; the latter, Christine's *Epistre*, in only six. The originals, however, of other texts here edited—the anonymous *Gesta Romanorum*, the *Horologium Sapientiae* of Henry Suso, the *Pèlerinage de l'âme* of Guillaume de Deguileville—survive in very many more copies, and even when the field of inquiry is restricted to copies known to have circulated in England, and even when modern editions exist, the task is, quite simply, huge.[26]

Yet the challenge must be faced, if we wish to avoid partiality and sometimes even error in what we say about the poems. Consider, for example, the first of the *Gesta* narratives in the *Series*. The only critical study thus far to consider this work in any detail, that by Mitchell, compared Hoccleve's copy in D with a Latin version of the story in MS London British Library Harley 2270 (Ha2), 'the most complete manuscript of the Anglo-Latin *Gesta*'. In so privileging Ha2, Mitchell was following an earlier edition, by Wallensköld, of the version of the text in Ha2. The latter had included the Ha2 version, without its concluding moralization, as part of a project to record versions of the medieval legend of the Roman Empress who preserved her chastity against repeated attempt from would-be seducers. In choosing Ha2, Wallensköld seems to have been following the view of J.A. Herbert, when he catalogued the romances in the British Library manuscript collections, that Ha2 was the best copy of a major group of manuscripts produced in England from the fourteenth century onwards.[27] Clearly, Hoccleve *could* have used this manuscript. But the 'best representative' of a manuscript tradition, or, in Mitchell's words, the 'most complete manuscript of the Anglo-Latin *Gesta*', is not necessarily, or self-evidently, Hoccleve's source;[28] still less is a modern printed edition a self-evidently trustworthy source.[29] Consider, for example, the opening words of the tale as preserved in Ha2:

> Menelaus in ciuitate Romana regnauit, qui filiam regis Hungarie in vxorem accepit, que erat pulcra et operibus misericordie plena [Menelaus reigned in the city of Rome, and married the daughter of the King of Hungary. She was beautiful and full of the works of mercy]

Here is the version preserved in MS Oxford Bodleian Library Douce 142 (D4) with variants from MSS Oxford Bodleian Library Douce 310 (D5) and London British Library Harley 5369 (Ha4) and Sloane 4039 (Sl):

> Gerelaus (Sl Ierelaus) in ciuitate Romana regnauit (Sl *adds* etc.), prudens valde [very prudent], qui filiam regis Vngarie in vxorem accepit, que erat pulcra, et oculis omnium graciosa [and gracious in the eyes of all], et (D5H4 *add* in omnibus) operibus misericordie (Ha4 *om.* misericordie) plena (Sl plena omni misericordia)

I make no attempt to arbitrate between these versions, but it should be immediately apparent that they provide a fuller version of the text than that in Ha2. For this material Hoccleve's copy in D gives us

In the *Romain actes* writen is thus:	*Gesta Romanorum*
Whilom an emperour in the citee	*once*

Of Roome regned, clept Iereslaus,	*called*
Which his noble estat and hy dignitee	
Gouerned wysly; and weddid had he	
The doghtir of the kyng of Vngarie,	
A fair lady *to euery mannes ye.*	*eye*

And for þat beautee in womman allone	*because*
Withouten bontee is nat commendable,	*goodness*
Shee was therto a vertuous persone,	*in addition*
And specially pitous and merciable	*compassionate and merciful*
In all hir wirkes, which ful couenable	*very fitting*
And pertinent is vnto wommanhede.	*a woman's estate*
Mercy causith good renon fer to sprede.	*reputation; far*
(VII.3.1–14)	

Without the fuller version in D4 and the other manuscripts, we should prob-ably have been forced to conclude that Hoccleve himself came up with the new name for the Emperor, and added the italicized phrase. There is certainly prece-dent for the change to the Emperor's name, in the many different names given to the Emperor in other versions of the story, including Merelaus and Octavianus, to say nothing of Hoccleve's probable readiness to tamper with the name of the prostitute in the second *Gesta* narrative.[30]

There is precedent for the added phrase, similarly, in the tendency of verse translations, medieval and post-medieval, to fill out lines with redundant expres-sions for the sake of rhyme and metre. Characteristically, such material reinforces the meaning of the original by echoing details from it, or draws atten-tion to the translator's mediation of the text by means of asseveration. Hoccleve certainly does this regularly in his translations. The more elaborate the rhyme scheme being followed—as in his translation for Chichele—the more padding that may be needed to secure the rhymes.[31] (To prove the point, we need only compare Hoccleve's prose versions of the moralizations of the *Gesta Romanorum* stories with his verse versions of the stories themselves.)

But the parallel version in D4 shows, on the contrary, that Hoccleve was, in all probability, acting precisely as he said he was when translating Christine's *Epistre*; not as an 'auctour' but simply as 'a reportour/Of folkes tales [a]s they seide' (VII.2.760–2). That is, Hoccleve's text cannot be understood without detailed reference to the textual traditions of the *Gesta Romanorum*, or at least of the Anglo-Latin copies of the work.[32] Admittedly, and regrettably, we have no hard evidence at present to connect Hoccleve's version with any one copy of the Latin—evidence, say, of his ownership of a particular copy of the Latin, or of the existence of a copy of the Latin which precisely mirrors his translation in respect of significant variation. Consequently, we should probably speak of 'analogues' rather than of actual sources for Hoccleve's work: which carries the further consequence that we need to be tentative in pronouncing on Hoccleve as translator and/or editor-critic of his sources. Even when he seems to be producing a reading of the sources which runs counter to them, the remote possibility exists that he is faithfully following a version of the original in which this counter-version first appeared.[33] The conclusions to be advanced in the following paragraphs therefore are probable rather than certain.

But there is still more to be observed about the quoted material. The holograph calls the Emperor 'Iereslaus', which is obviously closer to the 'Gerelaus' of D4 and its variants than to the version in Ha2. But 'Iereslaus' is not as close to 'Gerelaus' as the form found in the non-holograph copies of this text, in all of which the Emperor is called 'Gerelaus'.[34] We have two ways of explaining the discrepancy. The simplest is that the reading 'Gerelaus' derives from a version of Hoccleve's text anterior to D, and that D witnesses to second thoughts by Hoccleve about the Emperor's name.[35]

Of course, it would be foolish to build a whole case on the presence or absence of a single letter in a name prone to modification in the Latin text, and there are numerous instances in other Hoccleve texts where all or a significant number of non-holograph manuscripts share a reading which cannot derive from a version of the text anterior to the holograph, and which witness merely to later scribal activity, deliberate or inadvertent. The most dramatic instance of such scribal activity occurs in connection with Hoccleve's 'Epistre de Cupide', where we can show that six of the non-holograph copies derived from a copy which inadvertently miscopied its own exemplar by displacement of leaves.[36]

In many other instances, too, the holograph readings are closer to those of their sources than those of the other copies. Two examples from Hoccleve's 'Conpleynte paramont' will serve to demonstrate this. In this wonderfully florid lament, the Virgin Mary is begging for help from any and everybody—her ancestors, people who appeared earlier in the Gospel narrative, bystanders at the Crucifixion, the sun, moon and stars and even the earth —to release her son from his cruel torments. In particular, she calls on the woman in Luke 11.27 who once blessed her in her son's presence:

O womman þat among the peple speek,	*spoke*
How þat the wombe blessid was þat beer,	*bore (Christ)*
And the tetes þat yaf to sowken eek	*breasts; gave suck also*
The sone of God, which on hy hangith heer,	
What seist thow now, why comest thow no neer?	*nearer*

> Why n'art thow heer? O womman, wher art thow
> That nat ne seest my woful wombe now?
> (I.43–9)

For the 'wombe' of l. 49, the non-holograph manuscripts offer two readings, 'body' and 'herte'.[37] But 'wombe' must have been the original reading, not only because of the deliberate echo of the earlier line, itself translating the Biblical phrase 'beatus venter' [blessed the womb], but, more simply, because 'ventre' is almost certainly what the copy of Deguileville's text being used by Hoccleve contained.[38]

Similarly, a little later in the lyric, the scribes of several of the non-holograph manuscripts made very heavy weather of an extremely conceited passage in which the Virgin puns on the etymology of her own name. Hoccleve's own copy, by contrast, preserves the Deguileville conceits very accurately:[39]

Of sorwe talke may I nat ynow,	*enough*
Syn fro my name 'I' doon away is now.	*since; taken*
Wel may men clepe and calle me Mara	*call*
From hennesforward, so may men me call.	*henceforward*
How sholde I lenger clept be Maria,	*longer called*
Syn 'I', which is Ihesus, is fro me fall.	*which stands for; fallen*
This day al my swetnesse is into gall	
Torned, syn þat 'I', which was the beautee	*turned; since*
Of my name, this day bynome is me.	*is taken from*
(I.181–9)	

This is wonderfully witty writing, anticipating in the seventeenth century such poems as George Herbert's 'Love-Joy' or 'Jesu'. It focuses principally on the 'I' in Mary's name, which is also the marker to herself of her own selfhood, and at the same time a common manuscript abbreviation for the name of her son Jesus. With the death of her son, therefore, she loses both him and herself, and is left in bitterness, since her name has turned from 'Maria' into 'Mara' (etymologically, 'bitter') with the loss of that 'I'. The scribes of the other copies did not get the point, and mostly produced simpler readings so as to make sense of what they must have seen as a grammatical nonsense: even then, they did not always succeed, as the record of their variants for this line in Appendix 5 will show.

Yet even in the 'Conpleynte paramont', the evidence is not totally in favour of the holograph's readings. Comparison with the French original suggests that both the holograph and the archetype of the *Pilgrimage* copies modified different minor details of Hoccleve's original translation:[40] that is, both descend independently from a common ancestor, and both, in different ways, witness to second thoughts about the best wording for the text. (That is, the version in the holograph shows Hoccleve sometimes revising his original text, at places where the non-holograph copies show the preservation of an earlier version of the translation.) We shall observe this pattern in several of the other translated texts here edited.

In the 'Epistre', for example, we can observe a variation between the holograph and the non-holograph copies in respect of first person pronoun reference in the translation. Christine had used the plural form favoured by royalty at beginning and end of her letter, but in the body of the text had generally preferred the more intimate singular form. The holograph, for the most part, turns these latter into first person plural forms, and creates a fairly consistently royal presence for the speaker throughout. The non-holograph copies, by contrast, preserve the singular form of the pronoun in the middle of the text.[41] The easiest explanation for this variation must be that in copying out his text in the holograph Hoccleve has adapted it: in respect of this form, the non-holograph copies witness better to an earlier version of Hoccleve's text. Hence the inconsistency at VI.221, where the holograph switches from plural to singular pronoun within a single phrase.

It follows that we must take seriously the witness to Hoccleve's text provided by all the manuscripts, holograph and non-holograph alike. That witness, of course, differs from text to text, but a few general points are in order at the outset. (1) D seems to have been more widely read than either of the other holographs. Its copy of the second *Gesta* narrative was used by William Browne in 1614 for his version of the story.[42] Marginal notes indicate at least four later owners and/or readers of the manuscript.[43] Since these notes are absent from the material copied into the manuscript by Stowe in the sixteenth century (the whole of the first item and ll. 1–252 of the second) to replace missing material, it is probable that they predate Stowe's intervention. H1 and H2 attracted no comparable annotations. (2) Subgroups occur within the non-holograph manuscripts, but no one subgroup, much less any single surviving copy of any Hoccleve text, has greater authority than any other for the establishment of Hoccleve's 'first thoughts'. (3) Consequently, I am happiest to use the evidence of the non-holograph manuscripts to establish an earlier version of the text only when they agree unanimously against the holograph version and with the 'source' in respect of significant detail. That agreement, in what follows, I represent by the siglum *H. Since *H has a purely notional existence, I record its forms in modern English.

One text, Hoccleve's translation of the lyric from the Deguileville *Pèlerinage*, the 'Conpleynte paramont', presents problems of a very particular and pressing kind. The non-holograph copies of this work all appear at the appropriate point in a prose translation of the complete *Pèlerinage, The Pilgrimage of the Life of the Soul*, dated 1400/1413.[44] The textual relations of the poem correspond broadly to that of the *Pilgrimage* as a whole. The *Pilgrimage* is a most interesting work, and deserves to be more widely known.[45] In particular, the translation has responded to the formal intricacies of its original by translating into rhyme royal—the same stanza form used by Hoccleve for the 'Conpleynte paramont'— a number of speeches of the original, which it has inserted into the body of the prose translation at the appropriate points. The presence of the Hoccleve poem in the *Pilgrimage* has occasioned considerable debate about whether Hoccleve wrote some or all of the lyrics, or just the 'Conpleynte paramont'; whether, if so, he or another writer inserted them/it into the text of the *Pilgrimage*; or whether he translated the whole Deguileville work and later excerpted the 'Conpleynte paramont' to send it to the Countess of Hereford. As earlier noted, the holograph is generally more authoritative as a witness to Hoccleve's first thoughts than the copies in the *Pilgrimage*, so it would follow that, if Hoccleve translated the whole *Pilgrimage*, he must have revised the text of the 'Conpleynte paramont' when he added the poem to it. On the other hand, the other poems in the translation were almost certainly not written by Hoccleve, which makes it unlikely that he produced the whole work.[46] If so, the translator of the *Pilgrimage* must have known of the existence of Hoccleve's poem, and decided to incorporate it into his work. There is a parallel for this practice in the insertion of a lyric by Chaucer, the 'ABC', also a translation from an earlier Deguileville *Pèlerinage* (this time *Le pèlerinage de la vie de l'homme*), into an anonymous Middle English translation of that work.[47]

Even here, our difficulties with the text of the 'Conpleynte paramont' are not completely over. The holograph copy in H1 ends with a phrase which Hoccleve used elsewhere in H1 and H2 to mark the end of a poem: 'c'est tout'. But the copy of the poem in the *Pilgrimage* continues for another five stanzas, also translated without a break from Deguileville's text. These *might* have been written by Hoccleve, and cut from the version he sent the Countess, but their authorship is sufficiently uncertain to warrant their printing here as Appendix 1.[48]

Fortunately, the other texts do not present such a challenge to the reader. The non-holograph copies do, however, have considerable significance for the study of Hoccleve's works, on both micro- and macro-levels (that is, the levels of verbal detail and larger stucture). So we may now turn to their evidence, alongside that of the holographs, to see what they have to tell us.

V On Hoccleve's two holograph copies of the 'ars vtillissima'

The readiest place to begin, perhaps, is with the Hoccleve text which survives, as earlier noted, in two holograph copies, D and H2, and the seven non-holograph copies B, C, Ha1, L, R, S, and Y: the chapter translated from Suso's *Horologium* on preparing for one's death. Originally H2 looks to have carried a complete copy of the translation: now only ll. 1–672 survive. D positions the copy relative to the overall frame of the *Series* by reference to it in a previous section (VII.2.205–17), which probably indicates that the text had been composed earlier and was now being prepared for inclusion in the *Series*. The Suso text has clear relevance to major themes and structural principles of the *Series* as a whole: and, indeed, of the whole of Hoccleve's work. Its theme of suffering and death, as we shall see, has the force almost of an obsession with Hoccleve. Similarly, its use of framing and framed dialogues—the first between a disciple figure and Lady Wisdom, the second between the disciple and a young man whom the disciple imagines on the point of death—is a favoured structuring device in the work of Hoccleve, especially in the *Series*, and witnesses to Hoccleve's understanding that dialogue can function as a tool of self-discovery. In H2 the copy comes at the end of the MS, and, as earlier noted, is accommodated very differently to that collection by a pair of verses and a marginal note:

> After our song, our mirthe and our gladnesse
> Heer folwith a lessoun of heuynesse
> Salomon Extrema gaudii luctus occupat etc.
>   [Prov. 14.12: weeping occupies the ends of joy]

Comparison of these two copies with each other and with Suso's Latin shows that the version in D is generally closer to the Latin than that in H2.[49] At such points, therefore, D is probably closer to Hoccleve's original than H2: that is, Hoccleve in producing the latter version modified his original in small ways as he went along.[50] It is not so easy to decide the relation of H2 and D to one another where Hoccleve is not directly translating from Suso's Latin. However, H2's copy yields only three instances of possible superior readings.[51] Just possibly Hoccleve copied the version in H2 directly from D, though it is as likely that 'both copies radiated independently from a single lost exemplar'.[52]

Though minor, the changes in H2 throw into sharper relief a number of elements in Hoccleve's text. One such set of changes, also noted by Bowers, concerns the time scale of the events depicted and may serve to 'create a greater sense of urgency'—as we shall see, urgency similarly characterizes the *Gesta* narratives in the *Series*—in their appeal to the disciple-figure, and through him the reader, to repent while there is still time.[53] Similar reasoning may account for another change in H2, when (VII.4.322) the young man tells the disciple how he failed to do penance for his sins in the time loaned to him for that purpose; in D, by contrast, he was more secure, in that God *granted* him time in which to repent (cf. Lat. 'concessum').

Another change in H2 possibly witnesses to a greater drive for precision concerning the identity of the imagined young man. At first the narrative presents him unambiguously as a creation of the disciple's imagination (VII.4.87–90), but during the course of his conversation with the disciple he acquires a semi-independent existence, most strikingly when he invites the disciple to a further act of imaginative projection (VII.4.491–7), so that he becomes real relative to the fantasy he triggers. His departure from the scene leaves the disciple as bewildered and uncertain as the audience of a Pirandello play about the boundaries between the real and the fantastic (VII.4.753–4): one of the more exciting elements of what is, up till then, a fairly traditional exposition of the theme 'lerne to dye'. H2 alters a detail in D so as to make plain at the outset the imaginative character of the revelation-experience. In its version, Wisdom instructs the disciple to 'beholde inward [D now, Lat. nunc] the liknesse. . . of a man dyynge and talkyng with thee' (4.85–6).[54]

The changes to D in H2 may thus witness to two subtly different impulses on the part of a copyist of a text: a drive to heighten the effects of the original; a drive to make its meaning clearer. Both practices have ready parallels in medieval and later translation.

We can also see these, or similar, impulses at work in the non-holograph copies of the Suso text. I had hoped, when I began consulting these *H copies of the text, to find readings peculiar to their common ancestor *H and shared with Suso's Latin, so that I could use *H as a third independent witness to Hoccleve's translation, and (even) to produce a critical edition of the translation by recording the agreement of any two of the three versions, in D, H2 and *H, against the third.[55] Regrettably, I could not do so. *H agrees with D against H2 in most of the earlier-noted instances where the latter introduced error (exceptionally, *H shares an error with H2 at VII.4.220), as also where H2 may have preserved the correct reading. *H also shares a number of readings with H2 against D where the Latin provides no conclusive support for either reading.[56] It also includes a number of unique readings. Some of these are demonstrably erroneous;[57] the witness of others is uncertain. I have found only a few places where the *H version may be superior to that in D (they are VII.4.194, discussed below, and VII.4.445), and I am doubtful that they can bear much weight.

Nevertheless, unlikely though readings unique to *H are to be Hoccleve's, its copy of the Suso translation provides striking witness to what an early reader of the text, the scribe of *H, saw in it. *H is often more vigorous in its details than either D or H2. Thus at VII.4.662, where the dying man's breath begins to fail in both D and H2, it is his 'wind' which gives out in *H; again, at VII.4.778, near the end of the work, *H replaces the disciple's 'now wole Y voide [*remove*] fethirbeddes softe' in D (Lat. 'tolle tolle a me lectisterniorum mollitiem' [take away, take away from me the softness of couches])—an expression of the disciple's new-found determination to embrace the rigours of the spiritual life—with the much more dramatic 'o fy upon the featherbeds soft'.

A final change, from 'hardness' to 'hardiness' in the following quotation, is also worth lingering over:

> The way of trouthe Y lefte and drow to wrong.   *drew*
> On me nat shoon the light of rightwisnesse.   *shone*
> The sonne of intellect nat in me sprong.   *did not. . . rise*
> Y am weery [H2*H I weery am] of my wroght
>   wikkidnesse.
> Y walkid haue weyes of hardnesse[*H hardiness]*difficulty*
> And of perdicion. Nat kowde Y knowe
> The way of God.
> (VII.4.190–6)

This represents Suso's

> Erravi a via veritatis, et iustitiae lumen non luxit mihi, et sol intelligentiae non est ortus mihi. Lassatus sum in via iniquitatis et perditionis, et ambulavi vias difficiles; viam autem Domini ignoravi (Künzle 1977: 529) [I wandered from the way of truth, and the light of justice did not shine upon me. I have grown weary in the way of iniquity and perdition, and I have walked difficult paths. The way of the Lord I did not know]

Given the insistent repetitions of this passage, it is not easy to decide positively whether 'hardnesse' or 'hardinesse' is Hoccleve's original reading. It remains an outside possibility that the *H variant 'hardiness' translates 'iniquitatis', in which case it probably reflects an earlier version of the translation by Hoccleve, one which, in respect of this detail, he modified when producing the version in D and H2; more probably, DH2's 'weyes of hardnesse' translates Suso's 'vias difficiles', which means that the *H variant is scribal and not authorial. Either way, though, the *H variant generates a complexity wanting in the other versions and largely undeveloped in the Latin. Its account of the ways the sinner follows shows the sinner not so much suffering the penalty for his sins as hardening himself in the commission of those same sins.

In one minor respect, the Suso text in *H probably witnesses better to Hoccleve's original than either of the holographs: its glosses. D regularly and H2 occasionally provide marginal Latin glosses to the translation, as a check on the translation and an authorization of it. This feature also occurs elsewhere in the *Series*: in the 'Dialoge', where Hoccleve is translating from the Bible, from 'Bernard' (either Bernard of Cluny, or St Bernard of Clairvaux) and from Geoffrey of Vinsauf;[58] and in the moralizations to the two stories translated from the *Gesta Romanorum*, when Hoccleve is translating the Bible quotations embedded in the moralizations. The practice, which also characterizes manuscript copies of the *Regement*, presumably witnesses to Hoccleve's desire to provide his works with the paraphernalia of medieval scholarly editorial practice, so as to claim for himself, as Chaucer and Gower had done before him, the status of vernacular author.[59] The non-holograph copies take the practice much further than either of the holographs.

A notable instance occurs in 'My Compleinte', where, in an anticipation of the following dialogue with Hoccleve's friend, and of dialogues later in the *Series*, most notably the Suso text, Hoccleve reads from the *Synonyma* of Isidore of Seville.[60] In this text, a man lamenting his unfortunate situation is given good advice by the figure of Reason. Hoccleve translates the relevant speeches for us (VII.1.309–71). All *H MSS accompany the translation with extensive glosses from the Isidorean original, and scholars have generally taken the view that Hoccleve was responsible for them.[61]

Similarly, where comparison is possible, the glosses from the *Horologium* preserved in *H are sometimes closer to the accompanying verse translations or to Suso's Latin than are those in D.[62] Sometimes, too, where details are wanting in D, the glosses as preserved in *H stand in a closer relation to the translation than do the printed versions consulted.[63] This happens particularly when Suso is quoting from the Bible (e.g. VII.4.622–3, 844–6, 850–8). Given the many variants of these quotations that existed in copies both of the Bible and, probably, of the *Horologium*, it is difficult to decide at what point in the development of Hoccleve's text these last three glosses originated. It is even possible that they were made by a later scribe to bring the gloss into line with Hoccleve's own translation. Nevertheless, they are most likely to have originated with Hoccleve.

VI　The holographs versus the other copies: the case of the *Gesta* narratives

Marginal glosses are, it must be admitted, marginal to most readers' interests, but details of other texts in the *Series*, notably the two *Gesta* narratives, are much more important for an understanding of the *Series*: and, what is more, they argue for the probable superiority of ★H over D as witness to Hoccleve's first thoughts about those two narratives, since the versions in ★H are regularly closer to the analogues consulted, in respect of significant detail, than are those in D.[64]

Some of the changes to ★H in D's version of the first *Gesta* story are particularly noteworthy. At one point, not quite midway through the story, the saintly heroine has been banished as the result of a false accusation of murder. In D she rides off towards the east, to the accompaniment of an anxious commentary by the narrator:

> What leeue þat shee took ne woot I nat,
> Or þat shee fro þat place was ywent—　　　*before; had gone*
> The book maketh no mencion of that—
> But hir palfray shee hirself hath hent,　　　*horse; took*
> And so foorth rood toward the orient.
> O emperice, our lord God gye thee,　　　*guide*
> For yit thee folwith more aduersitee.
> (VII.3.428–34)

For D's weak connective 'so' (432), shared, admittedly, with a subgroup of ★H (C2DR), the other manuscripts of ★H offer the much more vivid 'sole', which parallels the reading of the analogues (Lat. 'sola'). It seems probable therefore that the holograph reading witnesses to second thoughts on the part of Hoccleve. Given how important solitude is as a theme of the story, and, indeed, of the *Series* as a whole, and given how often Hoccleve stresses the solitude of his protagonists, it is odd that he should have chosen in D to remove so obvious a pointer to this major theme. His modification is the odder since the moralization preserves the detail unchanged in both holograph and other copies at a point where the analogues again provide authority for its presence (VII.3.1039).

Hard on the heels of this change comes another, equally significant. As she rides away, the Empress spies a thief about to be hanged on a gallows, and bargains for his life in return for his service (he will repay her kindness by betraying her). The gallows appears in the holograph 'on hir right hand' (VII.3.435), but in the other MSS on her left hand. This reading, also shared by the analogues, well suggests the 'sinister' nature of the service the thief will later perform for the Empress: a point strengthened by the detail, shared by all manuscripts, and paralleled in the analogues, that the Empress was journeying 'toward the orient'. Where, therefore, the holograph situates the gallows, on the Empress's right hand, in the south, the non-holograph copies position them on her left hand and in the morally unpromising north. On the face of it, it is surprising that Hoccleve abandoned so obvious a moral marker when revising his text in the holograph. But maybe not: in common with the other moralized narratives of the *Gesta Romanorum*, the narrative of the virtuous Empress is so heavily signposted with moral markers, most of which D and *H share, that the absence of one of them may not be in itself especially significant. (And, of course, simple inattention may be enough to account for this and the previous change to the text in the holograph.)

Another change in the first *Gesta* narrative has a parallel of sorts with that earlier noted in the second holograph copy of the Suso translation. The *H scribes regularly include reference to the temporal context of the narrative, by means principally of the adverb 'now', a word which occurs with great frequency in the tales, not least as a marker of a new development in the narrative. The greater sense of immediacy that results links with a very distinctive element of the narrative, as, indeed, of the *Series* as a whole: haste.[65] Such changes are most strikingly focused in the single stanza near the start of the story when the wicked brother-in-law, the first of the men to attempt the Empress's virtue, is proposing to hang the Empress by her hair from a tree if she will not yield herself to him:

> 'But if þat thow consente wilt [*H *adds* now] to me,   *unless*
> In this foreste as swythe right [*H *adds* now] wole Y   *immediately*
> Hange thee by thyn heer vpon a tree,   *hair*
> Wher no wight shall thee fynde, and so,' quod he,   *person*
> 'Of wikkid deeth thow sterue shalt and die.   *you will die a wicked*
>   *death*
>
> Truste on noon [*H *adds* other] help at al
>   [BLSY *adds* now], ne remedie.   *no*
> (VII.3.219–24)

Whoever was responsible for these changes had a clear sense of the underlying dynamic of the whole volume.[66]

Another notable instance of variation concerns modifications in *H and/or D to Hoccleve's syntax. In the *Series*, as throughout his work, Hoccleve favours distinctive modifications to normal English word order, much in excess of what the constraints of his chosen verse form dictated—and one, it must be admitted, as my marginal glosses will indicate, which does not always make for easy communication of the sense. These include inversions of subject/direct object and verb, of auxiliary and infinitive/participle/adjective, and of preposition and verb; omission of adverbial 'to' as marker of an infinitive of purpose; position of negative particle before the verb; and a marked preference for absolute constructions modelled on Latin but often introduced into the translation where the analogues lack them.[67] I have argued elsewhere that these practices witness to Hoccleve's desire to achieve a high style.[68] We can support this view by observing a striking contrast with Hoccleve's practice in both translated and original prose in the *Series*. In his prose Hoccleve favours the placing of past participles at the end of phrases, but otherwise he hardly has recourse to unfamiliar word order, even though the religious subject-matter of the prose passages might have easily sanctioned recourse to high style. So this 'high' style seems to characterize Hoccleve's poetry rather than his prose. *H regularly, though by no means invariably, modifies the text of D so as to produce a less obviously artificial style.[69] Here it is not clear which manuscript tradition, D or *H, provides a better witness to the original version. If *H's less artificial style reflects Hoccleve's first thoughts better than D, it would follow that in producing D Hoccleve had actively heightened the syntactic strangenesses of the earlier version. If, on the other hand, the forms in *H witness to later scribal activity, then we must conclude that the *H scribe was trying to play down what he saw as his author's stylistic eccentricities.[70]

The portrait of Hoccleve's friend, so important an element in the development of the *Series*, as we shall see, also undergoes an interesting minor modification in the framing conclusion to the first *Gesta* narrative. As he did with his 'Compleinte', Hoccleve shows Friend his latest work, the first *Gesta* narrative, when, so to say, the ink is barely dry. Friend's reaction, at least as presented in D, is very positive: he questions Hoccleve about the omission of the tale's moralizing conclusion, but he finds the story 'wel vnto [his] lykyng' (VII.3.960). In *H, however, he expresses himself more cautiously: the story has been only 'sumdel' to his pleasure. This reading seems to me not scribal but authorial. If so, it might follow that Hoccleve had second thoughts, when revising the *Series* to submit it to the Countess of Westmoreland, about the role of Friend in his work and possible future readings of that work: though whether Friend grows more or less positive in his response as Hoccleve reworks him is an open question.

A last instance of variation, this time from the second *Gesta* narrative, is also worth noting briefly. Like the first *Gesta* narrative, this story, about the moral education of the prodigal Jonathas, functions by repetition: in this case, of Jonathas's foolish trust in the prostitute Fellicula, with whom he has taken up near the start of the story and who, each time he trusts her with another vital secret, betrays his trust once more. In the end the prodigal learns his lesson, and, to punish Fellicula, gives her to eat the fruit of a tree which had caused him to become leprous. The result is immediate and gruesome: 'hir wombe opned and out fil eche entraille/ That in hir was'. D accompanies this ending with a little moral: 'thus wrecchidly lo this gyle [*deceitful*] man dyde' (VII.5.664–6). As it stands in D, the latter phrase is a nonsense, since for Hoccleve 'dyde' must mean 'died',[71] and it is Fellicula, not Jonathas, who dies. *H, with support of the analogues, makes clear that the line should read, as Furnivall read it, 'thus wrecchidly, lo, this gyle woman dyde'.

VII   *Ordinatio* in the holograph and non-holograph copies of the *Series*

The non-holograph copies of the *Series* have a further importance for the reader at what I earlier called the macro-level of structure, and can show two subtly different ways of presenting the material, for both of which Hoccleve may have been responsible: and, as importantly, can show us ways of reading it.[72] To start with the holograph first: as edited by Furnivall from D, the *Series* consists of five items, which Furnivall numbers 20–24.[73] (1) The first item is 'My Compleinte', a name given to it near the beginning of the manuscript (rubric to VII.1.35 in both D and *H) and at the end of all *H manuscripts (rubrics to VII.1.35, VII.2.1).[74] 'My Compleinte' is itself preceded by a five-stanza prologue, so indicated in the rubric to VII.1.35 in all manuscripts. (2) The second item in D is 'A Dialoge' (so all *H MSS; D has the fuller title 'dialogus cum amico' [dialogue with a friend]). The dialogue functions in part as a prologue to the next two items in the anthology, since it includes comment on both. Thereafter, rubrics by Hoccleve authorize Furnivall's division of the rest of the text into: (3) the first of the two *Gesta* narratives, a 'fabula de quadam imperatrice Romana' [story of a certain Roman Empress]. This is followed by a brief linking passage of dialogue between Hoccleve and his friend, which serves to introduce the moral of the previous tale. (4) The moral is linked to the next tale by a rubric: 'explicit moralizacio, et incipit ars vtillissima sciendi mori' [here the moral ends, and the most useful art of knowing how to die begins]; the latter is marked off at the end by 'explicit illa pars per quam sciendum est mori' [here finishes that part by which you may learn to die]. What follows, though it wants rubrics in D, functions as a brief preface to a prose translation of the 'ixe lesson which is rad [read]/ In holy chirche vpon allhalwen [All Saints'] day' (VII.4.925–6), the so-called 'De caelesti Jerusalem'. (5) Lastly, we have a further passage of framing dialogue, which serves as prologue to the second tale from the *Gesta Romanorum*—it is so described in the rubric to VII.5.85 in D and in the rubric to the first line in all *H manuscripts (for this latter D offers 'hic additur alia fabula ad instanciam amici mei predilecti assiduam' [here another story is added at the earnest insistence of my special friend]). After the tale comes a prose moralization of the tale, not set apart from the tale itself by a rubric in D. If we except the rubric at the head of Furnivall's item 5, D seems to be using these rubrics so as to play down the sense of the anthology's frame, and throw emphasis on its major individual items.[75]

A similar understanding seems to be operating when four of the non-holograph MSS (BCLY) present the first *Gesta* story as the third chapter of an anthology, and subdivide both it and the following Suso text.[76] Precedent occurs for both practices: copies of *The Canterbury Tales* sometimes number their individual narrative items as continuous chapters of a book;[77] long texts like Chaucer's tales of the Knight, Clerk and Man of Law are regularly sectionalized, and Hoccleve's *Regement* treats its materials similarly. The removal of individual elements from the frame, and their copying into new manuscript collections, point in a similar direction: here parallels suggest themselves with the religious narratives of *The Canterbury Tales*.[78] Like the latter, it was the explicitly religious works which were excerpted: the two *Gesta* stories were anthologized three times, and once copied out on their own; the Suso was anthologized twice.[79] Two of the new anthologies, in D2 and R, join the *Gesta* stories to a copy of the *Regement*, like the non-holograph copies of the whole *Series* themselves. By this linking of the texts they may have sought to foreground the exemplary qualities to be found in all of them; alternatively, the royal associations of the *Gesta* narratives may have suggested their appearance in company with Hoccleve's manual of instruction for his princely reader.

At the same time, Hoccleve also structures his work, in the holograph, by means of large capital letters, in such a way as to suggest many more sections to the work. In addition to the main units identified by Hoccleve's rubrics, these capital letters also identify the following subsections: the passage linking the first *Gesta* narrative and its *moralizacio*; the *moralizacio* itself; the passage linking the Suso translation and the next piece, 'De caelesti Jerusalem'; and the 'De caelesti Jerusalem' itself. Strikingly, Hoccleve further subdivides the latter by means of a large capital at a point where he stops translating, and produces a brief summary—original, so far as we can presently tell—of the opposing pains of hell, almost as if he wished to help the reader distinguish his translated from his original writing.

The non-holograph MSS of the *Series* broadly conform to the pattern enunciated in the previous paragraph. They add a number of rubrics, which suggest that the scribe of their common ancestor saw the work's narrative frame as playing as important a part as its framed narratives. Thus, in addition to the 'prologues' to items 1 and 5 in D, the non-holograph MSS include rubrics which make the framing dialogue after the first *Gesta* tale the prologue to a new item, the moralization of the tale. They further present the framing speech after the Suso translation as a prologue to another new item, the 'ix lesson þat is red on all halow day'. One manuscript copy (S) indicates the importance of this new item by an illuminated capital on a par with those that it uses to introduce 'My Compleinte' and the 'Dialoge'. Lastly, they mark off the second *Gesta* narrative from its moralization in a way that suggests that this too functions as a separate item.[80]

Later readers also saw the material added to the Suso translation as a separate item in the anthology. Pits' account of Hoccleve's major works, quoted at the head of D, gives pride of place, at the head of the list, to the translation of the ninth lesson for All Saints' Day. He owes to Bale this distinctive understanding of the place of the translation in the *Series*, though Bale's list of Hoccleve's works, copied at the head of one of the *H MSS, Y, puts it in its proper place in the sequence. Bale called the work, as we have noted, 'De caelesti Jerusalem', and gave its opening line as 'tres alias libri partes nunc' [now the three other parts of the book], his version of the first line of what the *H MSS call the prologue to the 'ix lesson þat is red on all halow day': 'The othir iii partes which in this book' (VII.4.918). The offered title presumably derives from the prologue's account of 'the citee/ Called celestial Jerusalem' (VII.4.933–4).[81] Admittedly, Y also carries, above its copy of Bale's list, a later list in English of the works in the manuscript, which reads the 'De caelesti Jerusalem' as an appendix to the Suso translation ('To know how to learn to die with þe 9th lesson on Allhallows Day'). So the status of this text as a separate item remains unclear.

It is interesting that Hoccleve chose to partner or complete the Suso chapter with the 'De caelesti Jerusalem'. Had he been translating from a complete copy of the *Horologium*, which, as we shall see, he probably was not doing, he might have chosen to complete his translation of the 'ars vtillissima' with two earlier chapters in which Suso had produced a fine description of the pains of hell and joys of heaven (I.x-xi). However, a parallel of sorts exists for Hoccleve's practice in a MS (Lichfield Cathedral 16) first noted in this connection by Furnivall; in it the Latin and a Middle English prose translation of the Suso chapter is followed, first, by a copy of the *Pricke of Consience*, and then by Latin, Anglo-Norman and Middle English versions of the ps.-Anselmian *De Quatuordecim Partibus Beatitudinis*.[82]

VIII   Towards an interpretation of the *Series*

But the non-holograph manuscripts of the complete work not only suggest ways
in which Hoccleve may have thought of organizing the *Series*: they also show
us ways of reading it. This is immediately apparent from the rubrics they provide
for the two stories from the *Gesta Romanorum*. The rubrics at the start and end
of the first *Gesta* narrative in the non-holograph copies are close to those found
in the holograph,[83] and they produce a reading of the narrative which focuses
upon its literal, 'historical', dimension. This is a story about a noble—and, *H
adds, a virtuous—empress. The two traditions diverge slightly in their rubrics
for the second *Gesta* narrative: D reads it as the story of a wicked woman, the
prostitute Fellicula, whereas for *H it is the young man Jonathas, the story's
hero, who is at the story's heart. D's version of this second rubric suggests that
Hoccleve saw it as a contribution to the anti-feminist debate in which he had
previously been implicated by his translation of Christine's *Epistre*; that of *H
reflects more accurately the fictional circumstances of the commissioning of the
translation by Friend for his wild young son.

I shall have more to say about both versions later. What is striking about both
sets of rubrics is the contrast with their Anglo-Latin analogues. For example,
the copy of these narratives in the earlier-noted D5, whose verbal detail otherwise matches Hoccleve's translation quite closely, provides chapter headings
which foreground an allegorical reading of them:

> (for Ierelaus) de misericordia Dei super sentenciam suam contra pecca-
> torem [concerning the mercy of God in relation to his judgement against
> the sinner]
> (for Jonathas) de diuersis sibilacionibus siue suggestionibus diaboli contra
> audienciam verba Dei et vtilitatem, et est bona introduccio [concerning
> the different whisperings or suggestions of the devil against hearing the
> words of God and its usefulness, and it offers a good introduction]

We can see an immediate link between Hoccleve's view of the stories in D and
that of the scribe of D5. For the latter, the actions ascribed to God in the first
story, and the devil in the second, clearly originate with the good woman of the
first narrative and the bad woman of the second: good women and bad are, for
him, as for D, the trigger of the narrative and key to its meaning. But the differences are equally striking, and more significant. For the scribe of D5 the stories
exist as a stalking-horse for abstract moral teaching; for D and *H, the stories
seem to signify, as similar narratives did for Chaucer, as items of (admittedly
exemplary) history. More to the point, the lively interest the stories reveal in the

moral situation of their protagonists does not foreclose the question of their own interpretation. Readers, Hoccleve himself included, may find in them whatever speaks to their own situation. This possibly accounts for the initial omission of the moralization of the first *Gesta* narrative, and its subsequent inclusion, according to the rubric in *H, as a separate item, only after Friend has noted its absence.

The non-holograph manuscripts of the *Series* also offer readers another important interpretative key. They all follow the tale of Jonathas with a copy of Lydgate's 'Dance of Death'. Lydgate is not named as translator until the last stanza of the envoy, and the *H scribe may even have thought he was copying another text by Hoccleve: the language and the situation have clear echoes in the *Series*.[84] At all events, *H seems to have seen the *Series* as organized about the idea of death.[85] At the emotional, if not the literal, centre of the anthology comes the chapter from Suso, earlier anticipated in the 'Dialoge' where it is described as part, or the whole, of a 'small tretis' and entitled 'Lerne for to dye' (VII.2.205–6). This text attracts to itself in S a cluster of marginal annotations, and a striking illumination, reproduced as the frontispiece of this volume;[86] it also attracted a very different set of sixteenth-century annotations in D.[87] As a detail early in the chapter makes plain (VII.4.23–8), the chapter itself stands at the head of a set of four linked chapters (*Horologium* II.ii–v) instructing readers not only how to prepare for death (II.ii) but also how to live (II.iii) and how to prepare themselves, by way of reception of the Eucharist (II.iv) and heart-felt and constant praise of divine wisdom (II.v), for the joys of heaven. At the end of his translation of the first chapter (VII.4.918–24), Hoccleve admits his failure to 'touche' the 'othir iii partes which in this book/Of the tretice of deeth expressid be', which would have been well beyond his 'smal konnynge and symple art'. If he is here referring to *Horologium* II.iii–v, he brings into yet clearer focus the narrow range of the exercise.

Admittedly, the chapter on preparing for one's death enjoyed a widespread independent existence in manuscript, as also in the *Speculum Spiritualium*, sometimes with cuts to the beginning so as to leave it a more obviously free-standing work, and sometimes as part of an anthology organized about the theme of preparing for death;[88] so Hoccleve may not have known the chapter in its wider context but only in the narrower one, as indeed his earlier description of the text and offered title for it suggest, and would hence have been unable to qualify its unremitting negatives with the positives of Suso's later chapters.[89] But the fact that he chose to translate the chapter at all—and, moreover, that he translated the whole chapter, with its explicit announcement, at the start, of the more positive material to be discovered in the next three chapters—is significant.

As with the Suso, so throughout the *Series*. Death, and symbolic anticipations of it—solitude, sickness, misunderstanding—recur with great frequency in the *Series*. Death as a deserved punishment occurs in Suso and the tale of Jonathas; undeserved deaths figure prominently in the other *Gesta* narrative; sickness—deserved and undeserved, mental and physical, part of the divine purpose—appears in every part of the work;[90] solitude links the narrator of 'My Compleinte' with the protagonists of the *Gesta* narratives. To widen the focus of our discussion, solitude also characterizes the protagonists of other texts presented here, like the Virgin at the foot of the Cross in the 'Conpleynte paramont' (no. I), or Hoccleve himself in his celebrated 'Male Regle' (no. II); it also characterises the relationships of the sexes in Hoccleve's reworking of Christine de Pizan (no. VI). Fear of death joins the narrator of the 'Balade' for Chichele (no. IV) with the protagonist of the Suso translation. Hence the importance of the repeated motif of complaint:[91] of complaint by noble women against their faithless lovers ('Epistre'); by the Virgin Mary against all the forces, natural and human, that are failing to help her to release her son from his torment ('Conpleynte paramont'); by Hoccleve himself against his own excesses or his friends' neglect ('Male Regle', 'My Compleinte'). Complaint almost becomes a poetic style in the translation of Christine de Pizan, as Hoccleve's later comment on the translation seems to suggest (VII.2.772).

Also relevant in this connection, those important sixteenth-century students of Hoccleve, Stowe and Speght, may even have understood the title of the first item of the *Series* as applying to the whole work. They write of Hoccleve's enforced recantation for the alleged anti-feminist bias of the 'Epistre', in 'that booke of his, called *Planctus proprius*' [i.e. 'My Compleinte'].[92] If this reference is not a simple error on their part (for the recantation occurs in the 'Dialoge', not in the 'Planctus'), they may be drawing attention to an important thematic principle of the whole work. The production of the whole work, then, would function as a form of complaint, and its completion would witness to the resocializing for which the poet had prayed at the end of the 'Planctus' proper.

This solitude explains what we might call the several false endings of the *Series*. Hoccleve offers to end his writing career (VII.2.239–40), as a preparation for the end of his life, with the translation of Suso, which an unnamed 'devout man' has urged him to undertake. (As earlier noted, he has considered translating a military manual for the Duke of Gloucester, but decided against it.[93]) He is not able to start work immediately on the Suso. Friend reminds him of the need to placate the *gentil* female readership to whom his earlier translation of Christine de Pizan had given offence. The commission deflects Hoccleve from his Suso translation: only after he has completed the translation of the first *Gesta* story, within the fictional frame of things, is he able to get to the Suso. And his first ending of the *Gesta* story is itself a false ending, since, as we noted, his version turns out to be wanting the *moralizacio*, which Friend gets him to add from a copy he personally loans him.[94] The completion of the Suso is a further narrative tease, since the promised translation is cut short and replaced by the material describing the joys of heaven and the pains of hell: but at all events it offers a sort of *point final* to the work thus far. This ending reinforces the moralized ending of the previous *Gesta* story and contrasts strikingly with the ending of 'My Compleinte'. That had seemed to forecast the poet's reintegration into the community, and looked not for death but rather for the return of his old companions (VII.1.391); now, the ending of the Suso seems to leave Hoccleve with nowhere else to go but death and the last things, precisely as he had forecast (VII.2.239–52).

Unlike the comparable ending to Chaucer's more complex framed narrative collection, though, this ending is no sooner in place than it is disrupted by the return of Friend, with a request diametrically opposed to his previous one, for a work which will warn young men, most notably his own son, of the dangers of consorting with prostitutes. Hoccleve's fear that, in so doing, he will antagonize the very readers he was supposed to placate by his earlier translation leads Friend to turn his own earlier arguments on their head, and to endorse arguments very similar to those Hoccleve had previously advanced in his own defence. Hoccleve had argued that the scribe could not be held responsible for the faults of his author, whose work, he was convinced—as indeed it does— 'concludi[d] for' women (VII.2.779, cf. VI.463): not only that, but he had actually identified himself with his readers' cause in the way he wrote (VII.2.772). Following Hoccleve, Friend now argues that an author cannot be held responsible for the ways his readers misread his text.

This domestic version of the literary debate in the Prologue to Chaucer's *Legend of Good Women*, with putative royal readers to set against Chaucer's God of Love, serves once more to foreground the random nature of literary production and interpretation. In particular, it allows for a reading of the *Series* as a further contribution by Hoccleve to the anti-feminist debate.[95] So to approach the *Series* involves reading the 'Dialogue' as a prologue to the first *Gesta* narrative, and the second *Gesta* narrative as the story of a wicked woman who got her just deserts. Material probably added by Hoccleve to this latter, concerning the obedience and grief of Jonathas's widowed mother, provides a good female role model to set against that of Fellicula, and reinforces this approach to the tale, as does Hoccleve's slyly ironic view of women's abilities, in such situations, to 'putte vnto the flight/Al sorwe and wo and cacche ageyn confort' (VII.5.145–6).

The debate with Friend makes the further important point that 'faciendi plures libros nullus est finis' [of the making of many books there is no end].

Here, though, unlike Hoccleve's account of the process in the *Regement* (988–1029), and Chaucer's in *The House of Fame*, and unlike their ultimate source, the comments by Qoheleth in Ecclesiastes 12.12, Hoccleve does not seem to find the making of books wearisome to the body ('frequens meditacio, carnis afflictio est') or to endorse Qoheleth's view ('finem loquendi pariter omnes audiamus') that writers and readers should end with that vow of silence symbolized by Chaucer's *retracciouns*. The reason is simple. For Hoccleve, paradoxically, books are an item of mental as well of commercial currency, and their circulation joins readers and writers literally no less than metaphorically. Every text referred to in the *Series* is loaned or requested—or, in the case of 'My Compleinte', listened to—by a friend or promised to a patron. Hoccleve is in 'dette' to the Duke of Gloucester for a publication (VII.2.532); he submits D for approval to the Duchess of Westmoreland. Consequently, the *Series* as a whole dramatizes the reintegration into the community of the writer-as-solitary, a theme central both to 'My Compleinte' and to the ensuing dialogue.

In any case, books, both made and read, witness paradoxically to the principle of dialogue which ensures that, this side of death, no reader or writer is ever truly alone. Hence the importance of dialogue as both narrative and thematic element of Hoccleve's work. Hoccleve and the other scribes have a number of ways of indicating this important aspect of the work. Hoccleve makes much use of the paraph mark to distinguish the speakers in the different narratives of which D is composed.[96] Other scribes could not so use the paraph mark, since they had used it for stanza divisions, but they too draw the reader's attention to dialogue by regular glossing of lines in 'My Compleinte', the 'Dialogue' and the Suso translation so as to make plain the speakers of the glossed lines.[97]

A small detail from the 'Dialogue' further demonstrates the point that there is no end to the making of books. Like the narratives of the *Series* themselves, Hoccleve's framing monologue and dialogues carry frequent reminders of their own temporal dimension: notably, a date at the end of November when 'My Compleinte' was begun (VII.1.17); 'the holy seson. . . of Lente' (VII.2.662), a time of preparation for Easter by acts of self-denial, and the time when the first *Gesta* narrative was undertaken; an unspecified date 'a wike or two' after its completion (VII.3.953), when Friend returns to check on its progress; and the season of Easter, when Friend tells us he read the second *Gesta* narrative which he is now asking Hoccleve to translate (VII.5.4). These references may be as conventional and symbolic as comparable temporal markers in *The Canterbury Tales*; but, as earlier noted, they may also be straightforwardly factual.

One such is a detail from the 'Dialogue', in the course of which Hoccleve allows himself to be seen revising his own text. He has been making a distinction between his own illness, given by God and not caused by himself, and the ills of society, which proceed from the exercise of individual choice, like murder, extortion, heresy and falsifying of the currency (VII.2.64–72). Reference to falsifying of the currency triggers an attack on those guilty of the crime. If these people don't trim the coins or wash them, so that the purchaser gets less than he thinks he is paying for (VII.2.106–12), they counterfeit coins with 'golde, copir, clothe and tyn' (VII.2.143). King and commons alike suffer from the practice; yet the perpetrators seem to have escaped punishment. This passage reminds us, as only someone in a financially insecure position would feel the need to do, of the economic base of literary activity.[98] It is interrupted by a stanza which, as Burrow has shown, must have been composed later:[99]

Whanne I this wroot, many men [B a man,	*wrote*
D me] dide amis	
Thei weied gold, vnhad auctorite.	*weighed; without authority*
No statute made was þanne as þat nowe is.	
But sithen gold to weie charged nowe ben we,	*since; weigh; obliged*
Resoun axeth þat it obeied be.	*asks*
Nowe time it is vnto weiȝtes vs drawe,	*(to) take ourselves*
Sithen that the parlement hath maad it a lawe.	*since*
(VII.2.134–40)	

At first sight it appears, as with so much else in the *Series*, that the opening words of this stanza ('whanne I this wroot'), with their frame-breaking reminders of their own textuality, are a further marker of Hoccleve's debt to Chaucer.[100] There is, however, a vital difference between Chaucer's self-presentation as author and Hoccleve's. Even though he is known to have revised at least one of his own works (the Prologue to the *Legend*), Chaucer does not generally admit to doing so. Hoccleve, by contrast, is as ready to let himself be seen working in the now of textual production as he is willing, with his friend, to engage in the serendipitous now of conversation. It would be perfectly in character, then, if the various literary understandings which this Introduction has so far identified in the non-holograph manuscripts were, in fact, second and even third thoughts by Hoccleve about his own work.[101]

IX   Hoccleve and translations

Scribal comment also suggests another way of reading Hoccleve's texts: as translations. Among the rubrics which MSS of the *Series* provide for the accompanying Lydgate piece occur 'verba translatoris' [words of the translator], for the translator's voice in the first five stanzas (CLY) and final two stanzas ('l'envoy de translateur': all *H manuscripts). This rubric formally distinguishes the translator's voice from that of the author, whose voice it identifies at the start of the translation proper, in stanzas 6–7, by means of the phrase 'verba auctoris' [words of the author] (so all *H MSS). Except formally, though, this careful distinction between the two voices is a fiction: the translator's voice blurs with that of his source even as it frames it, most notably in his use of a mirror metaphor (31, 49), which, as we have seen, Hoccleve also makes much of. Yet more strikingly, the scribe of E completely obliterated the distinction between original and translated work in his copy of the first *Gesta* narrative, and identified Hoccleve as translator ('verba translatoris') in a passage where Hoccleve, so far as we know, is not translating from his source but acting as an author and commenting ironically on the gap between the real world and the ideal world of the story (VII.3.939–45). Here we find that same confusion between authorial and translatorial roles noted earlier. Hoccleve expressly identifies the last three items of the *Series*—four, if we reckon 'De caelesti Jerusalem' as a separate item—as translations (VII.2.211, 825, VII.4.930, VII.5.7, 26) and he talks of other projected translations (VII.2.561). We can further demonstrate the importance of translation for Hoccleve's work by reference to the incipits and explicits of several of them (in the present edition, nos. I, IV, and VI). It is therefore appropriate to recall earlier comments about medieval translation, as a prelude to a few concluding comments on Hoccleve as translator.

Underpinning Hoccleve's achievements in both his translated and many of his original works is a quality which, for want of a better word, we might call wit: the sort of wit you identify in Donne's 'Good Friday Riding Westward' rather than in the comic climaxes of Chaucer's fabliaux. The translations owe their wit in some measure, where they have it, to their sources, and, given that humour is perhaps the most difficult quality of a text to translate, Hoccleve deserves praise for his achievement.[102]

In the Deguileville translation, as earlier implied, the wit resides in the juxtaposition of the Virgin Mary's actual situation at the foot of the Cross and the hindsight enjoyed by the Christian reader. What she experiences as total disaster, the Christian can see as the necessary preliminary to a total triumph. This juxtaposition is a necessary part of any representation of the Crucifixion in which the writer reveals any interest in, or makes any concession to, the human situation of the protagonists. Deguileville goes much further than most medieval writers on the subject, and anticipates the Herbert of 'The Passion'. In the opening stanzas, for example, the Virgin condemns as so much waste of breath— at best, a pious fiction—the graces promised her before the birth of her son: for example,

O Gaubriel, whan þat thou come aplace   *into the place*
And madest vnto me thi salewyng   *salutation*
And seidist thus, 'Heil Mary, ful of grace',
Whi ne had thu gove me warnyng   *did not; give*
Of þat grace that veyn is and faylyng,   *transitory*
As thu now seest, and sey it weel before?   *saw; well before*
Sith my ioye is me rafte, my grace is lorne.   *since; taken from; lost*
(I.29–35)

Hoccleve not only carries much of Deguileville's wit over into his translation: by means of (probable) additions to the original, he even strengthens it.[103]

Wit is a rather different affair in the major narratives of the *Series*. In the first instance, we have to deal probably with at least one instance, and possibly with two instances, of humorous fictionalizing by Hoccleve of his relation to his sources: that is, the earlier-noted failure to translate the four linked chapters of Suso's *Horologium* as beyond the poet's competence, and the failure initially to translate the moralization of the first *Gesta* narrative because it was missing from the copy the poet was working from. More to the point, we can argue that, in treating his sources, like Chaucer before him, Hoccleve has exposed a latent irony in them and heightened it. I am not sure this feature is at all in evidence in the Suso translation, but it strongly colours the two translations from the *Gesta Romanorum*, especially in places where passages of direct address to the reader and other narratorial comment occur. Such material has no parallel in the analogues consulted, and, given the basically impersonal character of the narration in the analogues, I am pretty certain that all such material is Hoccleve's own invention.[104] The precedent here seems to be Chaucer's example in his two rhyme royal tales closest to Hoccleve's *Gesta* narratives, those of the Man of Law and the Clerk. Like Chaucer, Hoccleve uses these passages of added comment to loosen the unremitting moral grip of the narratives and to subject to comic scrutiny their insistent idealizations of their protagonists. In the first *Gesta* narrative, Hoccleve never directly satirizes his saintly heroine as Chaucer's Man of Law does his (cf. *CT* II.709–14), but, like Chaucer's Clerk, he casts a critical eye over the remoteness from the present of the events being narrated, and he draws on his earlier translation of Christine de Pizan to undermine the idealizations of the female role offered by her *Epistre* as well as by his immediate source.[105]

I have deferred till the end what was probably Hoccleve's first attempt to translate a witty author, Christine de Pizan, because it will be apparent from the concluding words of the previous paragraph, and from remarks earlier in this Introduction, that Hoccleve's engagement with Christine's *Epistre* is almost as long-standing as with Chaucer's work, and probably co-terminous with his entire poetic career. As earlier noted, the 'Dialoge' explicitly refers to it; the playful anti- (or pro-?) feminist asides in the *Regement* (5104–94) were arguably produced in Christine's shadow.[106] As if that were not enough, the non-holograph copies of both the 'Epistre' and the 'Dialoge' show that other scribes, and sometimes Hoccleve himself, continued the process of dialogue with Christine that he had first started in 1402. Consequently, we can use Hoccleve's on-going response to Christine's wit as a useful point at which to end this Introduction.

Unlike several of the other texts studied in this Introduction, Hoccleve's 'Epistre' has been the subject of on-going and lively critical debate, so I hope the reader will forgive the narrow focus and general feel of the following comments. For students coming to this exciting text for the first time, though, the comments appended by the copyist John Shirley to his copy of the work in Tr1 will possibly give some sense of it.[107] To begin with, Shirley provides a running title for the work, 'a parable [*var.* a gode parable] made by Occleve', which draws clear attention to the difficulties of interpretation generated by the text. Then, Shirley's incipit describes the work as

> a lytel traytis made and compyled by Thomas Occleue of þoffice of þe priue seel, specifying þe maners and þe conuersaciouns booþe of men and wymmen conuersaunte in þis lytell yle of Albyone.

Shirley's note does not make clear—but maybe he thought the title did—the identity of the principal speaker of the work; nor does it explain the scale or significance of the 'translation' of Christine's France to Hoccleve's 'Albyone'. But it does draw attention to the work's subject-matter (relations between men and women) as also, maybe, by its reference to 'maners. . . and conuersaciouns', to its distinctive blend of comedy and satire. And it draws attention to the central organizing principle of the work—and, as earlier comments have shown, of most of Hoccleve's writing: conversation. Admittedly, the conversations reported by Cupid in Hoccleve's 'Epistre' are pretty much a one-way affair. The men get all the direct speech, the women only indirect speech (VI.10–12, 17, 190–94); the men initiate, the women merely react.

I have written elsewhere, concerning Hoccleve's translation of Christine's wit, that Hoccleve tends to simplify its complexities and to flatten its distinctive contours, so as to produce a wit that is both broader and more traditional. As an obvious indication of this, we might note the vividly idiomatic speech, laced with *double entendres*, that Hoccleve gives his male seducers when they are in male company (fishing, taking a snack, one for the road: VI.100, 102, 109), by contrast with the courtly language they adopt when speaking to their ladies

(VI.29–35). In so Englishing Christine's courtly French idiom, Hoccleve distinguishes the men from the women in the poem more strongly than Christine does: in his 'Epistre' the women get to state their case only in the summary provided by the God of Love, and only in abstract and figurative (courtly?) language. In so presenting their speech, the God of Love makes ironic common cause with the male speakers he is officially condemning. He also identifies himself with the men, and against the women, by adopting their language, and using colloquialisms ('pot by the stele', VI.50), proverbs (VI.184–6) and possibly even euphemisms (VI.144 has been so read), all added by Hoccleve to his text. But colloquial and proverbial language, allied to euphemism, is a common marker, if not a defining feature, of fabliaux.[108] In so moving his original towards fabliau, Hoccleve is clearly simplifying its message: Christine had not distinguished so sharply between the language of the God and of his female complainants.

This simplification of Christine's original by Hoccleve has partly to do, as my earlier study suggested, with Hoccleve's use of Chaucer, principally Chaucer's *Legend of Good Women*, to gloss Christine, who had very possibly used the *Legend* herself as a gloss on the anti-feminist traditions she was attacking.[109] Hoccleve's recourse to Chaucer in the 'Epistre' contrasts with his use of Chaucer in the 'Dialoge'. In the latter, in the context of a reference to his earlier translation of Christine's work, he reads Christine through the same Chaucerian lens that she herself may have used as a secondary element in her *Epistre*: the *Prologue to the Wife of Bath's Tale*. Hoccleve's dependence on the *Legend*, when he was translating the *Epistre*, resulted in a simpler outline of Christine's work than he produced in the 'Dialoge' when he followed Chaucer and cited the Wife of Bath as an 'auctrice' (VII.2.694).

This intersection of Chaucer and Christine also affects the relation of the holograph (H2) and non-holograph (∗H) copies. Thus, for example, H2's condemnation of anti-feminist writing as 'wikkid bookes' (VI.197) almost certainly functions as an echo of a phrase in the *Prologue to the Wife of Bath's Tale*, against ∗H's tamer 'sorry books'. Similarly, H2's declaration that man's powers are too 'weyk' to declare fittingly the virtue of the Virgin Mary—that icon of female virtue, regularly used to conclude debate and produce a verdict in favour of women—possibly echoes a phrase in the prologue to the *Prioress's Tale*, an echo lost by ∗H with the adjective 'lean'.[110] Whether, however, these echoes were introduced by Hoccleve into the text at a late stage in its transmission or were part of the work from the very beginning there is at present no telling. Other occurrences in the 'Epistre' of the word 'wicked', especially at VI.230, where it is applied to the wicked sayings of the scholars against women, might support the view that its appearance at VI.197 faithfully represents what

Hoccleve wrote in an earlier draft of his text. If so, the version in *H witnesses to scribal second thoughts. On the other hand, Hoccleve's only explicit reference to the Wife of Bath occurs late in his poetic career, so just possibly the echo of the Wife of Bath at this point in H2 witnesses to later alteration by Hoccleve to an earlier text better preserved, in respect of this detail, in *H.

Elsewhere, too, the holograph and non-holograph copies divide over the precise interpretation of the work, specifically in respect of its presentation of what we might call the work's gendered ethical/social elements. Thus Cupid's power in H2 to set 'mennes hertes' on fire (VI.241) becomes in *H a power over 'folkis', of both genders presumably. Here H2 offers a reading, supported elsewhere in the text, of male crimes followed by their own humiliating reversals, most notably when the cynic falls in love. By contrast, *H widens the focus, as Christine had regularly done, to allow all human beings to be equally affected by desire.[111] Insofar as Hoccleve had restricted women's sexual role to the granting of pity (VI.43, 72), we may feel that this enlargement of the focus in *H cannot have been his.

One of the two instances of female 'pitee' in the text is itself the subject of further variation. At VI.72 women yield to their lovers as an expression of their 'pitee' in H2, but of their 'virtue' in *H, a term used elsewhere by Hoccleve only of the Virgin Mary (VI.405, 407) and as an encouragement to his female readers (VI.455–61) not to behave like prostitutes (VI.262). *H's use of the term is probably not authorial, then, but it complicates the simpler moral diagram H2 is presenting: as, strikingly, does its understanding of the term in VI.457–60. For these lines H2 offers us

> Vertu so noble is and worthy in kynde,   *(her) nature*
> þat vice and shee may nat in feere abyde.   *together*
> Shee puttith vice cleene out of mynde.
> Shee fleeth from him, shee leueth him behynde

and thus effects the same identification of women and virtue that Christine is working hard to create throughout the *Epistre*. *H replaces the feminine pronouns by masculine, and creates a more complex equation of virtue and maleness. This might have endeared the speaker to the early Church fathers, for whom the virtuous woman was often a sort of honorary male,[112] but not, possibly, to his female readers. Consequently, one might speculate that the disapproval by *gentil* women of Hoccleve's 'Epistre', which triggers his first translation from the *Gesta Romanorum*, was not simply a fictional effect—though obvious precedent exists for it in Chaucer's production of his *Legend* to atone for the alleged anti-feminist bias of earlier translations—but an actual occurrence, and that Hoccleve modified the version in H2 in the light of criticism.

Another modification, this time to the text of the 'Dialoge', may show him (re)acting differently. Here Hoccleve finds himself forced to defend his 'Epistre' against criticisms of female readers who are 'swart wrooth' with him for the translation's alleged anti-feminist bias. As part of his defence, Hoccleve recycles material earlier translated from Christine: notably, her use of the Genesis story of the creation of Adam and Eve.[113] Hoccleve uses Genesis 3.15, in which God curses both the woman and the serpent. God places the woman under the power of the man and gives the serpent power to bruise her heel, and grants her the reciprocal power over the serpent to bruise its head, a phrase conventionally applied to the Virgin Mary. This Biblical text was regularly used in pro- and anti-feminist writing. Hoccleve plays a wonderfully devious game with the text—as he had been less able to do when translating the *Epistre*—by applying it to the power modern wives have to break their husbands' heads:

> . . . God seide, 'This womman thyn heed   *head*
> Breke shal, for thurgh thyn [the serpent's]
>   enticement
> Shee hath ybroken my commandement.'
> Now [*H O], syn womman had of [*H on]
>   the feend swich might,   *since*
> To breke a mannes heed it seemeth light   *easy*
> (2.724–8);

a power they make as 'light' of—find it as 'light' to exercise—as, by implication, their husbands do not find it 'light' to endure. The playfulness continues in the following stanza, where, in an echo of the *Prologue to the Wife of Bath's Tale*, Hoccleve exposes women's 'reson' as, at best, *ex post facto* rationalization of instinct: 'hir reson axith haue of men maistrie' (VII.2.732, cf. *CT* III.441–2). This exercise of wit has strong overtones of Chaucer, to whom, in its ironic criticism of the male position and, at the same time, its thinly veiled attack on female excess, it is much closer than to Christine.

As with the 'Epistre', variants witness to second thoughts on the part of another scribe or of Hoccleve himself. Where the non-holograph MSS of this text describe how women, in the person of the Virgin Mary, have power over the devil, the holograph allows the bolder inference to be drawn that their power is derived *from* the devil. If the non-holograph reading provides witness to an earlier version by Hoccleve of his own text, it would follow that Hoccleve began traditionally enough, but made this detail of his text more radical in preparing it for its new reader, the Countess of Westmoreland. If, on the other hand, the non-holograph reading is not Hoccleve's, we have the picture of a scribe who took fright at the boldness of Hoccleve's irony and watered it down. Either way, Hoccleve emerges from this detail as a witty and adventurous writer, who nailed his colours to the anti-feminist mast more boldly in this later work than he was able to do in the holograph copy of the 'Epistre', when he identified virtue with the feminine principle.

X   Afterword

A last point is worth making, as an index both of the strengths and of the limitations of this most attractive writer. Leaving on one side the question of Hoccleve's metre, which, as earlier noted (n. 50), scribes seem to have found irregular and attempted to tidy up, the question remains of Hoccleve's language and imagery. We have already noted how Hoccleve's language is strongly marked by its preference for inversions of normal word order, juxtaposed with passages of idiomatic directness. Equally striking is the poet's readiness to operate within a relatively narrow range of verbal commonplaces. The notes will indicate a number of these. In the *Series*, the repeated turns of phrase bind the disparate elements of that work together and generate links in excess of those formally sanctioned by the overarching frame, and in excess of any links this Introduction has been able to suggest. Notwithstanding earlier remarks about the importance of community in Hoccleve's writing—and wit, after all, presupposes the existence of a community of shared understandings—Hoccleve's repetitions seem to me to function as obsessive expressions of an underlying preoccupation, a sense of personal insecurity and isolation. Like the newly bereaved, or like foreigners trying to make headway in a group of native speakers, it sometimes seems as if, for Hoccleve, conversation, like relationships, can only function satisfactorily on a one-to-one basis, as a purely temporary alleviation of a basic isolation. This makes for a striking contrast with Chaucer, whose major poem is organized about, and celebrates, the idea of group, or with Christine de Pizan, who locates and underpins her account of the struggle between the sexes in an awareness of the support offered individuals by their membership of a single-sex group. One might almost see in the solitude of the Hoccleve narrator a precursor of the narrators of Surrey's poems and Shakespeare's sonnets, and a figure who can speak very directly to our own uncertain and privatized age.

Notes

1.   For comment on St Bonaventura's formulation of these four levels (better, sites) of authorial activity, see Minnis 1984: 94, Wogan-Browne et al. 1999: Index s.v.

2.   For a single example of such a definition, see Johnson 1989: 71 and n. 10; for debates about translation at the end of the fourteenth century, Hudson 1975, Watson 1995.

3.   Hoccleve writes about Chaucer in *Regement* ll. 1961–74, 2077–107, 4978–5012 (for a modern edition, see Furnivall 1897).

4.   So Lawton 1985: 127–9.

5.   In the eighteenth century George Sewell still thought of the 'Epistre' as by Chaucer when he modernized it. (For an edition of his modernization, see Fenster and Erler 1990.)

6.   Mills 1996: 107 argues for links of the *Series* with *The House of Fame*.

7.   Burrow 1994: 219 [31]. For further comment on these two holographs, see Bowers 1989: 466 and Batt 1996₁: 7. Similarly, scribes regularly combined into a single volume the *Series*, in whole or in part, and the *Regement*, as if to make an edition of Hoccleve's major works comparable to that by Hoccleve of his minor poems.

8.   See, for example, Mitchell 1968: 1–19, Medcalf 1981 and especially Burrow 1981, 1982, 1984.

9.   For comment on the Lollards, see Catto 1985, Hudson 1988, Sargent 1992, Watson 1995, and the contributions of Simpson, Hanna III and Justice in Copeland 1996; on the deposition of Richard II, Jacob 1961: 1–65, 94–9, Scattergood 1971: 107–36, Strohm 1992: 75–94; for helpful summary account, Barr 1993: 1–5.

10.   On Henry V, for example, as 'prynce of preestes' (for this phrase, from Hoccleve's poem to Oldcastle, see Furnivall and Gollancz 1970: 17), see Haines 1971: 145, Pearsall 1994: 407.

11.   For this poem, see Furnivall and Gollancz 1970: 47–9, and, for judicious comment, Strohm 1998: 115–16, 122–3. Hoccleve's orthodoxy was questioned in the sixteenth century by John Bale, who cited a comment by Walsingham that Hoccleve was a follower of Berengarius and Wycliffe, but concealed his Protestant leanings for many years through fear of the Papists (1559: 537). In the seventeenth century Pits recycled the accusation, though unsure of its truth. Bale's comments appear at the head of MS Y, those of Pits at the head of D. On this point see further Toulmin Smith 1882 and Hudson 1988: 286 n. 47; and, for Foxe's post-Reformation linking of Hoccleve and Wycliffe, Cummings 1999: 848.

12.   On the barely concealed petitionary impulse behind the *Regement*, e.g. *Regement* 1779–87, 1902–4, cf. Hasler 1990.

13.   Quotation from Chaucer is from Benson 1988. Reference to *The Canterbury Tales* is by fragment and line number as given in Benson.

14.   On Chaucer as a translator, see Machan 1985, 1989, Cooper 1989, Copeland 1991: 186–201, Olsen 1999. Chaucer was early known as a 'grant translateur', a title given to him by his contemporary Eustache Deschamps. I use the term 'translation debate' loosely, but to read *The Canterbury Tales* as a debate on translation is probably almost as useful (so also Olsen) as to follow Kittredge in reading it as a debate on marriage.

15.   For a classic medieval formulation of these literary functions, see above n. 1. I have not sought to apply all four levels to Hoccleve's literary production, though it should be readily apparent that, when Hoccleve reads one work (say, the first *Gesta* narrative) with the assistance of others (the *Epistre* of Christine de Pizan, and the religious romances of *The Canterbury Tales*), he is functioning like a medieval compiler/commentator, as Chaucer

does, in his *Troilus and Criseyde*, when he uses the *Consolatio Philosophiae* of Boethius to gloss Boccaccio's *Il Filostrato*.

16. For the 'Inuocacio', see Furnivall and Gollancz 1970: 278. For another instance where Hoccleve may be drawing attention to the distinction, see below p. 27; for one where copies of a Lydgate translation do so, below pp. 34–5; for examples of similar practices by other translators, Ellis 1982.

17. Frantzen 1990 (the title of his book); Eagleton 1977: 72. The modern literature on translation theory is vast: for a few recent examples, see Bassnett 1991, Lefevere 1992, Robinson 1991, Venuti 1995.

18. Mills 1996: 90.

19. Pryor 1968: 84.

20. So Burrow 1994: 216 [28], but see also n. to VII.2.206–45 below.

21. Furnivall and Gollancz 1970: 8, 39, 41, 62, 308.

22. Dr Catherine Batt suggests that, even in producing a poem addressed to the Virgin Mary, Hoccleve may have been playing with the conventions of petitionary/epistolary form (private communication).

23. On the date for the Deguileville translation, see below p. 18; on that for 'Male Regle', Burrow 1994: 220 [32].

24. In so acting, of course, editors covertly privilege the author's own copy of his text over other copies. In making his own copy the author is also functioning as a scribe of his own text and is as liable to miscopy and/or alter his text as any other scribe.

25. In this connection, Windeatt's comment on 'the medieval poem' bears repeating: 'for the [modern] editor the medieval poem is. . . something of an aspiration, a hardest idea, somewhere between, behind, or above the network of available scribal variations in any given line' (1979: 139). See also comments on *Piers Plowman* by Kerby-Fulton 1999, esp. pp. 516–17.

26. With the notable exception of the edition of the *Epistre* by Fenster and Erler, editions of Hoccleve's originals are generally, if in different ways, unhelpful. Künzle's critical edition of the *Horologium*, and Stürzinger's of the *Pèlerinage*, provide few variant readings; the first editor of the Anglo-Norman original of the 'Balade' for Chichele, Sandison (1923), knew it only from an imperfect copy, and its most recent editor, Stokes (1995), edited from two other manuscripts only those portions of the text not included in Sandison's copy-text. As for the *Gesta* narratives, if we except the 1872 edition of Oesterley, of very limited use because it does not refer in any detail to Anglo-Latin textual traditions, we have only editions by Wallensköld and Mitchell, from the same manuscript, of the originals of Hoccleve's two tales. Fortunately, a modern edition of the Anglo-Latin *Gesta* is being undertaken from ten manuscripts of the work by Dr Diane Speed and Dr Philippa Bright.

27. Mitchell 1968: 86; Wallensköld 1907: 111–16; Ward and Herbert 1883–1910: 3.190.

28. Admittedly, Mitchell also writes in general terms of Hoccleve's following 'his original, the Anglo-Latin *Gesta*, in a straightforward manner', but he allows the inference to be drawn that this original is not, for practical purposes, distinct from the copy in Ha2.

29. Notwithstanding this caveat, I have, where possible in this study, used modern editions of originals translated by Hoccleve, especially where editors have provided a selection of variants: I have supplemented their variants as appropriate by reference to other copies of those originals. Where an editor has edited from a single MS, as Wallensköld did, I have consulted other MSS. For the Latin source of the second *Gesta* narrative, available in print only as edited from a single MS in a thesis I have been unable to consult, I have had to work directly from a selection of the MSS.

30. On this latter point, see n. to VII.5.634–6.

31. Apart from his prose translations, Hoccleve favours rhyme royal for all his translations except the Chichele text, where he uses an eight-line stanza form, ababbcbc, to match the

original's abababab. The latter is sustained, as Hoccleve's translation is not, over two eight-line stanzas. See further discussion of the latter in Stokes 1995.

32. Appendix 2A lists the major instances of readings shared by Hoccleve's *Gesta* narrative and the Anglo-Latin copies cited.

33. For other examples of this process, see Ellis 1994, Weitemeier 1996.

34. For a list of the non-holograph copies of this work, and comment on their textual relations, see Appendix 4; for variant readings, Appendix 5.

35. The alternative explanation is more complicated: it requires a scribe who indavertently or deliberately (because, say, he had access to the Latin source of the text) restored a link with the source which Hoccleve had sundered in the holograph. Cf. comments by Pearsall on authorial revisions by Chaucer to his *Troilus* (1992: 188–9).

36. For a list of the non-holograph copies of this poem, and comment on their textual relations, see Appendix 4; for variant readings, Appendix 5.

37. For a list of the non-holograph copies of this poem, and comment on their textual relations, see Appendix 4; for variant readings, Appendix 5.

38. See Stürzinger 1895: 211.

39. For other evidence of Hoccleve's awareness of the punning possibilities of proper names see nn. to III.14 (Henry Somer), VII.2.597 (Humphrey), and VII.5.634 (Fellicula).

40. H1 introduces error in its copy of the text with the rhyme at I.107, an occasional feature of other Hoccleve holographs (see V.80n.); and its readings at I.60, 166 and 240 may be less authoritative than the corresponding *Pilgrimage* MSS readings.

41. See Appendix 5, variants for VI.219.

42. Burrow 1994: 242 [54].

43. Owners and/or readers, all taken from Furnivall's footnotes, include Peter Hardy of Halifax (Furnivall and Gollancz 1970: 123); Thomas Kingston (140); John Hancock and Thomas Carter (both at one point apparently contesting ownership of the book: 156, cf. 181, 183–4); Thomas Hecker (194); and Thomas and William Wilton of Kirkland (187, 203, 218). Two dates are given, 1547 (239) and 1551 (226). The whole book was also read in 1666 by George Davenport (242). Annotations to the Suso translation will be discussed below, p. 30.

44. The two dates are given in the revision to Furnivall 1892 by Mitchell and Doyle (1970: lxxiii). For the date 1413, held to be more reliable by McGerr 1990: xxv, see Seymour 1981: xiv, and Ward/Herbert 1883–1910: 2.583.

45. The completion of McGerr's edition of the work, of which so far only Volume 1 has appeared (1990), will surely assist powerfully in realizing this desideratum.

46. So Burrow 1994: 212 [24] n. 96. For editions of these other poems, see Furnivall 1897: xxiii-lxii, and Smalley 1953.

47. For this text see Henry 1985: 140–4.

48. Burrow 1994: 212 [24] n. 95 argues against Hoccleve's authorship on grounds of the difference between their treatment of Deguileville's allegory and that in the body of the poem. Cf. I.35n. Other tests which might have helped decide the question proved inconclusive. These include (i) a comparison of the syntax of the added stanzas with the very distinctive syntax generally favoured by Hoccleve: similarities would strengthen the case for his authorship of the added stanzas; (ii) a comparison of the added stanzas with the body of the 'Conpleynte' in respect of the traditions of the French original: a different source for the added stanzas would probably indicate a different translator; (iii) rhymes: the other poems in the *Pilgrimage* rhyme '"etymological" -*y* [and] -*ye*', which Hoccleve himself avoids (Burrow's n. 96).

49. For examples, see Appendix 5 (variants for VII.4.85, 205, 220, 297, 322, 393) and note to VII.4.205. Errors in D are few, possibly only VII.4.695 and 738 (rhyme wanting in the latter case). For detailed and important comment on the relation of the two copies to each

other, which did not refer the two copies to their ultimate source, see Bowers 1989.

50. Pryor 1968: 123 also notes that some of the changes in H2 to the version in D 'give it advantage in rhythmical smoothness'. The drive to improve on what scribes saw as Hoccleve's faulty metrics may also have fuelled changes in non-holograph copies of other works by Hoccleve (for examples, see Appendix 5, variants for I.52, 93); Hoccleve himself admits to 'meetrynge amis' both in his 'Balade to the Duke of York' and in the *envoi* to the copy of the *Regement* presented to the Duke of Bedford (Furnivall 1970: 50, 57).

51. These are VII.4.231, 628 and the marginal note to 414–16: see variants for these lines in Appendix 5 (and, for 414–16, the relevant note to VII.4).

52. Bowers 1989: 458, followed by Burrow 1999: 111.

53. Examples include VII.4.117, 216, 231, 297, 377, 393, noted by Bowers 1989: 453, and Selman 1998: 213, who also notes the following example.

54. For a similar modification to a passage from the *Horologium* in the late fourteenth-century *Chastising of God's Children*, see Selman 1998: 117.

55. On the difficulties of any such attempt, see, for example, Greetham 1987. When a work is a translation, though, the source can function at least as a notional point of reference and guarantee of the exercise. Neither Bowers 1989 nor Burrow 1999 refers differences between the two versions to Suso's Latin.

56. These occur at VII.4.21, 69, 78, 193, 279, 301, 399, 451, 520, 583, 588, 667: see Appendix 5 for these readings.

57. Errors include VII.4.194, 225, 348, 452, 688, 758, and (probably) 768. All the *H MSS introduce error at 831, possibly by miscopying an ambiguous correct form in *H. At 597 D initially shared H2*H's erroneous omission of 'nat'. Consult Appendix 5 for these readings.

58. See nn. to VII.2.260–1, 638–41, 722–6.

59. On this general point see Copeland 1991, Minnis 1984; as applied specifically to Chaucerian glosses, Bowers 1989; as applied to glosses in Gower's *Confessio Amantis*, Pearsall 1989.

60. For the abbreviated version of the *Synonyma* which Hoccleve was almost certainly using, see Burrow 1998.

61. The glosses are missing in D, but their absence is not necessarily significant, because the whole of its copy of the 'Complainte' and of ll. 1–253 of the 'Dialoge' was at some time lost; D's version of the missing material was added to the manuscript in the sixteenth century by Stowe (according to Seymour 1981: 132, from S or a copy close to it).

62. For, VII.4.365, 414–16 and nn.; against, 4.556n.; divided, 4.709n.

63. Variants do occur, but I have been unable to trace them to any MSS of the *Horologium* consulted: these include MSS of the *Speculum Spiritualium*, in Part V of which the relevant Suso material occurs.

64. It is *prima facie* probable that the following readings of *H (or of selected MSS of *H) have greater authority than the corresponding D readings: VII.3.180, 432, 435, 904, VII.5.420, 424, 546, 666. At VII.3.351 and VII.5.547, by contrast, D appears more authoritative.

65. For fuller comment on this feature, see n. to VII.5.21.

66. This change also occurs regularly in the *H copies of the Suso translation, at VII.4.125, 127, 452 (error), 502, 516, 805. Hoccleve made such a change to his Suso text in H2 at 4.371. Some of the changes to the text of the 'Conpleynte paramont' in the non-holograph copies probably have a similar motive, to increase the immediacy of the situation and heighten its emotional appeal to the reader, by the addition of adverbs ('now', 'loo', 'here') and second person pronoun referents: see relevant readings in Appendix 5. On similar scribal changes to Chaucer's *Troilus and Criseyde*, see Windeatt 1979: 132.

67. For examples (all from *Series* VII.3, and at places where rhyme was not a consideration) see 362–3, 895 (inversion of subject and verb), 153, 360, 434 (direct object and verb), 42, 46, 92 (auxiliary and infinitive), 72, 84 (auxiliary and participle), 34, 485 (copula and adjec-

tive), 519, 696 (preposition and verb), 515, 784, 852 (infinitive of purpose without adverbial 'to'), 25, 55, 59, 392 (negative particle preceding verb), 19, 28, 111, 233 (absolute constructions).

68. Ellis 1996: 53–4. On one form of 'high' style, the so-called 'clergial'/'curial' style, see Bornstein 1977, Burnley 1983: 243 n. 18, Burnley 1986.

69. Examples (all from the first *Gesta* narrative): VII.3.233, 342, 422, 494, 519, 616, 626, 755, 782, 795 (against, 427, 658). I have not listed in Appendix 5 examples of infinitives of purpose where *H supplies adverbial 'to' and D does not, but they are common throughout the *Series*.

70. These changes are possibly scribal rather than authorial, since a comparison of the two holograph copies of the Suso translation shows that Hoccleve seldom revises his text in ways discussed in this paragraph (exception, VII.4.308). A similar situation obtains with the non-holograph MSS of the 'Conpleynte paramont' and 'Epistre'. On similar changes by scribes to the text of Chaucer's *Troilus*, see Windeatt 1979: 136–8.

71. On this point, see n. to VII.5.666.

72. The most recent study of the *Series*, by Mills (1996), does not refer to the manuscript traditions of the work, nor, in any detail, to the translations from Suso and the *Gesta Romanorum*, but its general view of the *Series*, and detailed comments on the 'Compleinte' and 'Dialoge', overlap at several points with my own.

73. Furnivall's numbers 1–19 were given to the copies of the poems in H1 and (18) the 'Epistre' edited from the copy in F.

74. For a Latin title, 'planctus proprius', offered by Stowe and followed by Speght, see Furnivall 1970: 92. This title may well be authorial, since the holograph uses Latin throughout for its rubrics and Stowe uses Latin for the introductory rubric to his copy of item 2.

75. This may explain how the work came to acquire in 1927, from Hammond, the infelicitous title, 'The Series', which it has carried ever since. For a possible earlier title of the work, see below p. 31.

76. For fuller comment on this point, see Appendix 4.

77. So Doyle and Parkes 1978: 193.

78. For further comment on these, see Silvia 1974.

79. The three stanzas linking the prose and verse sections of the Suso were copied with the rest of that text; otherwise, the framing stanzas were not copied.

80. Admittedly, the moralizations make only imperfect sense in isolation from the preceding narratives: following the analogues, Hoccleve's moralizations regularly cut short, by means of a repeated 'etc.', the recapitulated narratives on which they depend.

81. Bale provides Latin incipits for all items in the *Series* except the tale of Jonathas (Poole and Bateson 1902: 448, Bale 1559: 537, drawn to my notice by Hudson 1997: 325); Pits provides English incipits for the 'planctum proprium' and the 'de quadam Jonatha', and Latin incipits for the rest.

82. On Lichfield Cathedral 16, see Furnivall and Gollancz 1970: xlv–xlvi, Henry and Trotter 1994.

83. For further detail, see nn. to VII.2.826, VII.3.952.

84. In particular, the translator offers his work as a mirror to his readers (31; see further VI.179n.) and describes the work as a translation (23, 28) undertaken in response to the 'steryng and_. . . mocioun' of others (26, cf. VII.2.234–5). The plainness of the offered translation (28) also has a parallel in Hoccleve (VII.3.977). For an edition of the copy in S, and of a French version close to Lydgate's source, see Hammond 1927.

85. For an earlier expression of this point, and for similar treatment of much of the material in this section, see von Nolcken 1993, whose important work I discovered only after I had completed my own.

86. The illustration in S may be part of an evolving iconographic tradition. The translation of

the same Suso chapter in the Carthusian miscellany Ad6 includes a number of crudely drawn pictures of a dying man in bed menaced, and then stabbed, with a spear by Death, with Christ looking down from heaven. Initially, the disciple figure observes the action; later, he kneels in prayer, as a way of dramatizing the work's spiritual progression.

87. For comment on these annotations, see Appendix 3.

88. For examples and comment, see Künzle 1977: 194–5, 198, 230–9, 269; for brief comment on the *Speculum*, Edwards 1984: 156, Moyes 1984: 88 and n. 57, Westlake 1993: 21, 52.

89. Of course, Hoccleve generates his own positive, immediately afterwards, with his translation 'De caelesti Jerusalem'.

90. The marginalia of 'My Compleinte' and the Suso translation reinforce such links by their repeated metaphors of gold tested in the furnace (VII.1.358) and more valuable than philosophical treatises (VII.4.78), and by their repeated reference to the bitterness of death to those who live ill (VII.1.328) as well as to those who live in pleasure (VII.4.108).

91. The word 'complaint' and its cognates occur at I.31, 245 rubric, II.20, 341–2, VI.11, 16, 190, 277, VII.1.35 (rubric), 259, 285, 317, VII.2.1, 17, 23, 40, 200, 317, 772, VII.4.148, 265, 303, 642, VII.5.240.

92. Furnivall and Gollancz 1970: 92; cf. Green 1980: 123.

93. In this sense we may see the *Series* as outgrowing or abandoning the literary model of Hoccleve's earlier *Regement*, as of other earlier poems in which the poet gives advice to his social superiors.

94. One might have thought this device a palpable fiction to allow Hoccleve to comment on the unstable relation of narrative and interpretative comment to each other. But since the English version of the second *Gesta* narrative preserved in the commonplace book of Richard Hill (*c.*1520–30) also wants the 'moralite' (Dyboski 1907: xxxv), Hoccleve's claim may just possibly be true. (Dr Diane Speed confirms for me that the *moralizacio* is occasionally missing in other copies of the work too.) If so, we may need to reckon with the possibility of a separate textual tradition for the added *moralizacio*.

95. On this point see also Batt 1996₂: 59.

96. Paraph marks are used to indicate addressee(s) of the speakers at I.43, 50, 57, 71, 127, 134, 148, 190, 204, 211, 227; to mark off a speech, and draw attention to its subdivisions, at V.57, 64, 71, 75, 80, VII.3.389 (and cf. n.); to indicate citations from classical authors (e.g. VII.2.344) and vivid figures of speech (VII.2.400); and, in the first *Gesta* narrative, to mark passages of apostrophe (VII.3.169, 246, 253) and narratorial comment (VII.3.190). For comment on a comparable structural feature, the capitulum marks in the margins of Hoccleve's 'Epistre', see Fenster and Erler 1990: 205 (n. to l. 8).

97. See nn. to VII.1.309, VII.2.369, VII.4.15.

98. Cf. above p. 8 and n. 12. In this context Hoccleve's commonplace use of economic metaphors for spiritual salvation, and repeated reference in his *Gesta* narratives to the financial arrangements of his principal characters, may also acquire special resonance (cf. IV.134n.).

99. Burrow 1994: 215 [27], 1995: 366–72.

100. On the importance of textuality as theme in Hoccleve's work, see, for example, Greetham 1989, Simpson 1991.

101. The most striking instance of a near contemporary writer reissuing second and third thoughts is Langland, on whom see Kerby-Fulton 1999; other such writers include all of the so-called Middle English mystics, and Chaucer himself.

102. On the difficulties of translating humour, see, for example, Field 1989, Beer 1991.

103. For fuller comment on this point, see nn. to I.215, 221.

104. So too Mitchell 1968: 88–9.

105. For fuller comment on these points, see nn. to VII.3.190–6, 484–97, VII.5.138–47.

106. For analysis of this material in the *Regement*, see Batt 1996₂: 76–7.

107. For further comment on Shirley, see Griffiths and Pearsall 1989 (Index s.v.) and Connolly 1996.
108. For general comment on fabliaux, see Muscatine 1986; and on Chaucerian fabliaux, Hines 1993.
109. Ellis 1996: 38–40.
110. For fuller comment on these Chaucerian echoes, see nn. to VI.197, 407–10; for earlier comment, Ellis 1996: 49, 51.
111. This variation also occurs elsewhere in the poems here edited: see Appendix 5, readings for I.87, VII.4.588, VII.5.9, 207. In the last-cited instance, occurring in a text preoccupied, like the 'Epistre', by the question of relations between the sexes, the variation may be significant.
112. For further comment on this point, see Savage 1994.
113. On Christine's use of the Genesis story, cf. Ellis 1996: 33–6.

Editorial principles

1. The texts have been re-edited from the holographs, and emended where necessary against the non-holograph copies. Material missing from the holograph copies of the 'Conpleynte paramont', 'My Compleinte' and 'A Dialoge' has been supplied from non-holograph copies of the texts: the first from Eg, the second, following Seymour 1981, from S.

2. The texts have been edited with modern capitalization, but the original spelling. Punctuation is also modern, and occasionally as a result simplifies ambiguities of phrasing in the original. Except for Roman numerals, abbreviations are expanded silently, in accordance with Hoccleve's practice with uncontracted forms, so far as this can be determined. Paragraphing of Hoccleve's prose is also modern.

3. Appendix 5 exists principally to facilitate comparison of Hoccleve's holographs with the non-holograph copies of his works. Consequently, it provides a selection of substantive variants from non-holograph copies, in particular of substantive variants common to all of the latter and, presumably, originating in their common ancestor (*H). Since *H has a purely notional existence, these are given in modern spelling. Otherwise, except for major omissions of material, I have not recorded variants peculiar to individual manuscripts. Readings from the sources and analogues of translated works are included (abbreviated 'Fr.' and 'Lat.') for purposes of comparison. For editions of 'Item de Beata Virgine' and 'My Compleinte', full collations exist in the editions of Boyd and Seymour, so my collation supplements theirs, in the latter case by providing variants from D alone or in combination with the other MSS so as to make comparison easier with Furnivall's edition. For the opening six stanzas of the 'Conpleynte paramont' and ll. 1–252 of the 'Dialoge', I provide a fuller collation. Of the many marginal annotations in later hands, only those are noted which directly refer to the text: for the remainder in D, see Furnivall's edition.

A note on Hoccleve's language

In some ways Hoccleve's poetry looks very like Chaucer's, and seems as directly approachable; in other ways, its deliberate inversions of normal word order (noted above p. 24), especially those not called for by metre and rhyme, can present beginner readers with a very real challenge.

1. It can be hard to distinguish noun subjects and objects of verbs when normal word order is disturbed: examples include 'þat knowe mighte it euery creature' (I.96) and 'bite me the crowe' (VII.2.810), where only the context helps us recognize 'euery creature' and 'crow' as subjects and 'it' and 'me' as direct objects of their respective verbs. At VII.2.573–4, yet more strikingly ('Duc Henri, þat so worthy was and good/Folwith this prince, as wel in deede as blood'), we need a knowledge of the historical context to appreciate that Duke Henry is the object of imitation by Duke Humphrey ('this prince'), who is subject of the clause.

2. Less difficulty is created by the omission of infinitives of purpose and impersonal subject pronouns, though the result is sometimes strange enough to give a reader pause; for example, in the lines 'Why souffrest thow him, in the open sighte/Of the folk heer, vnkeuered abyde' (I.137; read ' to abide') and 'from al which song is good men hem to kepe' (II.240, read 'it is good').

As far as possible, I have used modern punctuation and marginal glosses to iron out these difficulties.

MINOR VERSE

I.

Conpleynte paramont

[*Superlative complaint*]

	O fader God, how fers and how cruel,	*fierce*
	In whom the list or wilt, canst þu the make.	*please*
	Whom wilt thu spare, ne wot I neuere a deel,	*not at all*
	Sithe thu thi sone hast to the deth betake,	*since; committed*
5	That the offended neuere ne dide wrake,	*harm*
	Or mystook him to the or disobeyde,	*acted wrongly*
	Ne to non other dide he harme or seide.	
	I had ioye entiere and also gladnesse	*entire*
	Whan þu betook him me to clothe and wrappe	*entrusted*
10	In mannes flesch. I wend, in sothfastnesse,	*thought; truth*
	Have had for euere ioye be the lappe.	*in my grasp*
	But now hath sorwe caught me with his trappe.	
	My ioye hath made a permutacioun	
	With wepyng and eek lamentacioun.	*also*
15	O holy gost, þat art alle confortoure	
	Of woful hertes that wofull be	
	And art hire veray helpe and counceyloure,	*their true; counsellor*
	That of hey vertue shadowist me	*with great power overshadowed*
	Whan þat the clernesse of thi diuinite	*brightness*
20	So shynyng in my feerful gost alight,	*spirit alighted*
	Which that me sore agasted and affright,	*alarmed; frightened*
	Whi hast thu me not in thi remembraunce	
	Now at this tyme right as thu had tho?	*then*

O, whi is it noght to thin pleasaunce   *pleasure*
25 Now for to shadwe me as weel also,   *overshadow; well*
That hid from me myght be my sones woo?
Wherof if þat I may no counfort haue,   *from which*
From dethis strok ther may nothing me save.   *stroke*

O Gaubriel, whan þat thou come aplace   *into the place*
30 And madest vnto me thi salewyng   *salutation*
And seidist thus, "Heil Mary, ful of grace",
Whi ne had thu gove me warnyng   *did not; give*
Of þat grace that veyn is and faylyng,   *transitory*
As thu now seest, and sey it weel beforne?   *saw; well before*
35 Sith my ioye is me rafte, my grace is lorne.   *since; taken from me; lost*

O thu Elizabeth, my cosyn dere,
The word[es] þat thu spak in the mowntayn
Be ended al in another maner   *are realized; altogether*
Than thu had wened. My blissyng into peyne   *thought*
40 Retorned is. Of ioye am I bareyne.   *turned*
I song to sone, for I sang be the morwe,   *sang; soon; in the dawning*
And now at even I wepe and make sorwe.

O womman þat among the peple speek,   *spoke*
How þat the wombe blessid was þat beer,   *bore (Christ)*
45 And the tetes þat yaf to sowken eek   *breasts; gave suck also*
The sone of God, which on hy hangith heer,
What seist thow now, why comest thow no neer?   *nearer*
Why n'art thow heer? O womman, wher art thow
That nat ne seest my woful wombe now?

50 O Simeon, thow seidest me ful sooth,   *truly*
The strook that perce shal my sones herte   *stroke; pierce*
My soule thirle it shal, and so it dooth.   *thrill*
The wownde of deeth ne may I nat asterte.   *escape from*
Ther may no martirdom me make smerte   *cause me pain*
55 So sore as this martire smertith me.   *suffering; pains*
So sholde he seyn þat myn hurt mighte see.

O Ioachim, o deer fadir myn,
And Seint Anne, my modir deer also,

	To what entente, or to what ende or fyn,	*purpose*
60	Broghten yee me foorth þat am greeued so?	*did you engender me*
	Mirthe is to me become a verray fo.	*true*
	Your fadir Dauid þat an harpour was	
	Conforted folk þat stood in heuy cas.	*who were grief-stricken*

	Me thynkith yee nat doon to me aright	*it seems to me; do; right*
65	þat wer his successours, syn instrument	*descendants; since*
	Han yee noon left wherwith me make light	*to make me cheerful*
	And me conforte in my woful torment.	
	Me to doon ese han yee no talent,	*desire*
	And knowen myn conforteless distresse.	*although you know*
70	Yee oghten weepe for myn heuynesse.	*ought to*

	O blessid sone, on thee wole I out throwe	*over; pour out*
	My salte teeres, for oonly on thee	
	My look is set. O thynke, how many a throwe	*time*
	Thow in myn armes lay and on my knee	
75	Thow sat and haddist many a kus of me.	*kiss*
	Eek thee to sowke on my brestes yaf Y,	*suck; permitted*
	Thee norisshyng fair and tendrely.	*fairly*

	Now thee fro me withdrawith bittir deeth	
	And makith a wrongful disseuerance.	*separation*
80	Thynke nat, sone, in me þat any breeth	
	Endure may þat feele al this greuance.	*grief*
	My martirdom me hath at the outrance.	*extremity*
	I needes sterue moot syn I thee see	*must die since*
	Shamely nakid, strecchid on a tree.	*shamefully*

85	And this me sleeth, þat in the open day	*kills; broad daylight*
	Thyn hertes wownde shewith him so wyde	*shows itself*
	þat alle folk see and beholde it may,	
	So largeliche opned is thy syde.	
	O wo is me, syn I nat may it hyde.	*since*
90	And among othre of my smerte greeues	*sharp griefs*
	Thow put art also, sone, amonges theeues,	

| | As thow wer an euel and wikkid wight. | *as if; person* |
| | And lest þat somme folk perauenture | *by chance* |

No knowleche hadde of thy persone aright,   *rightly*
95 Thy name Pilat hath put in scripture   *written on a notice*
þat knowe mighte it euery creature,
For thy penance sholde nat been hid.   *so that*
O wo is me, þat al this see betid.   *happen*

How may myn yen þat beholde al this   *eyes*
100 Restreyne hem for to shewe by weepynge   *keep themselves from showing*
Myn hertes greef? Moot I nat weepe? O yis.   *must; yes*
Sone, if thow haddist a fadir lyuynge
That wolde weepe and make waymentynge   *lamenting*
For þat he hadde paart of thy persone,   *a share in*
105 That wer a greet abreggynge of my mone.   *would be; abridgement*

But thow in eerthe fadir haddist neuere.
No wight for thee swich cause hath for to pleyne   *person; such; complain*
As þat haue I. Shalt thow fro me disseuere   *separate*
þat aart al hoolly myn? My sorwes deepe   *wholly*
110 Han al myn hertes ioie leid to sleepe.
No wight with me in thee, my sone, hath part.   *person*
Hoolly of my blood, deer chyld, thow art.   *wholly*

That doublith al my torment and my greef.
Vnto myn herte it is confusion
115 Thyn harm to see, þat art to me so leef.   *dear*
Mighte nat, sone, the redempcioun
Of man han bee withoute effusioun   *have been; pouring out*
Of thy blood? Yis, if it had been thy lust.   *yes; pleasure*
But what thow wilt be doon, souffre me must.   *I must endure*

120 O deeth, so thow kythist thy bittirnesse   *how; showest*
First on my sone and aftirward on me.
Bittir art thow and ful of crabbidnesse   *harshness*
That my sone hast slayn thurgh thy crueltee   *through*
And nat me sleest. Certein nat wole I flee.   *not; certainly*
125 Come of, come of, and slee me heer as blyue.   *come along; at once*
Departe from him wole I nat alyue.

O moone, o sterres, and thow firmament,
How may yee from wepynge yow restreyne   *prevent yourselves*

And seen your creatour in swich torment? *see; such*

130 Yee oghten troublid been in every veyne *to be disturbed*

And his despitous deeth with me conpleyne. *wretched*

Weepeth and crieth as lowde as yee may.

Our creatour with wrong is slayn this day. *unjustly*

O sonne, with thy cleere bemes brighte

135 þat seest my child nakid this nones tyde, *noontide*

Why souffrest thow him in the open sighte *do you allow; full view*

Of the folk heer vnkeuered abyde? *people; uncovered; to remain*

Thou art as moche or more, holde him to hyde *much; obliged*

Than Sem þat helid his fadir Noe *as Shem; covered*

140 Whan he espyde þat nakid was he. *saw*

If thow his sone be, do lyk therto. *similarly*

Come of, withdrawe thy bemes brightnesse. *come along*

Thow art to blame but if thow so do. *unless*

For shame, hyde my sones nakidnesse.

145 Is ther in thee no sparcle of kyndenesse? *spark; natural inclination*

Remembre he is thy lord and creatour.

Now keuere him for thy worsship and honour. *cover*

O eerthe, what lust hast thow to susteene *desire; support*

The crois on which he þat thee made and it *Cross*

150 Is hangid, and aourned thee with greene *decked*

Which þat thow werist? How hast thow thee qwit *wearest; repaid*

Vnto thy lord? O do this for him yit. *yet*

Qwake for doel and cleue thow in two, *grief*

And al þat blood restore me vnto

155 Which thow hast dronke. It myn is and nat thyn.

Or elles thus, withouten taryynge, *else; delay*

Tho bodyes dede whiche in thee þat lyn *those; dead; lie*

Caste out, for they by taast of swich dewynge *taste; moisture*

Hem oghte clothe ageyn in hir clothynge. *ought to clothe themselves; their*

160 Thow Caluarie, thow art namely *especially*

Holden for to do so. To thee speke Y. *obliged*

O deer sone, myn deeth neighith faste *approaches*

Syn to anothir thow hast youen me *since; given*

Than vnto thee. And how may my lyf laste
165 þat me yeuest any othir than thee?   *when you give me to*
Thogh he whom thow me yeuest maiden be   *givest; virgin*
And thogh by iust balance thow weye al,   *just; weigh*
The weighte of him and thee nat is egal.   *equal*

He a disciple is and thow art a lord.
170 Thow al away art gretter than he is.   *always*
Betwixt your mightes is ther greet discord.   *powers; difference*
My woful torment doublid is by this.
I needes mourne moot and fare amis.   *must; suffer misery*
It seemeth þat thow makist departynge   *separation*
175 Twixt thee and me for ay withoute endynge,

And namely syn thow me 'womman' callist,   *especially since*
As I to thee straunge wer and vnknowe.   *as if; foreign; unknown*
Therthurgh, my sone, thow my ioie appallist.   *by that means; weaken*
Wel feele I þat deeth his vengeable bowe   *vengeful*
180 Hath bent and me purposith doun to throwe.   *proposes; cast*
Of sorwe talke may I nat ynow,   *enough*
Syn fro my name 'I' doon away is now.   *since; taken*

Wel may men clepe and calle me Mara   *call*
From hennesforward, so may men me call.   *henceforward*
185 How sholde I lenger clept be Maria,   *longer called*
Syn 'I', which is Ihesus, is fro me fall.   *which stands for; fallen*
This day al my swetnesse is into gall
Torned, syn þat 'I', which was the beautee   *turned; since*
Of my name, this day bynome is me.   *is taken from*

190 O Iohn my deer freend, thow hast receyued
A woful modir, and an heuy sone
Haue I of thee. Deeth hath myn othir weyued.   *in you; carried off*
How may we two the deeth eschue or shone?   *avoid; shun*
We drery wightes two, wher may we wone?   *miserable people; dwell*
195 Thou art of confort destitut, I see,
And so am I. Ful careful been wee.   *all full of care are we*

Vnto our hertes deeth hath sent his wownde.
Noon of vs may alleggen othres peyne.   *lighten; the other's*

So manye sorwes in vs two habownde	*abound*
200 We han no might fro sorwe vs restreyne.	*power; to restrain ourselves*
I see noon othir, die moot we tweyne.	*must*
Now let vs steruen heer par conpaignie.	*die; for company's sake*
Sterue thow ther, and heere wole I die.	*die*
O angels, thogh yee mourne and waile and weepe,	
205 Yee do no wrong. Slayn is your creatour	
By tho folk þat yee weren wont to keepe	*those people*
And gye and lede. They to dethes shour	*guide; conflict*
Han put him. Thogh yee han wo and langour,	*grief*
No wondir is it. Who may blame yow?	
210 And yit ful cheer he had hem þat him slow.	*great kindness; to those; slew*
O special loue, þat me ioyned haast	
Vnto my sone, strong is thy knyttynge.	*fierce*
This day therin fynde I a bittir taast,	*in it (i.e. in the love)*
For now the taast I feele and the streynynge	*pressure*
215 Of deeth. By thy deeth feele I deeth me stynge.	
O poore modir, what shalt thow now seye?	
Poore Marie, thy wit is aweye.	
Marie? Nay, but 'marred' I thee calle.	
So may I wel, for thow art, wel I woot,	*know*
220 Vessel of care and wo and sorwes alle.	
Now thow art frosty cold, now fyry hoot,	*fiery hot*
And right as þat a ship or barge or boot	*boat*
Among the wawes dryueth steerelees,	*waves; rudderless*
So doost thow, woful womman, confortlees.	*comfortless*
225 And of modir haast thow eek lost the style.	*also; title*
No more maist thow clept be by thy name.	*called*
O sones of Adam, al to long whyle	
Yee tarien hens. Hieth hidir for shame.	*tarry; hasten here*
See how my sone for your gilt and blame	
230 Hangith heer al bybled vpon the crois.	*bloody; Cross*
Bymeneth him in herte and cheere and vois.	*lament; bearing*
His blody stremes see now and beholde.	
If yee to him han any affeccioun	

Now for his wo your hertes oghten colde.   *ought to grow cold*
235 Shewith your loue and your dileccioun.   *affection*
For your gilt makith he correccioun
And amendes right by his owne deeth.
That yee nat reewe on him, myn herte it sleeth.   *in that; have pity*

A modir þat so soone hir cote taar   *coat tore*
240 Or rente, sy men neuere noon or this,   *saw; before now*
For chyld which þat shee of hir body baar   *bore*
To yeue her tete, as my chyld þat heer is.   *give him her breast*
His cote hath torn for your gilt, nat for his,   *(he) has torn*
And hath his blood despent in greet foysoun,   *spent; plenty*
245 And al it was for your redempcioun.

C'est tout.   *This is all*

Ceste conpleynte paramont feust translatee au commandement de ma dame de Hereford, que Dieu pardoynt
[*This excellent complaint was translated at the commandment of my lady of Hereford; may God grant her pardon*]

Notes

In the following notes, readings from French MSS of the *Pèlerinage* (relevant lines, 6353–644) are given for comparative purposes. Three in particular (Ad2Ad4C2) are close to Hoccleve's source. Seymour notes the closeness of Ad2 to the translation (sigla C2L used below are from Stürzinger 1895). Neither Ad2 nor Ad4 can have been Hoccleve's actual source, since Hoccleve does not share their error at l55: Hoccleve's 'dronke' corresponds to Fr. 6525 'beu', not the Ad2Ad4 reading 'veu'. The work belongs to the medieval genre of Marian lament: for other examples, see Brown 1939 nos. 6–10, Davies 1961, and general discussion in Keiser 1985.

10 *flesch*: Fr. 'escorce' [bark]. Here and elsewhere (cf. 35, 243nn.) the translation suppresses the metaphor of Christ as the fruit taken from a green tree (the Virgin) and hung from a dry tree (the Cross).

13 *ioye*: Fr. 'gieu' [game]. Hoccleve's source may have read 'ioie'. Alternatively, Hoccleve was indulging in what Arn 1994 and Phillips 1994 have called homonym substitution. Another example may be 'remembraunce' (22), Fr. 'obumbres' [you overshadow], correctly translated elsewhere as 'shadwe' (25).

15–17 Cf. Fr. 'He saint esperit, conforteur/Des cuers [Ad2Ad4C2 *add* dolens] et vrai [Ad2Ad4C2 *om.* vrai] conseilleur'.

18, 25 Cf. Luke 1.35.

20 *alight* can carry several meanings ('to alight', 'to enlighten', 'to lighten'): Fr. 6373 'descendi' is closest to the first of these.

25 *also*: Fr. 'ainsi' (Ad2Ad4C2 aussi).

29 *aplace*: Seymour follows the Co reading 'apace', but there is precedent for the reading here followed from Eg, and shared by most of the MSS, in the medieval carol 'Nova nova Ave fit ex Eva' (Dyboski 1908: 5–6).

31 Cf. Luke 1.28.

35 Hoccleve here and elsewhere (cf. 113–19, 229–38nn.) loses Deguileville's

commonplace metaphor of the blood of Christ as a drink of power to inebriate those who will drink deeply of it: cf. Fr. 'succies… faites que yvres soies tous' [suck it… so that you are all drunk]. Here, for the second clause of the line, Deguileville writes 'la grace est jus espandue' [grace is a juice poured out]. But since Ad2Ad4C2 omit 'jus' at this point, and so lose the explicit point of the metaphor, Hoccleve may have been faithfully following a version of the original in which such material was absent. The omission is the more striking, if we reflect (a) how common such imagery is in late medieval English religious writing; (b) that Hoccleve is writing at a time when the Wycliffite attack on the Eucharist might have made it seem more necessary to underline the link between the Eucharist and the Crucifixion. Since the stanzas added to the *Pilgrimage* (see Appendix 1) do contain such material, they may have been based on another manuscript tradition than that followed by Hoccleve: which may suggest Hoccleve did not write them.

36–7 Cf. Luke 1.39–42.

41–2 A probable addition by Hoccleve to the text.

43–5 Cf. Luke 11.27. Hoccleve has added to Deguileville from the Bible text the second element of the woman's blessing ('and the tetes þat yaf to sowken eek'.)

50 Cf. Luke 2.35. The metaphoric sword referred to there (Fr. 6405 'glaive'; Hoccleve's 'strook') Deguileville glosses traditionally as the literal spear that pierced the side of Christ (John 19.34).

60 *H's 'engendred' is closer to Deguileville's 'engendrastes' than H1's 'broghten yee me foorth', but the agreement may not be significant.

62 On David as a harpist, cf. 1 Sam. 18.10. David is regularly represented iconographically, as author of the Psalms, with a harp in his hands.

71–2 In Deguileville, the Virgin proposes to speak to Christ, not to 'out throwe... salte teeres'.

86 The wounded heart of Christ, inspired by John 19.34, became a vital element in late medieval iconography and appears regularly in mystical writing (e.g. Richard Rolle and Julian of Norwich).

95 Cf. John 19.19.

97 Cf. Fr. 6452–3 'afin que a confusion/tu soies de tous cogneu'.

113–19 The first line of this stanza faithfully translates Deguileville ('si en est double mon tourment'): the rest represents only the general sense of the French, and suppresses its allegorical elements. Ad2Ad4 also lose the allegory at Fr. 6472: for the original's 'd'autre pomme ressaisi' they offer 'par aultre paine [Ad2 orig. pome?] rassaisi'.

134 Cf. Matt. 27.45 (the eclipse of the sun between noon and 3 p.m. at the Crucifixion). Deguileville, followed by Hoccleve, may imply that the sun responds to the cry of the Virgin by going into eclipse (cf. 142).

138 as moche or more: Fr. 6511 'autant et [C2 autant ou, Ad2Ad4 aucunement ou] plus'.

139–40 Cf. Gen. 9.23.

141 if thow his sone be: Fr. 6516 'si bon [L son] fil es [Ad2Ad4 om es]'.

149 crois. Here again Hoccleve loses the allegory: cf. Fr. 6520 'cel arbre sec'.

153 qwake for doel: Fr. 6523 'croule de dueil'.

153, 157–8 references to the prodigies which accompanied the death of Christ (an earthquake and the raising of dead bodies: cf. Matt. 27.51).

162ff. Cf. John 19.25–7. John, to whom Christ entrusted his mother, directing

her ('womman', 176) to take him as her son, was understood in the Middle Ages to have remained virgin (166) all his life. deere son (162): cf. Fr. 6533 'He [C2 adds doulz] fil'

174 departynge: Fr. 6544 'departement'.

182ff. Ad2Ad4 add material at this point, not followed by Hoccleve, to make explicit the identification of Maria/Mara with the bitterness (amara) which the name Mara connotes: 'on peut oster i de mon nom/et deuant .a. adiouster peut on/ appelle soie et nommer amara' [you could remove the 'i' from my name and add an 'a' before it, so that I shall be called bitter]. The first line of this addition corresponds to Fr. 6553 'ainsi ostant i de mon nom' [thus removing I from my name]. One MS of the English translation of the Pèlerinage (Co) loses the pun by miscopying 'Mara' as 'Maria' at 183.

186 Here, and again at 188–9, Hoccleve well represents—better than most of the other copyists of his text—Deguileville's punning etymology. For fuller comment, see Introduction p. 16. On the etymology of Maria, cf. Shepherd 1959: 46 (n. to 14/10); on its Biblical origins, Exod. 15.23 (so Seymour's n.), Ruth 1.20. One MS of the French also had difficulty with this passage: for Fr. 6557 'car i, c'est Ihesus', L reads 'car le bon jhesus' (cf. B3's 'swete Jhesus').

189 name/bynome: possibly Hoccleve intends an echo effect here, which *H loses by substituting 'byraft'. Admittedly, 'bynome' is much less common with Hoccleve than 'reft' (e.g. IV.156, VI.632, 1.229, 2.285, 396, 3.244, 4.906).

201 I see noon othir: 'I see no other course of action open to us but that', or 'I see noone else about' (cf. Fr. 6573 'povre assemblee en nous a').

202 A possible echo—if so, ironic—of Chaucerian fabliaux (see CT I.3839, 4167).

215 In both H1 and *H this line, by its imprecise division of phrases (a characteristic feature of Hoccleve's syntax) and repeated use of the word 'death', suggests the intimate connections between Christ's literal and actual experience of death and the Virgin's subjective and quasi-metaphoric

experience of the same process. The use of the word 'stynge' echoes St Paul ('the sting of death is sin', 1 Cor. 15.56) and thus makes the Virgin a figure of those for whose sin Christ's death must atone. It is a bold stroke, though not unprecedented in the original, to have made the Virgin a figure of unredeemed and suffering humanity. The version in *H makes the effect stronger by setting the two deaths immediately after each other.

218–26 Hoccleve did his best to preserve the Deguileville pun at the outset (*Marie/marrie*) but, in what follows, he does not preserve the complex puns on 'amer/amere/a mer/mere'. Deguileville had written (6589–96) how Mary should not be called mother ('mere') so much as bitterness ('amere'); love made Mary love ('amer') and filled her with such bitterness that from sea to sea ('de mer a mer') one cannot find her better. Hoccleve develops the one detail ('de mer a mer') into the metaphor, an echo of Chaucer, of Mary as a courtly lover (221n.) adrift on a sea of misfortune (222–4, cf. *Troilus* I.416). This latter image has the effect of recalling the speech of Gabriel at the Annunciation (29–31 above) whose promised 'grace' now turns out to be 'veyn… and faylyng'.

221 *frosty cold… fyry hoot*: this figure, a commonplace of courtly writing (cf. *Troilus* I.420), is also used in a more general sense by Hoccleve to describe an individual's experience of the vagaries of life (cf. *Series* 1.154n.) The echo of *Troilus* is reinforced by the following metaphor of the Virgin as a rudderless ship (222–4, cf. *Troilus* I.416–18), though the latter might also contain an echo of the rudderless ship in *The Man of Law's Tale*, abbreviated *MLT*, on which see Kolve 1984: 325ff.

229–38 Here again the central Deguileville metaphor of the 'jus' flowing from the wounds of Christ is lost, and replaced by the simpler metaphor of the blood streaming from the wounds of Christ as the object of compassionate attention.

243 *cote*: Hoccleve's repetition of this word from 239 loses the allegory again (Fr. 6611 escorce [bark]).

245 (rubric) *que Dieu pardoynt*: these words indicate that the dedicatee had died between the time when Hoccleve received the commission from her and the time when he made the copy. She died in 1419. For further information about her, see Seymour.

II

Cy ensuyt la male regle de T. Hoccleue

[Here follows the unruly life of Thomas Hoccleve]

O precious tresor inconparable!
O ground and roote of prosperitee!
O excellent richesse commendable
Abouen all þat in eerthe be!

5 Who may susteene thyn aduersitee?   *opposition*
What wight may him auante of worldly welthe,   *man; boast*
But if he fully stande in grace of thee,   *unless; in your grace*
Eerthely god, piler of lyf, thow helthe?   *pillar*

Whil thy power and excellent vigour,
10 As was plesant vnto thy worthynesse,
Regned in me, and was my gouernour,
Than was I wel, tho felte I no duresse.   *then; hardship*
Tho farsid was I with hertes gladnesse.   *stuffed*
And now my body empty is, and bare
15 Of ioie and ful of seekly heuynesse,   *sickly*
Al poore of ese and ryche of euel fare.   *in things bringing ease; in misfortune*

If þat thy fauour twynne from a wight,   *separate*
Smal is his ese and greet is his greuance.   *distress*
Thy loue is lyf. Thyn hate sleeth doun right.   *kills immediately*
20 Who may conpleyne thy disseuerance   *lament; departure*
Bettre than I þat, of myn ignorance,
Vnto seeknesse am knyt, thy mortel fo?   *sickness*
Now can I knowe feeste fro penaunce,   *distinguish feasting*
And whil I was with thee, kowde I nat so.

25 My grief and bisy smert cotidian   *anxious daily pain*
    So me labouren and tormenten sore
    þat what thow art now wel remembre I can,
    And what fruyt is in keepynge of thy lore.   *profit; teaching*
    Had I thy power knowen or this yore,   *long before this*
30 As now thy fo conpellith me to knowe,
    Nat sholde his lym han cleued to my gore,   *lime; clung; clothing*
    For al his aart, ne han me broght thus lowe.

    But I haue herd men seye longe ago,
    Prosperitee is blynd and see ne may,
35 And verifie I can wel it is so,
    For I myself put haue it in assay.   *to the proof*
    Whan I was weel, kowde I considere it? Nay,   *well*
    But what me longed aftir nouelrie,   *I yearned; novelty*
    As yeeres yonge yernen day by day,   *those young in years*
40 And now my smert accusith my folie.   *hurt; censures*

    Myn vnwar yowthe kneew nat what it wroghte,   *ignorant; was doing*
    This woot I wel, whan fro thee twynned shee.   *know; separated*
    But of hir ignorance hirself shee soghte,
    And kneew nat þat shee dwellyng was with
        thee,
45 For to a wight wer it greet nycetee   *person; would be; folly*
    His lord or freend wityngly for t'offende,   *knowingly*
    Lest þat the weighte of his aduersitee
    The fool oppresse and make of him an ende.   *constrain*

    From hennesfoorth wole I do reuerence
50 Vnto thy name, and holde of thee in cheef,   *be your tenant*
    And werr make and sharp resistence   *war*
    Ageyn thy fo and myn, þat cruel theef,
    þat vndir foote me halt in mescheef,   *holds; wretchedness*
    So thow me to thy grace reconcyle.   *restore*
55 O now thyn help, thy socour and releef,   *now (grant)*
    And I for ay misreule wole exyle.   *ever; banish*

    But thy mercy excede myn offense,   *unless; surpass*
    The keene assautes of thyn aduersarie   *assaults*
    Me wole oppresse with hir violence.   *their*

60   No wondir thogh thow be to me contrarie.
     My lustes blynde han causid thee to varie   *desires; pass*
     Fro me thurgh my folie and inprudence,
     Wherfore I wrecche curse may and warie   *curse*
     The seed and fruyt of chyldly sapience.   *childish wisdom*

65   As for the more paart, youthe is rebel   *for the most part*
     Vnto reson, and hatith hir doctryne,   *teaching*
     Regnynge which, it may nat stande wel
     With yowthe, as fer as wit can ymagyne.   *far*
     O yowthe, allas, why wilt thow nat enclyne,   *bow*
70   And vnto reuled resoun bowe thee,   *the rule of reason*
     Syn resoun is the verray streighte lyne   *since; true*
     þat ledith folk vnto felicitee?   *happiness*

     Ful seelde is seen þat yowthe takith heede   *seldom*
     Of perils þat been likly for to fall,   *dangers; occur*
75   For, haue he take a purpos, þat moot neede   *once he has taken; must needs*
     Been execut. No conseil wole he call.   *carried out; advice; call (for)*
     His owne wit he deemeth best of all,   *judges*
     And foorth therwith he renneth brydillees,   *runs; unbridled*
     As he þat nat betwixt hony and gall   *like one who*
80   Can iuge, ne the werr fro the pees.   *war*

     All othir mennes wittes he despisith.
     They answeren nothyng to his entent.   *correspond not at all*
     His rakil wit only to him souffysith.   *rash; alone; suffices*
     His hy presumpcioun nat list consente   *pleases not to agree*
85   To doon as þat Salomon wroot and mente,
     þat redde men by conseil for to werke.   *advised; on advice; act*
     Now, youthe, now thow sore shalt repente
     Thy lightlees wittes dull, of reson derke.   *benighted; dark (for want) of*
     reason

     My freendes seiden vnto me ful ofte
90   My misreule me cause wolde a fit,
     And redden me in esy wyse and softe   *advised; manner*
     A lyte and lyte to withdrawen it,   *little by little*
     But þat nat mighte synke into my wit,
     So was the lust yrootid in myn herte.   *pleasure rooted*

95 And now I am so rype vnto my pit	*ready for my grave*
þat scarsely I may it nat asterte.	*I may escape it*
Whoso cleer yen hath, and can nat see,	*bright eyes*
Ful smal, of ye, auaillith the office.	*very little; eye; exercise*
Right so, syn reson youen is to me	*since; given*
100 For to discerne a vertu from a vice,	
If I nat can with reson me cheuice,	*know how to; get on with*
But wilfully fro reson me withdrawe,	*willingly*
Thogh I of hir haue no benefice,	*benefit*
No wondir, ne no fauour in hir lawe.	*nor that I find no favour*
105 Reson me bad, and redde as for the beste,	*advised*
To ete and drynke in tyme attemprely,	*moderately*
But wilful youthe nat obeie leste	*was not pleased to obey*
Vnto þat reed, ne sette nat therby.	*advice; nothing by it*
I take haue of hem bothe outrageously,	*to excess*
110 And out of tyme. Nat two yeer or three,	*out of (due) time*
But xxti wyntir past continuelly,	*twenty years*
Excesse at borde hath leyd his knyf with me.	*table*
The custume of my repleet abstinence,	*abstaining only when full*
My greedy mowth, receite of swich outrage,	*receiver; excess*
115 And hondes two, as woot my negligence,	*knows*
Thus han me gyded and broght in seruage	*servitude*
Of hir þat werreieth euery age,	*wars against*
Seeknesse, Y meene, riotoures whippe,	*the scourge of the riotous man*
Habundantly þat paieth me my wage,	
120 So þat me neithir daunce list, ne skippe.	*I . . . please*
The outward signe of Bachus and his lure,	
þat at his dore hangith day by day,	
Excitith folk to taaste of his moisture	
So often þat men can nat wel seyn nay.	
125 For me, I seye I was enclyned ay	
Withouten daunger thidir for to hye me	*holding off; hasten*
But if swich charge vpon my bak lay	*unless such a load*
That I moot it forber as for a tyme,	*forego*

Or but I wer nakidly bystad | *unless; placed like one naked*
130 By force of the penylees maladie, | *penurious sickness*
For thanne in herte kowde I nat be glad,
Ne lust had noon to Bachus hows to hie. | *desire; hasten*
Fy! Lak of coyn departith conpaignie, | *separates*
And heuy purs, with herte liberal, | *generous heart*
135 Qwenchith the thristy hete of hertes drie, | *thirsty*
Wher chynchy herte hath therof but smal. | *stingy; little benefit of it*

I dar nat telle how þat the fressh repeir | *lively company*
Of Venus femel lusty children deer | *pleasing female*
þat so goodly, so shaply wer, and feir, | *shapely*
140 And so plesant of port and of maneere, | *carriage*
And feede cowden al a world with cheere, | *with a look*
And of atyr passyngly wel byseye, | *attire; surpassingly; provided*
At Poules Heed me maden ofte appeere, | *(the tavern of) Paul's Head*
To talke of mirthe and to disporte and pleye.

145 Ther was sweet wyn ynow thurghout the hous, | *enough; throughout*
And wafres thikke, for this conpaignie | *wafers*
þat I spak of been sumwhat likerous. | *is fond of good food*
Wheras they mowe a draght of wyn espie, | *where; may*
Sweete, and in wirkynge hoot for the maistrie | *powerfully hot*
150 To warme a stommak with, therof they drank.
To suffre hem paie had been no courtesie. | *let; would have been churlish*
That charge I took, to wynne loue and thank. | *thanks*

Of loues aart yit touchid I no deel. | *had no contact*
I cowde nat, and eek it was no neede. | *didn't know how; also*
155 Had I a kus, I was content ful weel, | *kiss; well*
Bettre than I wolde han be with the deede. | *sexual act*
Theron can I but smal, it is no dreede. | *Of it I know only a little; doubt*
Whan þat men speke of it in my presence | *spoke*
For shame I wexe as reed as is the gleede. | *grew; red; glowing coal*
160 Now wole I torne ageyn to my sentence. | *turn; matter*

Of him þat hauntith tauerne of custume, | *resorts to; frequently*
At shorte wordes, the profyt is this: | *briefly*
In double wyse his bagge it shal consume | *twice over; (money) bag*
And make his tonge speke of folk amis,

165 For in the cuppe seelden fownden is *seldom is it found*
þat any wight his neigheburgh commendith. *man; neighbour*
Beholde and see what auantage is his *advantage*
þat God, his freend and eek himself offendith. *who; also*

But oon auantage in this cas I haue: *one*
170 I was so ferd with any man to fighte, *afraid*
Cloos kepte I me. No man durste I depraue *quiet; dared*
But rownyngly I spak, nothyng on highte. *whisperingly; aloud*
And yit my wil was good, if þat I mighte, *i.e. speak aloud*
For lettynge of my manly cowardyse, *(save) for hindering*
175 þat ay of strokes impressid the wighte, *always; (with fear) of; person*
So þat I durste medlyn in no wyse. *fight; way*

Wher was a gretter maistir eek than Y, *master also*
Or bet aqweyntid at Westmynstre yate, *better; known; gate*
Among the tauerneres namely *especially*
180 And cookes, whan I cam eerly or late? *early*
I pynchid nat at hem in myn acate, *found no fault with; purchase*
But paied hem as þat they axe wolde, *ask*
Wherfore I was the welcomer algate *always*
And for a verray gentilman yholde. *true; reckoned*

185 And if it happid on the someres day *happened*
þat I thus at the tauerne hadde be,
Whan I departe sholde and go my way
Hoom to the Priuee Seel, so wowed me *home; Privy Seal; enticed*
Hete and vnlust and superfluitee *disinclination; excess*
190 To walke vnto the brigge and take a boot *boat*
þat nat durste I contrarie hem all three,
But dide as þat they stired me, God woot. *knows*

And in the wyntir, for the way was deep, *covered with mud*
Vnto the brigge I dressid me also, *wharf; went*
195 And ther the bootmen took vpon me keep, *boatmen; took note of me*
For they my riot kneewen fern ago. *long since*
With hem I was itugged to and fro, *pulled*
So wel was him þat I with wolde fare, *happy he was; travel*
For riot paieth largely eueremo. *generously*
200 He styntith neuere til his purs be bare. *ceases*

Othir than maistir callid was I neuere
Among this meynee, in myn audience.   *troop; hearing*
Methoghte I was ymaad a man for euere,   *I seemed made*
So tikelid me þat nyce reuerence   *tickled; senseless*
205 þat it me made larger of despense   *in spending*
Than þat I thoghte han been. O flaterie,   *intended to be*
The guyse of thy traiterous diligence   *way*
Is, folk to mescheef haasten and to hie.   *to hasten and hurry*

Albeit þat my yeeres be but yonge,
210 Yit haue I seen in folk of hy degree,
How þat the venym of faueles tonge   *the flatterer's*
Hath mortified hir prosperitee   *poisoned; their*
And broght hem in so sharp aduersitee   *into*
þat it hir lyf hath also throwe adoun.
215 And yit ther can no man in this contree   *region*
Vnnethe eschue this confusioun.   *scarcely; escape*

Many a seruant vnto his lord seith
þat al the world spekith of him honour
Whan the contrarie of þat is sooth, in feith,   *true*
220 And lightly leeued is this losengeour.   *easily believed; flatterer*
His hony wordes wrappid in errour   *honey-sweet*
Blyndly conceyued been, the more harm is.   *understood*
O, thow fauele, of lesynges auctour,   *flattery; author of lies*
Causist al day thy lord to fare amis.   *go wrong*

225 Tho combreworldes clept been enchantours,   *those wastes of space; called*
In bookes as þat I haue, or this, red,   *before; read*
That is to seye, sotil deceyuou[r]s,   *cunning*
By whom the peple is misgyed and led   *led and directed wrongly*
And with plesance so fostred and fed   *pleasure*
230 þat they forgete hemself, and can nat feele   *forget*
The soothe of the condicion in hem bred,   *truth*
No more than hir wit wer in hir heele.   *than if their brains*

Whoso þat list in the book Of Nature   *whoever pleases*
Of Beestes rede, therin he may see,
235 If he take heede vnto the scripture,   *writing*
Wher it spekth of meermaides in the see,   *speaks*

How þat so inly mirie syngith shee   *inwardly merry*
þat the shipman therwith fallith asleepe,
And by hir aftir deuoured is he.
240 From al swich song is good men hem to keepe.   *such; for men to guard*
                                                                   themselves

Right so the feyned wordes of plesance   *pleasure*
Annoyen aftir, thogh they plese a tyme   *disturb*
To hem þat been vnwyse of gouernance.   *govern themselves unwisely*
Lordes, beeth waar, let nat fauel yow lyme.   *wary; flattery; ensnare*
245 If þat yee been enuolupid in cryme,   *enwrapped*
Yee may nat deeme men speke of yow weel,   *judge; well*
Thogh fauel peynte hir tale in prose or ryme.
Ful holsum is it truste hir nat a deel.   *wholesome; not at all*

Holcote seith vpon the book also   *(in his commentary) on*
250 Of Sapience, as it can testifie,   *Wisdom*
Whan þat Vlixes saillid to and fro   *Ulysses*
By meermaides this was his policie: *near*
Alle eres of men of his conpaignie
With wex he stoppe leet, for þat they noght   *wax; had blocked*
255 Hir song sholde heere, lest the armonye   *their*
Hem mighte vnto swich deedly sleep han broght, *so fatally deep a sleep*

And bond himself vnto the shippes mast.   *bound*
Lo, thus hem all saued his prudence.
The wys man is of peril sore agast.   *sorely afraid*
260 O flaterie, o lurkyng pestilence!
If sum man dide his cure and diligence   *care*
To stoppe his eres fro thy poesie,
And nat wolde herkne a word of thy sentence,   *listen to; meaning*
Vnto his greef it wer a remedie.   *it would be a cure*

265 A, nay. Althogh thy tonge wer ago,   *lost*
Yit canst thow glose in contenance and cheere.   *deceive; expression*
Thow supportist with lookes eueremo   *continually*
Thy lordes wordes in eche mateere,
Althogh þat they a myte be to deere,   *little*
270 And thus thy gyse is, priuee and appert,   *way; secretly; openly*
With word and look among our lordes heere

Preferred be, thogh ther be no dissert.   *to be preferred; deserving*

But whan the sobre, treewe, and weel auysid   *serious; prudent (man)*
With sad visage his lord enfourmeth pleyn   *serious; plainly*
275 How þat his gouernance is despysid   *rule*
Among the peple, and seith him as they seyn,   *reports their words to him*
As man treewe oghte vnto his souereyn,
Conseillynge him amende his gouernance,
The lordes herte swellith for desdeyn,
280 And bit him voide blyue with meschance.   *bids; depart at once; bad luck*

Men setten nat by trouthe nowadayes.   *loyalty*
Men loue it nat. Men wole it nat cherice.   *nurture*
And yit is trouthe best at all assayes.   *in all situations*
When þat fals fauel, soustenour of vice,   *flattery; supporter*
285 Nat wite shal how hir to cheuyce,   *know; see to herself*
Ful boldely shal trouthe hir heed vp bere.
Lordes, lest fauel yow fro wele tryce,   *from well-being snatch*
No lenger souffre hir nestlen in your ere.   *let*

Be as he may, no more of this as now,   *be that as it may; for now*
290 But to my misreule wole I refeere,   *return*
Wheras I was at ese weel ynow,   *where; well enough*
Or excesse vnto me leef was and deere,   *before; beloved*
And, or I kneew his ernestful maneere,   *and (when); before; earnest*
My purs of coyn had resonable wone: *expectation/abundance*
295 But now therin can ther but scant appeere.
Excesse hath ny exyled hem echone.   *nearly; them (i.e. coins) all*

The feend and excesse been conuertible,   *devil; interchangeable*
As enditith to me my fantasie.   *suggests; imagination*
This is my skile, if it be admittible: *reasoning; admissible*
300 Excesse of mete and drynke is glotonye;
Glotonye awakith malencolie;
Malencolie engendrith werre and stryf;
Stryf causith mortel hurt thurgh hir folie.
Thus may excesse reue a soule hir lyf.   *take from*

305 No force of al this. Go we now to wacche   *matter; stay awake*
By nyghtirtale out of al mesure,   *night-time*

For, as in þat, fynde kowde I no macche   *in that respect*
In al the Priuee Seel with me to endure,
And to the cuppe ay took I heede and cure,   *paid attention and care*
310 For þat the drynke apall sholde noght,   *so that; grow weak*
But whan the pot emptid was of moisture
To wake aftirward cam nat in my thoght.

But whan the cuppe had thus my neede sped,   *answered*
And sumdel more than necessitee,   *somewhat; I needed*
315 With repleet spirit wente I to my bed,
And bathid ther in superfluitee.   *wallowed; excess*
But on the morn was wight of no degree   *no person of any rank*
So looth as I to twynne fro my cowche,   *get up*
By aght I woot. Abyde; let me see.   *for anything; know*
320 Of two as looth I am seur kowde I towche.   *sure; touch (upon)*

I dar nat seyn Prentys and Arondel
Me countrefete, and in swich wach go ny me,   *copy; such vigils*
But often they hir bed louen so wel   *their*
þat of the day it drawith ny the pryme   *near; first hour*
325 Or they ryse vp. Nat tell I can the tyme   *before*
Whan they to bedde goon, it is so late.
O helthe, lord, thow seest hem in þat cryme,
And yit thee looth is with hem to debate,   *you are unwilling*

And why I not. It sit nat vnto me   *don't know; is unfitting for*
330 þat mirour am of riot and excesse
To knowen of a goddes pryuetee,   *secrets*
But thus I ymagyne and thus I gesse:
Thow meeued art, of tendre gentillesse,   *moved; because of; courtesy*
Hem to forber, and wilt hem nat chastyse,
335 For they, in mirthe and vertuous gladnesse,   *because*
Lordes reconforten in sundry wyse.   *comfort*

But to my purpos. Syn þat my seeknesse,   *since*
As wel of purs as body, hath refreyned   *held back*
Me fro tauerne and othir wantonnesse,
340 Among an heep my name is now desteyned,   *large number; dishonoured*
My greuous hurt ful litil is conpleyned,   *not at all; lamented*
But they the lak conpleyne of my despense.   *spending*

Allas, þat euere knyt I was and cheyned
To excesse, or him dide obedience.

345 Despenses large enhaunce a mannes loos   *expenditures; reputation*
Whil they endure, and whan they be forbore   *dispensed with*
His name is deed. Men keepe hir mowthes cloos, *closed*
As nat a peny had he spent tofore.   *as if; before*
My thank is qweynt, my purs his stuf hath lore, *(their) thanks; quenched; lost*
350 And my carkeis repleet with heuynesse.   *body*
Bewaar, Hoccleue, I rede thee therfore,   *advise*
And to a mene reule thow thee dresse.   *moderate regime; apply*

Whoso, passynge mesure, desyrith,   *beyond*
As þat witnessen olde clerkes wyse,
355 Himself encombrith oftensythe, and myrith,   *often hinders; bemires*
And forthy let the mene thee souffyse.   *therefore; suffice*
If swich a conceit in thyn herte ryse   *such; thought*
As thy profyt may hyndre, or thy renoun,   *damage; reputation*
If it wer execut in any wyse,   *carried out; way*
360 With manly resoun thriste thow it doun.   *thrust*

Thy rentes annuel, as thow wel woost,   *annuities; know*
To scarse been greet costes to susteene,
And in thy cofre, perdee, is cold roost,   *by heaven; roast*
And of thy manuel labour, as I weene,   *expect*
365 Thy lucre is swich þat it vnnethe is seene   *payment; such; scarcely*
Ne felt. Of yiftes seye I eek the same.   *gifts (of money); also*
And stele, for the guerdoun is so keene,   *to steal; reward; sharp*
Ne darst thow nat, ne begge also for shame.   *dare*

Than wolde it seeme þat thow borwid haast   *borrowed*
370 Mochil of þat þat thow haast thus despent   *much; spent*
In outrage and excesse, and verray waast.   *intemperance; pure waste*
Auyse thee, for what thyng þat is lent   *consider; whatever*
Of verray right moot hoom ageyn be sent.   *must*
Thow therin haast no perpetuitee.   *over it; perpetual right*
375 Thy dettes paie, lest þat thow be shent,   *destroyed*
And or þat thow therto conpellid be.   *before*

Sum folk in this cas dreeden more offense | *situation; fear; (their) offence*
Of man, for wyly wrenches of the lawe, | *cunning twists*
Then he dooth eithir God or conscience,
380 For by hem two, he settith nat [an] hawe. | *cares not at all*
If thy conceit be swich, thow it withdrawe, | *thought; such; remove*
I rede, and voide it clene out of thyn herte, | *advise; expel; completely*
And first of God, and syn of man, haue awe, | *then*
Lest þat they bothe make thee to smerte. | *cause; suffer*

385 Now lat this smert warnynge to thee be, | *pain; (a) warning*
And if thow maist heeraftir be releeued,
Of body and purs so thow gye thee | *(in respect) of; conduct*
By wit þat thow no more thus be greeued.
What riot is, thow taastid haast, and preeued. | *experienced; tested*
390 The fyr, men seyn, he dreedith þat is brent, | *fears; burnt*
And if thow so do, thow art wel ymeeued. | *directed*
Be now no lenger fool, by myn assent. | *longer; I advise*

Ey, what is me, þat to myself thus longe | *Oh, what is with me*
Clappid haue I? I trowe þat I raue. | *chattered; believe; am raving*
395 A, nay, my poore purs and peynes stronge
Han artid me speke as I spoken haue. | *compelled*
Whoso him shapith mercy for to craue | *whoever prepares*
His lesson moot recorde in sundry wyse, | *must repeat; ways*
And whil my breeth may in my body waue, | *draw*
400 To recorde it vnnethe I may souffyse. | *scarcely; suffice*

O God! o helthe! vnto thyn ordenance,
Weleful lord, meekly submitte I me. | *blessed*
I am contryt and of ful repentance | *fully repentant*
þat euere I swymmed in swich nycetee | *was immersed; such folly*
405 As was displesaunt to thy deitee. | *unpleasing*
Now kythe on me thy mercy and thy grace. | *show*
It sit a god been of his grace free. | *is fitting for; generous*
Foryeue, and neuere wole I eft trespace. | *forgive; hereafter sin*

My body and purs been at ones seeke, | *once; sick*
410 And for hem bothe, I, to thyn hy noblesse, | *nobility*
As humblely as þat I kan, byseeke, | *beseech*
With herte vnfeyned, reewe on our distresse. | *have pity*

Pitee haue of myn harmful heuynesse.
Releeue the repentant in disese.   *afflicted penitent*
415 Despende on me a drope of thy largesse,   *expend; liberality*
Right in this wyse if it thee lyke and plese.   *way; please*

Lo, lat my lord the Fourneval, I preye,   *let; lord Furnivall*
My noble lord þat now is tresoreer,   *treasurer*
From thyn hynesse haue a tokne or tweye   *highness; two*
420 To paie me þat due is for this yeer   *what*
Of my yeerly x li. in th'eschequeer,   *ten pounds; exchequer*
Nat but for Michel terme þat was last.   *only for last Michaelmas term*
I dar nat speke a word of ferne yeer,   *years gone by*
So is my spir[i]t symple and sore agast.   *sorely afraid*

425 I kepte nat to be seen inportune   *would not care; importunate*
In my pursuyte. I am therto ful looth.   *very reluctant*
And yit þat gyse ryf is, and commune   *yet; custom; widespread*
Among the peple now, withouten ooth.   *oath*
As the shamelees crauour wole, it gooth,   *shameless beggar wishes*
430 For estaat real can nat al day werne,   *royal estate; refuse*
But poore shamefast man ofte is wrooth,   *shy; angered*
Wherfore, for to craue, moot I lerne.   *beg; must*

The prouerbe is, the doumb man no lond getith.
Whoso nat spekith and with neede is bete,   *whoever; afflicted*
435 And thurgh arghnesse his owne self forgetith,   *cowardice*
No wondir, thogh anothir him forgete.
Neede hath no lawe, as þat the clerkes trete,   *tell*
And thus to craue artith me my neede,   *beg; compels*
And right wole eek þat I me entremete,   *justice wishes also; involve*
440 For þat I axe is due, as God me speede.   *ask; prosper*

And þat that due is, thy magnificence
Shameth to werne, as þat I byleeue.   *refuse*
As I seide, reewe on myn inpotence,   *have pity; weakness*
þat likly am to sterue yit or eeue,   *die; before*
445 But if thow in this wyse me releeue.   *unless; way*
By coyn, I gete may swich medecyne   *such*
As may myn hurtes all, þat me greeue,
Exyle cleene, and voide me of pyne.   *completely; rid myself; pain*

Notes

This work, dated 1405–6, is a witty parody of the penitential lyric which accommodates mock repentance for a mis-spent past with requests for overdue payment of annuities. It has formal parallels with traditions of Goliardic satire, and with petitionary poems by Deschamps, whom Hoccleve may have read (for comment on the latter, see Burrow 1997: 45–9). Parallels also exist with the *Regement*, e.g. 4376–89. For further comment see especially Thornley 1967, Burrow 1994: 195–6, 202–3 [7–8, 14–15]. Fragments exist of this text in Canterbury Cathedral Archives Register O ff. 207v-8r (Burrow 1994: 241 [53]), but the many variants in this copy are most probably scribal.

31 'he should never have so attached himself to me' (using the metaphor of a hand clinging to another person's clothing).

34 A commonplace with echoes of a number of Chaucerian passages (e.g. *Troilus* I.211, III.820ff). Whiting 1968: 206, 475 offers a parallel in Heywood ('prosperity maketh us blind') and a parallel proverb ('fortune is blind').

42–4 The copy in the Canterbury Archive changes the feminine pronouns to masculine in these lines, a feature characterizing other Hoccleve texts (e.g. the 'Epistre', and cf. VI.171–2n. and Introduction p. 39). It also turns first person into third at 109, and suppresses Hoccleve's address to himself at 351, possibly so as to widen the reference and relevance of the text.

65ff. With this characterization of youth, cf. *Regement* 596ff., *Series* 5.12–21, and the presentations of the *imago mortis* in the Suso translation (4.91, 112, 144 etc.) and of Jonathas in the second *Gesta* narrative (5.156–7n.).

85–6 Cf. *Series* 2.391n.

91 'in esy wyse and softe' could refer to the friends' advice or to the narrator's withdrawal of himself from misrule.

95 Cf. *Series* 1.266.

129–30 This extension of the prevailing metaphor of health and sickness suggests that poverty is also a form of illness, just as, in the opening sections of the *Series* (e.g. 1.21), introspective thought can be.

133–6 Cf. the early episodes of the second *Gesta* narrative, on a young man similarly given over to misrule.

160 With this characteristic rhetorical figure, made much of in the first *Gesta* narrative (e.g. 3.729), cf. Chaucer's *Nun's Priest's Tale*, abbreviated *NPT* (*CT* VII.3374).

171 *cloos* (cf. 347): a word with particular resonance in the *Series*. See 1.32, 145, 2.28, 3.284, 495, 5.195, 291.

173–6 The sense is that Hoccleve would willingly have got into fights but was too cowardly—ironically, a mark of his manhood—to get involved, for fear of the blows that he would receive.

194 For the reading of 'brigge' as 'wharf', see Seymour's n.

233–40 On the identification of this text as Theobaldus, *Physiologus de naturis xii animalium*, see Seymour's n., and cf. *NPT*, especially (*CT* VII.3325–30) for the address to the 'lordes' (below, l. 244).

249 Robert Holcot the Dominican wrote a commentary on the Old Testament book of Wisdom (*Super Sapientiam Salomonis*, Hoccleve's 'vpon the book… of wisdome'), also used by Chaucer in *NPT* (Benson 1988: 936). The episode of Ulysses (so Seymour's n.) comes from section 64 of Holcot's commentary. Seymour also identifies a borrowing at 300–4 (from Holcot's section 84).

262 With this equation of flattery and poetry, and (266) with 'glosing', cf. Boethius *Consolatio Philosophiae* Bk I pr. 1.

264 This line develops the medical metaphors earlier applied to money, and implies the interrelationship of money, deceit and illness.

269 *deere*: Seymour glosses 'grievous', referring not to the financial but to the moral cost of the flattery to the lord and/or the flatterer.

272 The undeserved preferment 'with word and look' thus parallels the flatterer's support of his lord, which the latter does not deserve either.

273–88 On flattery, see also *Regement* 547–53, 1912–43, and comment in Scattergood 1971: 312–13, Pearsall 1994: 409.

297 *conuertible*: cf. *CT* I.4395 and *Regement* 1563.

321 *Prentys and Arondel*: younger colleagues of Hoccleve. Cf. Furnivall and Gollancz 1970: xxxv, Richardson 1985–6: 320.

324 *by the pryme*: Furnivall and Seymour both gloss '9 a.m.'

331 *a goddes pryuetee*: this phrase Hoccleve may owe to Chaucer who uses it in the context of fabliau (*Miller's Tale*, *CT* I.3164), as he did with the word

'conuertible' 297n. above.

350 *repleet*: a condition which earlier (113) ironically induced abstinence (and cf. 315), here becomes its own negative and leaves, in its absence, only a superfluity of care.

367–8 For comment on this possible echo of Luke 16.3, a detail from the parable of the unjust steward, also used by Langland in a parallel context, what she calls 'epistle mendicant' [begging letter], see Kerby-Fulton 1997: 95.

393 ends a soliloquy which began at 353: on the role of soliloquy in other poetry of Hoccleve, see *Series* 1.33n.

401ff. Here the appeal to the God of Health takes the explicit form of a parodic act of penitence. On this dimension of the poem, see Thornley 1967.

417 The real point of the poem is an appeal to the treasurer, Lord Fourneval, to pay the poet his annuity of £10 from the Exchequer (421), and a reminder that previous sums are also owing (423).

422 D glosses 'Annus ille fuit annus restrictionis annuitatum' [that year was the year in which the annuities were restricted].

433 proverbial: Wilson 1970 offers a parallel from Gower's *Confessio Amantis* 6.318, and two sixteenth-century examples.

437 Cf. the comic treatment of this theme by the 'yonge... scolers' in *The Reeve's Tale* (*CT* I.4026, 4179)

III

Cestes balade et chanceon ensuyantes feurent faites a mon meistre H. Somer, quant il estoit souztresorer

[This balade and song that follow were made for my master Henry Somer, when he was undertreasurer]

The sonne, with his bemes of brightnesse,	
To man so kyndly is and norisshynge	
þat, lakkyng it, day nere but dirknesse.	*would be; only*
To day he yeueth his enlumynynge,	*gives*
5 And causith al fruyt for to wexe and sprynge.	*grow*
Now, syn þat sonne may so moche auaille,	*since; is of such power*
And moost with somer is his soiournynge,	*summer*
That sesoun bonteuous we wole assaille.	*plentiful; assay*
Glad cheerid somer, to your gouernaille	*bright-faced; governance*
10 And grace we submitte al our willynge.	*desires*
To whom yee freendly been, he may nat faille	*the man to whom*
But he shal haue his resonable axynge.	*request*
Aftir your good lust, be the sesonynge	*pleasure; by; ripening*
Of our fruytes this laste Mighelmesse,	*Michaelmas (29 September)*
15 The tyme of yeer was of our seed ynnynge,	*(the) harvesting*
The lak of which is our greet heuynesse.	
We truste vpon your freendly gentillesse,	*courtesy*
Ye wole vs helpe and been our suppoaille.	*support*

Now yeue vs cause ageyn this Cristemesse   *give; again/before*
20 For to be glad. O Lord, whethir our taille   *may it be our tally*
Shal soone make vs with our shippes saille
To port salut? If yow list we may synge,   *haven of safety; please*
And elles moot vs bothe mourne and waille,   *otherwise; must we*
Til your fauour vs sende releeuynge.   *relief*

25 We, your seruantes, Hoccleue and Baillay,
Hethe and Offorde, yow beseeche and preye,
'Haastith our heruest as soone as yee may.'   *hasten*
For fere of stormes our wit is aweye,
Wer our seed inned, wel we mighten pleye,   *gathered*
30 And vs desporte and synge and make game,   *entertain; merriment*
And yit this rowndel shul we synge and seye   *yet*
In trust of yow and honour of your name.

Somer, þat rypest mannes sustenance   *ripens*
With holsum hete of the sonnes warmnesse,
35 Al kynde of man thee holden is to blesse.   *every race; bound*

Ay thankid be thy freendly gouernance,
And thy fressh look of mirthe and of gladnesse.
Somer etc

To heuy folk of thee the remembrance   *the memory of you*
40 Is salue and oynement to hir seeknesse.   *their*
Forwhy, we thus shul synge in Cristemesse,   *therefore*
Somer etc

Notes

Another witty begging poem, probably composed in 1408: see Burrow 1994: 203–4 [15–16].

14 Hoccleve develops the basic conceit (summer/Somer) with this reference to Michaelmas, the time when harvests are brought in and when clerks of the Privy Seal ought to have received half of their yearly annuities.

21 a further pun, since 'the great noble, [a coin] valued at a half-mark, … [was] stamped with a large ship' (Seymour's n.); this image is further developed possibly in the 'fere of stormes' at 28.

25–6 friends of Hoccleve at the Privy Seal: see Richardson 1985–6: 318–21.

IV

Ceste balade ensuyante feust translatee au commandement de mon meistre Robert Chichele

[*This following ballade was translated at the commandment of Master Robert Chichele*]

As þat I walkid in the monthe of May
Besyde a groue in an heuy musynge,   *sombre meditation*
Floures dyuerse I sy, right fressh and gay,   *saw*
And briddes herde I eek lustyly synge,   *birds; pleasantly*
5   þat to myn herte yaf a confortynge.   *gave comfort*
But euere o thoght me stang vnto the herte,   *one; pierced*
þat dye I sholde and hadde no knowynge
Whanne, ne whidir, I sholde hennes sterte.   *hence start*

Thynkynge thus, byfore me I say   *saw*
10   A crois depeynted with a fair ymage.   *cross depicted*
I thoghte I nas but asshes and foul clay.   *was only*
Lyf passith as a shadwe in euery age,   *shadow*
And my body yeueth no bettre wage   *gives*
Than synne which the soule annoyeth sore.   *sorely grieves*
15   I preyde God mercy of myn outrage,   *excess*
And shoop me him for t'offende no more.   *planned*

On God to thynke it yeueth a delyt,   *gives pleasure*
Wel for to doon and fro synne withdrawe,   *to act virtuously*
But for to putte a good deede in respyt   *deferral*
20   Harmeth. Swich delay is nat worth an hawe.   *such; hawthorn berry*

Wolde God, by my speeche and by my sawe,   *would to God; saying*
I mighte him and his modir do plesance,   *pleasure*
And to my meryt folwe Goddes lawe,   *reward; follow*
And of mercy, housbonde a purueance!   *cultivate a provision*

25 Modir of Ihesu, verray God and man,   *true*
   þat by his deeth victorie of the feend gat,   *got*
   Haue it in mynde, thow blessid womman,
   For the wo which vnto thyn herte sat   *about*
   In thy sones torment (forgete it nat).
30 Grante me grace to vertu me take,   *to betake myself*
   Synne despyse, and for to hate al that   *to despise*
   That may thy sone and thee displesid make.

Mercyful lord Ihesu, me heer, I preye,   *hear me*
   þat right vnkynde and fals am vnto thee.
35 I am right swich. I may it nat withseye.   *such; deny*
   With salte teeres craue I thy pitee,
   And herte contryt. Mercy haue on me
   þat am thy recreant caytyf traitour.   *cowardly; wretched*
   By my dissertes oghte I dampned be,
40 But ay thy mercy heetith me socour.   *promises*

Lady benigne, our souereyn refuyt,   *refuge*
   Seur trust haue I to han, by thy prayeere,   *sure*
   Of strengthe and confort so vertuous fruyt,
   That I shal sauf be, Crystes modir deere.   *saved*
45 My soules ship gouerne thow, and steere.
   Let me nat slippe out of thy remembrance,
   Lest, whan þat I am rype vnto my beere,   *ready for my grave*
   The feend me assaille, and haue at the outrance.   *with greatest force*

To thanke thee, Lord, hyly holde I am,   *greatly obliged*
50 For my gilt, nat for thyn, þat woldest die.
   Who souffrid euere swich a martirdam?
   Yit thy deeth gat of the feend the maistrie,   *obtained; mastery*
   And þat al kynde of man may testifie.   *human nature*
   O, blessid be thy loue charitable,
55 þat list so deer our synful soules bie,   *pleased; dearly; to buy*
   To make vs sauf wher we weren dampnable.

Now thy socour, o Heuenes Emperice.   *(grant) your help*
Fro me, wrecche, torne thow nat thy face.
Theras I deepe wrappid am in vice,   *where*
60   Gretter neede haue I thyn help to purchace.
Vnto the souerain leche preye of grace,   *supreme healer; beg for*
þat he my wowndes vouchesauf to cure,   *will vouchsafe*
So þat the feend my soule nat embrace,
Althogh I haue agilt ouer mesure.   *sinned; to excess*

65   Wel oghten we thee thanke, gracious lord,
þat thee haast humbled, for to been allied
To vs. Auctour of pees and of concord,   *author*
On the crois was thy skyn into blood died.   *Cross; dyed with blood*
Allas! why haue I me to synne applied?
70   Why is my soule encombrid so with synne?   *burdened*
Lord, in al þat I haue me misgyed,   *misconducted myself*
Foryeue, and of my trespas wole I blynne.   *desist*

Lady, wardeyn of peple fro ruyne,   *guardian*
þat sauedest Theofle and many mo,   *more*
75   Of thy grace, myn herte enlumyne.   *in/with your grace; enlighten*
For, as I trowe, and woot it wel also,   *believe; know*
Thy might is me to warisshe of my wo.   *power; heal*
Of thy benigne sone mercy craue,
Of þat forueyed haue I, and misgo.   *for what; done wrong; mistaken*
80   His wil is thyn my soule keepe and saue.   *to preserve*

Lord Ihesu Cryst, I axe of thee pardoun.   *ask*
I yilde me to thee, lord souereyn.   *yield myself*
My gilt confesse I, lord. Make vnioun
Betwixt thee and my soule, for in veyn
85   My tyme haue I despendid in certeyn.   *spent; certainly*
Some of the dropes of thy precious blood
þat the crois made as weet as is the reyn,   *Cross; wet*
Despende on me, lord merciable and good.

Lady, þat clept art modir of mercy,   *called*
90   Noble saphir, to me þat am ful lame
Of vertu, and am therto enemy,   *enemy of it*
Thy welle of pitee, in thy sones name,

Lete on me flowe to pourge my blame,
Lest into despeir þat I slippe and falle.
95   For my seurtee to keepe me fro blame,
Of pitee mirour, I vnto thee calle.   *mirror of pity (Mary)*

Synne, þat is to euery vertu fo,
Betwixt God and me maad hath swich debat,   *such*
þat my soule is dampnyd for eueremo,
100 But if þat mercy which hath maad th'acat   *unless; purchase*
Of mannes soule, þat was violat   *violated*
By likerous lust and disobedience,   *lustful desires*
For which our lord Ihesu was incarnat,
Me helpe make the feend resistence.   *(against) the devil*

105 Lady, þat art of grace spryng and sours,   *source*
Port in peril, solas in heuynesse,
Of thy wont bontee keepe alway the cours.   *accustomed goodness*
Lat nat the feend at my deeth me oppresse.
Torne the crois to me, noble princesse,
110 Which vnto euery soor is the triacle.   *disease; medicine*
Thogh my dissert be naght, of thy goodnesse,   *I do not deserve it*
Ageyn the feendes wrenches make obstacle.   *wiles*

Lord, on thy grace and pitee myn herte ay
Awaitith to purchace thy mercy.
115 Allas, I caytif, wel I mourne may,   *wretch*
Syn the feend serued oftensythe haue Y.   *often*
It reewith me. Do with me graciously,   *I repent it*
For I purpose to stynte of my synnes,   *propose; cease*
What ageyn thee mistake hath my body.   *against; done wrong*
120 My soule keepe fro the feendes gynnes.   *tricks*

Blessid virgyne, ensample of al vertu,   *example*
þat peere hast noon, of wommanhode flour,   *equal; flower*
For the loue of thy sone, our Lord Ihesu,
Strengthe vs to doon him seruice and honour.
125 Lady, be mene vnto our sauueour,   *intermediary*
þat our soules þat the feend waytith ay
To hente, and wolde of hem be possessour,   *seize*
Ne sese hem nat in the vengeable day.   *(he) many not seize; day of*
                                                       vengeance

The flessh, the world and eek the feend my fo,   *also*
130 My wittes alle han at hir retenance.   *in their retinue*
They to my soule doon annoy and wo.   *cause grief*
Forwhy, Lord, dreede I me of thy vengeance.   *therefore; I fear*
With mercy, my soule into blisse enhance.   *raise*
Worthy merchant, saue thy marchandie,
135 Which þat thow boghtest with dethes penance.   *pain*
Lat nat the feend haue of vs the maistrie.

Excellent lady, in thy thoght impresse
How and why thy chyld souffrid his torment.
Preye him to haue on vs swich tendrenesse
140 þat in the feendes net we be nat hent.   *seized*
At the day of his steerne iugement,   *stern judgement*
Lat nat him leese þat he by deeth boghte.   *lose what*
I woot wel therto hath he no talent.   *know; for that; desire*
Mynge him theron, for thee so to doon oghte.   *remind; you ought*

145 Whan in a man synne growith and rypith,   *ripens*
The fruyt of it is ful of bittirnesse,
But penitence cleene away it wypith,   *completely*
And to the soule yeueth greet swetnesse.   *gives*
O, steerne iuge, with thy rightwisnesse   *stern; righteousness*
150 Medle thy mercy and shewe vs fauour.   *mix*
Unto oure soules, maad to thy liknesse,
Graunte pardoun of our stynkyng errour.

O glorious qweene, to the repentaunt
þat art refuyt, socour and medecyne,   *refuge*
155 Lat nat the foule feend make his auaunt   *boast*
þat he hath thee byreft any of thyne.   *stolen from you*
Thurgh thy preyer, thow thy sone enclyne   *move*
His merciable grace on vs to reyne.   *pour*
Be tendre of vs, o thow blissid virgyne,
160 For if thee list, we shuln to blisse atteyne.   *please*

C'est tout.   *This is all*

Notes

On the genre of this poem, see Burrow 1994: 213 [25]; for fuller comment, Stokes 1995: 80–1, kindly drawn to my notice by Professor Burrow. The text begins with the conventional elements of a *chanson d'aventure* (the poet walking in a May morning in a grove and observing the burgeoning life of nature), but then applies them to a religious theme.

title on Chichele, 'brother of the Archbishop of Canterbury [and] ... a prosperous member of the London Grocers company' (so Burrow). See also Seymour 1981: xv-xvi, and Sandison 1923: 236–8.

2 The 'heuy musynge' of the narrator (Fr. 'pensant') has more in common with Hoccleve's self-presentation in 'My Compleinte' or the *Regement* than with the courtly *aventure* which the beginning seems to promise. Similarly, the narrator's obsession with death links him with the protagonists of the *Series* (see following n.). Both Hoccleve and his source, however, link the comforts of the spring (5) with the comfort of thinking on God (17).

12 This image also occurs elsewhere in Hoccleve, invariably in a moral-religious context and often translated from the sources (so here and at I.18, 25, translating Deguileville, *Series* 1.321 translating Isidore of Seville, 2.276, and 4.199, translating Suso).

25 Hoccleve introduces this stanza and stanza 10 (73–4) with the translation of the last lines of the previous stanzas in the Fr., and thus makes clearer the overarching structure of alternating address to Christ and the Virgin.

45 *soules ship*: for comment on this phrase, see Stokes 1995: 81 and 4.235n.

47 *rype vnto my beere*: with this image, cf. 145, II.95, *Series* 1.266, 2.247, 808, 4.53, 144, 356.

74 For brief comment on the popular figure of Theophilus, who 'sold his soul to the devil and was afterward saved by our

lady', see Boyd 1964: 6, 8, 127–9; and, for Middle English versions of his story, Ross 1940: 260.33–261.8, Boyd 1964: 68–87.

77 With this medical metaphor, a Biblical commonplace, cf. 110, 154 (the latter translating 'medicine mettez a ma greuance' [bring medicine for my pain]), and, in other works, II.264n., 446, *Series* 1.237, 2.93. Medicine occurs as a narrative element at the end of the two *Gesta* stories (3.925, 5.622).

89ff. On the traditional metaphors applied to the Virgin in this poem and the prologue to no. V, cf. Davies 1963: Appendix.

134 This distinctive version of the economy of salvation, with Christ as a merchant, has Biblical roots (cf. Matt. 13.44–6, Prov. 31.14, the latter explicitly applied to Christ in Wenzel 1989: 286). Hoccleve is here translating the original's 'trecher marchaunt' (Stokes 1995: 82). The phrase echoes others added to the translation (e.g. 24, 55, 60, 88, 100, 114, 142), and reflects a major economic preoccupation of the poet. The original makes much less of the metaphor (but cf. l. 87 'quant si chere mauez chate' [seeing you have bought me so dearly], not translated by Hoccleve). Parallels occur in the *Series* (4.911–17), including parallels, or parodies, in key events in the two *Gesta* narratives (ships' captains who sell merchandise or agree a price to transport the protagonist from one place to another; a king who rewards the hero for healing him, etc.).

V

Item de beata Virgine

[*Another piece about the blessed Virgin*]

	Whoso desirith to gete and conquere	*acquire*
	The blisse of heuene, needful is a guyde	
	Him to condue and for to brynge him there,	*conduct*
	And so good knowe I noon for mannes syde,	*defence*
5	As the roote of humblesse and fo to pryde,	*humility*
	That lady, of whos tetes virginal	*breasts*
	Sook our redemptour, the maker of al.	*sucked; redeemer*
	Betwixt God and man is shee mediatrice	
	For our offenses mercy to purchace.	
10	Shee is our seur sheeld ageyn the malice	*against*
	Of the feend þat our soules wolde embrace	
	And carie hem vnto þat horrible place	
	Wheras eternel peyne is, and torment,	*where*
	More than may be spoke of, thoght or ment.	*or told/complained of*
15	Now syn þat lady noble and glorious	*since*
	To al mankynde hath so greet cheertee	*affection*
	That in this slipir lyf and perillous	*slippery*
	Staf of confort and help to man is shee,	
	Conuenient is þat to þat lady free	*fitting; noble*
20	We do seruice, honour and plesance,	*pleasure*
	And to þat ende heer is a remembrance.	

Explicit prologus et incipit fabula   [*here ends the prologue and begins the tale*]

Ther was whilom, as þat seith the scripture,   *once; book*
In France a ryche man and a worthy,
That God and holy chirche to honure
25 And plese enforced he him bisily,   *took pains*
And vnto Crystes modir specially,
þat noble lady, þat blissid virgyne,
For to worsshipe, he dide his might and pyne.   *(all in) his power; (took) pain*

It shoop so þat this man had a yong sone,   *happened*
30 Vnto which he yaf informacion,   *instruction*
Euery day to haue in custume and wone   *practice*
For to seye at his excitacion   *arising*
The angelike salutacion   *the Ave Maria*
L sythes in worsship and honour   *fifty times*
35 Of Goddes modir, of vertu the flour.

By his fadres wil a monk, aftirward,
In th'abbeye of Seint Gyle maad was he,   *St Giles; made*
Wheras he in penance sharp and hard   *where*
Obserued wel his ordres duetee,   *his religious duties*
40 Lyuynge in vertuous religioustee,   *religious life*
And on a tyme, him to pleye and solace,   *amuse and comfort*
His fadir made him come hoom to his place.

Now was ther, at our ladyes reuerence,
A chapel in it maad and edified,   *made and built*
45 Into which the monk, whan conuenience
Of tyme he had awayted and espied,
His fadres lore to fulfille him hied,   *instruction; hastened*
And L sythes with deuout corage   *fifty times; heart*
Seide Aue Marie as was his vsage.   *wont*

50 And whan þat he had endid his preyeere,
Our lady, clothid in a garnement   *garment*
Sleeuelees, byfore him he sy appeere,   *without sleeves; saw*
Wherof the monk took good auisament,   *careful note*
Merueillynge hym what þat this mighte han ment,   *might mean*
55 And seide, 'O goode lady, by your leeue,
What garnament is this, and hath no sleeue?'   *that has*

And she answerde and seide, 'This clothynge
Thow hast me youen, for thow euery day   *given*
L sythe Aue Maria seyynge,   *fifty times*
60 Honured hast me. Hensfoorth, I the pray,
Vse to treble þat by any way,   *make it a custom*
And to euery xthe Aue ioyne also   *tenth*
A Pater Noster. Do thow euene so.   *Our Father*

'The firste Lti wole I þat seid be   *fifty; wish*
65 In the memorie of the ioie and honour
That I had whan the angel grette me,   *greeted*
Which was right a wondirful confortour   *truly*
To me whan he seide the redemptour   *redeemer*
Of al mankynde I receyue sholde.
70 Greet was my ioie whan he so me tolde.

'Thow shalt eek seyn the seconde lty   *fifty*
In honur and in mynde of the gladnesse   *memory*
That I had whan I baar of my body   *bore*
God and man withouten wo or duresse.   *hardship*
75 The iiide lty in thyn herte impresse,   *third fifty*
And seye it eek with good deuocioun
In the memorie of myn assumpcion,   *Assumption*

'Whan þat I was coroned queene of heuene,   *crowned*
In which my sone regneth, and shal ay.'
80 Al this was doon þat I speke of and meene,   *refer to*
As the book seith, vpon an halyday.   *holy day*
And than seide our lady, the glorious may,   *maid*
'The nexte halyday wole I resorte
To this place thee to glade and conforte.'''   *gladden*

85 And therwithal fro thens departed shee,   *with that*
The monk in his deuocion dwellynge,   *remaining*
And euery day Aue Maria he
Seide aftir hir doctryne and enformynge.   *teaching; instruction*
And, the nexte haliday aftir suynge,   *holy day; following*
90 Our lady fresshly arraied and wel
To the monk cam, beynge in þat chapel,   *as he was*

And vnto him seide, 'Beholde now
How good clothyng and how fressh apparaille   *apparel*
That this wyke to me youen hast thow.   *week; given*
95   Sleeues to my clothynge now nat faille,   *are not wanting*
Thee thanke I, and ful wel for thy trauaille   *labour*
Shalt thow be qwit heer, in this lyf present,   *rewarded*
And in þat othir whan thow hens art went.   *have departed*

'Walke now and go hoom vnto th'abbeye.
100   Whan thow comst, abbot shalt thow chosen be,
And the couent teche thow for to seye
My psalter as byforn taght haue I thee.   *before; taught*
The peple also thow shalt in generaltee   *general*
The same lessoun to myn honur teche,
105   And in hir hurtes wole I been hir leche.   *their; doctor*

'Viie yeer lyue shalt thow for to do   *seven; carry out*
This charge and whan tho yeeres been agoon,   *those; have gone*
Thow passe shalt hens and me come vnto,
And, of this, doute haue thow right noon.
110   By my psalter shal ther be many oon   *many a one*
Saued, and had vp to eternel blisse,   *brought*
þat, if þat ner, sholden therof misse.'   *were not; be deprived of it*

Whan shee had seid what lykid hir to seye,   *pleased*
Shee vp to heuene ascendid vp and sty.   *went*
115   And soone aftir, abbot of þat abbeye
He maad was, as þat tolde him our lady.
The couent and the peple deuoutly   *convent*
This monk enformed and taghte hir psaltccr,
For to be seid aftir þat viie yeer.   *seven*

120   Tho yeeres past, his soule was betaght   *those; entrusted*
To God. He heuene had vnto his meede.   *as his reward*
Who serueth our lady, leesith right naght.   *loses nothing*
Shee souffissantly qwytith euery deede.   *sufficiently; repays*
And now heeraftir the bettre to speede,   *succeed*
125   And in hir grace cheerly for to stonde,   *lovingly*
Hir psalteer for to seye let vs fonde.   *try*

    Explicit.   *the story ends*

Notes

For comment on the genre of this poem, a miracle of the Virgin, and for other related examples, one of which, that in the Auchinleck MS, may have been known to Hoccleve, see Boyd 1964. The poem survives in three copies: for detailed textual comment, see Boyd 1956. For other poems by Hoccleve about, or directed to, the Virgin, see I, IV above and nos. 7, 10 of Furnivall's edition and 5 of Gollancz's (Furnivall 10 is printed by Seymour and O'Donoghue). The title refers to the fact that this is the third poem in a sequence of religious poems in H2 addressed to or written about the Virgin Mary. The title in the copy in Tr2 locates the miracle in a monastery of St Egidius in France, and its concluding words might have been preferred for the work's title: 'inuentio psalterii beate Marie' [invention of the psalter of the blessed Virgin Mary] (cf. its opening title: 'quomodo psalterium beate marie primo erat inuentum' [how the Psalter of the blessed Virgin Mary was made], a title closely paralleled by the version of the legend in MS Oxford Bodleian Library Digby 86: 'coment le sauter noustre dame fu primes cuntroue', Furnivall 1901: 777).

1 margin: 'Ce feust faite a l'instance de T. Marleburgh.' [This was made at the request of T. Marleburgh.] For information about Marleburgh, see Furnivall and Gollancz1970: 272, Doyle and Parkes 1978: 198, Seymour 1981: xv, and Griffiths and Pearsall 1989: Index *s.v.*

13 *eternel*: the variant 'ay during' has a parallel in the *Series*, where D generally prefers 'ay' to *H's 'euere' (thus at 2. 327, 372, 721).

18 *staf*: a traditional metaphor also used at *Series* 3.195, 4.188.

33 i.e. the Ave Maria, so called because its first phrases derive from the greeting of the angel Gabriel to the Virgin Mary at the Annunciation. See also following note.

65–6 i.e. commemorating the Annunciation (cf. I.31n.).

80 The holograph loses the rhyme at this point, while ChTr2 ('nevene') preserve it. Hoccleve occasionally miscopies or omits rhymes in other texts: see I.107, 3.245, 4.738.

102 the Psalter of the Virgin: the Rosary (i.e. 150 Ave Marias and 10 Our Fathers). On the Rosary, cf. Boyd 1964: 118–19.

VI

L'epistre de Cupide

[*The letter of Cupid*]

'Cupido, vnto whos commandement		
The gentil kynrede of goddes on hy	*noble kindred; above*	
And peple infernal been obedient,	*denizens of hell*	
And the mortel folk seruen bisyly,	*earthly*	
5 Of goddesse Sitheree sone oonly,	*Venus*	
To all tho þat to our deitee	*those*	
Been sogettes, greetynges senden we.	*subjects*	

'In general we wole þat yee knowe — *wish you to know*
þat ladyes of honur and reuerence,
10 And othir gentil wommen, han isowe — *gently born; sown*
Swich seed of conpleynte in our audience, — *such; hearing*
Of men þat doon hem outrage and offense,
þat it oure eres greeueth for to heere,
So pitous is th'effect of hir mateere. — *pitiful; substance; complaint*

15 'And, passyng alle londes, on this yle — *above; island*
That clept is Albioun they moost conpleyne. — *called*
They seyn þat ther is croppe and roote of gyle, — *deceit*
So can tho men dissimulen and fcyne, — *those; dissimulate*
With standyng dropes in hir yen tweyne, — *tears; their two eyes*
20 Whan þat hir herte feelith no distresse,
To blynde wommen with hir doublenesse.

'Hir wordes spoken been so sighyngly,
And with so pitous cheere and contenance, — *pitiful appearance; bearing*

That euery wight þat meeneth trewely   *person; is honourably disposed*
25   Deemeth þat they in herte han swich greuance.   *judges; grief*
They seyn so importable is hir penance,   *intolerable*
þat, but hir lady list to shewe hem grace,   *please*
They right anoon moot steruen in the place.   *forthwith must die*

"'A, lady myn", they seyn, "I yow ensure,   *promise*
30   Shewe me grace, and I shal euere be,
Whyles my lyf may lasten and endure
To yow as humble in euery degree   *respect*
As possible is, and keepe al thyng secree,   *everything discreet*
As þat yourseluen lykith þat I do,   *it may please you*
35   And elles moot myn herte breste on two."   *otherwise; may; break in*

'Ful hard is it to knowe a mannes herte,   *very*
For outward may no man the truthe deeme,   *by outward signs; judge*
Whan word out of his mowth may ther noon   *none; issue*
    sterte,
But it sholde any wight by reson qweeme.   *please*
40   So is it seid of herte, it wolde seeme.   *from the heart*
O feithful womman, ful of innocence,
Thow art betrayed by fals apparence.   *appearances*

'By procees wommen meeued of pitee,   *in course of time; moved by*
Weenyng al thyng wer as þat tho men seye,   *thinking; everything; those*
45   Granten hem grace of hir benignitee,   *in their kindness*
For they nat sholden for hir sake deye,   *lest they should; die*
And with good herte sette hem in the weye
Of blisful loue, keepe it if they konne.   *happy; know how to*
Thus othir whyle been the wommen wonne.   *at other times*

50   'And whan the man the pot hath by the stele,   *handle*
And fully of hir hath possessioun,
With þat womman he keepith nat to dele   *cares; deal*
Aftir, if he may fynden in the toun
Any womman his blynd affeccion
55   On to bestowe. Foule moot he preeue!   *foully may; prosper*
A man, for al his ooth, is hard to leeue.   *oath; believe*

'And for þat euery fals man hath a make,   *friend*
As vnto euery wight is light to knowe,   *person; easy*
Whan this traitour the womman hath forsake,   *left*
60   He faste him speedith vnto his felowe.   *hastens*
Til he be ther his herte is on a lowe.   *on fire*
His fals deceit ne may him nat souffyse,   *suffice*
But of his treson tellith al the wyse.   *way*

'Is this a fair auant, is this honour,   *boast*
65   A man himself to accuse and diffame?   *defame*
Now is it good confesse him a traitour,   *to confess himself*
And brynge a womman to a sclaundrous name,
And telle how he hir body hath doon shame?   *(to) her body*
No worsship may he thus to him conquere,   *gain for himself*
70   But ful greet repreef vnto him and here.   *reproof; her*

'To her, nay, yit was it no repreef,   *yet; reproof*
For al for pitee was it þat shee wroghte,   *did*
But he þat breewid hath al this mescheef,   *brewed up; misfortune*
þat spak so fair and falsly inward thoghte,
75   His be the shame, as it by reson oghte,   *rightly ought to be*
And vnto her thank perpetuel,   *endless*
þat in a neede helpe can so wel.   *crisis*

'Althogh þat men, by sleighte and sotiltee,   *deceit; cunning*
A cely, symple and ignorant womman   *innocent*
80   Betraye, is no wondir, syn the citee   *since*
Of Troie, as þat the storie telle can,
Betrayed was thurgh the deceit of man,   *through*
And set afyr, and al doun ouerthrowe,   *on fire*
And finally destroyed, as men knowe.

85   'Betrayen men nat remes grete and kynges?   *kingdoms*
What wight is þat can shape a remedie   *person; ordain*
Ageynes false and hid purposid thynges?   *secretly planned*
Who can the craft tho castes to espye,   *has the skill; those plans*
But man whos wil ay reedy is t'applie   *always ready; apply (itself)*

90 To thyng þat sovneth into hy falshede?   *tends towards; falsehood*
Wommen, bewaar of mennes sleighte, I rede.   *deceit; advise*

'And, ferthermore, han the men in vsage   *as a custom*
þat wheras they nat likly been to speede,   *where; succeed*
Swiche as they been with a double visage   *(one) such*
95 They procuren for to pursue hir neede.   *advance their cause*
He preyeth him in his cause proceede,
And largely him qwytith his trauaille.   *generously; rewards; work*
Smal witen wommen how men hem assaille.   *little know*

'To his felawe anothir wrecche seith,   *companion*
100 "Thow fisshist fair. Shee þat hath thee fyrid,   *enflamed*
Is fals and inconstant and hath no feith.
Shee for the rode of folk is so desyrid,   *ride; by people*
And as an hors fro day to day is hyrid,   *hired*
That whan thow twynnest from hir conpaignie,   *depart*
105 Anothir comth, and blerid is thyn ye.   *blinded. . . eye (i.e. deceived)*

'"Now prike on faste and ryde thy iourneye.   *spur; day's travel*
Whyl thow art ther, shee, behynde thy bak,   *there (i.e. away)*
So liberal is shee can no wight withseye,   *person; refuse*
But qwikly of anothir take a snak,   *bite (with sexual overtone)*
110 For so the wommen faren, al the pak.   *behave; pack*
Whoso hem trustith, hangid moot he be!   *may*
Ay they desiren chaunge and noueltee."   *always*

'Wherof procedith this but of enuye?
For he himself here ne wynne may,   *her*
115 Repreef of here he spekth, and villenye,   *reproof; speaks*
As mannes labbyng tonge is wont alway.   *blabbing*
Thus sundry men ful often make assay   *attempt*
For to destourbe folk in sundry wyse,   *disquiet*
For they may nat accheuen hir empryse.   *achieve; their undertaking*

120 'Ful many a man eek wolde for no good,   *also; good (purpose)*
þat hath in loue spent his tyme and vsid,
Men wiste his lady his axyng withstood,   *knew; opposed his requests*
And þat he wer of his lady refusid,   *had been by;*
Or waast and veyn wer al þat he had musid,   *wasted; projected*

125 Wherfore he can no bettre remedie,   *knows*
    But on his lady shapith him to lie.   *against; prepares*

    '"Euery womman", he seith, "is light to gete.   *easy*
    Can noon seyn nay if shee be wel isoght.   *entreated*
    Whoso may leiser han with hire to trete,   *whoever; leisure; deal*
130 Of his purpos ne shal he faille noght,
    But on maddyng he be so deepe broght   *unless; madness; deeply*
    þat he shende al with open hoomlynesse.   *ruin; plain speaking*
    þat louen wommen nat, as þat I gesse."

    'To sclaundre wommen thus what may profyte,   *slander; it profit*
135 To gentils namly þat hem armen sholde,   *gentlmen; especially; themselves*
    And in deffense of wommen hem delyte,
    As þat the ordre of gentillesse wolde.   *due practice; gentility requires*
    If þat a man list gentil to be holde,   *wishes; a gentleman; reckoned*
    Al moot he flee þat is to it contrarie.   *must*
140 A sclaundryng tonge is therto aduersarie.   *slandering; opposed to it*

    'A foul vice is of tonge to be light,   *easy of speech*
    For whoso mochil clappith gabbith ofte.   *much chatters; lies*
    The tonge of man so swift is and so wight   *powerful*
    þat wan it is areisid vp on lofte,   *raised; aloft (i.e. aloud)*
145 Reson it sueth so slowly and softe   *follows*
    þat it him neuere ouertake may.
    Lord, so the men been trusty at assay!   *how; when tested*

    'Al be it þat men fynde o womman nyce,   *although; one; foolish*
    Inconstant, rechelees or variable,   *careless; changeable*
150 Deynous or prowd, fulfillid of malice,   *scornful*
    Withoute feith or loue and deceyuable,   *deceitful*
    Sly, qweynte and fals, in al vnthrift coupable,   *cunning; malpractice; guilty*
    Wikkid and feers and ful of crueltee,
    It folwith nat swiche alle wommen be.   *follows; such*

155 'Whan þat the hy God angels fourmed hadde,
    Among hem all whethir ther was noon
    þat fownden was malicious and badde?
    Yis, men wel knowen ther was many oon   *a one*
    þat for hir pryde fil from heuene anoon.   *their; fell; immediately*

160 Shal man therfore alle angels prowde name?   *call*
     Nay, he þat that susteneth is to blame.   *supports that view*

     'Of xii apostles oon a traitour was.   *the twelve*
     The remanaunt yit goode wer and treewe.   *remainder*
     Thanne, if it happe men fynden par cas   *happen that; by chance*
165 O womman fals, swich is good for t'escheewe,   *one; such; avoid*
     And deeme nat þat they been alle vntreewe.   *judge*
     I see wel mennes owne falsenesse
     Hem causith wommen for to truste lesse.

     'O, euery man oghte han an herte tendre   *loving*
170 Vnto woman, and deeme hir honurable,   *judge*
     Whethir his shap be eithir thikke or sclendre,   *shape; thick-set*
     Or he be badde or good, this is no fable.   *fiction*
     Euery man woot þat wit hath resonable,   *knows; rational*
     þat of a womman he descendid is.   *from*
175 Than is it shame spek of hir amis.   *to speak ill of her*

     'A wikkid tree good fruyt may noon foorth
        brynge,
     For swich the fruyt is as þat is the tree.   *such*
     Take heede of whom thow took thy begynnynge.
     Lat thy modir be mirour vnto thee.
180 Honure hir if thow wilt honurid be.
     Despyse thow nat hir in no maneere,   *way*
     Lest þat therthurgh thy wikkidnesse appeere.   *through it*

     'An old prouerbe seid is in Englissh:
     Men seyn þat brid or foul is deshonest,   *bird; dishonourable*
185 Whatso it be, and holden ful cherlissh,   *whatever, reckoned most ill-bred*
     þat wont is to deffoule his owne nest.   *accustomed; defile*
     Men to seye of wommen wel it is best,   *for men to speak well*
     And nat for to despise hem ne depraue,
     If þat hem list hir honur keepe and saue.   *they wish; their*

190 'Ladyes eek conpleynen hem on clerkis,   *also; scholars*
     þat they han maad bookes of hir deffame,   *defaming them*
     In whiche they lakken wommennes werkis,   *find fault with; actions*
     And speken of hem greet repreef and shame,   *reproof*

And causelees hem yeue a wikkid name.   *without cause; give; reputation*
195 Thus they despysid been on euery syde,   *everywhere*
And sclaundred and belowen on ful wyde.   *slandered; belied; very widely*

'Tho wikkid bookes maken mencion,   *those*
How they betrayeden, in special,   *particular*
Adam, Dauid, Sampson and Salomon,
200 And many oon mo. Who may rehercen al   *another more; recite*
The tresoun þat they haue doon and shal?
Who may hir hy malice conprehende?   *their; great*
Nat the world, clerkes seyn, it hath noon ende.   *say; it (their malice)*

'Ouyde, in his book callid *Remedie*
205 *Of Loue* greet repreef of wommen writith,   *criticism*
Wherin I trowe he dide greet folie,   *believe*
And euery wight þat in swich cas delitith.   *man; such a case*
A clerkes custume is whan he endytith   *scholar's; writes*
Of wommen, be it prose, rym or vers,   *rhyme; verse*
210 Seyn they be wikke, al knowe he the reuers.   *to say; wicked; although; opposite*

'And þat book scolers lerne in hir childhede,   *i.e. the Remedia Amoris*
For they of wommen be waar sholde in age,   *so that; wary; when old*
And for to loue hem euere been in drede,   *to be afraid*
Syn to deceyue is set al hir corage.   *since; inclination*
215 They seyn peril to caste is auantage,   *forecast; advantageous*
Namely swich as men han in be trappid,   *especially such*
For many a man by wommen han mishappid.   *suffered misfortune*

'No charge what so þat the clerkes seyn.   *matter; say*
Of al hir wrong wrytyng do we no cure.   *their; do not care*
220 Al hir labour and trauaille is in veyn,
For, betwixt vs and my lady Nature,
Shal nat be souffred, whyl the world may dure,   *endured; last*
Clerkes, by hir outrageous tirannye,
Thus vpon wommen kythen hir maistrye.   *to show*

225 'Whilom ful many of hem wer in our cheyne   *formerly; very*
Tyd, and lo now, what for vnweeldy age,   *tied; impotent*
And for vnlust, may nat to loue atteyne,   *lack of appetite; attain*

And seyn þat loue is but verray dotage.　　　　　*nothing but folly*
Thus, for þat they hemself lakken corage,　　　　*(sexual) energy*
230　They folk excyten by hir wikked sawes,　　　　*their; sayings*
For to rebelle ageyn vs and our lawes.　　　　　*against*

'But maugree hem þat blamen wommen moost,　*in spite of*
Swich is the force of oure impressioun　　　　　*such; onslaught*
þat sodeynly we felle can hir boost　　　　　　*bring to nought; boast*
235　And al hir wrong ymaginacioun.
It shal nat been in hir elleccioun,　　　　　　*choice*
The foulest slutte in al a town refuse,
If þat vs list, for al þat they can muse,　　　　*we please; for all their plans*

'But hir in herte as brennyngly desyre　　　　　*burningly*
240　As thogh shee wer a duchesse or a qweene:
So can we mennes hertes sette on fyre,
And, as vs list, hem sende ioie and teene.　　　*we please; hurt*
They that to wommen been iwhet so keene,　　*against women; sharpened*
Our sharpe strokes, how sore they smyte,
245　Shul feele and knowe, and how they kerue and　*cut; wound*
　　byte.

'Pardee, this greet clerk, this sotil Ouyde,　　*by God; clever*
And many anothir, han deceyued be
Of wommen, as it knowen is ful wyde,　　　　　*by women; very widely*
What, no men more, and þat is greet deyntee.　*a great pleasure*
250　So excellent a clerk as þat was he,
And othir mo þat kowde so wel preche,　　　　　*many others*
Betrappid wern for aght they kowde teche.　　*were trapped in spite of anything*

'And trustith wel þat it is no meruaille,
For wommen kneewen pleynly hir entente.　　　*their intention*
255　They wiste how sotilly they kowde assaille　　*knew; cunningly*
Hem, and what falshode in herte they mente,
And tho clerkes they in hir daunger hente.　　*their power; seized*
With o venym anothir was destroyed,　　　　　*another (poison)*
And thus the clerkes often wer anoyed.　　　　*troubled*

260　'This ladyes ne gentils nathelees　　　　　　*gently born; nevertheless*
Weren nat they þat wroghten in this wyse,　　*acted; way*

But swiche filthes þat wern vertulees: *such sluts; immoral*
They qwitten thus thise olde clerkes wyse.   *repaid*
To clerkes forthy lesse may souffyse   *therefore; suffice*
265 Than to depraue wommen generally,   *defame*
For honur shuln they gete noon therby.   *none by this means*

'If þat tho men þat louers hem pretende,   *those; pretend themselves*
To wommen weren feithful, goode and treewe,
And dredden hem to deceyue and offende,   *feared*
270 Wommen to loue hem wolde nat escheewe,   *refuse*
But euery day hath man an herte neewe.
It vpon oon abyde can no whyle.   *one (object); remain; time*
What force is it swich oon for to begyle?   *matter; such; deceive*

'Men beren eek the wommen vpon honde,   *also; accuse the women*
275 þat lightly, and withouten any peyne,   *easily; difficulty*
They wonne been. They can no wight   *are won; man*
    withstonde,
þat his disese list to hem conpleyne.   *pleases; to complain of*
They been so freel, they mowe hem nat restreyne,   *frail; may*
Bot whoso lykith may hem lightly haue,   *pleases; easily*
280 So been hire hertes esy in to graue.   *to make an impression on*

'To maistir Iohn de Meun, as I suppose,
Than it was a lewde occupacioun,   *ignorant business*
In makynge of the *Romance of the Rose*:
So many a sly ymaginacioun   *cunning plot*
285 And perils for to rollen vp and doun,
So long procees, so many a sly cautele,   *process; trick*
For to deceyue a cely damoisele!   *ignorant maiden*

'Nat can we seen ne in our wit conprehende,
þat art and peyne and sotiltee may faille   *labour; cunning*
290 For to conquere, and soone make an ende,
Whan man a feeble place shal assaille,
And soone also to venquisshe a bataille,   *overcome (in)*
Of which no wight dar make resistence,   *where no man*
Ne herte hath noon to stonden at deffense.

295 'Than moot it folwen of necessitee,   *must*
Syn art askith so greet engyn and peyne,   *since; requires; skill*
A womman to deceuye, what shee be,   *whatever*
Of constance they been nat so bareyne   *constancy; bare*
As þat some of tho sotil clerkes feyne,   *those clever*
300 But they been as þat wommen oghten be,
Sad, constaunt and fulfillid of pitee.   *steadfast; full*

'How freendly was Medea to Iasoun,
In the conqueryng of the flees of gold.   *gaining; Golden Fleece*
How falsly quitte he hir affeccion,   *repaid*
305 By whom victorie he gat, as he hath wold.   *as he wished*
How may this man for shame be so bold
To falsen hir þat from deeth and shame   *play her false*
Him kepte, and gat him so greet prys and name?   *reputation*

'Of Troie also the traitour Eneas,
310 The feithlees man, how hath he him forswore   *perjured himself*
To Dydo þat queene of Cartage was,
þat him releeued of his greeues sore!
What gentillesse mighte shee do more   *nobility; show*
Than shee, with herte vnfeyned, to him kidde,   *showed*
315 And what mescheef to hire of it betidde!   *misfortune; for it; befell*

'In our legende of martirs may men fynde,
Whoso þat lykith therin for to rede,   *whoever pleases in it*
That ooth noon, ne byheeste, may men bynde.   *promise*
Of repreef ne of shame han they no drede.   *reproof*
320 In herte of man conceites treewe arn dede.   *thoughts*
The soile is naght; ther may no trouthe growe.   *wicked*
To womman is hir vice nat vnknowe.   *their; unknown*

'Clerkes seyn also ther is no malice
Vnto wommannes crabbid wikkidnesse.   *compared to*
325 O womman, how shalt thow thyself cheuyce,   *look after*
Syn men of thee so mochil harm witnesse?   *since; much evil*
Yee, strah, do foorth, take noon heuynesse.   *straw; carry on*
Keepe thyn owne, what men clappe or crake,   *whatever; chatter or croak*
And some of hem shuln smerte, I vndirtake.   *suffer*

330 'Malice of wommen, what is it to drede?   *why; to be feared*
They slee no men, destroien no citees.   *slay*
They nat oppressen folk, ne ouerlede,   *tyrannize over (them)*
Betraye empyres, remes ne duchees,   *kingdoms; duchies*
Ne men byreue hir landes ne hir mees,   *deprive of their; dwellings*
335 Folk enpoysone or howses sette on fyre,   *poison*
Ne fals contractes maken for noon hyre.

'Trust, parfyt loue and enteer charitee,   *perfect; entire*
Feruent wil and entalentid corage   *passionate inclination*
To thewes goode as it sit wel to be,   *virtues; is fitting*
340 Han wommen ay of custume and vsage,   *practice*
And wel they can a mannes ire asswage   *allay*
With softe wordes, discreet and benigne.   *kindly*
What they been inward shewith owtward signe.

'Wommannes herte to no creweltee
345 Enclyned is, but they been charitable,
Pitous, deuout, ful of humilitee,   *pitiful*
Shamefast, debonair and amiable,   *modest; gentle*
Dreedful and of hir wordes mesurable.   *timid; moderate*
What womman thise hath nat, per auenture,   *by chance*
350 Folwyth nothyng the way of hir nature.   *not at all*

'Men seyn our firste modir, nathelees,   *nevertheless*
Made al mankynde leese his libertee,   *lose*
And nakid it of ioie, douteless,   *stripped; certainly*
For Goddes heeste disobeied shee,   *commandment*
355 Whan shee presumed to ete of the tree
Which God forbad þat shee nat ete of sholde,
And nad the feend been, no more she wolde.   *had not; devil; would have*

'Th'enuyous swellyng þat the feend our fo   *growing envy*
Had vnto man in herte for his welthe
360 Sente a serpent and made hir to go
To deceuye Eeue, and thus was mannes welthe
Byreft him by the feend, right in a stelthe,   *stolen from; an act of theft*
The womman nat knowyng of the deceit.   *ignorant*
God woot, ful fer was it from hir conceit.   *knows; far; thought*

365 'Wherfore we seyn, this good womman Eeue
    Our fadir Adam ne deceyued noght.   *forefather*
    Ther may no man for a deceit it preeue   *prove*
    Proprely but if þat shee in hir thoght   *unless*
    Had it conpassid first or it was wroght,   *projected; before*
370 And, for swich was nat hire impressioun,   *intended effect*
    Men call it may no deceit, by resoun.

    'No wight deceyueth but he it purpose.   *person; unless; plans*
    The feend this deceit caste, and nothyng shee.   *planned; not at all*
    Than is it wrong for to deeme or suppose   *judge*
375 þat shee sholde of þat gilt the cause be.   *that she was the cause*
    Wytith the feend and his be the maugree,   *blame; penalty*
    And for excusid haue hir innocence,   *hold her innocence excused*
    Sauf oonly þat shee brak obedience.   *except; broke (her vow of)*

    'Touchynge which, ful fewe men ther been—   *concerning*
380 Vnnethes any, dar we saufly seye,   *scarcely; safely*
    Fro day to day, as men mowe wel seen—   *may*
    But þat the heeste of God they disobeye.   *command*
    This haue in mynde, sires, we yow preye.
    If þat yee be discreet and resonable,
385 Yee wole hir holde the more excusable.   *forgivable*

    'And wher men seyn in man is stidfastnesse,   *constancy*
    And womman is of hir corage vnstable,   *heart*
    Who may of Adam bere swich witnesse?   *such*
    Tellith on this, was he nat changeable?
390 They bothe weren in a cas semblable,   *similar case*
    Sauf willyngly the feend deceyued Eeue.   *except that*
    So dide shee nat Adam, by your leeue.

    'Yit was þat synne happy to mankynde.
    The feend deceyued was, for al his sleighte.   *cunning*
395 For aght he kowde him in his sleightes wynde,   *anything (i.e. all that); ensnare*
    God, to descharge mankynde of the weighte   *discharge*
    Of his trespas, cam doun from heuenes heighte,
    And flessh and blood he took of a virgyne
    And souffred deeth, man to deliure of pyne.   *deliver from pain*

400 'And God, fro whom ther may no thyng hid be,
    If he in womman knowe had swich malice   *known; such*
    As men of hem recorde in generaltee,   *generally*
    Of our lady, of lyf reparatrice,   *she who was restorer*
    Nolde han be born. But for þat shee of vice   *would not*
405 Was voide, and of al vertu wel, he wiste,
    Endowid, of hir be born him liste.   *well supplied; he pleased*

    'Hir hepid vertu hath swich excellence   *accumulated*
    þat al to weyk is mannes facultee   *weak; mind*
    To declare it and therfore, in suspense,   *abeyance*
410 Hir due laude put moot needes be.   *must*
    But this we witen verraily, þat shee,   *know truly*
    Next God, the best freend is þat to man longith. *belongs*
    The keye of mercy by hir girdil hongith,   *hangs*

    'And of mercy hath euery wight swich neede,   *person; such*
415 þat, cessyng it, farwel the ioie of man!   *in its absence*
    Of hir power it is to taken heede.   *due note should be taken*
    Shee mercy may, wole, and purchace can.   *obtain*
    Displese hir nat. Honureth þat womman,
    And othir wommen all for hir sake,
420 And, but yee do, your sorwe shal awake.   *unless*

    'Thow precious gemme, martir Margarete,
    Of thy blood dreddist noon effusioun.   *feared no pouring out*
    Thy martirdom ne may we nat foryete.   *forget*
    O constant womman, in thy passioun   *suffering*
425 Ouercam the feendes temptacioun,   *(you) overcame*
    And many a wight conuerted thy doctryne   *person; teaching*
    Vnto the feith of God, holy virgyne.

    'But vndirstondith, we commende hir noght
    By encheson of hir virginitee.   *reason*
430 Trustith right wel, it cam nat in our thoght,
    For ay we werreie ageyn chastitee,   *always; war; against*
    And euere shal, but, this leeueth wel yee,   *believe this well*
    Hir louyng herte and constant to hir lay,   *faith*
    Dryue out of remembrance we nat may.

435 'In any book also wher can yee fynde
þat of the wirkes, or the deeth or lyf
Of Ihesu spekth or makith any mynde,   *speaks; calls at all to mind*
þat wommen him forsook for wo or stryf?
Wher was ther any wight so ententyf   *person; attentive*
440 Abouten him as wommen? Perdee, noon.   *by heavens*
Th'apostles him forsooken euerichoon.   *all*

'Wommen forsook him noght, for al the feith
Of holy chirche in womman lefte oonly.   *remained; (one) woman alone*
This is no lees, for thus holy writ seith.   *lie*
445 Looke, and yee shuln so fynde it, hardily.   *we may swear*
And therfore it may preeued be therby,   *proved by this*
That in womman regneth al the constaunce,   *constancy*
And in man is al chaunge and variaunce.   *variation*

'Now holdith this for ferme and for no lye,   *as a truth*
450 þat this treewe and iust commendacioun
Of wommen is nat told for flaterie,
Ne to cause hem pryde or elacioun,   *vainglory*
But oonly, lo, for this entencioun,
To yeue hem corage of perseuerance   *encouragement*
455 In vertu and hir honur to enhaunce.

'The more vertu, the lasse is the pryde.   *(the) virtue; less*
Vertu so noble is and worthy in kynde,   *(her) nature*
þat vice and shee may nat in feere abyde.   *together*
Shee puttith vice cleene out of mynde.
460 Shee fleeth from him, shee leueth him behynde.
O womman, þat of vertu art hostesse,
Greet is thyn honur and thy worthynesse.

'Than thus we wolen conclude and deffyne: *bring our dispute to end*
We yow commaunde, our ministres echoon,   *each one*
465 þat reedy been to our heestes enclyne,   *commands; (to) submit*
þat of tho men vntreewe, our rebel foon,   *against those; foes*
Yee do punisshement, and þat anoon.   *immediately*
Voide hem our court and banisshe hem for   *expel them from*
    euere,
So þat therynne they ne come neuere.

470 'Fulfillid be it, cessyng al delay.   *without any*
     Looke ther be noon excusacion.   *excuse*
     Writen in th'eir the lusty monthe of May,   *pleasant*
     In our paleys, wher many a milion
     Of louers treewe han habitacion,
475 The yeer of grace ioieful and iocounde,   *pleasant*
     Millesimo CCCC and secounde.'   *1402*

        Explicit epistula Cupidinis.   *here ends the letter of Cupid*

Notes

For fuller comment on Hoccleve's version of the witty parody by Christine de Pizan of anti-feminist commonplaces, see Fleming 1971, Fenster and Erler 1990 (the former responsible for Christine's text, the latter for Hoccleve's), Ellis 1996. The relation of Hoccleve's to Christine's work has occasioned much debate: Hoccleve provides the precedent for this debate (cf. Introduction pp. 9, 40 and *Series* 2.772n.) by declaring that, whereas some gentlewomen have read it as a satire on women, any satire belongs to his source, and that his identification with the female position has led him to write 'conpleynyngly' in support of women. For a sixteenth-century copy of four stanzas from the work, probably from the version included by Thynne in his 1532 edition of Chaucer's works, see Muir 1944–7: 278–9 (his numbers 43–4, 48), and brief comment in Burrow 1999: 807. For possibly relevant comment on the ways in which Lancastrian texts generally present women, see Strohm 1998: 161.

1–8 Hoccleve follows Christine in giving Cupid, as a king (of Love) the appropriate royal style for the letter he is directing to his loyal servants. On the conventions of such a letter, and the wider context of such letters, see Fenster and Erler 1990: 167–8.

10 On Hoccleve's changes to Christine's presentation of women, see Ellis 1996. In Hoccleve gentle birth characterizes both the women (10, 260) and their lovers (135, 138).

16 Here and at the end of the work (476) Hoccleve adapts Christine's time (1399) and place (France) to his own time (1402) and place ('Albion': in S2 'Britane'). The bad reputation of Englishmen as lovers will become a commonplace later in the century, in the writings of Malory and Caxton. What Venuti (1995) calls the 'domestication' of translation is also seen in Hoccleve's explicit use of an English proverb (183).

24 This line has an echo of Chaucer: cf. *Troilus* 3.1147–8. The lover who offers to die to prove his faith (35) also has parallels in *Troilus*.

26ff. The elements of orthodox religion appropriated by courtly love, or *fin amor*, include 'penance' (26), humility (32) and the need for grace (27, 30). Other elements include secrecy (33, broken by the boastful lover at 63), 'daunger' (257n.), and, for loyal women betrayed by faithless lovers, a form of martyrdom (316n.).

41–2 Although this figure appears in Christine, Hoccleve gives it a distinctive slant by invoking a Chaucerian model, the innocent heroines of the *Legend*, moved by pity (72) to grant favour, and addressed directly by the narrator in an attempt to put them on their guard (41–2, 91, cf. *LGW* 1254, 2559). Similarly, like the heroes of the *Legend*, Hoccleve's male figures are presented more negatively and more simply than Christine's (cf. 54, 59, 62–3).

50 This, Hoccleve's version of Christine's 'quant ainsi les ont enveloppees' (Fr. 106)[when they have thus entrapped them], is both more vigorous and—paradoxically, given the translation's emphasis on noble women—more domestic than the French. See further comment, Introduction p. 38.

62 i.e. it isn't enough for him to have betrayed the woman; he has to tell his friend about it (and so break his earlier promise of secrecy).

65 The man accuses himself (or exposes himself unwittingly: Fensler and Erler 1990: 168 n. 7, 206n. to l. 65) by exposing his own falseness.

82 *the deceit of man*: Sinon.

94–5 The use of a go-between is not found in Christine, but has overtones of Chaucer's *Troilus*, which most clearly implies the two-faced nature of the go-between in the invocation to Janus (*Troilus* II.77).

100, 103, 106, 110 These and other animal metaphors (e.g. 184) are not found in Christine. (For comments on those in 102, 106, see Fensler and Erler 1990). Hoccleve uses those in 103 and 110 to good effect, contrasting the lover, departing on horseback (106), with the faithless woman who allows herself to be hired out and ridden like a horse (102–3).

105 See Fensler and Erler 1990 for a parallel to this line in Chaucer's *Reeve's Tale* (*CT* I.4049).

131 'unless he is made so deeply mad'. In H2 'he' has been added above the line; as first copied, without it, the text shared S2's reading: 'but be made so deeply mad'.

141 Cf. 127, where women were 'light' to win over.

144 The sense must be that the tongue is so quick in the utterance (i.e. 'wan it is areisid vp on lofte') of falsehood or the rationalizing of the speaker's appetites that the promptings of reason are left behind (reading 'on lofte' as parallel to 'on highte'; cf. II.172). Mitchell 1968: 23 and Fensler and Erler 1990: 208 find *double entendre* in the stanza, presumably in the words 'areisid vp on lofte... softe', which, if present, depends on the commonplace use of the tongue as a bawdy euphemism for the penis (e.g. Webster's *Duchess of Malfi* I.ii).

148–54 Much of this stanza translates Christine closely (Fr. 185–92), with the exception of 'feers', which may, by homonym substitution (cf. I.13n.), be Hoccleve's version of Christine's 'fieres' (proud).

162–3 Not in Christine, and derived (so

Fensler and Erler 1990: 208) from Chaucer's *Canon's Yeoman's Tale* (*CT* VIII.1001–5). See also Ellis 1996: n. 22.

171–2 The scribe of T found these lines odd enough to emend the male pronominal reference to female.

176 Cf. Matt. 7.17, *Series* 1.204n. For a parallel with Chaucer's *Legend* (2394–5), see Fensler and Erler 1990: 208.

178–82 Cf. Exod. 20.12 (also cited *Regement* 569–70), Prov. 1.8, 6.20.

179 *mirour*: part of material added by Hoccleve to Christine, this is a recurring image in his work (cf. Torti 1991). See also II.330, *Series* 2.409, 608, 646, 5.76, *Regement* 690; and, from the translations (the image added by Hoccleve in each instance), IV.96, *Series* 3.697, 727, 4.295, 455, 5.637. See also variant readings at V.35 and *Series* 2.67. The figure exists as an element of the narrative in *Series* 1.157, 162.

183 For comment on this proverbial figure, see Fensler and Erler 1990: 208.

189 The Fr. shows that 'hir' refers to the men; it could, of course, refer to the women whose honour men, in this poem, regularly betray (so that in preserving women's honour men, at the same time, preserve their own).

191 *books of hir diffame*: on the anti-feminist literature to which Christine is objecting, see Fenster and Erler 1990, Fleming 1971 and Miller 1977. Named figures include Ovid (204–5, 246) and Jean de Meun (281–3), author, with Guillaume de Lorris, of the enormously influential *Roman de la rose*. Christine attacked the latter in her contribution to the celebrated *Querelle de la rose*: for a modern printing and discussion, see Fenster and Erler 1990. In making the God of Love a literary censor Christine may have been influenced by Chaucer's presentation of the God of Love in the *Legend*, since the latter attacks the poet-translator Chaucer for translating the *Romance of the Rose*.

197 *wikkid bookes*: not so named by Christine ('en vers dient', 267), and probably deriving from *The Prologue to the Wife of Bath's Tale*, abbreviated *ProlWBT* (*CT* III.685), where, however, not the authors of the books, as here, but their subject matter ('wives') is so named. Given that Christine herself may have used *ProlWBT* similarly (Ellis 1996, cf. 225–31n. below), this rewriting of an anti-feminist commonplace shows Hoccleve more deeply responsive to Christine's ironies than is usually the case.

199 These Old Testament figures regularly appear as men deceived by women. See *Sir Gawain and the Green Knight* 2416–17 (Burrow 1977 contains the lines and provides a note), and fuller comment in Fenster's n. to *Epistre* 267–70 (Fenster and Erler 1990: 84).

202–3 The non-holograph MSS offer a reading which might have been Hoccleve's original: at all events, it preserves an ambiguity in the referent of the pronoun 'it' (203)—the world? women?—slightly better than the version in the holograph.

204 i.e. the *Remedia Amoris*.

209 The distinction between 'rym' and 'vers' Hoccleve owes to Christine (261). It does not appear to signify for him as much as that between prose and verse: cf. II.247, *Series* 3.977, 4.930.

215 *they*: H2 has an interlinear gloss 'scilicet libri' (i.e. books like Ovid's *Remedia*, above 204, 211).

221 The relation between Love and Nature, a parody of that between God and Nature—for Chaucer's presentation of Nature as 'vicaire of the almyghty Lord' cf. *CT* VI.19–26, *Parlement of Foules* 379–81—is given clearest expression in the *Roman de la rose* (cf. Benson 1988: 999, n. to *PF* 303).

225–31 These lines, translating Christine (Fr. 493–504), have a striking parallel in Chaucer (*ProlWBT*, *CT* III.707–10).

233 *impressioun*: so Fr. Chaucer uses the word tellingly, though not only, in fabliau contexts (*CT* I.3613, IV.1978, cf. IV.2178).

257 *daunger*: a property of the courtly heroine, variously defined 'standoffish-ness', 'disdain', 'hesitation'.

258 For the best reading of this line, that women use one poison (their deceiving of the scholars, 247) to drive out (destroy) another (the scholars' attempts to deceive them, 254–6), see Skeat's n. (D1D3 found the line problematical, and replaced 'venym' by the easier reading 'women'.)

266 Since Hoccleve does not use the word

'worship' elsewhere in this text, and does use 'honour' regularly (9, 63, 170, 180, 189, 418, 455), the *H reading appears to be scribal.

281 Tr1 glosses this line 'id est autour of þe Romans of þe Roos'.

299 *feyne*: TTr1 read 'seyn', which is closer to Christine's phrase ('comme aucuns dit', 406), but the stronger version common to the other non-holograph MSS and to H2 must be Hoccleve's. (Rhymes in '-eyn' are particularly prone to variation in the MSS.)

302 *Medea* provides a possible further link between Christine and Chaucer's *Legend*, since she and Dido (311) both occur in the *Legend*, and its official pro-feminist agenda leads to a similar rewriting of her and Dido's stories so as to exonerate the women's characters and blacken the men's, much as in Christine's work.

316 This addition by Hoccleve presumably refers to Chaucer's *Legend of Good Women* (so Skeat's n.), a work commissioned by the God of Love to commemorate women faithful in love to the point of self-inflicted death: hence its title, 'Legend', which usually refers to a saint's life (cf. Benson 1988: 842, n. to *CT* I.3141). The death of such women counts as a sort of martyrdom.

323 T glosses (later hand) 'fæminae malitia'.

327 In context, this line recalls the envoy of the *Clerk's Tale*, abbreviated *ClT*, which similarly encourages women to break out of the mould created for them by pro-feminist writing and run true to anti-feminist type (*CT* IV.1177–212).

341 Cf. Prudence, the heroine of Chaucer's *Tale of Melibee*, who similarly assuages her husband Melibee's wrath. Parallels exist in other texts: see Strohm 1992: 95–119.

351 Tr1 glosses 'id est Eua'.

360 On the serpent as feminine in medieval inconography, see Benson 1988: 860 (n. to *CT* II.360–1), Ross 1940: 294 and *Series* 5.159n.

359–62 The *H rhymes wealth/health/stealth are used again by Hoccleve in *Series* 4.877–80.

393 An echo of the traditional medieval view of the 'happy sin' (*felix culpa*) which brought about the birth of Christ: see Skeat's n.

398 The birth of Christ of a virgin is often advanced as the clinching argument against the anti-feminist position: cf. the Middle English 'The Thrush and the Nightingale' (Dickins and Wilson 1951).

407–10 A possible echo of Chaucer's *Prioress's Tale* (*CT* VII.460, 475, 481–2).

417 *may, wole, and … can*: on a possible Trinitarian echo in this formulation, see *Series* 1.108n. below.

421–7 Various reasons have been advanced, none entirely satisfactory (cf. Fenster and Erler 1990: 163 and n. to l. 421), for this addition by Hoccleve to Christine's text. On St Margaret, see the *Legenda Aurea* of James of Varaggio; her legend was translated by Hoccleve's near-contemporary Bokenham. Her inclusion here involves the speaker in a hasty qualification in the next stanza, and thus serves to undermine his authority somewhat after the manner of the Prologue to Chaucer's *Legend*.

426 *doctryne*: Erler reads 'edifying example') Fenster and Erler 1990: 211).

431–2 Tr1 glosses 'id est Cupide'.

434 *out of remembrance*: a dash between the words 'of' and 'remembrance' in the holograph might imply a missing possessive. Most copies read 'my' (cf. Introduction p. 17); Erler emends, on authority of usage elsewhere in H2, to 'our' (Fenster and Erler 1990: 198).

439 *Ententyf* (Fr. 566 'entalente') may glance at Chaucer's use of the word in a similarly ironic context in the *Merchant's Tale*, abbreviated *MerchT* (*CT* IV.1288).

441 Cf. Matt. 26.56.

442–4 Women are prominent as witnesses of the Passion and, subsequently, of the Resurrection. For Christine and for most of her contemporaries it was the Virgin Mary, who appears in the Gospel accounts of the Passion and Resurrection only in John 19.26–7, who embodied *par excellence* the faith of the Church (cf. 443, where Fr. 571 reads 'toute la foy remaint en une femme'; Tr1 glosses this line 'id est in oure ladye Marye'; cf. Ross 1940: 322.1–12 and n. According to the ps.-Bonaventuran *Meditationes Vitae Christi* she was the first to greet Christ after the Resurrection; for the recently founded Brigittine Order, Mary headed the nascent Church between the Resurrection and Pentecost (Ellis 1984: 27); closer parallels exist with Love's *Mirror of the Blessed Life of Jesus Christ* (Sargent 1992: 193) and the anonymous *Speculum Devotorum* (Hogg 1973–4: 307), both noted by Selman 1998: 177.

VII. THE SERIES

1. My compleinte

Aftir þat heruest inned had hise sheues,	*autumn; brought in*
And that the broun sesoun of Mihelmesse	*Michaelmas*
Was come, and gan the trees robbe of her leues,	*proceeded; (to) rob; their*
That grene had ben and in lusty freisshenesse,	*pleasing*
5 And hem into colour of ȝelownesse	
Had died and doun throwen vndirfoote,	*dyed*
That chaunge sanke into myn herte roote.	
For freisshly brouȝte it to my remembraunce	
That stablenesse in this worlde is ther noon.	
10 Ther is noþing but chaunge and variaunce.	*alteration*
Howe welthi a man be or wel begoon,	*prosperous*
Endure it shal not. He shal it forgoon.	*lose*
Deeth vndirfoote shal him þriste adoun.	*thrust down*
That is euery wiȝtes conclucioun,	*person's*
15 Wiche for to weyue is in no mannes myȝt,	*refuse*
Howe riche he be, stronge, lusty, freissh and gay.	*however; vigorous*
And in the ende of Nouembre, vppon a niȝt,	
Siȝynge sore, as I in my bed lay,	*sighing*
For this and oþir þouȝtis wiche many a day,	*thoughts*
20 Byforne, I tooke, sleep cam noon in myn ye,	*before; eye*
So vexid me the þouȝtful maladie.	*i.e. melancholia*
I sy wel, sithin I with siknesse last	*saw; since*
Was scourgid, cloudy hath bene þe fauour	
That shoon on me ful briȝt in times past.	*shone; very brightly*
25 The sunne abated, and þe dirke shour	*diminished; dark*
Hilded doun riȝt on me, and in langour	*poured*
Me made swymme, so that my spirite	

To lyue no lust had, ne no delyte.   *pleasure*

The greef aboute myn herte so sore swal   *swelled*
30   And bolned euere to and to so sore   *swelled; more and more*
That nedis oute I muste therwithal.   *necessarily; (burst) out; with it*
I thou3te I nolde kepe it cloos no more,   *would not; secret*
Ne lete it in me for to eelde and hore,   *age; grow grey*
And for to preue I cam of a womman,   *prove; was born*
35   I braste oute on þe morwe and þus bigan.   *burst; next day*

     Here endith my prolog and folwith my compleinte.

Almy3ty God, as liketh his goodnesse,   *pleases*
Vesiteþ folke alday, as men may se,   *visits; continually*
With los of good and bodily sikenesse,
And amonge othir, he for3at not me.   *others; forgot*
40   Witnesse vppon the wilde infirmite
Wiche þat I hadde, as many a man wel knewe,
And wiche me oute of mysilfe caste and threwe.

It was so knowen to þe peple and kouthe   *familiar*
That counseil was it noon, ne not be mi3t.   *secret*
45   Howe it wiþ me stood was in euery mannes
         mouþe,
And þat ful sore my frendis affri3t.   *sorely; frightened*
They for myn helþe pilgrimages hi3t,   *promised*
And sou3te hem, somme on hors and somme
         on foote,
God 3elde it hem, to gete me my boote.   *reward them for it; health*

50   But alþou3 the substaunce of my memorie
Wente to pleie as for a certein space,   *for a time*
3it the lorde of vertue, the kyng of glorie,   *yet*
Of his hi3e my3t and his benigne grace,
Made it for to retourne into the place
55   Whens it cam, wiche at Alle Halwemesse   *went out; All Saints'*
Was fiue 3eere, neither more ne lesse.   *five years ago*

And euere sithin, thankid be God oure Lord   *since*
Of his good and gracious reconsiliacioun,   *for*

My wit and I haue bene of suche acord *as well agreed*
60 As we were or the alteracioun *before*
Of it was, but by my sauacioun, *salvation*
Sith þat time haue I be sore sette on fire *since*
And lyued in greet turment and martire. *suffering*

For þouȝ that my wit were hoom come aȝein, *had returned again*
65 Men wolde it not so vndirstonde or take. *accept*
With me to dele hadden they disdein. *scorn*
A rietous persone I was and forsake. *dissolute; abandoned*
Min oolde frendshipe was al ouershake. *shaken off*
No wiȝt with me list make daliaunce. *person; pleased to converse*
70 The worlde me made a straunge countinaunce, *showed; the face of a stranger*

Wi[c]h þat myn herte sore gan to tourment,
For ofte whanne I in Westmynstir Halle,
And eke in Londoun, amonge the prees went, *also; crowd*
I sy the chere abaten and apalle *saw; faces grow dejected; pale*
75 Of hem þat weren wonte me for to calle *those; accustomed*
To companie. Her heed they caste awry, *to join them; their heads; aside*
Whanne I hem mette, as they not me sy. *as if; saw*

As seide is in þe sauter miȝt I sey, *Psalter*
'They þat me sy, fledden awey fro me'. *saw*
80 Forȝeten I was al oute of mynde awey, *forgotten*
As he þat deed was from hertis cherte. *dead; (far) from; love*
To a lost vessel lickned miȝte I be, *likened*
For manie a wiȝt aboute me dwelling *person; in my vicinity*
Herde I me blame and putte in dispreisyng. *and censure*

85 Thus spake manie oone and seide by me: *about*
'Alþouȝ from him his siiknesse sauage *wild*
Withdrawen and passed as for a time be,
Resorte it wole, namely in suche age *return; will; specially*
As he is of,' and thanne my visage *face*
90 Bigan to glowe for the woo and fere. *burn; grief*
Tho wordis, hem vnwar, cam to myn eere. *those; without their knowledge*

'Whanne passinge hete is,' quod þei, 'trustiþ this, *extreme; believe*
Assaile him wole aȝein that maladie.'

And ȝit, parde, thei token hem amis.   *by heaven; were wrong*
95   Noon effecte at al took her prophecie.   *their*
Manie someris bene past sithen remedie   *are; since*
Of that God of his grace me purueide.   *in his grace; provided with*
Thankid be God, it shoop not as þei seide.   *happened*

What falle shal, what men so deme or gesse,   *whatever; happen; judge*
100   To him that woot euery hertis secree,   *knows; secret*
Reserued is. It is a lewidnesse   *an ignorance*
Men wiser hem pretende þan thei be,   *to pretend themselves*
And no wiȝt knowith, be it he or she,
Whom, howe, ne whanne God wole him vesite.   *visit*
105   It happith often whanne men wene it lite.   *expect; not at all*

Somtime I wende as lite as any man   *thought; little*
For to han falle into that wildenesse,   *to have fallen*
But God, whanne him liste, may, wole and can   *it pleases*
Helthe withdrawe and sende a wiȝt siiknesse.   *person*
110   Thouȝ man be wel this day, no sikernesse   *certainty*
To hym bihiȝte is that it shal endure.   *promised*
God hurte nowe can, and nowe hele and cure.

He suffrith longe but at the laste he smit.   *endures; smites*
Whanne þat a man is in prosperite,
115   To drede a falle comynge it is a wit.   *mark of wisdom*
Whoso that taketh hede ofte may se   *whoever*
This worldis chaunge and mutabilite
In sondry wise, howe nedith not expresse.   *different ways; to declare*
To my mater streite wole I me dresse.   *immediately; address myself*

120   Men seiden I loked as a wilde steer,   *looked like; ox*
And so my looke aboute I gan to throwe.   *cast*
Min heed to hie, anothir seide, I beer: *head; carried*
'Full bukkissh is his brayn, wel may I trowe.'   *very like a buck; believe*
And seide the thridde, 'And apt is in þe rowe   *(he) is fit; row (i.e. company)*
125   To site of hem that a resounles reed   *sit; senseless piece of advice*
Can ȝeue: no sadnesse is in his heed.'   *give; soundness*

Chaunged had I m[y] pas, somme seiden eke,   *pace; moreover*
For here and there forþe stirte I as a roo,   *started; roe*

Noon abood, noon areest, but al brainseke. *resting; stopping; brainsick*
130 Another spake and of me seide also, *concerning*
My feet weren ay wauynge to and fro, *moving*
Whanne þat I stonde shulde and wiþ men talke, *stand (still)*
And þat myn yen souȝten euery halke. *eyes; sought; corner (of room)*

I leide an eere ay to as I by wente, *gave an ear to this constantly*
135 And herde al, and þus in myn herte I caste: *reflected*
'Of longe abidinge here I may me repente.
Lest that of hastinesse I at the laste *in hastiness*
Answere amys, beste is hens hie faste, *wrongly; to depart quickly*
For if I in þis prees amys me gye, *crowd; misbehave myself*
140 To harme wole it me turne and to folie.' *and (make me) a laughing-stock*

And this I demed wel and knewe wel eke, *judged; also*
Whatso þat euere I shulde answere or seie, *whatever*
They wolden not han holde it worth a leke. *held; leek*
Forwhy, as I had lost my tunges keie, *therefore; as if; tongue's key*
145 Kepte I me cloos, and trussid me my weie, *private; took myself off*
Droupinge and heuy and al woo bistaad. *drooping; woebegone*
Smal cause hadde I, meþouȝte, to be glad.

My spirites labouriden euere ful bisily
To peinte countenaunce, chere and look, *appearance; face*
150 For þat men spake of me so wondringly, *because*
And for the verry shame and feer I qwook. *shook*
Thouȝ myn herte hadde be dippid in þe brook, *even if; been plunged*
It weet and moist was ynow of my swoot, *wet; enough; with my sweat*
Wiche was nowe frosty colde, nowe firy hoot. *hot as fire*

155 And in my chaumbre at home whanne þat I was
Mysilfe aloone I in þis wise wrouȝt. *way; did*
I streite vnto my mirrour and my glas, *(went) straight*
To loke howe þat me of my chere þouȝt, *my expression seemed to me*
If any othir were it than it ouȝt, *at all other*
160 For fain wolde I, if it not had bene riȝt, *gladly*
Amendid it to my kunnynge and myȝt. *to have improved; according to; knowledge*

Many a saute made I to this mirrour,   *leap*
Thinking, 'If þat I looke in þis manere
Amonge folke as I nowe do, noon errour
165 Of suspecte look may in my face appere.   *suspicious*
This countinaunce, I am sure, and þis chere,   *appearance; expression*
If I it forthe vse, is nothing repreuable   *abroad; not; objectionable*
To hem þat han conceitis resonable.'   *understandings*

And therwithal I þouȝte þus anoon: *thereupon; at once*
170 'Men in her owne cas bene blinde alday,   *their; situation; continually*
As I haue herde seie manie a day agoon,   *before this*
And in that same plite I stonde may.   *danger*
Howe shal I do? Wiche is the beste way
My troublid spirit for to bringe in rest?
175 If I wiste howe, fain wolde I do the best.'   *knew; gladly; my best*

Sithen I recouered was, haue I ful ofte   *since*
Cause had of anger and inpacience,
Where I borne haue it esily and softe,   *calmly; gently*
Suffringe wronge be done to me, and offence,   *enduring*
180 And not answerid aȝen, but kepte scilence,   *back*
Leste þat men of me deme wolde, and sein,   *judge*
'Se howe this man is fallen in aȝein.'   *in(to his sickness); again*

As that I oones fro Westminstir cam,   *once*
Vexid ful greuously with þouȝtful hete,   *burning thought*
185 Thus thouȝte I, 'A greet fool I am,
This pauyment adaies thus to bete,   *daily; beat (upon)*
And in and oute laboure faste and swete,   *everywhere; sweat*
Wondringe and heuinesse to purchace,   *gain*
Sithen I stonde out of al fauour and grace.'   *since*

190 And thanne þouȝte I on þat othir side,
'If that I not be sen amonge þe prees,   *throng*
Men deme wole that I myn heed hide,   *judge*
And am werse than I am, it is no lees.'   *lie*
O Lorde, so my spirit was restelees.
195 I souȝte reste and I not it fonde,   *found*
But ay was trouble redy at myn honde.   *always*

	I may not lette a man to ymagine	*prevent; from imagining*
	Fer aboue þe mone, if þat him liste.	*far; moon; please*
	Therby the sothe he may not determine,	*truth*
200	But by the preef ben thingis knowen and wiste.	*proof; grasped*
	Many a doom is wrappid in the myste.	*judgement; hidden as in*
	Man by hise dedis and not by hise lookes	*deeds*
	Shal knowen be. As it is writen in bookes,	
	Bi taaste of fruit men may wel wite and knowe	*know*
205	What that it is. Othir preef is ther noon.	*proof*
	Euery man woote wel that, as þat I trowe.	*knows; believe*
	Riȝt so, thei that deemen my wit is goon,	*judge*
	As ȝit this day ther deemeth many oon	*many a one*
	I am not wel, may, as I by hem goo,	
210	Taaste and assay if it be so or noo.	
	Uppon a look is harde men hem to grounde	*(it) is; for men to determine*
	What a man is. Therby the sothe is hid.	*truth*
	Whethir hise wittis seek bene or sounde,	*are*
	By countynaunce is it not wist ne kid.	*known; made public*
215	Thouȝ a man harde haue oones been bitid,	*has once experienced hardship*
	God shilde it shulde on him contynue alway.	*forbid*
	By commvnynge is the beste assay.	*conversation; test*
	I mene, to commvne of thingis mene,	*converse; ordinary*
	For I am but riȝt lewide, douteles,	*uneducated*
220	And ignoraunt. My kunnynge is ful lene.	*knowledge; very slight*
	Ȝit homely resoun knowe I neuerethelees.	*yet; ordinary reasoning*
	Not hope I founden be so resounlees	*think; (to) be found; foolish*
	As men deemen. Marie, Crist forbede!	*judge; St Mary; forbid*
	I can no more. Preue may the dede.	*know; prove (this); deed*
225	If a man oones falle in drunkenesse,	*once*
	Shal he contynue therynne eueremo?	
	Nay, þouȝ a man do in drinking excesse	*drink to excess*
	So ferforþe þat not speke he ne can, ne goo,	*far*
	And hise witts welny bene refte him fro,	*are almost all taken*
230	And buried in the cuppe, he aftirward	
	Cometh to hymsilfe aȝeine, ellis were it hard.	*otherwise it would be*

Riȝt so, þouȝ þat my witte were a pilgrim,

And wente fer from home, he cam aȝain.   *far; returned*

God me deuoided of the greuous venim   *emptied; poison*

235 That had enfectid and wildid my brain.   *maddened*

See howe the curteise leche moost souerain

Vnto the seke ȝeueth medicine   *sick (man) gives*

In nede, and hym releueth of his greuous pine.   *torment*

Nowe lat this passe. God woot, many a man   *let; knows*

240 Semeth ful wiis by countenaunce and chere   *appearance; expression*

Wiche, and he tastid were what he can,   *tested; knows*

Men miȝten licken him to a fooles peere,   *compare; mate*

And som man lokeþ in foltisshe manere   *like a fool*

As to þe outwarde doom and iugement,   *judged externally*

245 That, at þe prefe, discreet is and prudent.   *when tested*

But algatis, howe so be my countinaunce,   *all the same; however*

Debaat is nowe noon bitwixe me and my wit,   *disagreement*

A[l]þouȝ þat ther were a disseueraunce,   *separation*

As for a time, bitwixe me and it.

250 The gretter harme is myn, þat neuere ȝit   *yet*

Was I wel lettrid, prudent and discreet.   *educated*

Ther neuere stood ȝit wiis man on my feet.   *wise*

The sothe is this, suche conceit as I had   *truth; thoughts*

And vndirstonding, al were it but smal,   *although; only*

255 Bifore þat my wittis weren vnsad,   *unstable*

Thanked be oure Lorde Ihesu Crist of al,   *for all*

Suche haue I nowe, but blowe is ny oueral   *blown; nearly everywhere*

The reuerse, wherþoruȝ moche is my mornynge,   *through which*

Wiche causeth me thus syȝe in compleinynge.   *sigh*

260 Sithen my good fortune hath chaungid hir chere,   *since; look*

Hie tyme is me to crepe into my graue.   *for me*

To lyue ioielees, what do I here?   *joyless*

I in myn herte can no gladnesse haue.

I may but smal seie but if men deme I raue.   *only a little; unless; judge*

265 Sithen oþir þing þan woo may I noon gripe,   *since; grasp*

Vnto my sepulcre am I nowe ripe.   *for; ready*

My wele, adieu, farwel, my good fortune.   *wealth*
Oute of ȝoure tables me planed han ȝe.   *removed*
Sithen welny eny wiȝt for to commvne   *since almost; person; talk*
270 With me loth is, farwel prosperite.   *unwilling*
I am no lenger of ȝoure liuere.   *longer; livery*
Ȝe haue me putte oute of ȝoure retenaunce.   *retinue*
Adieu, my good auenture and good chaunce.   *fortune; luck*

And aswithe aftir, thus biþouȝte I me: *immediately; reflected*
275 'If þat I in this wise me dispeire,
It is purchas of more aduersite.   *purchase*
What nedith it my feble wit appeire,   *need is there; to weaken*
Sith God hath made myn helþe home repeire,   *since; return*
Blessid be he? And what men deme and speke,   *whatever; judge*
280 Suffre it þenke I and me not on me wreke.'   *(to) endure; think; (to) avenge*

But somdel had I reioisinge amonge,   *somewhat; between whiles*
And a gladnesse also in my spirite,
That þouȝ þe peple took hem mis and wronge,   *judged; amiss; wrongly*
Me deemyng of my siiknesse not quite,   *judging; freed*
285 ȝit for they compleined the heuy plite   *regretted; plight*
That they had seen me in wiþ tendirnesse
Of hertis cherte, my greef was the lesse.   *love*

In hem putte I no defaute but oon.   *found no fault; one*
That I was hool, þei not ne deme kowde,   *whole; judge*
290 And day by day þei sye me bi hem goon   *saw; go*
In hete and coolde, and neiþer stille or lowde   *silent or speaking*
Knewe þei me do suspectly. A dirke clowde   *(to) act suspiciously; dark*
Hir siȝt obscurid withynne and wiþoute,   *their sight*
And for al þat were ay in suche a doute.   *(they) were; uncertainty*

295 Axide han they ful oftesithe, and freined   *asked; often; inquired*
Of my felawis of the Priue Seel,   *fellows; Privy Seal*
And preied hem to telle hem wiþ herte vnfeined,   *sincere*
Howe it stood with me, wethir yuel or wel.
And they the sothe tolde hem euery del,   *completely*
300 But þei helden her wordis not but lees.   *reckoned their; nothing; lies*
Thei miȝten as wel haue holden her pees.   *kept their peace*

This troubly liif hath al to longe endurid.　　*troublesome*
Not haue I wist hou in my skyn to tourne.　　*known*
But nowe mysilfe to mysilfe haue ensurid　　*I myself; guaranteed*
305 For no suche wondringe aftir this to mourne.　　*amazement; repine*
As longe as my liif shal in me soiourne　　*remain*
Of suche ymaginynge I not ne recche.　　*care*
Lat hem deeme as hem list and speke and drecche.　　*judge; please*

This othir day a lamentacioun
310 Of a wooful man in a book I sy,　　*saw*
To whom wordis of consolacioun
Resoun ʒaf spekynge effectuelly,　　*gave; to good effect*
And wel esid myn herte was therby,　　*eased; by it*
For whanne I had a while in þe book reed,　　*read*
315 With the speche of Resoun was I wel feed.　　*nourished*

The heuy man wooful and angwisshous　　*anguished*
Compleined in þis wise, and þus seide he:
'My liif is vnto me ful encomborus,　　*burdensome*
For whidre or vnto what place I flee,
320 My wickidnessis euere folowen me,
As men may se the shadwe a body sue,　　*shadow; follow*
And in no manere I may hem eschewe.　　*avoid*

'Vexacioun of spirit and turment
Lacke I riʒt noon. I haue of hem plente.
325 Wondirly bittir is my taast and sent.　　*amazingly; smell*
Woo be þe time of my natiuite.　　*accursed*
Vnhappi man, that euere shulde I be.
O deeth, thi strook a salue is of swetnesse　　*stroke; ointment*
To hem þat lyuen in suche wrecchidnesse.

330 'Gretter plesaunce were it me to die,　　*pleasure would it be for me*
By manie foolde than for to lyue so.　　*many times over*
Sorwes so manie in me multiplie
That my liif is to me a verre foo.　　*very; foe*
Comforted may I not be of my woo.
335 Of my distresse see noon ende I can.
No force howe soone I stinte to be a man.'　　*matter; cease*

    Thanne spake Resoun, 'What meneth al this   *behaviour*
      fare?
    Thouȝ welþe be not frendly to thee, ȝit   *yet*
    Oute of thin herte voide woo and care.'   *cast*
340 'By what skile, howe, and by what reed and wit,' *counsel; skill*
    Seide this wooful man, 'miȝte I doon it?'   *do*
    'Wrastle,' quod Resoun, 'aȝein heuynesse   *struggle; sadnesses*
    Of þe worlde, troublis, suffringe and duresse.   *hardships*

    'Biholde howe many a man suffrith dissese,
345 As greet as þou and alaway grettere,   *continually*
    And þouȝ it hem pinche sharply and sese,   *though; them; seize*
    ȝit paciently thei it suffre and bere.   *endure; bear*
    Thinke hereon and the lesse it shal þe dere.   *injure*
    Suche suffraunce is of mannes gilte clensinge,   *purification*
350 And hem enableth to ioie euerelastinge.   *enables them (to attain)*

    'Woo, heuinesse and tribulacioun
    Comen aren to me[n] alle and profitable.   *common*
    Thouȝ greuous be mannes temptacioun,
    It sleeth man not. To hem þat ben suffrable   *kills; those who; patient*
355 And to whom Goddis strook is acceptable   *stroke*
    Purueied ioie is, for God woundith tho   *ordained; those*
    That he ordeined hath to blis to goo.

    'Golde purgid is, thou seest, in þe furneis,   *purified*
    For þe finer and clenner it shal be.   *purer*
360 Of þi dissese the weiȝte and þe peis   *burden*
    Bere liȝtly, for God, to prove the,   *easily*
    Scourgid þe hath wiþ sharpe aduersite.
    Not grucche and seie, "Whi susteine I this?"   *complain*
    For if þou do, thou the takest amis.   *act wrongly*

365 'But þus þou shuldist þinke in þin herte,
    And seie, "To þee, lorde God, I haue agilte   *done wrong*
    So sore I moot for myn offensis smerte,   *grievously; must; suffer*
    As I am worthi. O Lorde I am spilte,   *destroyed*
    But þou to me þi mercy graunte wilte.   *unless*
370 I am ful sure þou maist it not denie.
    Lorde, I me repente, and I the mercy crie."'   *beg mercy of you*

Lenger I þouȝte reed haue in þis book,   *longer; to have read*
But so it shope þat I ne miȝte nauȝt.   *happened*
He þat it ouȝte aȝen it to him took,   *owned; back*
375   Me of his hast vnwar. ȝit haue I cauȝt   *haste; unaware; taken*
Sum of the doctrine by Resoun tauȝt
To þe man, as above haue I said.
Wel þerof I holde me ful wel apaid,   *with it; satisifed*

For euere sithen sett haue I the lesse   *since*
380   By the peples ymaginacioun,
Talkinge this and þat of my siknesse
Wich cam of Goddis visitacioun.   *from*
Miȝte I haue be founde in probacioun   *when tested*
Not grucching but han take it in souffraunce,   *complaining; patience*
385   Holsum and wiis had be my gouernaunce.   *would have been; self-control*

Farwel my sorowe, I caste it to the cok.   *? away (to the cock)*
With pacience I hensforþe thinke vnpike   *(to) undo*
Of suche þouȝtful dissese and woo the lok,   *(i.e.) melancholia; lock*
And lete hem out þat han me made to sike.   *them (my thoughts); sigh*
390   Hereafter oure Lorde God may, if him like,   *please*
Make al myn oolde affeccioun resorte,   *feeling; return*
And in hope of þat wole I me comforte.

Thoruȝ Goddis iust doom and his iugement   *through; just*
And for my best, nowe I take and deeme,   *my greatest (profit); reckon*
395   ȝaf þat good lorde me my punischement.   *gave*
In welthe I tooke of him noon hede or ȝeme,   *attention*
Him for to plese and him honoure and queme,   *please; gratify*
And he me ȝaf a boon on for to gnawe,   *bone*
Me to correcte and of him to have awe.

400   He ȝaf me wit and he tooke it away   *gave*
Whanne that he sy that I it mis dispente,   *saw; used it amiss*
And ȝaf aȝein whanne it was to his pay.   *profit*
He grauntide me my giltis to repente,
And hensforwarde to sette myn entente   *intention*
405   Vnto his deitee to do plesaunce,   *to please his godhead*
And to amende my sinful gouernaunce.   *way of life*

Laude and honour and þanke vnto þee be,
Lorde God, that salue art to al heuinesse.   *sadness*
Thanke of my welthe and myn aduersitee.   *thanks for*
410 Thanke of myn elde and of my seeknesse.   *age; sickness*
And thanke be to thin infinit goodnesse
And thi ȝiftis and benefices alle,   *gifts; benefits*
And vnto thi mercy and grace I calle.

Notes

The form and force of this complaint depend to some extent on the work it cites, the *Synonyma* of Isidore of Seville (on which, see Rigg 1970, Burrow 1998). See also comment by Burrow 1994: 194 [6] on links between 'My Compleinte' and other writing of Hoccleve, as well as formal similarities with petitions presented by private individuals seeking redress for wrongs done them, and handled by the Office of the Privy Seal, where Hoccleve was a clerk (on the importance of petition as a tool of medieval government, see Green 1980: 42). Clear links exist with the *Regement* in the person of the solitary narrator visited by God's judgement (in the *Regement*, the old beggar is so visited, 668–70, and nearly loses his wit, 1328) and misunderstood by his friends (cf. 1.46n.). Burrow 1994: 215 [27] dates this and the following piece 1419–20 (see also 2.134n.).

title from rubric to l. 35.

1–21 For comment on the ways in which this opening parodies the conventions of the *General Prologue to the Canterbury Tales*, see relevant nn. in Seymour 1981, Burrow 1977; and for links with French *dits*, Burrow 1997: 44 n. 32).

23 With this metaphor, cf. Chaucer's *Monk's Tale*, abbreviated *MkT* (*CT* VII.2766).

33 I have read 'let' in the sense 'permit'; Burrow 1977 favours the sense 'hinder' and translates the phrase 'to dam it up inside myself.' For further instances of the important motif of thought/soliloquy in 'My Compleinte', see 134–40, 162–75, 185–93, 274–80, 372; see also Burrow 1977, n. to 169–75.

46 On the role of friendship (both positive and negative) in the *Series*, as in other poems here edited, cf. 2, epilogue to 3 and prologue to 5 *passim*; see also 1.68, 338, 3.449, 529, 924, 4.15n, 151, 424–32, 467, 498–514, 534–41, 690, 708–15, 5.157, 506, and *Regement* 715–19.

55 The feast of All Saints, November 1.

79 A gloss in BCSY shows the source of this quotation, elements of which can be seen in the rest of the stanza, as Ps.

30.12 (so Seymour 1981, Burrow 1977); for the full quotation, see Rigg 1970: 565, who later cites a parallel passage in the *Synonyma* of Isidore of Seville, a text used directly at several points in 'My Compleinte' and indirectly at many others.

100 Against this line occurs the first of several marginal 'nota bene nota' in S (others are 113, 211, 225, 239, 379, 393).

104 If 'whom' is accepted (and not emended—see Burrow 1977, n.—to 'where') it must be understood pleonastically as anticipating 'him' in the same line.

108 There may be an echo here of the conventional representation of the Trinity as power ('may'), will ('wole') and wisdom ('can'), qualities appropriated respectively to the Father, Spirit and Son.

113 Cf. *Regement* 4422–4, on God's 'long suffrance', a Biblical commonplace.

114 BY gloss this comment on the way 'prosperite' can prelude 'a falle comynge' with a quotation from 'Bernardus' on the dangers of good rather than ill fortune, since, presumably, the former can blind people to the truth of their situations. See Rigg 1970: 565 for the quotation. 'Bernardus' may refer either to Bernard of Cluny, author of *De Contemptu Mundi*, or to St Bernard of Clairvaux, under whose name circulated the *Meditationes Piissimae de Humanae Condicionis*, sometimes also entitled *De Contemptu Mundi* (*PL* 184.485–508). I have not been able to trace the quotation. Burrow 1999 (n. to l. 115) offers parallels in Peter of Blois (*PL* 207.989) and Gregory the Great (*PL* 75.679–80).

123 *bukkissh*: cf. *Regement* 604.

124–6 I follow Burrow 1977 in giving this whole speech to the third bystander. Seymour reads only the last clause as so spoken, and has the rest, in parenthesis, as spoken by the narrator against the third speaker. Burrow's reading has the support of a later repetition of the word 'resoulnes' (222).

154 With this collocation, cf. 2.355–6, 5.320–1, *Regement* 108. The fire of hell, source of both cold *and* heat in the ninth *lectio* for All Saints' Day, though not as translated by Hoccleve (cf. 4.958n.) is juxtaposed similarly with the cold sweat of fear it induces in 4.789–91.

157 Burrow 1977 reads 'streight' as past tense of the verb 'stretch', in which case the sense 'reached (for)' would be preferred.

178–80 Possibly an echo of Prov. 15.1. Rigg 1970: 572 offers Ps. 38.[2–3] from the *Synonyma* as a parallel. Neither text contains all the elements of this passage.

188 *wondringe and heuinesse* could both be applied to the narrator: if so, the former means 'distress' (cf. Burrow 1977, n.). Alternatively, the former might refer to the reaction of the bystanders (cf. 150 above).

195 may echo Matt. 12.43 (Burrow 1977, n.) or Boethius, *Consolatio* Bk. III pr.3 (cf. Benson 1988: 996, n. to *PF* 90–1).

204 Glossed in BLSY by the Latin of Matt. 7.16 ('a fructibus eorum cognoscetis [S congnoscetis] eos', cf. Rigg 1970: 565). This metaphor may be still operative at the end of the stanza, where 'taaste', though carrying the primary sense 'test, put to the proof' (Burrow 1977, n.), can also be understood quasi-metaphorically (and cf. Ps. 34.9).

211–14 Hoccleve's poem to Oldcastle

similarly speaks of the difficulty of judging a person accurately on the basis only of appearances (Furnivall and Gollancz 1970: 19.353–5). Contrast Christine de Pizan's assertion that women are as they seem to be (VI.343).

252 With this self-presentation, cf. *Regement* 1236–9.

268 Burrow's note on this line (1977) explains that 'writing was removed from wax tablets by smoothing ("planing") the surface.'

271 *liuere* i.e. of your household as a retainer (hence, as Burrow 1977 notes, the reading 'retenaunce' in the following line).

308 *drecche*: variously glossed by Furnivall ('vex'), Seymour ('slander'), Burrow 1977 ('speculate'). OED gives the sense 'be troubled in their sleep' (cf. MED *s.v.* 'drecchinge' 1b), which may depend on an acceptance of D's reading 'dreme' earlier in the line. 'Dreme' might, however, be authorial, given its echo of a similar collocation in Chaucer (*CT* VII.2884).

309 The *H MSS gloss 'hic est lamentacio hominis dolentis' [this is the lamentation of a grieving man], and carefully distinguish the speakers in the following dialogue by further marginal notes: 'racio' [*var.* Reason] 312, 337, 342, 'homo' 317, 340. These last Stowe ascribes in D to 'Thomas [Hoccleve]' (earlier noted by von Nolcken 1993: 47 (n. 34)), and thus achieves a blurring of levels of voicing in the text analogous to that regularly produced by Chaucer in *CT*. The following passage (309–64) is heavily glossed in the MSS: see Rigg 1970.

310 For detailed comment on the 'book', the *Synonyma* of Isidore of Seville, and its use by Hoccleve in 'My Compleinte', see Rigg 1970.

318 Rigg 1970: 565 cites Baruch 3.1 as source of the Latin behind this line.

328–9 Cf. Ecclus. 41.3. These lines (Rigg 1970: 565) are glossed in LSY 'o mors quam dulcis es male uiuentibus' [o death how sweet you are to those who live badly], 'male' presumably in error for 'amare' of source, the latter translated by Hoccleve as 'wrechednes'.

330 Cf. Jonah 4.8 (so Rigg 1970: 568).

337, 340, 342, 351, 356, 358 For

accompanying glosses in *H MSS, all taken from the *Synonyma*, see Rigg 1970: 545.

356 Cf. Heb. 12.6; Rigg 1970: 545 adds Prov. 3.12, Apoc. 3.19 as parallels.

358 With this passage, cf. Prov. 17.3, 27.21, Ecclus. 2.5, all noted by Rigg. The image is a Biblical commonplace.

360 *wei3te and... peis*: this collocation recurs in the 'Dialoge' (2.54, 417). Weighing is a common metaphor in Hoccleve (cf. I.167–8, II.47, *Regement* 60, 1689.) The metaphor is literalized when Hoccleve talks about currency fraud (2.105–6).

400 An echo of Job 1.21.

2. Here endith my compleynt and begynneth a dialoge

And, endid my compleinte in this manere,	*having ended*
Oon knockid at my chaumbre dore sore	*someone; hard*
And criede alowde, 'Howe, Hoccleue, art þu here?	
Open thi dore. Me thinketh ful ȝore	*a long time*
5 Sithen I the sy. What, man, for Goddis ore	*since; saw; mercy*
Come oute, for this quarter I not the sy,	*(last) three months; saw*
By ouȝt I woote': and oute to hym cam I.	*anything; know*
This man was my good frende of fern agoon,	*long standing*
þat I speke of, and þus he to me seide:	
10 'Thomas, as thou me louest, telle anoon	*at once*
What didist þou whanne I knockede and leide	*beat*
So faste vppon þi dore?' And I obeide	
Vnto his wil: 'Come in', quod I, 'and see.'	
And so he dide; he streit wente in wiþ me.	*at once*
15 To my good frende not þouȝte I to make it queinte,	*difficult*
Ne my labour from him to hide or leine,	*conceal*
And riȝt anoon I redde hym my compleinte,	
And, that done, þus he seide: 'Sin we tweine	*since*
Ben here, and no mo folke, for Goddis peine,	*are; more*
20 Thomas, suffre me speke and be not wrooth,	*let; angry*
For the to offende were me full looth.	*I should be; most reluctant*
'That I shal seie shal be of good entente.	*what; well-meant*
Hast þou maad þis compleint forth to goo	*to be circulated*
Amonge þe peple?' 'ȝe, frende, so I mente.	
25 What ellis?' 'Nay, Thomas, war, do not so.	*else; beware*

If þou be wiis, of that matter ho.   *wise; stop*
Reherse þou it not ne it awake.   *recite; stir up*
Kepe al that cloos for thin honours sake.   *secret*

'Howe it stood with thee leide is al aslepe.
30 Men han forʒete it. It is oute of mynde.   *forgotten*
That þou touche therof I not ne kepe.   *should handle it (again); care*
Lat be, þat reede I, for I cannot finde   *advise*
O man to speke of it. In as good a kinde   *one; way*
As þou hast stonde amonge men or this day   *before*
35 Stondist þou nowe.' 'A, nay,' quod I, 'nay, nay.

'Thouʒ I be lewide I not so ferforthe dote.   *foolish; am not totally mad*
I woote what men han seide and seien of me.   *know*
Her wordis haue I not as ʒit forgote.   *their; yet*
But greet meruaile haue I of ʒow, that ʒe
40 No bet of my compleint avisid be,   *better; have thought*
Sithen, mafey, I not redde it vnto ʒow   *since, on my word*
So longe agoon, for it was but riʒt now.   *ago; even*

'If ʒe took hede, it maketh mencioun
That men of me speke in myn audience   *spoke; hearing*
45 Ful heuily. Of ʒoure entencioun   *gravely; (good) intention*
I thanke ʒou, for of beneuolence,
Woote I ful wel, procedeþ ʒoure sentence,   *know; opinion*
But certis, good frende, þat þing þat I heere,   *certainly*
Can I witnesse and vnto it refeere.

50 'And whereas that ʒe me counseile and rede   *where; advise*
That for myn honour shulde I by no weie
Anyþing mynge or touche of my wildhede,   *at all; recall; wildness*
I vnto þat answere thus and seie:
Of Goddis strook howe so it peise or weie,   *stroke; however; weigh*
55 Ouʒt no man to þinke repreef or shame.   *ought; reproof*
His chastisinge hurtiþ no mannes name.

'Anothir þing ther meueþ me also: *moves*
Sithen my seeknesse sprad was so wide   *since; spread*
That men knewe wel howe it stood with me þo,   *then*
60 So wolde I nowe vppon þat othir side   *to the contrary*

Wist were howe oure lorde Ihesu, wich is gide   *might be known*
To all releef and may alle hertis cure,
Releued hath me sinful creature.

'Had I be for an homicide iknowe   *been; known*
65   Or an extorcioner or a robbour,
Or for a coin clipper as wide yblowe   *noised abroad as widely*
As was my seeknesse, or a werriour   *warrior*
Aȝein þe feith, or a false maintenour   *against; supporter*
Of causes, þouȝ I had amendid me,   *even if*
70   Hem to han mynged had ben nicete.   *recalled; would have been folly*

'And whi? for þo proceden of freelte   *those*
Of man hymsilfe. He brewith alle þo.   *stirs up; those*
For siþen God to man ȝoue hath liberte,   *since; given*
Wiche chese may for to do wel or no,   *who may choose*
75   If he myschese he is his owene foo,   *choose wrong*
And to reherse his gilte wich him accusiþ,   *recite*
Honour seith nay there he scilence excusiþ.   *where; (by) silence excuses*
                                                        himself

'But this is al another caas, sothly.   *truly*
This was the strook of God; he ȝaf me þis.   *stroke; gave*
80   And sithen he hath withdrawe it curteisly,   *since; withdrawn; kindly*
Am I not holden it out? O ȝis.   *bound to declare it; yes*
But if God had þis þanke it were amis.   *unless*
In feith, frende, make I thenke an open shrifte,   *I think to make; confession*
And hide not what I had of his ȝifte.   *gift*

85   'If that a leeche curid had me so—   *doctor*
As they lacken alle þat science and miȝt—   *though; knowledge; power*
A name he shulde han had for eueremo,   *ever*
What cure he had doon to so seek a wiȝt.   *sick; person*
And ȝit my purs he wolde haue made ful liȝt.
90   But curteis Jhesu of his grace pacient   *courteous; longsuffering*
Axith not but of gilte amendement.   *asks only; wrong*

'The benefice of God not hid be sholde.   *benefits*
Sithen of myn heele he ȝaf me þe triacle,   *since; health; medicine*
It to confesse and þanke hym, am I holde,   *bound*

95 For he in me hath shewid his miracle.
His visitacioun is a spectacle   *mirror*
In wiche that I biholde may and se,
Bet þan I dide, howe greet a lord is he.   *better*

'But, freend, amonge þe vicis þat riȝt now
100 Rehercid I, oone of hem, dar I seie,   *recited; one; dare*
Hath hurte me sore, and I woote wel ynow   *know; enough*
So hath it mo, wiche is feble moneie.   *more; poor*
Manie a man þis day, but þei golde weie,   *weigh out*
Of men not wole it take ne resceiue,
105 And if it lacke his peis þei wole it weiue.   *weight; reject*

'Howe may it holde his peis whanne it is wasshe *weight; washed*
So that it lacke sumwhat in thiknese?
The false peple nothing hem abaisshe   *are not at all ashamed*
To clippe it eke. It in brede and roundenesse   *trim; also; breadth*
110 Is than it shulde be alweie the lesse.
The pore man amonge alle othir is   *amongst; others*
Ful sore anoied and greued in this.   *sorely troubled*

'If it be golde and hool that men him profre   *whole; offer*
For his laboure or his chaffre lent,   *or goods he has loaned*
115 Take it if him list and putte it in his cofre,   *please; chest*
For, waisshinge or clipping, holde him content   *whether he hold himself*
Or leue, he gete noon othir paiement.   *leave (off); (will) get*
It semeth but smal; othir is ther.   *another (thing)*
Trouþe is absent, but falsheed is not fer.   *far*

120 'Howe shal þe pore do if in his holde   *poor man; dwelling*
No more moneie he ne haue at al
Par cas but a noble or halpenie of golde,   *perhaps; halfpenny*
And it so thynne is and so narowe and smal   *slight*
That men the eschaunge eschewen oueral?   *exchange; refuse completely*
125 Not wil it goo but miche he theronne leese.   *unless; much; lose*
He moot do so, he may noon other chese.   *must; choose*

'I mysilfe in this caas ben haue, or this,   *case; before*
Wherfore I knowe it a greet dele þe bet.   *better*
He that in falsing of coyn gilty is,   *counterfeiting*

130 Hath greet wronge þat he nere on þe gebet.   *is wrongly spared the gallows*
It is pitee that he therfrom is let,   *kept from it*
Sithen he therto hath so greet title and riȝt.   *since; entitlement*
Regne, Iustice, and preue on him thi myȝt.   *prove; power*

'Whanne I this wroot, many men dide amis.   *wrote*
135 Thei weied gold, vnhad auctorite.   *weighed; without authority*
No statute made was þanne as þat nowe is.
But sithen gold to weie charged nowe ben we,   *since; weigh; obliged*
Resoun axeth þat it obeied be.   *asks*
Nowe time it is vnto weiȝtes vs drawe,   *(to) take ourselves*
140 Sithen that the parlement hath maad it a lawe.   *since*

'Yit othir shrewis doon a werse gyn,   *villains; do; trick*
And tho bene they þat þe coyn countirfete,   *those are*
And thei that with golde, copir, clothe and tyn,   *cloth*
To make al seme golde, þei swinke and swete   *toil and sweat*
145 In helle for to purchace hem a sete.   *obtain; seat*
If thidre lede hem her false couetise,   *thither; their; greed*
That purchas maad was in a fooltisch wise!   *made; foolish manner*

'What causith, trowen ȝe, all this mischaunce?   *do you think*
What coumforte ȝouen is to this vntrouþe?   *given*
150 In feith, men sein it is the maintinaunce
Of grete folke, wich is a greet harme and rouþe.   *pity*
God graunte herafter that ther be no slouþe,   *sloth*
Of this tresoun punischement to do,   *for; exact*
Riȝt suche as that is partinent therto.   *appropriate*

155 'Thei þat consenten to that falsehede,
As wel as the werkers, wiþ peine egal   *equal*
Punischid ouȝten be as þat I rede.   *advise*
Nowe, maintenours, biwar nowe of a fal.
I speke of no persone in special.   *particular*
160 In countrees diuerse is ther many oon   *regions*
Of ȝow, and hath be many a day agoon.   *since*

'Allas, that to oure kingis preiudice   *detriment*
And harme to alle hise lege peple trewe,   *loyal*
Contynue shal þis foule and cursid vice

165 Of falsing of coyn, not bigonne of newe,   *counterfeiting; recently*
Wiche, and it forþe goo, many oon shal it rewe.   *if; advance; one; regret*
God and oure kyng remedie al this greef,
For to þe peple it is a foule mischeef.

'Bi comoun harme is not smal to sett.   *small store is not to be set*
170 That venym ouere wide and brood spredith.   *too widely; broadly*
Greet merite were it suche þing stoppe and lett,   *would it be; (to) stop; hinder*
As þat the comoun into mischef leedith.   *as leads the commons*
The vois of þe peple veniaunce on ȝow gredith,   *vengeance; cries*
ȝe cursid men, ȝe false moneyours,   *money-changers*
175 And on ȝoure outereris and ȝoure maintenours.   *those who publish and*
maintain you

'O this I drede alweie, this heuieþ me   *makes me heavy*
Many a sithe, that punischement   *time*
Noon falle shal on this cursid meine.   *troop*
Howe trewe so be her enditement,   *however true be; indictment*
180 Oure lige lorde shal be so innocent   *ignorant (of it)*
That vnto him shall hid be þe notice.   *from him*
Vnwaisshen gold shal waisshe awey þat vice.   *unwashed; wash*

'Enformed shal be his hie excellence   *informed; high*
By menes, whom þat þe lady Moneye   *intermediaries*
185 Hath rowned with, and shewid euidence   *whispered; provided*
In plate, þat al wronge is þat men seie   *coin*
Of þat false folke. My soule dar I leie,   *dare; wager*
Tho meenes shullen haue no deffectif plate: *those*
Her receit shal be good and fin algate.   *the quantity (of coins); fine; by*
all means

190 'Nowe in good feith I drede ther shal be
Suche multitude of þat false secte
Wiþynne þis twoo ȝeere, or ellis thre,
But if þis stinking errour be correcte,   *unless; righted*
That so moche of this land shal be infecte   *infected*
195 Therwiþ þat trouþe shal adoun be þrowe,   *with it; be cast down*
And that cursid falsheed it oueregrowe.   *will surpass it*

'Lo, frende, nowe haue I myn entent vnreke.   *revealed my intentions*

Of my longe tale, displese ȝow nouȝt.'   *account*
'Nay, Thomas, nay, but lat me to the speke.   *let*
200 Whanne þi compleinte was to the ende ybrouȝt,   *brought*
Cam it ouȝt in þi purpos and þi thouȝt   *at all*
Ouȝt ellis therwith to han maad þan that?'   *anything; in addition; made*
'Ȝe, certein, frende.' 'O nowe, good Thomas,   *certainly*
    what?'

'Frende, þat I shal telle as blyue, ywys.   *at once; certainly*
205 In Latyn haue I seen a smal tretice,   *treatise*
Wiche Lerne for to Die callid is.
A bettir restreint knowe I noon fro vice,
For whanne þat deeth shal man from hennes trice   *hence; snatch*
But he þat lessoun lerned haue or thanne,   *unless; before*
210 War that, for deeth comeþ woot þere no wiȝt   *beware of; knows no man*
    whanne.

'And that haue I purposid to translate,   *intended*
If God his grace list therto me lene,   *please; to that end; (to) loan*
Siþen he of helþe hath opened me þe ȝate,   *since*
For where my soule is of vertu al lene,   *bare*
215 And þoruȝ my bodies gilte foule and vnclene,
To clense it sumwhat by translacioun
Of it shal be myn occupacioun.

'For I not oonly but, as that I hope,   *think*
Many another wiȝt eke therby shal   *person; also; by it*
220 His conscience tendirly groope,   *mercifully; examine*
And wiþ himsilfe acounte and recken of al   *make account; reckon up*
That he hath in this liif wrouȝt, greet or smal,
While he tyme hath, and freissh witt and vigour,   *youthful*
And not abide vnto his deeþis hour.   *delay*

225 'Man may in þis tretiis hereaftirward,
If þat hym like rede and biholde,   *if he pleases to*
Considre and see wel þat it is ful hard
Delaie acountis til liif bigynne to colde.   *giving his reckoning; grow cold*
Shorte tyme is þanne of hise offensis oolde   *there is little time*
230 To make a iust and trewe reckenynge.
Sharpnesse of peine is therto greet hinderinge.   *in addition/of it*

'Not hath me stirid my deuocioun   *stirred*
To do this labour, ȝe shullen vnderstonde,
But at the excitinge and mocioun   *stirring; inspiration*
235   Of a deuoute man, take I here on honde   *I undertake*
His labour, and, as I can, wole I fonde   *attempt*
His reed, þoruȝ Goddis grace, to parforme,   *advice; through; carry out*
Thouȝ I be bare of intellecte and forme.   *devoid; knowledge of rules*

'And whanne that endid is I neuere þinke
240   More in Englissh after be occupied.   *thereafter to be*
I may not labour as I dide, and swinke,   *toil*
My lust is not therto so wel applied   *I do not take such pleasure in it*
As it hath ben: it is ny mortified.   *nearly dead*
Wherfore I cesse þinke, be þis doon.   *think to end, once this is done*
245   The niȝt approcheþ. It is fer past noon.   *far*

'Of age am I fifty wintir and three.
Ripenesse of deeth faste vppon me now hastiþ.   *Maturity*
My lymes sumdel now vnweldy be;   *members; somewhat; weak*
Also my siȝt appeiriþ faste, and wastiþ,   *grows worse; wastes away*
250   And my conceit adaies nowe not tastiþ   *thought; nowadays; savours*
As it hath doon in ȝeeris precedent.   *previous years*
Nowe al another is my sentement.   *different; feeling*

'More am I heuy now vpon a day   *in a (single) day*
Than I sumtyme was in dayes fyue.
255   Thyng þat or this methoghte game and play   *before this seemed to me*
Is ernest now. The hony fro the hyue
Of my spirit withdrawith wondir blyue.   *amazingly quickly*
Whan al is doon, al this worldes swetnesse
At ende torneth into bittirnesse.

260   'The fool, thurgh loue of this lyf present   *through; life*
Deceyued is, but the wys man woot weel   *knows*
How ful this world of sorwe is, and torment,
Wherfore in it he trustith nat a deel.   *not at all*
Thogh a man this day sitte hye on the wheel,   *wheel (of Fortune)*
265   Tomorwe he may be tryced from his sete.   *plucked*
This hath be seen often among the grete.   *been*

'How fair thyng or how precious it be
þat in the world is, it is lyk a flour,
To whom nature yeuen hath beautee   *given*
270 Of fressh heewe and of ful plesant colour,
With soote smellynge also, and odour,   *sweet*
But, as soone as it is bicomen drye,
Farwel colour, and the smel gynneth dye.   *begins to*

'Rial might and eerthely magestee,   *royal*
275 Welthe of the world, and longe and fair dayes,
Passen as dooth the shadwe of a tree.   *pass (away); shadow*
Whan deeth is come ther be no delayes.
The worldes trust is brotil at assayes.   *worldly; fragile; when tested*
The wyse men wel knowen this is sooth.   *true*
280 They knowen what deceit to man it dooth.   *does*

'Lond, rente, catel, gold, honour, richesse,   *chattels; riches*
þat for a tyme lent been to been ouris,
Forgo we shole sonner than we gesse.   *shall sooner*
Paleises, maners, castels grete and touris   *towers*
285 Shal vs bireft be by deeth þat ful sour is.   *(from) us be taken*
Shee is the rogh besom which shal vs all   *rough broom*
Sweepe out of this world, whan God list it fall.   *pleases (to let) it happen*

'And syn þat shee shal of vs make an ende,   *since*
Holsum is hir haue ofte in remembrance,   *(it) is (to) have*
290 Or shee hir messager seeknesse vs sende.   *before*
Now, my freend so good, yeue yow good   *may good fortune be yours*
       chaunce,
Is it nat good to make a purueance   *provision*
Ageyn the comynge of þat messageer,   *against*
That we may stande in conscience cleer?'   *with a clear conscience*

295 'Yis, Thomas, yis, thow hast a good entente,   *yes; intention*
But thy werk hard is to parfourme, I dreede.   *perform; dread*
Thy brayn, par cas, therto nat wole assente,   *perhaps; to that; agree*
And wel thow woost, it moot assente neede   *know; must needs assent*
Or thow aboute brynge swich a deede.   *before; such*
300 Now, in good feith, I rede as for the beste,   *advise*
þat purpos caste out of thy myndes cheste.

'Thy bisy studie aboute swich mateere   *such matters*
Hath causid thee to stirte into the plyt   *leap; plight*
That thow wer in, as fer as I can heere.   *hear*
305 And thogh thow deeme thow be therof qwyt,   *judge; freed from it*
Abyde, and thy purpos putte in respyt   *wait; delay your purpose*
Til þat right wel stablisshid be thy brayn,   *fully restored*
And therto thanne I wole assente fayn.   *to that; gladly*

'Thogh a strong fyr þat was in an herth late,   *fire; a hearth; recently*
310 Withdrawen be and swept away ful cleene,
Yit aftirward, bothe the herth and plate
Been of the fyr warm, thogh no fyr be seene
There as þat it was, and right so I meene.   *where it was*
Althogh past be the grete of thy seeknesse   *great (part); sickness*
315 Yit lurke in thee may sum of hir warmnesse.'   *yet*

'O what is yow, freend, benedicitee?   *what ails you; God bless you*
Right now, whan I yow redde my conpleynte,   *read; complaint*
Made it nat mynde it standith wel with me?   *did it not remind (you)*
Myn herte with your speeche gynneth feynte.   *because of; begins to*
320 Shuld we be now al neewe to aqweynte,   *newly; to grow acquainted*
þat han so wel aqweynted be ful yore?   *for a long time*
What, han yee now lerned a neewe lore?   *have; lesson*

'Han yee lerned your freend for to mistruste,
And to his wordes yeue no credence?   *to give*
325 If your frendshipe cancre so and ruste,   *grow corrupt*
Sore wole it trouble myn innocence,
þat ay yow holden haue in existence
A verray freend. Certes, sore am I greeued,   *sorely*
That yee nat leeue how God me hath releeued.   *do not believe*

330 'Whoso nat leeueth what þat a man seith   *whoever; believes*
Is signe þat he trustith him but lyte.   *(it) is a sign; little*
A verray freend yeueth credence and feith   *true; gives*
Vnto his freend, whatso he speke and wryte.   *whatever*
Frendshipes lawe nat worth wer a myte   *would not be worth*
335 If þat vntrust vnto it wer annexid.   *mistrust; joined*
Vntrust hath many a wight ful sore vexid.   *person; sorely*

'I with myseluen made foreward   *an agreement*
Whan with the knotte of frendshipe I me knytte   *knitted myself*
Vnto yow, þat I neuere aftirward
340 Fro þat hy bond departe wolde, or flitte,   *would depart, or shift*
Which keepe I wole ay. O, your wordes sitte
Ny to myn herte, and, thogh yee me nat loue,   *near; (even) though*
My loue fro yow shal ther no wight shoue.

'Tullius seith þat frendshipe verray   *Cicero; true friendship*
345 Endurith euere, howso men it assaill.   *however; attack*
Frendshipe is noon to loue wel this day,   *It is no friendship*
Or yeeres outhir, and aftirward faill.   *either*
A freend to freend his peyne and his trauaill   *for (his) friend*
Dooth ay, frendshipe to keepe and conserue   *always; preserve*
350 Til dethes strook þat bond asondir kerue.   *stroke; cut in pieces*

'To this matir accordith Salomon—   *With this position agrees*
Yee knowe it bet than I by many fold—   *better; many times over*
Ones freend, and holde euere thervpon.   *once; to it*
In your frendshipe wer a slipir hold   *would be; slippery*
355 If it abate wolde and wexe cold   *diminish; grow*
þat vnto now hath been bothe hoot and warm.   *until; hot*
To yow wer it repreef, and to me harm.   *would it be (a) reproach*

'If þat me list in this mateer dwelle,   *I pleased; to linger*
And it along for to drawe and dilate,   *draw it out and dilate upon it*
360 Auctoritees an heep kowde I yow telle   *a huge number of authorities*
Of frendshipe, but stynte I moot algate,   *cease; must; anyhow*
Or elles wole it be ful longe and late   *else; will*
Or I haue endid my purposid werk,   *before; planned work*
For feeble is my conceit, and dul and derk.   *understanding; darkened*

365 'But as þat I seide eer, and sooth it is,   *before; true*
My sclendre wit feele I as sad and stable   *slender; settled*
As euere it was at any tyme or this,   *before*
Thankid be our lord Jhesu merciable.'   *merciful*
'Yit, Thomas, herkne a word, and be souffrable,   *Yet; listen to; patient*
370 And take nat my speeche in displesance.   *amiss*
In me shalt thow fynde no variance.   *inconstancy*

'I am thy freend as þat I haue ay been,   *always*
And euere wole, doute it nat al,   *will, be in no doubt of it*
But truste wel, it is but seelden seen   *seldom*
375 þat any wight þat caght hath swich a fal   *person; has taken such a fall*
As thy seeknesse was, þat aftir shal   *sickness; that (such a one)*
Be of swich disposicioun and might   *such*
As he was erst, and so seith euery wight.   *before; person*

'Of studie was engendred thy seeknesse,   *from (overmuch) study; born*
380 And þat was hard. Woldest now agayn   *Would you*
Entre into þat laborious bisynesse,
Syn it thy mynde and eek thy wit had slayn?   *since; also*
Thy conceit is nat worth a payndemayn.   *idea; anything*
Let be, let be, bisye thee so no more,   *busy yourself*
385 Lest thee repente and reewe it ouer sore.   *you repent; grieve for;*
    excessively

'My reed procedith nat of froward wil,   *advice; ill*
But it is seid of verray freendlyhede,   *true friendliness*
For if so causid seeknesse on me fil   *sickness thus caused; fell*
As dide on thee, right euene as I thee rede,   *advise*
390 So wolde I do myself, it is no drede.   *without doubt*
And Salomon bit aftir conseil do,   *commands (us); advice; (to) act*
And good is it conforme thee therto.   *(to) conform yourself to it*

'He þat hath ones in swich plyt yfall,   *once; peril; fallen*
But he wol rule him may in slippen eft.   *unless; again*
395 This rede I thee, for aght þat may befall,   *advise; anything*
Syn þat seeknesse God hath thee byreft,   *since; sickness; taken from you*
The cause eschue, for it is good left,   *avoid*
Namely, thyng of thoghtful studie kaght,   *especially; caught*
Perillous is, as þat hath me been taght.

400 'Right as a theef þat hath eschapid ones   *once escaped*
The roop, no dreede hath eft his art to vse   *rope; fear; after*
Til þat the trees him weye vp, body and bones,   *gallows; bear*
So looth is him his sory craft refuse,   *unwilling he is; unhappy trade*
Sa farest thow. Ioie hastow for to muse   *so; ponder*
405 Vpon thy book, and therin stare and poure,   *in it; pore*
Til þat it thy wit consume and deuoure.

'I can no more. The latter errour   *know; last*
Wers is, rede I, than þat þat was beforn.   *worse; advise; before*
The smert of studie oghte be mirour   *pain; ought to be a mirror*
410   To thee. Let yit thy studie be forborn.   *yet; put by*
Haue of my wordes no desdeyn or scorn,   *disdain*
For þat I seye, of freendly tendrenesse   *what I say; tenderness*
I seye it al, as wisly God me blesse.   *God bless me in his wisdom*

'If thee nat list vpon thyself to reewe,   *you please not; to have pity*
415   Thomas, who shal reewe vpon thee, I preye?
Now do foorth, let see, and thyn harm reneewe,   *carry on; renew*
And heuyer shal it peise and weye   *heavier; weigh (twice)*
Than it dide eer—therto my lyf I leye—   *before; on that; I wager*
Whiche thee wolde ouermochil harme and   *overmuch*
        greeue.'
420   'Freend, as to þat, answer I shal by leeue.   *with (your) permission*

'Whereas þat yee deemen of me, and trowe   *judge; believe*
That Y of studie my disese took—
Which conceit eek among the peple is sowe—   *thought; also; people; sown*
Trustith right wel, þat neuere studie in book   *trust*
425   Was cause why my mynde me forsook,
But i[t] was causid of my long seeknesse,
And othirwyse nat in soothfastnesse.   *truth*

'And forthy neuere aftir this, preye Y yow,   *therefore*
Deemeth no more so, ne nat it mynge.   *judge; nor bring it to mind*
430   That men kneew I had seeknesse is ynow.   *knew; enough*
Thogh they make of the cause no serchynge,   *no inquiry into the cause*
Ther cometh but smal fruyt of swich deemynge.   *little; such judgement*
To yow told haue I treewely the cause.
Now let vs stynten heer and make a pause.   *cease at this point*

435   'In this keepe I no replicacioun.   *I care (to make) no reply*
It is nat worth; the labour is in veyn.   *of no worth*
Shal no stirynge or excitacioun   *persuasion; influence*
Lette me of this labour, in certeyn.   *hinder me from; certainly*
Trustith wel, this purpos is nat sodeyn.   *trust; hasty*
440   Vpon my wittes stithie hath it be bete   *anvil; been beaten*
Many a day. Of this no lenger trete.   *talk about this no more*

'I haue a tyme resonable abide   *waited*
Or that I thoghte in this laboure me,   *before; to take pains*
And, al to preeue myself, I so dide.   *prove*
445   A man in his conceit may serche and see   *thought*
In v yeer what he do may, pardee,   *five years; by God*
And aftir þat take vpon him, and do,   *undertake and do (it)*
Or leue. Reson accordith heerto.'   *leave off; agrees with this*

'O Thomas, holdist thow it a prudence   *a (mark of) prudence*
450   Reed weyue, and wirke aftir thyn owne wit? *(to) shun advice*
Seide Y nat eer þat Salomons sentence   *before; wise saying*
To do by reed and by conseil men bit?   *act; advice; bids*
And thow desdeynest for to folwen it.   *you scorn to follow*
What, art thow now presumptuous become,   *arrogant*
455   And list nat of thy mis been vndirnome?'   *please; for your wrong;*
                                                       reproved

'Nay freend, nat so, yee woot wel, elleswhere   *elsewhere*
Salomon bit, "Oon be thy conseillour   *bids; (let) one*
Among a ml", and if þat yee were   *thousand*
As constant as yee han been or this hour,   *before*
460   By yow wolde I be red, but swich errour   *advised; such*
In your conceit I feele now, sanz faille,   *thought; without fail*
That in this cas yee can nat wel consaille.   *case; give advice*

'For, God woot, a blynd counseillour is he   *knows*
Which þat conseille shal in a mateere,   *who will give advice*
465   If of a soothe him list nat lerned be,   *truth; he won't be instructed*
And euene swich oon fynde I yow now heere.   *such a one*
I pleynly told yow haue the maneere
How þat it with me standen hath, and stant,   *it has been, and is, with me*
But of your trust to meward be yee scant.   *towards me; chary*

470   'Han yee aght herd of me in communynge   *have; anything; conversation*
Wherthurgh yee oghten deeme of me amis?   *judge*
Haue I nat seid reson, to your thynkynge?'   *spoken; as it seems to you*
'Forsoothe, Thomas, to my conceit, yis,   *as it seems to me, yes*
But euere I am agast, and dreede this,   *afraid*
475   Thy wit is nat so mighty to susteene
That labour as thow thyself woldest weene.'   *think*

'Freend, as to þat, he lyueth nat þat can
Knowe how it standith with another wight   *person*
So wel as himself. Althogh many a man
480   Take on him more than lyth in his might   *undertake; lies*
To knowe, þat man is nat ruled right   *directed rightly*
þat so presumeth in his iugement.
Beforn the doom, good wer auisament.'   *judgement; would be; careful*
                                                  consideration

'Now, Thomas, by the feith I to God owe,
485   Had I nat taastid thee, as þat I now   *tested (had experience of)*
Doon haue, it had been hard, maad me to trowe   *to make me believe*
The good plyt which I feele wel þat thow   *condition*
Art in. I woot wel thow art wel ynow,   *know; enough*
Whatso men of thee ymagyne or clappe.   *whatever; chatter*
490   Now haue I God, me thynkith, by the lappe.   *it seems to me; in my grasp*

'But al so hertly as I can or may,   *as heartily; know how to*
Syn þat thow wilt to þat labour thee dresse,   *since; set yourself*
I preye thee in al maneere way   *in every way possible*
Thy wittes to conserue in hir fresshnesse.   *their*
495   Whan thow therto goost, take of hem the lesse.   *to it (i.e. work); make use of*
To muse longe in an hard mateere   *ponder; matter*
The wit of man abieth it ful deere.'   *pays for; at a high price*

'Freend, I nat medle of matires grete.   *do not involve myself in*
Therto nat strecche may myn intellect.   *to them*
500   I neuere yit was brent with studies hete.   *burnt up; heat of studying*
Let no man holde me therin suspect.   *let no man suspect me of that*
If I lightly nat cacche may th'effect   *easily; grasp*
Of thyng in which laboure I me purpose,   *to labour*
Adieu my studie! Anoon my book I close.   *at once*

505   'By stirtes, whan þat a fressh lust me takith,   *starts; desire*
Wole I me bisye now and now a lyte,   *little*
But whan þat my lust dullith and asslakith,   *pleasure; abates*
I stynte wole and no lenger wryte,   *will cease; longer*
And, pardee, freend, þat may nat hyndre a myte, *by God; hinder at all*
510   As þat it seemeth to my symple auys.   *judgement/opinion*
Iugeth yourself. Yee been prudent and wys.'   *Judge (it); are*

'Sikir, Thomas, if thow do in swich wyse   *certainly; act; such (a) way*
As þat thow seist, I am ful wel content
þat thow vpon thee take þat empryse   *undertake that work*
515 Which þat thow hast purposed and yment.   *proposed and intended*
Vnto þat ende yeue Y myn assent.   *give*
Go now therto, in Jhesu Crystes name,   *begin that work*
And, as thow haast me seid, do thou þat same.

'I am seur þat thy disposicioun   *sure*
520 Is swich þat thow maist more take on hoonde   *such; undertake more*
Than I first wende in myn oppinioun   *thought*
By many fold, thankid be Goddes soonde.   *times; providence*
Do foorth, in Goddes name, and nat ne woonde   *proceed; hesitate*
To make and wryte what thyng þat thee list.   *whatever pleases you*
525 þat I nat eer kneew, now is to me wist.   *before; known*

'And of o thyng now wel I me remembre,   *one*
Why thow purposist in this book trauaille.   *propose; to labour*
I trowe þat in the monthe of Septembre   *believe*
Now last, or nat fer from, it is no faille—   *near to it; without doubt*
530 No force of the tyme: it shall nat auaille   *no matter about; profit*
To my mateer, ne it hyndre or lette—   *disrupt*
Thow seidist of a book thow wer in dette   *you owed a book*

'Vnto my lord þat now is lieutenant,
My lord of Gloucestre, is it nat so?'
535 'Yis, soothly, freend, and as by couenant   *as we had agreed*
He sholde han had it many a day ago,
But seeknesse and vnlust and othir mo   *weariness; similar pressures*
Han be the causes of impediment.'   *have caused my delay*
'Thomas, than this book haast thow to him   *then; intended for him*
        ment?'

540 'Yee sikir, freend, ful treewe is your deemynge.   *certainly; judgement*
For him it is þat I this book shal make.
As blyue as þat I herde of his comynge   *soon*
Fro France, I penne and ynke gan to take,
And my spirit I made to awake
545 þat longe lurkid hath in ydilnesse
For any swich labour or bisynesse.   *for (want of); such*

'But of sum othir thyng fayn trete I wolde,   *I would gladly write*
My noble lordes herte with to glade,   *gladden*
As therto bownden am I deepe, and holde.   *deeply; obliged/loyal*
550 On swich mateer, by God þat me made,
Wolde I bestowe many a balade,   *ballade*
Wiste I what. Good freend, telle on what is best   *if I knew*
Me for to make, and folwe it am I prest.   *for me; to follow; ready*

'Next our lord lige, our kyng victorious,
555 In al this wyde world lord is ther noon
Vnto me so good ne so gracious,
And haath been swich yeeres ful many oon,   *such for very many years*
God yilde it him. As sad as any stoon   *reward; (for) it; solid*
His herte set is, and nat change can   *heart; cannot turn aside*
560 Fro me, his humble seruant and his man.

'For him I thoghte han translated Vegece   *to have; Vegetius*
Which tretith of the art of chiualrie,
But I see his knyghthode so encrece   *increase*
þat nothyng my labour sholde edifie,   *not at all; profit (him)*
565 For he þat art wel can for the maistrie.   *knows; in the highest degree*
Beyonde, he preeued hath his worthynesse,   *abroad; has proved*
And, among othre, Chirburgh to witnesse.   *as; other places; can witness*

'This worthy prynce lay beforn þat hold,   *before; stronghold*
Which was ful strong, at seege many a day,   *besieiging it*
570 And thens for to departe hath he nat wold,   *thence; he did not wish*
But knyghtly ther abood vpon his pray   *waited; against; prey*
Til he by force it wan, it is no nay.   *won; there is no denying it*
Duc Henri, þat so worthy was and good,
Folwith this prince as wel in deede as blood.

575 'Or he to Chirburgh cam in iourneyynge,   *before; his military campaign*
Of Constantyn he wan the cloos and yle,   *Cotentin; won; close*
For which laude and honur and hy preysynge
Rewarden him and qwyten him his whyle.   *repay him for his trouble*
Thogh he beforn þat had a worthy style,   *before; title/reputation*
580 Yit of noble renoun is þat encrees.   *that (his winning of Cotentin)*
He is a famous prince, doutelees.

'For to reherce or telle in special   *repeat*
Euery act þat his swerd in steel wroot there
And many a place elles—I woot nat al—   *else; know*
585 And thogh euery act come had to myn ere,
To e[x]presse hem my spirit wolde han fere
Lest I his thank par chaunce mighte abregge   *praise; cut short*
Thurgh vnkonnynge if I hem sholde allegge.   *ignorance; cite in evidence*

'But this I seye, he callid is Humfrey
590 Conueniently, as þat it seemeth me,   *fittingly*
For this conceit is in myn herte alwey: *thought*
Bataillous Mars in his natiuitee   *warlike*
Vnto þat name of verray specialtee   *as a sign of special favour*
Titled him, makynge him therby promesse   *gave him title; by it; promise*
595 þat strecche he sholde into hy worthynesse,   *rise*

'For Humfrey as vnto myn intellect   *as (it seems) to my thinking*
"Man make I shal", in Englissh is to seye,   *means in English*
And þat byheeste hath taken treewe effect   *promise*
As the commune fame can bywreye.   *report; reveals*
600 Whoso his worthy knyghthode can weye   *if anyone; weigh*
Duely in his conceites balaunce   *the scales of his thought*
Ynow hath wherof his renoun enhaunce.   *enough; (to) exalt*

'To cronicle his actes wer a good deede,   *would be*
For they ensaumple mighte and encorage   *give an example; inspire*
605 Ful many a man for to taken heede
How for to gouerne hem in the vsage   *practice*
Of armes. It is a greet auauntage
A man before him to haue a mirour,
Therin to see the path vnto honour.

610 'O Lord, whan he cam to the seege of Roon   *Rouen*
From Chirburgh, whethir fere or cowardyse   *was it*
So ny the walles made him for to goon   *near*
Of the town as he dide? I nat souffyse   *don't have the ability*
To telle yow in how knyghtly a wyse   *manner*
615 He logged him ther, and how worthyly   *lodged*
He baar him. What, he is al knyght, soothly.   *conducted himself; truly*

'Now, good freend, shoue at the cart, I yow   *lend a helping hand*
    preye.
What thyng may I make vnto his plesance?   *to please him*
Withouten your reed noot I what to seye.'   *advice; I don't know*
620   'O, no, pardee, Thomas, o no, ascaunce.'   *by heaven; not at all*
'No, certein, freend, as now no cheuissance   *at present no device*
Can I. Your conseil is to me holsum.   *know*
As I truste in yow, mynystreth me sum.'

'Wel, Thomas, trowest thow his hy noblesse   *believe*
625   Nat rekke what mateere þat it be   *does not care; matter*
þat thow shalt make of?' 'No, freend, as I gesse,
So þat it be mateere of honestee.'   *decency*
'Thomas, and thanne I wole auyse me.   *think upon (your request)*
For whoso reed and conseil yeue shal,   *advice; will give*
630   May nat on heed foorth renne therwithal.   *ahead; straight forward*

'And þat so noble a prince, namely,   *what; especially*
So excellent, worthy and honurable
Shal haue, needith good auys, soothly,   *advice*
þat it may be plesant and agreable
635   To his noblesse. It is nat couenable   *nobility; suitable*
To wryte to a prince so famous
But it be good mateer and vertuous.   *unless*

'Thow woost wel, who shal an hous edifie   *knowest; build*
Gooth nat therto withoute auisament   *deliberation*
640   If he be wys, for with his mental ye   *inner eye*
First is it seen, purposid, cast and ment,   *proposed, forecast and planned*
How it shal wroght been, elles al is shent.   *destroyed*
Certes, for the deffaute of good forsighte,   *certainly; lack*
Mistyden thynges þat wel tyde mighte.   *happen wrong; might happen well*

645   'This may been vnto thee in thy makynge
A good mirour. Thow wilt nat haaste, I trowe,
Vnto thy penne, and therwith wirke heedlynge,   *(with) headlong (haste)*
Or thow auysed be wel and wel knowe   *before; advised*
What thow shalt wryte. O, Thomas, many a   *time*
    throwe

650 Smertith the fool for lak of good auys, *feels pain; advice*
But no wight hath it smerted þat is wys, *person; hurt*

'For wel is he waar or he wryte or speke *aware before*
What is to do or leue. Who by prudence
Rule him shal, nothyng shal out from him breke
655 Hastily ne of rakil negligence.' *rash*
'Freend, þat is sooth. O now, your assistence
And help. What I shal make, I yow byseeche.
In your wys conceit, serche yee and seeche.' *understanding; seek*

He a long tyme in a studie stood, *abstracted*
660 And aftir þat thus tolde he his entente: *intention*
'Thomas, sauf bettre auys I holde it good, *in the absence of*
Syn now the holy seson is of Lente, *since*
In which it sit euery man him repente *is fitting for; (to) repent*
Of his offense and of his wikkidnesse,
665 Be heuy of thy gilt, and the confesse, *sad for; make confession*

'And satisfaccioun do thow for it. *make atonement*
Thow woost wel, on wommen greet wyt and lak *know; blame and reproach*
Ofte haast thow put. Bewaar lest thow be qwyt. *repaid*
Thy wordes fille wolde a quarter sak *sack*
670 Which thow in whyt depeynted haast with blak. *white; painted*
In hir repreef, mochil thyng haast thow write *their reproof; many things*
That they nat foryeue haue ne foryite. *forgiven; forgotten*

'Sumwhat now wryte in honour and preysynge
Of hem. So maist thow do correccioun
675 Sumdel of thyn offense and misberynge. *somewhat; misconduct*
Thow art cleene out of hir affeccioun. *completely; their*
Now syn it is in thyn eleccioun *since; choice*
Whethir thee list hir loue ageyn purchace *you please; their*
Or stonde as thow doost, out of loue and grace,

680 'Bewar, rede I: cheese the bettre part. *advise; choose*
Truste wel, this women been fell and wyse. *these; fierce*
Hem for to plese lyth greet craft and art. *requires*
Wher no fyr maad is, may no smoke aryse. *made*
But thow haast ofte, if thow thee wel auyse, *reflect carefully*

685   Maad smoky brondes: and for al þat gilt   *brands*
      Yit maist thow stonde in grace, if þat thow wilt.   *find favour*

      'By buxum herte and by submissioun   *obedient*
      To hir graces, yildinge thee coupable,   *confessing yourself blameworthy*
      Thow pardon maist haue and remissioun,
690   And do vnto hem plesance greable.   *pleasure which will satisfy them*
      To make partie art thow nothyng able.   *make good your cause*
      Humble thy goost, be nat sturdy of herte.   *spirit; rebellious*
      Bettre than thow art han they maad to smerte.   *have; suffer*

      'The Wyf of Bathe take I for auctrice   *female authority*
695   þat wommen han no ioie ne deyntee   *have; pleasure*
      þat men sholde vpon hem putte any vice.   *allege against them*
      I woot wel so, or lyk to þat, seith shee.
      By wordes writen, Thomas, yilde thee.   *(to be) written; surrender*
      Euene as thow by scripture hem haast offendid,   *by (your) writing*
700   Right so, let it be by wrytynge amendid.'

      'Freend, thogh I do so, what lust or pleisir   *delight or pleasure*
      Shal my lord haue in þat? Noon, thynkith me.'   *it seems to*
      'Yis, Thomas, yis, his lust and his desir
      Is, as it wel sit to his hy degree,   *suits*
705   For his desport and mirthe, in honestee   *pleasure*
      With ladyes to haue daliance,   *familiar conversation*
      And this book wole he shewen hem par chance.   *perhaps*

      'And syn he thy good lord is, he be may   *since; may be*
      For thee swich mene þat the lightlyere   *such an intermediary; more easily*
710   Shuln they foryeue thee. Putte in assay   *forgive; put to the proof*
      My conseil. Let see, nat shal it thee dere.   *advice; harm*
      So wolde I doon if in thy plyt I were.   *plight*
      Leye hond on thy breest if thow wilt so do
      Or leue. I can no more seyn therto.   *give (it) up; on this point*

715   'But thogh to women thow thyn herte bowe,
      Axynge hir graces with greet repentance   *asking their*
      For thy giltes, thee wole I nat allowe
      To take on thee swich rule and gouernance   *such (a)*

As they thee rede wolde, for greuance   *would advise you; harm*
720 So greet ther folwe mighte of it, par cas,   *follow; perhaps*
That thow repente it sholdest ay, Thomas.'

'Adam begyled was with Eeues reed,   *deceived; advice*
And sikir so was shee by the serpent,   *certainly*
To whom God seide, "This womman thyn heed   *head*
725 Breke shal, for thurgh thyn enticement
Shee hath ybroken my commandement."
Now, syn womman had of the feend swich might,   *power over/from the devil*
To breke a mannes heed it seemeth light.   *easy*

'For why, let noon housbonde thynke it shame   *therefore*
730 Ne repreef vnto him, ne vilenye,   *reproof*
Thogh his wyf do to him þat selue same.   *self-same (thing)*
Hir reson axith haue of men maistrie.   *(to) have; over; mastery*
Thogh holy writ witnesse and testifie
Men sholde of hem han dominacioun,   *over them*
735 It is the reuers in probacioun.   *when put to the proof*

'Hange vp his hachet and sette him adoun,   *cease from his labours; sit down*
For wommen wole assente in no maneere   *way*
Vnto þat poynt ne þat conclusioun.'
'Thomas, how is it twixt thee and thy feere?'   *woman*
740 'Wel, wel,' quod I, 'what list yow therof heere?   *does it please; to hear*
My wyf mighte haue hokir and greet desdeyn   *scorn*
If I sholde in swich cas pleye a soleyn.'   *play so unsociable a part*

'Now, Thomas, if thee list to lyue in ese,   *you please*
Prolle aftir wommennes beneuolence.   *prowl about for*
745 Thogh it be dangerous, good is hem plese,   *difficult; to please them*
For hard is it to renne in hir offense.   *incur their*
Whatso they seyn, take al in pacience.   *whatever*
Bettre art thow nat than thy fadres before,   *forefathers*
Thomas, han been. Be right wel waar therfore.'

750 'Freend, hard it is wommen to greeue, I grante,
But what haue I agilt, for him þat dyde?   *what wrong have I done; died*
Nat haue I doon why, dar I me auante,   *nothing; dare to boast*
Out of wommennes graces slippe or slyde.'   *(I should) slip*

'Yis, Thomas, yis, in th'epistle of Cupyde
755 Thow haast of hem so largeliche said   *spoken so broadly*
That they been swart wrooth and ful euele apaid.'   *black with rage; not at all pleased*

'Freend, doutelees sumwhat ther is therin   *doubtless*
þat sowneth but right smal to hir honour,   *tends; very little; their*
But as to þat, now, for your fadir kyn,   *for (the sake of); father's*
760 Considereth, therof was I noon auctour.   *author*
I nas in þat cas but a reportour
Of folkes tales. As they seide, I wroot.
I nat affermed it on hem, God woot.   *against them*

'Whoso þat shal reherce a mannes sawe,   *recite/repeat; words*
765 As þat he seith moot he seyn and nat varie,   *the one; the other must*
For, and he do, he dooth ageyn the lawe   *if*
Of trouthe. He may tho wordes nat contrarie.   *those; oppose*
Whoso þat seith I am hir aduersarie
And dispreise hir condicions and port,   *bearing*
770 For þat I made of hem swich a report,

'He misauysed is, and eek to blame.   *wrongly advised; also*
Whan I it spak I spak conpleynyngly.   *in the style of a complaint*
I to hem thoghte no repreef ne shame.   *wished them neither reproof*
What world is this? How vndirstande am I?   *(mis)understood*
775 Looke in the same book. What stikith by?   *is evident there?*
Whoso lookith aright therin may see   *truly*
þat they me oghten haue in greet cheertee,   *they (women); ought; affection*

'And elles woot I neuere what is what.   *otherwise*
The book concludith for hem, is no nay,   *in their favour undeniably*
780 Vertuously, my good freend, dooth it nat?'
'Thomas, I noot, for neuere it yit I say.'   *don't know; saw*
'No, freend?' 'No, Thomas.' 'Wel trowe I, in fay, *believe; in faith*
For had yee red it fully to the ende,
Yee wolde seyn it is nat as yee wende.   *thought*

785 'Thomas, how so it be, do as I seide.
Syn it displesith hem, amendes make.   *since*
If þat some of hem thee therof vpbreide,   *reproach*

Thow shalt be bisy ynow, I vndirtake,   *enough*
Thy kut to keepe. Now I thee bytake   *portion; entrust*
790 To God, for I moot needes fro thee weende. *must*
The loue and thank of wommen God thee seende.

'Among, I thynke thee for to visyte   *from time to time*
Or þat thy book fully finisshid be,   *before; is finished*
For looth me wer thow sholdest aght wryte   *I would be loath; anything*
795 Wherthurgh thow mightest gete any maugree, *ill-will*
And for þat cause I wole it ouersee.
And, Thomas, now adieu and fareweel.
Thow fynde me shalt also treewe as steel.'

Whan he was goon, I in myn herte dredde   *feared*
800 Stonde out of wommennes beneuolence,   *(to) stand*
And, to fulfill þat þat he me redde,   *what he advised*
I shoop me do my peyne and diligence   *prepared to*
To wynne hir loue by obedience.
Thogh I my wordes can nat wel portreye,   *represent*
805 Lo, heer the fourme how I hem obeye.

My ladyes all, as wisly God me blesse,   *as I hope for God's blessing*
Why þat yee meeued been can I nat knowe.   *moved (with anger)*
My gilt cam neuere yit to the ripnesse,   *maturity*
Althogh yee for your fo me deeme and trowe.   *believe*
810 But I your freend be, byte me the crowe.   *Unless; let the crow bite me*
I am al othir to yow than yee weene.   *entirely; think*
By my wrytynge hath it and shal be seene.

But nathelees, I lowly me submitte   *nevertheless*
To your bontees, as fer as they han place   *virtues*
815 In yow. Vnto me, wrecche, it may wel sitte *be fitting*
To axe pardoun thogh I nat trespace.   *ask*
Leuer is me with pitous cheere and face   *I prefer; piteous countenance*
And meek spirit, do so than open werre   *than (that); war*
Yee make me, and me putte atte werre.   *give me a worse time of it*

820 A tale eek which I in the Romayn deedis   *also; (the Gesta Romanorum)*
Now late sy, in honur and plesance   *recently saw*
Of yow, my ladyes, as I moot needis,   *must needs*

Or take my way for fer into France,   *fear*
Thogh I nat shapen be to prike or prance,   *shaped; spur a horse*
825 Wole I translate and þat shal pourge, I hope,
My gilt as cleene as keuerchiefs dooth sope.   *soap cleans kerchiefs*

Notes

This work resembles formally, in respect of its blend of social criticism and personal comment, the introductory dialogue between Hoccleve and the beggar in Hoccleve's *Regement of Princes* (so also Pryor 1968: 78). For further comment, see Burrow 1994: 213–14 [25–26]. Precedent for the dialogue between commissioning editor (Friend) and scribe (Hoccleve) does occur in Chaucer's *Legend*, but Hoccleve's contribution to the genre has a much stronger flavour of the randomness and serendipity of actual conversation; on this latter point, see brief comment (on the *Regement*) in Kerby-Fulton 1997: 85.

Title from BLY (S *om.*; D 'dialogus cum amico'). C provides the fullest title 'hic finit questus siue planctus Thome Occleue, et incipit quidam dialogus inter eundem Thomam et quemdam amicum suum etc.' [here ends the complaint of Thomas Hoccleve and begins a certain dialogue between the same Thomas and a certain friend of his]

67–8 *or a werriour/Aȝein þe feith*: on Hoccleve's repeated awareness of the dangers of heresy before and after the failed Oldcastle rebellion, see Mitchell 1968: 48–9, Green 1980: 183–5. See also 2.190–96 for his use of the metaphor of heresy, if indeed it is a metaphor, and not an equation between Lollards and coin clippers as enemies of the realm (on this point see esp. Strohm 1998: ch. 5); for similar equations of heresy and covetousness, see Ross 1940: 210.6–16, and of heresy as, like felony, 'promulgator... of civic unrest', Staley 1994: 175, Strohm 1998: 120. On Lollards generally, see Hudson 1988.

81 BLY seem not to have appreciated that 'out' can function as a verb, though Y copies it correctly at 5.43.

102–98 With this section, attacking those who debase the coinage by clipping and issuing of counterfeit coin, cf. Burrow 1999: 120–4, Strohm 1998: 142–5; Scattergood 1971: 125, quoting a song from MS Oxford Bodleian Library Digby 102 (edited in EETS OS 124),

and Haines 1975: 152. For comment on its literary implications, see Strohm 1999: 649–50.

110 D makes 109–10 refer to the intention of the coin clippers rather than to the outcome of their actions.

134 *whanne I this wroot*: Burrow 1994: 215 [27] rightly concludes from this reference that the rest of the 'Dialoge' (so too the 'Compleinte' which precedes it) must have been written before this stanza, and that the statute referred to in 136 (see following n.) thus provides a *terminus ad quem* for its composition. See also n. to 533 below.

136 *statute*: i.e. of Henry V (Burrow 1994: 215 [27] dates 2 May 1421); for a French translation see *Statutes of the Realm* 2 (1816), 208–9.

155–7 For comment on the legal maxim behind these lines ('Consencientes et agentes pari pena punientur' [those who consent shall be punished with same pain as those who do (the same deed)]), see Burrow 1999 n.

162 i.e. Henry V (other references to him are at 167, 180, 183, 554).

173 BLSY gloss: 'vox populi (S popoli) vox dei.' [the voice of the people is the voice of God]. Cf. *Regement* 2885–6.

175 *outereris* (D *outeris*, LY *outrers*): those who utter (i.e. circulate false coin. Scribal difficulties with the word are shown yet more clearly by the readings of B (*entrers*) and C (*actores*).

179 *enditement*: CD read 'entendement', presumably ironically (i.e. the 'entendement' of the guilty is not at all 'trewe').

182 BLY gloss: 'nota bene nota' (cf. S 253, LS 772). At 309 S and at 400 LSY use the phrase to draw attention to a vivid metaphor ('exemplum').

183–9 The implication of this stanza is that the King will be deceived about the fraud by intermediaries acting for pecuniary gain (personified as 'Lady Moneye', cf. Lady Meed in *Piers Plowman*) so that the coins they present will not be 'deffectif' but 'good and fin'.

206–17 Hoccleve's proposed translation is produced later in the *Series* (see further headnote to 4). Recent comment follows Pryor in arguing for the Duke of Gloucester (cf. 533n. below) as intended first reader of this work and of the first *Gesta* narrative: hence, effectively, of the whole *Series* (Selman 1998: 219).

213 *of helþe… þe ʒate*: cf. 4.615, 909 (death and God at the gate) and 5.516 (Jonathan procuring the 'chartre of helthe' for the leprous King).

220 On 'groping' applied ironically to investigations of conscience, cf. Chaucer's *Summoner's Tale* (*CT* III.1817).

238 'Form' presumably functions broadly as an equivalent for 'intellect', rather in the way that in Chaucer it functions as the opposite of 'matter' (*LGW* 1582, 2228).

260–1 Quoted in their original Latin in the margin and in *H ('fallitur insipiens vite presentis amore etc.' [the fool is deceived by love of this present life]). According to *H, these words—noted by Burrow 1999 as 'a rhyming hexameter couplet of wide currency'—are taken from the *De Contemptu Mundi* (on the problems of identifying this text see above 1.114n.); they come from the ps.-Bernardine 'Carmen Paraeneticum' (*PL* 184.1308), a text also known, from its opening word, as the *Chartula*. On the role of this text in the standard schoolbook for advanced Latin studies, the *Auctores Octo*, see Woods-Copeland 1999: 384. Pryor compares Boethius, *Consolatio* Bk. III pr.8, but the parallel is not close.

265 Cf. Chaucer's *MkT* (*CT* VII.3322).

276 Cf. Chaucer's *Shipman's Tale* (*CT* VII.9).

282 *lent*: cf. 4.322 (H2's reading).

325 The collocation of *cancre* and *ruste* occurs elsewhere in Hoccleve (cf. *Regement* 4003) and as late as Dr Johnson (OED s.v. *canker* v.).

344 Cf. Cicero, *De Amicitia* chs. 5, 6, 13, 17, noted by Pryor and, in the context of Chaucer's *Romaunt of the Rose* 5201, by Benson 1988 and earlier editors of Chaucer.

351–3 Pryor relates these commonplaces on friendship to Ecclus. 6.1–17; *H MSS have a marginal gloss from Prov. 17.17, 'omni tempore diligit qui amicus est' [always he loves who is a friend]. Neither passage is particularly close to Hoccleve's version. Subsequent references to Solomon (391, 457, q.v.) continue this pattern and give a distinctive, traditional colouring to the dialogue. Since Solomon is adduced in support of both sides of the argument, references to him contribute to a secondary theme of the *Series*: the problematic nature of interpretation.

354 *hold* could refer to hand-, foot- or strong-hold

369 BLY gloss 'Amicus' (repeated by L at 449); the other speaker is similarly glossed, though not actually speaking there, at 415 ('Thomas', LY). LY gloss 'Thomas' in the middle of a passage translated from Ecclesiastes at 457, and make it seem as if Friend is addressing Hoccleve ('vnus sit tibi consiliarius Thomas inter mille'), though 'Thomas' indicates the speaker rather than the addressee. Similar glosses establish speakers in the Suso text. Ready parallels occur in other near-contemporary texts, e.g. Chaucer's *Troilus* (see Windeatt 1984: 123–5); see also apparatus to I. 568, 582, 596 etc.).

391 Hoccleve may owe this quotation, and its ascription to Solomon (cf. Ecclus. 32.24), to Chaucer, or may have derived it, like Chaucer, from Albertano of Brescia (for comment on its use by Chaucer, see Benson 1988: 847, 924, nn. to I.3530, VII.1003). A marginal comment in *H offers a Latin version of the quotation: 'omnia fac cum consilio'.

407 *H glosses (Matt. 27.64): 'nouissimus error peior priori' [S priore, L priorius].

450 Cf. *Regement* 194–8.

457 D's marginal comment (also in *H) gives as the ultimate Latin original of this quotation, in Eccles. 7.29, 'Vnus sit tibi consiliarius inter mille'. This quotation, like the earlier-noted 'quotation' from Solomon (391), is also found in Chaucer's *Melibee*.

533 Pryor notes that Duke Humphrey was twice lieutenant or regent in the period before the poem's composition, first during 1419–21, and then in 1422. The reference to the Duke's coming from France (543) is established by a marginal note in D, wanting in the *H MSS, as his second return from France ('scilicet de secundo reditu suo de Francia'). The duke was three times in France during the years 1415–22, and his 'second return' occurred in late November-December 1419: which explains Hoccleve's emphasis on the Duke's campaigns in France during the period 1417–19 (2.566–76, 610–16, noted Burrow 1994: 214 [26]). The marginal note makes best sense if composed after the Duke's third return in 1422 (Burrow 1994: 218 [30]).

561–2 *Vegece*: Vegetius, fourth-century author of work on military strategy (*De re militari*, cf. 562 'the art of chiualrie') which was widely translated in the later Middle Ages (for fuller details, see the notes of Seymour and Hammond) and recommended reading for the nobility (so Hoccleve's poem to Oldcastle, Furnivall and Gollancz 1970: 14.196; see also Green 1980: 144–5). C omits the name, as, originally, did S. Hoccleve may have decided against producing a translation if he knew of the translation of Vegetius undertaken in 1408 for the Duke of Berkeley by John of Trevisa or John Walton, both of whom produced translations for the Duke or members of his family; see Edwards 1984: 138–9.

574 *Duc Henri*: father-in-law of John of Gaunt (so Seymour's n.). The *Regement* expresses similar praise of him (2647–53, 3347–51) and of John of Gaunt (512–20) and Henry IV (3352–3). Hoccleve identifies 'this prince' (Duke Humphrey) with the virtues of his illustrious ancestor Duke Henry. For further comment on Hoccleve's 'web of Lancastrian compliment', see Pearsall 1994: 390,

Strohm 1999: 644.

583 BLY lose the metaphor of the Duke writing his own fame with his sword.

586 *expresse*: Seymour reads 'xepresse' (though the form of the letter does not suggest 'x' to me) and emends to the *H reading 'expresse', Furnivall 'yepresse' with emendation to 'expresse' queried. In the context of Hoccleve's fear of providing inadequate witness to Duke Humphrey's valour, the *H reading 'expresse' is probably warranted, though 'represse' (the initial letter a confusion of two forms of the letter 'r', if so) is almost as good.

588 *allegge* can also be read as meaning 'allay' (Seymour) and 'lighten' (Hammond). Hammond reads the whole phrase 'if I should enumerate (i.e. understate) them'. Cf. MED *alleggen* 2. The general sense is that the poet doubts his ability adequately to represent the bravery of the Duke, and fears, if he makes a poor attempt ('thurgh vnkonnynge'), that he will diminish the Duke's praise.

597 This punning etymologizing of names— here Duke Humphrey's name is taken to mean 'homme ferai' [I shall make man], because he is a superlatively well-made man—is a common medieval practice, whose ultimate model is Isidore of Seville. For other examples, cf. I.186n., 5.634–6. A later annotation in L draws attention to the passage: 'diffenition de ceste mesme [? nosme] Hounfrey'. For further comment on the Duke up to the time of Hoccleve's poem, see Scattergood 1971: 142–6; and on the Duke's possible adverse reaction to Hoccleve's proposal, Green 1980: 173.

610ff. Hammond notes a parallel contemporary account of the siege of Rouen which similarly praises Gloucester's bravery. See also Scattergood 1971: 60–9.

638–41 derive from a proverb in the *Poetria Nova* of Geoffrey of Vinsauf, as evidenced by the marginal gloss in both D and *H ('Si quis habet fundare domum, non currit ad actum impetuosa manus etc.'[if anyone intends to build a house, the hasty hand does not rush to the work]). Cf. Chaucer's *Troilus* I.1065–71 and n. (Benson 1988: 1030), though Hoccleve was not dependent on

Chaucer's version (so Mitchell 1968: 120, and Pryor). Within the terms of the fiction, it is Friend who acts as translator of the proverb, and Hoccleve, acting as scribe of his own work, who supplies the marginal gloss.

669 i.e. (so Seymour) a sack capable of holding a quarter (8 bushels) of grain (in Furnivall's words, a double sack).

691 *make partie*: I read 'make partie' as parallel to 'hold party' i.e. dispute (MED *party* 6a, which cites this line).

694–7 For this reference, cf. *ProlWBT* (*CT* III.662, noted by Seymour); on the Wife of Bath's *auctorite* (the easier reading of BC for Hoccleve's nonceword 'auctrice' and LSY's 'auct(o)rice'), cf. *CT* III.1, IV.1685–7.

722–6 D*H's marginal quotation establishes this as Hoccleve's version of Gen. 3.15 ('Genesis: Ait dominus ad serpentem, ipsa conteret caput tuum etc.'); a marginal quotation to the following stanza, against 733–5, derives from Gen. 3.16 ('Eodem capitulo, Sub viri potestate eris, et ipse dominabitur tui etc.') I have punctuated the lines so that 722–38 are spoken by Hoccleve. Furnivall reads them as spoken by Friend, but the paraph mark at 739 suggests a new speech for Friend begins there, which would mean that Hoccleve must have begun speaking at 722, Friend having addressed him in the previous line, and 722 itself marked by a paraph mark. For a different interpretation of this detail, see Burrow 1999 n.

727–8 For comment on these lines, see Introduction p. 40; Green 1980: 113, 122.

754 This literary self-deprecation, which is at the same time self-display, has frequent precedents in Chaucer's work: cf. the prologue to *The Man of Law's Tale*, abbreviated *MLT* (*CT* II.47–50).

755 *Largeliche* probably means 'fully' (MED 4b) but a subsidiary sense 'improperly/inaccurately' (cf. MED 6a: 'presumptuously, disparagingly') may also be hinted at.

759 *for your fadir kyn*: MED describes as an oath or an asseveration and cites examples from Chaucer.

761–7 This claim (cf. Furnivall's n.) has precedent in Chaucer: cf. Introduction pp. 8–9.

772 i.e. he followed Christine's 'Epistle' in uttering a complaint not against but on behalf of women (Hammond reads 'conpleynyngly' 'under protest'). A marginal note in *H ('nota') finds this line significant (C 'Nota bene', L 'nota bene nota').

820–6 These comments, that the act of translation can purge the translator's guilt, comically rework earlier comments on Hoccleve's proposed translation of Suso (2.215–17).

826 H* MSS end 'explicit dialogus et incipit quedam fabula de quadam bona et nobili (C nobile) imperatrice romana'; BCLY add 'capitulo tercio' [here ends the dialogue and begins a story about a certain good and noble Roman empress; third chapter].

3. Fabula de quadam imperatrice Romana
[*The story of a certain Roman Empress*]

	In the *Romain actes* writen is thus:	*Gesta Romanorum*
	Whilom an emperour in the citee	*once*
	Of Roome regned, clept Iereslaus,	*called*
	Which his noble estat and hy dignitee	
5	Gouerned wysly; and weddid had he	
	The doghtir of the kyng of Vngarie,	
	A fair lady to euery mannes ye.	*eye*
	And for þat beautee in womman allone	*because*
	Withouten bontee is nat commendable,	*goodness*
10	Shee was therto a vertuous persone,	*in addition*
	And specially pitous and merciable	*compassionate and merciful*
	In all hir wirkes, which ful couenable	*very fitting*
	And pertinent is vnto wommanhede.	*a woman's estate*
	Mercy causith good renon fer to sprede.	*reputation; far*
15	Now in my tale foorth wole I proceede.	
	As þat this emperour in his bed lay	
	Vpon a nyght, a thoght gan in him breede	*began to grow in him*
	Vnto the Holy Land to take his way,	
	And on the morwe, left lenger delay,	*morning; without longer*
20	His wyf and his brothir he made appeere	
	Before him, and hem seide in this maneere:	*as follows*
	'My deere wyf, myn hertes ioie and hele,	*well-being*
	þat thyng þat stablisshid in myn herte is,	*fixed*
	I can nat hyde fro thee ne concele,	
25	Ne nat ne wole, and shortly it is this:	*nor wish to*
	Vnto the Holy Land I wole ywis,	*wish (to go) certainly*

And forthy make I thee principally   *therefore*
Of al th'empire, me absent, lady,   *in my absence, (first) lady*

'Bytakynge and committynge vnto thee   *entrusting*
30 Of peple and land the charge special,   *of (my) people; care*
And vndir thee my brothir heer shal be
Steward of it to rule and gouerne al
That to me and my peple, greet and smal,
Profitable is, by conseil and assent   *counsel*
35 Algate of thee and thyn auysament.   *always; advice*

'Althogh thee thynke this purpos sodeyn,   *to you seems*
Yit be nat heuy, but in gree it take.   *yet; in good part*
With Goddes grace my comynge ageyn
Shal nat be longe to. I for thy sake   *too long*
40 Wole the shorter abood ther make.   *will; stay*
Truste me weel, as blyue as þat I may   *quickly*
Haaste I me wole fro thennes away.'

To whom with spirit of humilitee
She seide, 'Syn it is your good plesance   *pleasure*
45 To departe hens and go to þat contree,
I take moot algates, in souffrance,   *must always bear patiently*
Your wil and shal, with hertes obeissance.   *obedience*
As treewe as turtle þat lakkith hir feere   *a dove; mate*
In your absence I shal be, my lord deere.

50 'Ful sore I am agast and greetly dreede   *sorely; afraid*
þat neuere yee shuln thennes with your lyf   *shall thence*
Retorne, almighty God yow saue and speede.'   *return; prosper*
He hir yaf wordes confortatyf,   *gave; comforting*
And kiste hir, and seide, 'Farewel, wyf.
55 Be nat abassht, ne nat dreedith, I preye,'   *fear not*
And foorth he hastith him in his iourneye.

The sorwe of herte and cheer of heuynesse   *saddened countenance*
Which this good lady at his departynge
Made, the book nat can telle or expresse,
60 Wherfore of þat haue I no knowlechynge.   *information*
Eek kepte I nat the belle of sorwe out rynge,   *Moreover, I would not care*

Thogh þat I kneew wel euery circumstance
Of hir wo and hir heuy contenance.   *sad appearance*

But whan this emperour was thus agoon,   *had thus departed*
65 His brothirs herte was so eleuat   *puffed up*
And so prowd þat by wight ne sette he noon.   *he set store by no person*
Himself forgat he for his hy estat.
The pore and simple folk this potestat   *potentate*
Oppressid sore and dide hem greet duresse.   *hardship*
70 The riche he robbid eek of hir richesse.   *as well; their*

And yit this wikkid man, this seneschal,   *steward*
Meeued was werse, and to fulfill it thoghte.   *was moved (to do) worse*
He dide his might and his peyne total   *all his pain*
And all weyes serchid he and soghte,
75 And to brynge it aboute he faste wroghte,
Althogh he faillid at preef and assay.   *at (the) test*
He was knyt vp with a wommanly nay.   *repulsed; refusal*

He day by day lay on this emperice   *importuned*
To make hir vnto him flesshly consente,   *yield her body to him*
80 But shee answerde, 'It wer ouer greet vice *would be too great (a)*
To me, if I therto myn herte bente.   *to it*
Nay, brothir, nay, God woot I neuere it mente, *knows; meant such a thing*
Ne neuere shal. I truste in Goddes grace.
Yee goon wrong, yee mischosen han your place. *go; have abused*

85 'In al your lyf yee neuere, ne noon othir,   *nor any other*
Shal make me consente to þat synne.
For shame, fy, þat yee, my lordes brothir,
And whom þat he right feithful trust hath inne,
Sholde any swich tale to me begynne,   *such*
90 Which wer ageyn his and your honestee,
And myn, þat am his wyf, wel knowen yee.

'A treewe wyf I lyue wole and dye.
His wole I be, to whom þat I am bownde
Whyle he lyueth and I, withouten lye.
95 Trustith wel, it noon othir shal be fownde.' *no other outcome will be seen*
But, for al this, at euery tyme and stownde   *occasion*

He stired hire whan he fond hir soul   *tempted; found; alone*
Vnto this deede vicious and foul.

And whan shee sy shee mighte haue no reste—   *saw*
100 Nat wolde he stynte of his iniquitee—   *cease*
Shee aftir three or four of the gretteste
Of al th'empire sente, and thus spak shee:
'Sires, the cause þat hath meeued me   *moved*
For yow to sende is this, as I shal seyn,   *say*
105 Of which I sore encombred am, certeyn.   *am sorely troubled, truly*

'Yee woot wel þat my lord the emperour   *know*
In his absence hath maad me principal
Of th'empire, and his brothir gouernour
And steward vndir me for to rule al,
110 With this addicioun þat he nat shal
Wirke, my conseil and assent vnhad.   *without my advice and consent*
This was my lordes wil, and thus he bad.   *commanded*

'And, nathelees, the poore he hath oppressid
And robbid ryche folk, yee woot, I trowe,   *know; believe*
115 And werse thyng which shal nat been expressid
As now he wolde han doon—myself it knowe—   *just now*
Wherfore vpon the feith which þat yee owe
To my lord, and on his part, I yow charge   *in his name*
Enprisone him. Let him nat goon at large.   *go*

120 'Fettreth him faste.' And they answerden thus,
'Madame, he hath doon many a wikkid deede
Syn our lord wente, it wel knowe is to vs.   *since; known*
To your commandement, as we moot neede,   *must needs*
We wole obeie, but withoute dreede   *without doubt*
125 Yee muste in this warrante vs and allowe,   *authorize us*
Lest our lord whan he comth vs disallowe.'   *returns; should blame us*

'What, sires,' quod shee, 'doutith yow right noght,   *have no fear at all*
For if my lord kneew as mochil as I,   *much*
That he hath doon sholde be deer boght.   *what; dearly paid for*
130 þat I yow charge wole I stande by.'   *what; charge (to do)*
They made anoon areest on his body,   *at once they seized*

And into prison they him threew and caste,
And fettred him in yren bondes faste,

Wher he abood til þat word comen was,   *remained; arrived*
135 How þat the emperour was hoom comynge.   *home*
Thanne he thus thoghte, 'How shal I doon, allas? *what*
Now knowe shal my lord, by enquerynge,
The verray cause of myn enprisonynge,   *true*
Wherthurgh his grace I vttirly shal leese,   *through which; lose*
140 Or par cas my lyf. I ne shal nat cheese.   *perhaps; (be able to) choose*

'In feith, if I may it shal nat be so.'
A messager as blyue ordeyned he,   *as quickly as possible*
And made him to the emperice go,   *Empress*
And byseeche hir, of hir hy bontee,   *great goodness*
145 Syn shee had ay been of hir grace free,   *since; always; generous*
þat shee so mochil grace wolde him do   *much*
As come and speke a word with him or two.

Vnto the dore of his prison shee cam.
Withouten danger shee therto obeide.   *grudging; acceded to (his request)*
150 'What is your wil?' quod shee. 'Lo, heer I am.'
He lookid pitously and meekly preide,   *piteously*
'O gracious lady, reewe on me,' he seide;   *have mercy on me*
'If þat my lord me fynde heer in prison,
My deeth wole it been and confusion.

155 'My gentil lady, what shal yow profyte   *noble; (it) profit you*
To do me of a mescheuous deeth sterue?   *make; wretched; (to) die*
If þat I lyue may, wole I me qwyte   *clear myself*
Treewely to yow and your thank disserue.   *deserve*
What yow list me commande, I wole obserue   *please*
160 And do as humblely as any man
þat in this world lyueth do may or can.'   *may or knows how to do*

And she anoonright, meeued of pitee,   *at once; moved*
Seide, 'If I wiste þat of thy folie   *knew*
Thow stynte woldest, and amende thee   *cease*
165 Hensfoorth, and thee vnto vertu applie,
My grace wolde I nat to thee denye.'

He seide and swoor al þat he cowde swere,
Amende he wolde and wel aftir him bere.   *afterwards conduct himself*

O noble lady, symple and innocent,
170 Trustynge vpon his ooth and his promesse,   *oath*
Ful wo is me for thy wo consequent.   *I am deeply grieved; coming*
Often happith wommannes tendrenesse   *(it) happens (that)*
Torneth hir vnto harm and to duresse.   *turns; hardship*
This emperice fond it so by preef,   *found; proof*
175 Whom þat forsworn man greet harm dide, and
greef.

This man shee took out of the prison hous,
And made him bathid been, and fresshly shaue,   *shaved*
And dide him clothe in clothes precious,   *had him clothed*
And a fressh courser eek she made him haue,   *also*
180 And seide, 'Now, brothir, so God yow saue!
Takith your hors, and ryde foorth with me
Toward my lord'; and foorth with hir rood he.   *rode*

And as they riden right in the hy way
Ny a foreste, an hert before hem ran.   *hart*
185 Ther nas but 'Ryde on, ryde' and 'Hay, dogge,
hay'.
Euery man dooth his peyne in what he can,   *takes pains; all that; knows how*
The hert to sue. Ther lefte no man   *chase; remained*
With this good lady sauf this wikkid wight,   *save; creature*
This steward which brak al þat he had hight.   *broke; promised*

190 Par auenture men wole han meruaille   *perhaps; marvel*
That damoisele with hir had shee noon.   *maiden; none*
No force of þat: the book withouten faille   *no matter for*
Makith no mynde as mochil as of oon.   *mentions not even one*
This chaunce shoop many a yeer agoon.   *accident happened; ago*
195 That tyme, par cas, was no swich array   *perhaps; arrangement*
As þat in sundry contrees is this day.   *regions*

Whan this knyght sy ther was noon but they two,   *saw; the two of them*
To th'emperice he seide in this maneere: *as follows*
'It is ago fern syn I spak yow to   *long since*

200 Of loue. Come on now, my lady deere,
With me into this priuee foreste heere,   *secret*
That Y of yow may haue my talent.   *desire*
Now shal be doon þat I longe haue ment.'   *what; intended*

'What, fool, took I thee nat out of prisoun
205 No lenger hens than yistirday,' quod shee,   *as recently as yesterday*
'In trust and hope of thy correccioun,
As thow swoor and behightest vnto me,   *promised*
And now to thy folie and nycetee   *stupidity*
Retourne woldest thow? Nay, doutelees,
210 It shal nat be. Stynte and holde thy pees.   *cease*

'Ther neuere shal man do with me þat deede,
Sauf my lord th'emperour, which þat of right   *except; duly*
Licenced is therto. O, God forbeede   *has those rights over me; forbid*
þat by myn honestee sette I so light.   *I should set so little*
215 Peyne thee nat therto, for in thy might   *make no effort*
Shal it nat be thy wil for to perfourme.
By no way wole I me therto confourme.'   *in no way; to it (i.e. to your demands)*

And he answerde and spak vnreuerently: *crudely*
'But if þat thow consente wilt to me,   *unless*
220 In this foreste as swythe right wole Y   *immediately*
Hange thee by thyn heer vpon a tree,   *hair*
Wher no wight shall thee fynde, and so,' quod he,   *person*
'Of wikkid deeth thow sterue shalt and die.   *you will die a wicked death*
Truste on noon help at al, ne remedie.'   *no*

225 'By thy manaces sette I nat a myte,'   *threats; pin*
Shee seide. 'Of hem haue I no dreede at al.   *fear*
Thogh thow me thretne myn heed of to smyte,
And do me what torment thow canst, I shal
Thee werne ay þat. This for answer final   *refuse always*
230 Take if thee list, for, to þat poynt me dryue,   *please; (to) force me*
Thow neuere shalt whyles I am on lyue.

'Thow woost wel in effect thus seide I eer.'   *know; before*
He strypid hir anoon, left al delay,   *stripped; at once, without delay*

	Vnto hir smok, and heeng hir by hir heer	*hung; hair*
235	Vpon an ook, and by hir hir palfray	*palfrey*
	He stonde leet, and foorth on deuel way	*left stand; in cursed wise*
	Rood this tirant, this man malicious,	
	This cruel-herted man enuenymous.	*poisonous*

	And whan he had his felawshipe atake,	*fellows; overtake*
240	He bleew and blustred and made heuy cheere,	*blew; looked sad*
	And a strong lesyng he gan to hem make.	*he lied greatly to them*
	He seide, 'Allas, þat I nere on my beere,	*I wish I were dead*
	So wo is me for þat my lordes feere,	*I am so sad; because; wife*
	My lady, is me reft by force of men.'	*taken from me; (a) band*
245	God yeue him sorwe, and all swiche! [Amen.]	*give; such*

	O false lyer, o thow cofre and cheste	*coffer*
	Of vnclennesse, o styknynge aduoutour,	*adulterer*
	In wil, seye I, and willy to inceste,	*eager to commit*
	O false man to God, and thow traitour	
250	To thy lord and brothir, the emperour,	
	O enemy to wyfly chastitee,	
	And in thy wirkes ful of crueltee,	

	O cursid feendly wrecche, why hast thow	*devilish*
	Deceyued and betrayed innocence?	
255	What wilt thow seye and how wilt thow looke, how,	
	Whan thow comest to thy lordes presence,	
	And art opposid by his excellence,	*questioned; excellency*
	How þat it with his lady hath betid?	*what has happened with his lady*
	I am seur þat the trouthe shal been hid.	*sure*

	For as wel as þat to thy conpaignie	*company*
260	Thow lyedist whan thow hem ouertook,	
	As lowde wilt thow vnto thy lord lye,	
	I woot wel, and that with bold face and look.	
	Nathelees, of this tretith nat the book,	*nevertheless; tells*
265	Wherfore to my tale wole I go,	*return*
	Of this lady and foorth telle of hir wo.	*continue with*

Whan þat shee so had hanged dayes three,
By þat foreste rood ther on huntynge
An erl, þat was of a strange contree,

270 Beforn whos howndes was a fox rennynge,   *before*
And they aftir it blyue folewynge,   *quickly*
And as þat they ran, they hadden a sent   *scent*
Of the lady, and thidir be they went,   *they went there*

And theras shee heeng, they stood at a bay.   *where; hung; baying*
275 This erl, of þat meruaillynge him greetly,
Thidir him hyeth in al þat he may,   *hastens there with all the speed*
And whan he hir ther hangynge sy,   *saw*
He seide, 'Womman, what art thow, and why
Hangest thow in this wyse vpon the tree?'
280 'A strange womman, sir, am I,' quod shee,   *foreign*

'Of fer parties. How into this place   *parts*
I cam, God woot.' Shee wolde by no way
Deskeuere what shee was, ne what fallace   *reveal; deception*
Was doon to hir. Cloos shee kepte hir ay,   *secret*
285 And tolde nat o word of hir affray.   *(the) attack (on) her*
Than axed hir the erl, 'Whos hors is this   *asked*
þat by thee standith?' Quod shee, 'Myn it is.'

Wherby the erl anoonright vndirstood   *at once*
þat it noon othir wyse mighte be
290 But shee sum gentil womman was of blood,   *a woman of noble blood*
And in his herte routhe of hir had he,   *pity for*
And seide to hir, 'If it lyke thee,   *please*
Vnto my wil thee confourme and enclyne,   *to conform yourself and yield*
Deliure wole I thee out of thy pyne.   *deliver; pain*

295 'Lo, this I meene, this is myn entente.   *intention*
A yong doghtir haue I, in soothfastnesse,   *truth*
Of which I wolde, if þat thee list assente,   *would wish; pleased to agree*
Thow took on thee to be gouerneresse,   *would undertake*
And teche hir as longith to a maistresse   *is fitting; governess*
300 þat lordes children han in gouernaille,   *governance*
And wel wole I thee qwyte thy trauaille.   *repay*

'Myn entente is þat, and othir right noon.'
'Sire,' quod shee, 'gladly wole I obeye
To yow in þat,' and shee was take anoon   *taken at once*
305 Doun fro the tree, and, shortly for to seye,
With him to his castel shee rood hir weye,
And of the chyld shee took the gouernance,
Which torned hir, aftir, to greet nusance.   *brought her. . . great harm*

Shee with this yong chyld in the chambre lay
310 Euery nyght wher lay th'erl and the contesse,
Betwixt whos beddes brente a lampe alway,   *burned*
And wel beloued for hir hy goodnesse
Of euery wight was, bothe more and lesse,   *person*
This emperice til vpon a nyght,
315 Giltlees, hir good loos refte a wikkid wight.   *though innocent; reputation;*
                                                 stole; person

Ther was a styward in this erles hous
þat to hir ofte had spoke of flesshly loue,
To whom seide ay this lady gracious,
'Maad haue I an avow to God aboue   *made; vow*
320 Loueres alle fro myn herte shoue,   *to repel*
Sauf oonly him whom, of Goddes precept,   *save; commandment*
To loue I holde am, and þat shal be kept.   *I am bound*

'I truste in God. Myn herte shal nat change
Fro þat, whil my lyf shal soiourne in me.'
325 'O, wilt thow so, wilt thow make it so strange?   *make such difficulties*
Wilt thow noon othir wyse do?' quod he.   *way*
'þat I seid haue I wole holde,' quod shee.
And whan he sy noon othir remedie,   *saw*
He wroothly wente out of hir conpaignie,

330 And fro thensfoorth conpassid in his wit   *planned; mind*
How to be venged vpon hir and wroken,   *revenged; avenged*
And on a nyght, vnhappyly shoop it   *it occurred*
Left was the erles chambre dore vnstoken,   *unfastened*
To which he cam, and fond it was nat loken,   *found; locked*
335 And theefly in staal this wikkid persone,   *nefariously; stole*
Wheras he fond hem slepynge euerychone.   *where; all*

And he espyde by the lampes light
The bed wheras þat lay the emperice   *where*
With th'erles doghtir, and as blyue right   *immediately*
340 This feendly man his purposid malice   *proposed*
Thoghte for to fulfill and accomplice.   *accomplish*
And so he dide. A long knyf he out drow   *drew*
And therwithal the mayden chyld he slow.   *with it; slew*

Hir throte with þat knyf on two he kutte,
345 And as this emperice lay slepynge,
Into hir hand this bloody knyf he putte
For men sholde haue noon othir deemynge   *so that; opinion*
But shee had gilty been of this murdrynge.   *but that she was; murder*
And whan þat he had wroght this cursidnesse,
350 Anoon out of the chambre he gan him dresse.   *he took himself*

The contesse aftir, of hir sleep awakid,   *woken from sleep*
To th'emperices bed gan caste hir look,
And sy the bloody knyf in hir hond nakid,   *saw*
And for the fere shee tremblid and qwook,   *quaked*
355 And rogged on hir lord and him awook,   *shook; awoke*
Preyynge him to the bed he looke wolde
And ther a meruaillous thyng seen he sholde.   *frightful*

Whan he was wel awakid of his sleep,
He lookid therto as shee him besoghte,   *towards the bed; begged*
360 And it byheeld, and of it took good keep,   *observed it carefully*
And of þat meschief him sore forthoghte,   *misfortune; was greatly grieved*
Deemynge þat this cursid deede wroghte   *judging*
This emperice, as þat it was ful lyk   *very likely*
To been, and vp he threew an heuy syk,   *uttered; sigh*

365 And hir awook, and thus to hir he cryde,
'Womman, what is þat in thyn hand I see?
What hast thow doon, womman? For him þat
   dyde,
What wikkid spirit hath trauaillid thee?'   *laboured*
And, as soone as þat adawid was shee,   *awake*
370 The knyf fil out of hir hond in the bed   *fell*
And shee byheeld the clothes al bybled,   *covered with blood*

And the chyld deed: 'Allas!' shee cryde, 'allas!
How may this be? God woot al, I noot how.   *knows; do not know*
I am nat pryuee to this heuy cas.   *a party to; dreadful event*
375 The gilt is nat myn. I the chyld nat slow.'   *slew*
To which spak the contesse, 'What seist thow?
Excuse the nat. Thow maist nat seyn nay.
The knyf al bloody in thyn hand I say.'   *saw*

And thus vnto hir lord shee cryde anoon: *at once*
380 'Slee this cursid feend þat our chyld hath slayn.
Lat hir no lengere on lyue goon.   *longer live*
þat Y neuere had hir seen wolde I ful fayn,   *would (wish); very gladly*
But or shee heer cam þat shee had be flayn,   *before; flayed*
For so greet wo cam neuere to myn herte.
385 Slee hir as blyue. Lat nat hir asterte.'   *at once; escape*

Althogh þat shee wer in this cas vengeable,   *might be; case; vengeful*
For causes two me thynkith it smal vice   *it seems to me*
(Shee was in þat in partie excusable):   *in that respect; part*
Oon is shee wende þat the emperice   *thought*
390 Hir chyld had slayn of purposid malice,   *deliberate*
And so it seemed as by liklyhede,   *to all intents*
Albeit þat nat wer it so in dede;

þat othir cause, as woot euery man,   *knows*
In the world so louynge tendrenesse
395 Is noon as is the loue of a womman,
To hir chyld namely, and, as I gesse,   *especially*
To hir housbonde also, wherof witnesse
We weddid men may bere if þat vs lyke,   *it please us*
And so byhoueth a thank vs to pyke.   *it is useful; to gain their favour*

400 Now foorth, how the erl to th'emperice him   *conducted himself*
    hadde,
And how þat he gouerned þat mateere,
Herkneth. With heuy cheere and wordes sadde   *countenance; serious*
To hir he spak and seide in this maneere:
'Womman, with my swerd slee wolde I thee heere,
405 Sauf for awe of God, at whos reuerence   *except*
þat deede wole I putte in abstinence.   *abstain from carrying out*

'Thow haue shalt, for me, noon harm at al,   *as far as I am concerned*
But whoso trustith on the curtesie
Of thee, ful soone he deceyued be shal.
410   Whan þat thow wer on a tree hangid hye,
Wheras thow likly haddest been to dye,   *where*
Thow woost wel, therfrom I deliured thee   *know; from it*
And with my doghtres deeth thow qwit hast me.   *repaid*

'Vnkynde womman, walke on foorth thy way.   *Unnatural; go forth*
415   Hye thee hens, and neuere see my face.   *hasten*
For if þat I heeraftir thee see may—
Outhir in this or eny othir place   *either*
Of my lordshipe—thow noon othir grace
Shalt han, but die a deeth ful villenous,
420   Thow wikkid woman, fals and traiterous.'

This innocent lady no word ageyn   *in reply*
Spak, for shee spoken had ynow beforn,   *enough*
Excusynge hir, but al was in veyn,
For whan þat shee had al yseyd and sworn,   *said*
425   Shee with the erl and his wyf was doun born,   *overwhelmed in argument*
And, sikirly, wheras þat no credence   *certainly; where*
May been had, wysdam conseilith silence.

What leeue þat shee took ne woot I nat,
Or þat shee fro þat place was ywent—   *before; had gone*
430   The book maketh no mencion of that—
But hir palfray shee hirself hath hent,   *horse; took*
And so foorth rood toward the orient.
O emperice, our lord God gye thee,   *guide*
For yit thee folwith more aduersitee.

435   As shee rood, on hir right hand shee espyde
A galwe tree to which men a theef ledde   *gallows*
Hanged to been, and to hir horses syde
The spore gooth. Shee faste hir thidir spedde.   *spur; hastened there*
For verray routhe hir thoghte hir herte bledde,   *true pity*
440   And to the officers meekly shee preide
In this wyse, and right thus shee to hem seide: *way*

'Sires, if yow list this mannes lyf saue   *please*
I reedy am to yeue yow good meede.'   *give; reward*
'We wole wel,' quod they. 'What shul we haue?
445 What lykith yow for his lyf vs to beede?   *pleases it; to offer us*
Paieth therfore wel, and yee shul speede.'   *prosper*
They of the paiement accorded were.   *about; reached agreement*
Shee paide, and this man foorth shee took with
     here.

'Be to me treewe now,' quod she, 'my freend,
450 Syn fro thy deeth deliured haue Y thee.'   *since*
'Yis, certes, lady, elles to the feend   *certainly; else*
Body and soule bytake Y,' seide he.   *commit*
'Noon othir wolde I for al Cristientee
Been vnto yow,' and foorth shee rood hir way,
455 And on his foot this man hir folwith ay,   *followed continually*

Til þat they drow vnto a citee ny,   *drew*
Whidir beforn shee bad him for to go   *where beforehand; ordered*
And take hir in, so þat shee honestly   *secure lodging for her*
Mighte inned been, and he dide right so,   *lodged*
460 And taried nat his lady longe fro,
But ageyn hir as blyue right this man   *towards; immediately*
To brynge hir thidir faste wente and ran.

Shee cam into hir in, and abood ther   *dwelt*
Dayes dyuerse for hir ese and reste,   *several*
465 And in the citee fame wydewher   *report everywhere*
Sprang, how a lady, the womanlycste
Of cheer, port, shap and eek the faireste   *appearance; carriage; also*
That any wight beholde mighte or see,   *person*
Was come and inned hir in the citee.   *lodged*

470 Many a lusty man, in loues art   *handsome*
Expert and sotil, drow hem to hir in,   *skilful; drew; dwelling*
Weenynge han geten þat of which no part   *thinking to obtain*
They gete kowde, for noon art ne gyn.   *or cunning*
To th'ententes corrupt þat they wer in   *corrupt purposes*
475 Shee wolde for no thyng bowe and enclyne.   *yield*
Hir hertes castel kowde they nat myne.   *undermine*

As fer as the boundes of honestee   *far*
Requeren, shee made hem disport and cheere,   *demand; entertainment*
But passynge it, for al hir sotiltee,   *beyond those bounds; cleverness*
480 For profre of meede ne for fair preyeere,   *offered reward; entreaty*
Shee change nolde hir vertuous maneere.
The lessons þat they in Ouyde had red
Halp hem right noght. They wenten thens vnsped.   *helped; without success*

O yee þat seyn wommen be variant,   *changeable*
485 And can nat sad been if they been assaillid,   *constant*
Yee been ful vnkonnynge and ignorant,   *unwise*
And of the soothe foule yee han faillid.   *truth; foully*
Constance is vnto wommanhode entaillid.   *constancy; bestowed inalienably*
Out of þat fee they nat be dryue may.   *inheritance; may not be driven*
490 Swich hir nature is, thogh sum men sayn nay.   *such*

They stidefast been, as fer as Y woot,   *steadfast; far; know*
But it be wher they take han a purpos   *except*
þat naght is, which, be it neuere so hoot,   *wicked; passionate*
They change, lest it hurte mighte hir loos,   *reputation*
495 And keepen it secree, couert and cloos,   *secret; close covered*
Vnexecut, thogh of hem nat a fewe   *unexecuted*
The reuers doon. What, the feend is a shrewe.   *devil; villain*

Let al this passe. Ther cam to the port
Of this citee a ship with marchandyse
500 Charged, wherof hir man made report   *loaded*
To his lady. Shee bad him in al wyse   *by all means possible*
Go thidir and see, and him wel auyse   *take due note*
What thyng therin was, and word hoom hir
   brynge,
Withoute any delay or taryynge.

505 He thidir wente, and clothes precious
Amonges othir thynges ther he fond.   *found*
Ful ryche was the stuf, and plenteuous,
Of the ship, and the maistir by the hond
He took and seide, 'Ga we to the lond,
510 To my ladyes in. Shee wolde bye,   *dwelling*
If þat yow list, sum of your marchandie.'

'I wole gladly,' seide the shipman,
And to the ladyes in they bothe two
Goon, but before dressith him hir man   *beforehand went*
515 And reported hir as him oghte do,   *to her; he ought*
What he had in the ship seen, and, therto,   *in addition*
That the shipman was comen he hir tolde,   *had come*
Axynge hir if shee with him speke wolde.   *asking*

'Yis,' quod shee, 'let him in come, I the preye.'
520 He entred, and vnto him thus spak shee:
'Sire, yee han in your ship, heer Y seye,   *I hear said*
Dyuerse precious clothes, and if yee
Wolden some of hem brynge hidir to me,
As þat we mighte accorde, wolde Y paye   *and we might reach agreement*
525 In honde, and nat your paiement delaye.'

'Madame, I grante,' he seide, and took his leeue,
And with him hir seruant to the ship wente,
To whom the shipman by the way gan meeue,   *exhort*
'Freend, I am set on a certein entente,   *course of action*
530 Vnto the whiche if þat thow wilt assente
And do thy deuer and my conseil hyde,   *duty*
That thow me kneew thow blysse shalt the tyde. *bless; time*

'O may I truste, may I truste in thee?
Thow helpe me maist, and no wight but thow.
535 If thow wilt so in this necessitee,
Gold and siluer wole I thee yeue ynow.'   *give enough*
'Yis,' quod this seruant, 'that I make avow
To God, if þat it in my power lye,
Myn help to thee ne wole Y nat denye.

540 'If thow heeraftir fynde þat I gabbe,   *have spoken idly*
Of my promesse thanne dokke me.   *(your) promise to me; curtail*
I neuere was yit of my tonge a labbe.   *in speech a blabbermouth*
þat thyng þat me told is in priuetee   *confidence*
Keepe I can wel. Be in noon aweertee,   *doubt*
545 But anoon to me telle out al thy gole,   *the words in your mouth*
For treewe and trusty be to thee Y wole.'

'Grant mercy,' seide the shipman, 'iwis.   *many thanks; certainly*
Now feele I confort. Now dar Y bywreye   *reveal*
To thee myn hertes secree, which is this: *secret*
550 Swich excellence of beautee is, Y seye,
In thy lady, þat but if thow purueye   *arrange*
For me þat Y hir loue may obteene,
Ful shorte shuln my dayes been, Y weene.'   *will*

Quod this seruant, 'Looke how Y may profyte   *make progress*
555 In this. Let see and me sette in the way   *show me*
How Y shal do, and so shal Y me qwyte   *acquit myself*
þat Y thy thank disserue shal for ay.
Al shal be doon right to thyn owne pay.   *profit*
Telle on, how wilt thow þat I me gouerne?'
560 The shipman seide, 'And þat I wole as yerne.   *at once*

'On my behalue to thy lady weende   *behalf; journey*
And to hir seye þat in no maneere   *under no circumstances*
Clothes out of my ship may I hir seende.
If hir good lust be in my ship appeere,   *pleasure; to appear*
565 Shee shal seen what hir list with ful good cheer,   *she pleases*
But out of my ship wole Y nothyng selle.
Right euene thvs vnto hir seye and telle.

'But of o thyng thow must thee wel auyse—   *take good care*
Good heede therof take and nat ne faille—
570 Be thow wel waar, in al maneere wyse,   *in any event*
þat the wynd thanne be good, hens to saille.   *for setting sail*
Al þat thow doost elles may nat auaille.   *otherwise*
For lede hir hoom wole Y to my contree.
Lo, this is al þat Y desire of thee.'

575 Ful sooth is seid, the fals and coueitous   *truly*
Been soone accordid. Allas, this onhede   *agreed; unity*
Synful shal be wikkid and treccherous.
O emperice, God the gye and lede.   *guide you*
Thow haast, or this, had trouble greet and drede,   *before*
580 And yit a sharp storm is vnto thee shape,   *prepared*
But, thankid be God, al thow shalt eschape.

Now to purpos. Than seide this seruant   *to the point*
To the shipman, 'Come of, yeue me meede,   *along; give; payment*
For heer Y swer and make couenaunt   *agreement*
585 This shal be doon. Haue therof no dreede.'   *fear*
He had Y not what, the deuel him speede,   *don't know; bad luck to him!*
For his labour to be doon in this caas,
And to his lady dressith he his paas.   *he takes his way*

He tolde hir how the shipman wolde naght
590 Deliure clothes out of his vessel,
But, if it lykid hir to bye aght,   *pleased; buy anything*
Thidir shee muste come, and he ful wel
With hir wolde do. She kneew no del   *part*
Of the treson purposid twixt hem two,   *proposed*
595 And seide, 'In Goddes name it shal be do.   *done*

'I reedy am to go whan þat Y shal,
Syn þat thow seist it may noon othir be,   *since; no other way*
But outhir moot Y goon or leuen al.   *either; must*
Let vs go thidir as swythe,' quod shee.   *at once*
600 'A nay, madame, it may nat be,' seide he.
'Swich occupacion hath he this day,   *so busy is he*
That he vnto yow nat entende may.   *attend*

'Madame, vs muste abyden his leisir.   *await; leisure*
Theron I wole awayte bysyly.   *wait*
605 And whan tyme is yee shuln han your pleisir.   *time is (right); shall have*
Often vpon him awayte moot Y,
To wite and knowe wel and redily   *know*
The tyme whan we shal vs thidir dresse.   *take ourselves there*
Madame, for yow this best is, Y gesse.'

610 This humble lamb, this lady innocent,
Of al this treson no notice hauynge,
Seide, 'As þat thow doost, holde Y me content.'   *according to what*
Thus hir seruant delayed hir goynge
Til þat the wynd wel stood the ship to brynge
615 Out of the port, and thidir he hir spedde,   *hurried*
And þat in haaste. Hir he to the ship ledde.

Whan shee withyn the shipbord entred was,   *on board ship*
Vp gooth the sail at the top of the mast.
Hir man, of purpos, lefte on londe, allas.   *purposely remained*
620 Quod shee, 'Nat was Y waar of this forcast,'   *plan*
And therwithal out to weepe shee brast,   *burst out weeping*
And seide, 'What treson doost thow, shipman,
To me?' 'Nay,' quod he, 'no treson, womman,

'Nat meene I, but thus, lo, thus wole I do,
625 Flesshly the knowe and aftir wedde thee.'   *have sexual dealings with you*
'A vow,' quod shee, 'maad haue I God vnto
þat neuere so shal ther man do to me,
For thyng in this world, outake oonly he   *anything; except*
To whom Y am ybownden to and knyt.
630 The labour is in vein to speke of it.'

'Keepe in thy wordes, womman, I thee rede,'   *restrain; advise*
Quod he. 'Considere and thynke wel, þat thow
Of thy lyf standist in peril and drede,
For in middes of the see been we now.
635 To me conforme—it shal be for thy prow—   *adapt yourself; profit*
Elles into the see wole I thee caste.   *or*
Truste me wel, so wole Y do as faste.'

'Now wel,' quod shee, 'syn Y may nat asterte   *escape*
My deeth but Y your entente fulfille,   *design*
640 Althogh it be greetly ageyn myn herte,   *against*
Yit rather than þat yee me sle or kille,
Wole Y assente, so it be your wille   *provided you are willing*
In the ende of the ship for to ordeyne
An honest place and pryuee for vs tweyne.   *private*

645 'It is nat, as I hope, your entente   *intention*
In open sighte of folk do with me so.   *full view*
Hard were it make me therto consente,   *it would be hard; to it*
For þat a greet encrees were of my wo.   *would greatly increase*
Yit leuer wer it me my lyf forgo.   *I should rather*
650 A pryuee place, as I seide, purueye   *provide*
For vs, þat folk see nat how we foleye.'   *behave foolishly*

He in the ship, wheras was his plesance,   *where he pleased*
A place ordeyned, curtyned aboute,
Into the which with heuy contenance,
655 Whyles he speek with his meynee withoute,   *crew*
Shee entred hath, and anoon gan to loute   *bow*
To God. Right on hir knees shee hir prayeere
Made as I to yow shal rehercen heere.   *repeat*

'O God, our lord, Ihesu, our saueour,
660 þat fro my youthe haast kept me to this day,
Curteys Ihesu, me keepe now this hour
From al pollucioun so þat Y may,
With herte cleene in this woful affray,   *assault*
My soule yilde to thy deitee.   *yield*
665 Mercyful lord, of this byseeche Y thee.'

Nat endid was hir orison vnnethes   *scarcely*
But swich a tempest aroos in the see
þat the ship brast and ther took hir dethes   *broke up; their deaths*
They þat therin weren, the hool meynee,   *crew*
670 Sauf oonly this maistir shipman and shee.   *save*
By oon of the bordes shee faste hir heeld,
Which from hir deeth was hir deffense and
     sheeld,

And broghte hir vp vnto the land saufly.
To anothir bord this maistir shipman
675 Eek claf, and was sauf. This fil wondirly.   *also clung; saved; was a miracle*
Many maistries our lord God do can.   *works of power*
And þat this lady, this noble womman
Was sauf, this maistir shipman kneew no deel,   *not at all*
Ne shee þat he fortuned had so weel.   *had been so fortunate*

680 Of this shipman speke Y no more as now,   *for now*
But this lady vnto a nonnerie
þat was but ther faste by hir drow,   *close; took herself*
Wher the ladyes of hir conpaignie   *company*
Wer ful glad, and of hir genterie   *in their courtesy*
685 Receyued hir, althogh þat no notice
They hadde of hir estat of emperice.   *of her royal breeding*

And ther abood shee a long tymes space   *remained*
In holy lyf and vertuous clennesse,   *purity*
Vnto whom God yaf and shoop swich a grace   *gave and fashioned such*
690 þat shee kowde hele folk of hir seeknesse,   *their*
What so it wer, and thidir gan hem dresse   *whatever; betook themselves*
From euery part and euery contree
They þat felten any infirmitee.

Than shoop it he þat to the emperour   *happened*
695 Was brothir, which this lady on a tree
By hir heer vp heeng, þat cursid traitour,   *hair; hung*
Mirour of malice and iniquitee,
As foul a leepre was as mighte be.   *leper*
Lo, thogh God him to wreke a whyle abyde,   *Himself; avenge; waits*
700 The fals and wikkid qwytith he sum tyde.   *repays; at some time*

The knyght eek which the erles doghtir slow,   *slew*
The emperice and shee bothe sleepynge
As Y before told haue vnto yow,
Was blynd and deef, and also the tremblynge
705 Of palesie sore gan him wrynge.   *palsy; sorely; distress*
No force how sore swich a wrecche smerte   *no matter; suffer pain*
That to wommen so cruel is of herte.

The theef which to the maistir of the ship
Betrayed th'emperice, his lady, als   *also*
710 From harm ne greef kowde nat make a skip—
God sheelde he sholde, he þat was so fals   *forbid*
To hir þat from the roop kepte his hals—   *rope; neck*
Potagre and gowty and halt he was eek,   *gouty; lame; also*
And was in othir sundry wyse seek.   *ways sick*

715 The shipman had also the franesie   *dementia*
þat with this emperice hadde ment
Fulfillid his foul lust of aduoutrie   *(to have) fulfilled; desire; adultery*

Which was in him ful hoot and ful feruent.   *hot and burning*
See how all hem þat to this innocent,
720 This noble lady, had ydoon greuance,   *done wrong*
Our lord God qwitte with strook of vengeance.   *repaid; stroke*

Yee men, whos vsage is, women to greeue,   *custom*
And falsely deceyue hem and bytraye,
No wondir is thogh yee mishappe and cheeue.   *have bad luck and suffer harm*
725 God qwyte yow wole and your wages paye   *repay*
In swich wyse þat it yow shal affraye.   *such a way; terrify*
Let Goddes wreches hensfoorth yow miroure,   *punishments; be a mirror to*
For, but if yee do, yee shul bye it soure.   *unless; pay for; bitterly*

Now to the emperour torne wole Y,
730 Which, whan he herde þat in an abbeye
Of nonnes was a womman so holy
And therto so konnynge, he herde seye,   *in addition; wise*
That voide kowde shee and dryue aweye   *rid*
Seeknesses alle, of what kynde or nature   *sicknesses*
735 They weren, and hem hele wel and cure,

Right thus vnto his brothir seide he tho: *then*
'To this holy womman best is þat we,
As faste as we may make vs reedy, go,   *ready*
Syn so good and so gracious is shee   *since*
740 þat of thy leepre shee may cure thee.'   *leprosy*
This was assentid. They hem haaste and hye
In what they may vnto þat nonnerie.   *as fast as possible*

Knowen vnto th'abbesse and hir couent   *when it was known; convent*
How þat the emperour was ny comynge,   *approaching*
745 Ageyn him in processioun arn they went   *towards; they went*
Hir seruice ful deuoutly syngynge,   *their*
And dide al þat was to swich cas longynge,   *such a case; appropriate*
And, whan he in th'abbeye was alight,   *dismounted*
Thus of th'abbesse he axid anoonright: *asked; at once*

750 'Is ther any swich womman in this hous   *such*
As folkes hele kan of hir seeknesse?   *their*
Men seyn, heer is a womman merueillous.
Shal it be fownden so,' he seide, 'abbesse?'
And shee answerde, 'Sir, in soothfastnesse
755 A good womman dwellynge is with vs heere
Which in vertu we knowen noon hir peere.'   *equal*

Shee dide hir come anoon to his presence,   *made; at once*
But with hir veil hir face hid had shee,
To been vnknowe, and dide him reuerence,
760   As longid vnto his hy dignitee.   *was fitting*
And right as blyue of hir axid he,   *quickly; asked*
'Can yee my brothir of his maladie
Of leepre cure, and of meselrie?   *leprosy; leprosy*

'If þat yee can, now tell on, Y yow preye,
765   For your labour ful wel qwyte wole Y.'   *reward*
But or þat shee aght wolde answer and seye   *before; anything*
Shee caste hir look aboute, and ther sy   *saw*
The emperoures brothir stande by
þat leepre was, and eek tho othir three   *also those*
770   þat had hir doon so greet aduersitee,

That is to seyn, the knyght, theef and shipman,
And thanne shee spak and seide in this wyse,   *way*
'Sire, noon þat is heer Y cure can.
I may nat take vpon me þat empryse—   *undertaking*
775   Therto may nat my konnynge souffyse—   *my knowledge is inadequate*
But if þat they an open shrifte make   *unless; confession*
Of hir offenses dirke and synnes blake.'   *their; dark*

To his brothir than spak this emperour:
'Among all vs thee openly confesse.
780   Spare nat to deskeuere thyn errour,   *reveal*
Syn þat thow therby maist of thy seeknesse   *since*
Cured be. Telle out al thy wikkidnesse.
Be nat abassht. It manly is to synne,
But feendly is longe lye therynne.'   *to lie long in it*

785   For forme a confession made he,   *appearances' sake*
Swich as it was, but how the emperice   *such*
His lordes wyf he heeng vpon a tree   *hung*
By hir heer, tolde he nat þat curside vice,   *hair*
For torne it sholde him into preiudice   *turn; to his disadvantage*
790   And harm also. Deskeuere kepte he noght.   *he didn't care to reveal it*
Yit aftirward he therto was ybroght.   *to that point*

Whan þat his lewde shrifte was ydo,   *wicked confession; done*
'Sire,' quod shee, 'laboure Y sholde in veyn,
If aght I leide your brothir vnto   *anything; placed. . . upon*
795 For he maad haath noon hool shrifte ne pleyn.'   *complete confession*
This emperour vnto him spak ageyn:
'Woost thow nat weel thow art a foul mesel?   *know; leper*
Telle out, let see, shryue thee cleene and wel,   *confess completely*

'Or truste me weel, for þat encheson   *reason*
800 Thow voide shalt out of my conpaignie.'   *be expelled*
'O lord,' he seide, 'but if your pardon   *unless*
Yee me promette, I dar nat specifie   *promise*
O word of my gilt. I yow mercy crye.'   *one*
Quod th'emperour, 'What, haast thow agilt me?'   *wronged*
805 'Certes, right greeuously, my lord,' seide he.

'Now,' quod the emperour, 'and haast thow so?'
And of the emperice he thoghte nat,
But, weenynge shee many a day ago   *thinking*
Deed had been, seide, 'What offense is that?
810 Be nat aferd, but telle on plein and plat.   *blunt*
For what so þat it be, Y foryeue al.   *forgive*
Truste wel, þat Y seye, Y holde shal.'   *what; do*

Therwithal was his brothir herted weel.   *with that; greatly encouraged*
Al how the emperice had he betrayed
815 Before hem al he tolde out euerydeel,   *every part*
Wherof the emperour was sore affrayed.
His brothres reward had nat been vnpayde   *(due) reward*
Nad promesse of the emperour him bownde   *had not*
To pardoun, for which, wo was him þat   *he was grieved; time*
     stownde.

820 Almoost he was out of himself, certeyn—
So seith the book, and þat was no meruaille.   *wonder*
What lord is þat if swich a word sodeyn   *unexpected*
To him cam of his wyf, whos gouernaille   *self-control*
Was hires lyk, but ny, to, sholde him faille   *like hers; nearly, as well*
825 His wit and his good disposicioun
For the sodeyn woful impression?

For falle anoon sholde in his remembrance
Hir vertuous manere and wommanhede,
Hir beautee, shap, good cheer and daliance.   *conversation*
830 Al this considered, withouten drede,   *doubt*
Out of the weye of ioie him wolde lede
The mis of so vertuous a persone,   *loss*
And yit nat for þat enchesoun allone,   *reason*

But also the vnkyndely tresoun   *unnatural*
835 Of his brothir þat him to him had qwit   *had acquitted himself*
So falsely, me thynkith by resoun   *it seems to me only right*
Stike right ny vnto his herte oghte it   *to stick near*
And causen him ful many an heuy fit: *feeling*
But nathelees, wit axith, and prudence,   *nevertheless; requires*
840 Al thyng þat fallith take in pacience.   *everything; befalls to take*

Now to my purpos. Th'emperour tho spak   *then*
To his brothir and thus he to him seide:
'Thow cursid wrecche, thow demoniak!
þat our lord God which for vs all deide   *died*
845 The strook of his vengeance vpon thee leide   *stroke*
No wondir is. Had Y this beforn wist,   *before; known*
Thy body sholde han the grownd swept and kist,   *dragged along*

'And therto eek as sharp punisshement   *in addition; also*
As þat dyuyse ther kowde any wight   *devise; person*
850 Thow sholdest han ypreeued by the sent,   *feeling*
But holde wole Y þat Y thee haue hight.'   *keep; what; promised*
And thanne confesse him began the knyght   *to confess*
þat the erles doghtir slow as shee sleep.   *slew; slept*
Lo, thus he seide, takith now good keep.   *heed*

855 'Notice noon,' seide he, 'ne knowlechynge   *knowledge*
Haue Y of þat lady, ne who it is,   *nor*
But as my lord the erl rood on huntynge   *rode*
In a foreste ones, wel woot Y this,   *once; know*
A fair lady he fond hangynge, iwis,   *certainly*
860 On a tree by hir heer and, of pitee
And routhe meeued, hir adoun took he   *compassion; moved; down*

'And to his castel with him hir he ladde,   *led*
And the charge bytook to hir and cure   *entrusted; care*
To keepe a yong doghtir which þat he hadde,
865 Hir to teche and to lerne norture.   *instruct in good manners*
But to me shoop ther a misauenture.   *befell; misfortune*
I bisyed me to haue by hir leyn,   *busied; lain*
And al my labour ydil was and veyn.   *wasted*

'For any craft þat euere kowde Y do,   *trick*
870 To me shee wolde assente by no way.   *agree*
I kowde in no wyse brynge hir therto.   *to that point*
Hir answer was euere oon, and that was nay,   *the same*
Which was nothyng vnto my lust and pay.   *not at all; pleasure; profit*
Wherfore meeued was Y nat a lyte   *moved; little*
875 But ful greetly, and hir Y thoghte qwyte,   *to repay*

'And in hir bed as shee lay on a nyght,
This yonge maide and shee sleepynge faste,
I kilde the chyld and therwith, foorthright   *at once*
The bloody knyf into the hand Y thraste   *thrust*
880 Of the lady, for þat men sholde caste   *reckon*
And suppose how þat no wight but shee
Mighte of this slaghtre and murdre gilty be,   *slaughter*

'And thens my lord maade hir voide anoon,   *depart at once*
But wher shee becam am Y nat priuee.   *what became of her; don't know*
885 God woot þat knowleche haue Y therof noon.'
Than spak the theef. 'Y noot whom meene yee,   *don't know*
But a lady of excellent beautee
Allone and soul cam by the way rydynge   *solitary*
Whan for my gilt Y led was to hangynge,

890 'And whan þat this lady benigne and good
Had hir look toward me cast, and espyed
From afer in what mescheef þat Y stood,
Hir herte anoon of pitee was applyed   *in pity; directed*
Me to socoure and helpe, and hath hir hyed   *hastened*
895 Vnto the place wher deed sholde Y be,
And payde for my lyf, and saued me.

'And aftirward, I as a fals traitour
Ageyn hir gentillesse and hy bontee   *gentle breeding; high goodness*
To a shipman which was a foul lecchour
900 Betrayed hir, and to his contree
Him shoop lede hir this man delauee,   *planned; dissolute*
And fer into the see Y saw hem saille,   *far*
But what fil aftir woot Y nat sanz faille.'   *happened; without*

'Swich a fair lady, certein, Y receyued   *such*
905 Into my ship,' seide the shipman tho,   *then*
'And thoghte haue hir deffoulid and deceyued   *planned; debauched*
Amiddes the see, but shee preide so   *in the middle of*
To God þat my desyr was Y put fro.
I mighte nat acheeue my purpoos.
910 Whan shee had preid an hidous storm aroos,   *arose*

'And shortly of this for to speke and telle,
The wynd ful sore in the sail bleew and haf,   *rose*
And the wawes began to bolne and swelle,   *waves; rise up*
And our taklynge brast, and the ship claf   *tackle broke; clove*
915 In two. Of seurtee loste Y ny the staf.   *security; almost*
Vndir the watir wenten euerychone.   *everyone*
Myself except, knowe Y no sauf persone.   *no person saved*

'By a bord of the ship, heeld Y me faste,   *timber; held*
And as þat my fortune shoop þat tyde   *ordained; time*
920 The wawes me sauf vpon the land caste.'   *waves; safe*
This emperice list no lenger hyde   *pleased; longer*
What þat shee was, but spak and sumdel cryde   *somewhat*
On hy and to hem seide in this maneere: *aloud*
'Now been yee cleene shryuen, freendes deere.   *completely confessed*

925 'Now shul yee all haue of me medecyne.'
Shee dide hir art and helid euery wight   *practised; person*
Of his seeknesse and voidid al his pyne,   *removed; suffering*
And from hir heed shee hath hir veil yplight   *plucked*
And hem hir face shewid anoonright.   *immediately*
930 And as swythe as the emperour hir sy   *soon; saw*
þat shee his wyf was, kneew he verraily,   *truly*

And withoute delay to hir he sterte   *rushed*
And hir embraced in his armes tweyne
And kiste hir often with vnfeyned herte,   *honest*
935 But fro weepynge he kowde him nat restreyne,
Thogh it nat causid wer of greef and peyne,   *even though*
But of the inward ioie which þat stownde   *time*
He took, bycause he had his wyfe yfownde.   *found*

O, many a wrecche is in this lond, Y weene,   *expect*
940 þat thogh his wyf lenger had been him fro,   *longer; from*
No kus, but if it had been of the spleene   *kiss; caused by sadness*
Shee sholde han had, and forthermore also
Fyndynge of hir had been to him but wo,   *nothing but*
For him wolde han thoght þat swich a fyndynge   *it would have seemed to him;*
945 To los sholde han him torned, and harmynge.   *loss*

No force of þat, my tale I now thus eende.   *no matter about*
Hoom vnto his paleys this emperour   *palace*
And his good lady th'emperice weende   *went*
And lyueden in ioie and hy honour
950 Til þat the tyme of deeth cam, and his hour,
Which þat no wight eschue may, ne flee: *person; escape*
And whan God list, also dye shul we.   *please*

Explicit fabula de quadam imperatrice Romana.
[here ends the story of a certain Roman Empress]

My freend, aftir, I trowe, a wike or two   *think; week*
That this tale endid was, hoom to me cam,
955 And seide, 'Thomas, hastow almoost do?   *finished*
To see thy werk, hidir comen Y am.'
My tale anoon Y fette, and he it nam   *fetched; took*
Into his hand and it al ouersy,   *oversaw*
And aftirward he seide thus therby: *about it*

960 'Thomas, it is wel vnto my lykyng,   *it pleases me well*
But is ther aght þat thow purposist seye   *anything; intend*
More on this tale?' 'Nay, my freend, nothyng.'
'Thomas, heer is a greet substance aweye.   *matter missing*
Wher is the moralizynge, Y yow preye,

965 Bycome heerof? Was ther noon in the book
Out of the which þat thow this tale took?'

'No, certes, freend, therin ne was ther noon.'
'Sikirly, Thomas, therof I meruaille.   *am amazed*
Hoom wole Y walke and retourne anoon—   *at once*
970 Nat spare wole Y for so smal trauaille—   *labour*
And looke in my book. Ther Y shal nat faille
To fynde it. Of þat tale it is parcel,   *a part*
For Y seen haue it ofte, and knowe it wel.'

He cam therwith, and it vnto me redde,
975 Leuynge it with me and hoom wente ageyn.
And to this moralyzynge I me spedde,   *moralization; hastened*
In prose wrytynge it hoomly and pleyn,
For he conseillid me do so, certeyn,   *certainly*
And lo, in this wyse and maneere it seith,   *way; speaks*
980 Which to þat tale is good be knyt, in feith.   *to be joined*

Hic incipit moralizacio
[*here begins the moralization*]

This emperour þat Y spak of aboue is our lord Ihesu Cryst. His wyf is the
soule. Th'emperoures brothir is man, to whom God committed and bytook
[*entrusted*] the cure [*care*] and the charge of his empire, þat is to seyn, of
his body, and nathelees [*nevertheless*] principally of the soule. But the wrec-
985 chid flessh ful oftensythe [*often*] stireth and excitith the soule vnto synne.
But the soule þat entierly loueth God abouen alle thynges makith euere
resistence vnto synne, and takith his mightes and powers (þat is to seye,
reson, wil, intellect and conscience) and makith swich inobedient flessh to
the spirit [*spiritually disobedient flesh*] to been enprisoned in the prisoun of
990 penance til it obeye in alle thynges to reson.

Th'emperour (þat is to seye, Cryst) is to come to the synner, and thanne
the flessh cryeth, axynge [*asking*] grace, and as often as he hath mercy he
hath hope, and for trust and hope of mercy, the rather [*more quickly*] wole
he synne. Ageyn swiche folk spekith holy scripture in this wyse [*way*]:
995 'Accursid is or be þat man þat synneth in hope.' To which the soule is
oftensythe [*often*] enclyned. Shee letith the flessh goon out of the prisoun

of penance. Shee wasshith and pourgith the flessh of the filthes of synne, clothynge it with good vertues, and makynge it ascende and worthe [*get up*] vp on the steede of charitee to ryde in goode wirkes and deedes, þat it 1000 may meete with God in the holy day of Estren. But allas and weleaway [*woe*], oftensythe [*often*] the synner offendith and trespaceth by the way in þat holy tyme, wherof the hert [*hart*] rysith (þat is to seyn, delectacioun of synne) and alle the wittes rennen [*run*] aftir synne, and the howndes (þat is to seyn, the wikkid thoghtes) alway berken [*bark*], and maken swich insti-1005 gacion þat man (þat is to seyn, the flessh and the soule) been togidere left withouten any vertu, and the flessh, apparceyuynge [*perceiving*] þat, solic-itith and bysyeth hir, stirynge the ful noble soule, which is Crystes spowse, vnto synne. But nathelees [*nevertheless*] the soule þat is wel beloued of God, and vnto Cryst weddid and oned [*united*], wole nat forsake God and 1010 consente to synne, wherfore the wrecchid flessh despoillith [*strips*] often and robbith the soule of hir clothes (þat is to seyn, goode vertues) and hir hongith [*hangs her*] on an ook (þat is to seyn, worldly delyt and delecta-cioun) by the heeres (þat is to seyn, by wikkid concupiscences and desirs) til the erl (þat is to seyn, the prechour or discreet confessour) hunte in the 1015 foreste of this world with vertuous sarmonynge [*sermons*] and prechynge, yeuynge [*giving*] conseil and reed [*counsel and advice*] to do goode and vertuous deedes, berkynge [*barking*] (þat is to seyn, pronouncynge the wordes of holy scripture). And thus the discreet confessour or prechour ledith the lady (þat is to meene, the soule) vnto the hows of holy chirche 1020 for to teche and norisshe the maiden (þat is to seyn, to hele the conscience with the wirkes of mercy.

The erl before his bed hath a laumpe: þat is to seyn, the discreet confes-sour, prelat or prechour hath alway beforn [*before*] the yen [*eyes*] of his herte the laumpe of holy scripture in which he seeth the griefs and annoyes [*hurts*] 1025 of the soule, and tho [*those*] thynges eek [*also*] þat therto been profitable and necessarie (þat is to seyn, drawynge or plukkynge out of it vices and puttynge or ympynge [*grafting*] in it vertues). The styward [*steward*] þat excited and stired hir to synne, certein, þat is pryde of lyf, which is the styward of this world, by whom many folk been deceyued and begyled, but 1030 the soule of God beloued wole nat consente to pryde. What dooth therfore worldly pryde? Certein, it takith the knyf of auarice, whan shee profrith a man a purs ful of moneye, castynge it beforn the yen of a man, and so shee sleeth the maiden (þat is to seyn, good conscience), wherof it is writen thus: 'Yiftes [*gifts*] or meede [*reward*] blynden the iuges yen and peruerten wyse 1035 men', so þat equitee or euenehede [*equality*] mighte nat entre but stood al

afer [*afar off*], and the iugement was torned vpsodoun. [*upside-down*]
Swiche been they þat been, or oghte been, put out of the chirches lappe or
bosom.

The lady rood soul [*solitary*] or allone, and apparceyuynge [*perceiving*] a
1040 man led to the galwes [*gallows*] etc. This man may be led to his deeth by
deedly synne wirkynge. Let vs therfore do as dide þat lady. Shee smoot
[*smote*] hir hors with hir spores [*spurs*]. So sholde we do. We sholden prikke
our flessh with the spores of penance and helpe and socoure our neighburgh in his necessitee, nat oonly with goodes temporel [*of the world*] but
1045 also with goodes spirituel. Whereof seith Salomon: 'Wo is þat man þat lyth
soul [*alone*] in synne and hath no wight to be holpen [*helped*] by or
conforted.' O hye [*hasten*] thee man, hye thee, areise or rere [*raise*] vp thyn
neighburgh þat is doun fall, [*fallen*] for the brothir þat is holpen of [*helped
by*] his brothir is lyk a strong or sad [*secure*] citee. 'Whoso [*whoever*] oonly
1050 yeueth [*gives*] cold watir to his brothir to drynke, he shal nat leese his meede.'
[*reward*] But manye vnkynde [*unnatural*] folk ther been, as was the theef
þat betrayed his lady aftir shee had saued him from his deeth. Some men
yilden [*repay*] euel ageyn [*in exchange for*] good to hem doon [*done to them*],
wherof spekith Ysaye thus: 'Wo be to hem þat callen good euel and euel
1055 good'.

The maistir of the ship is the feend, by whom many folk been deceyued in
the see, þat is to seyn, in this world. 'All thynges been vanitee', seith
Ecclesiastes, but the ship is broken as ofte as any wight [*person*] cheesith
[*chooses*] wilful pouert [*voluntary poverty*] and he þat obeieth to his prelat
1060 in alle thynges for God, thanne hatith he the world and the concupiscence
of it. It is impossible to plese the world and God.

The lady wente to the abbeye: so torned the soule to holy lyf fro worldly
tribulaciouns, wherthurgh alle the wittes, by whiche the soule vexed was
and troubled, been infect with dyuerse seeknesses, as ye [*eye*] by the concu-
1065 piscence of yen [*eyes*], heerynge by detraccioun, and so foorth, wherfore
the soule may nat openly be seen of [*by*] Cryst hir spowse til þat alle the
wittes [*sins commited by the senses*] be confessed openly, and thanne,
doutelees, the soule may be led to the ioie of paradys, to which he vs brynge
þat starf [*died*] for our redempcioun, amen.

Explicit moralizacio [*here ends the moralization*]

Notes

This, and the final item of the *Series*, are translations of two stories from the major late medieval source of allegorized narratives of the Roman emperors, the *Gesta Romanorum*. Though Hoccleve's precise source has not been discovered, his version is close to Latin and Middle English versions of the story: for the Latin version from Ha2, see Wallensköld 1907: 111–16; for another printed Latin version, from a German MS, Oesterley 1872: 648–57; for a Middle English version, Herrtage 1879: 311–321, modernized in Blamires 1992: 270–7. In the analogues this story usually occurs near the end of the volume, and thus functions broadly like the story of Griselda as used by Boccaccio in *The Decameron*. Selected readings from MSS of the Latin are included in Appendix 2A. Parallels with Chaucer's treatment of the same theme, in *MLT*, include a heroine unjustly accused of murder (344–50, cf. *CT* II.596–602) and preserved from an attempt on her virtue while at sea (666–70, cf. *CT* II.918–24).

2   *whilom*: D's conventional beginning is used again to introduce the second *Gesta* narrative (5.85). *H prefers 'sometime', but since elsewhere 'whilom' is preferred (V.22, VI.225) *H's reading is likely to be scribal.

7–10 expands on the version in the analogues with an echo of *ClT* (*CT* IV.210–12) so as to create a hierarchy of physical and spiritual beauty.

12–13 Hoccleve's account of the qualities appropriate to a good woman (specifically, mercy, 11, 14) has echoes of his version of Christine de Pizan's *Epistre* (for whom also the 'spread' of a woman's 'good renoun' is a crucial question), so that, as in Chaucer's *MLT*, his heroine will be presented as an exemplar of courtliness.

15   Hoccleve's narratives are punctuated by such references to the circumstances of their own narration (e.g. 400, 498, highlighted by rubrication in *H), and (a motif derived from Chaucer, especially *MLT*) to the gaps in the source which his version cannot make good (57–63, 190–6 and n., 264, 428–30). Hoccleve

also points future narrative developments more clearly than the analogues (e.g. 308, 434), a feature with parallels in *MLT*.

36–42 an added stanza with possible echoes of *ClT* in Jereslaus' 'sodeyn' purpose (cf. *CT* IV.316), which the Empress must take 'in gree' (*CT* IV.1151). The following stanza makes the Empress's response (more clearly in the analogues) a figure of that of the Virgin Mary at the Annunciation (Luke 1.38), as was that of Grisilde (*CT* IV.361). Hoccleve's speech for the Empress at 150 similarly contains an echo of the Virgin at the Annunciation.

50–1 may recall Dorigen in *The Franklin's Tale*, abbreviated *FrkT*, though the immediate origin is probably the Latin source (cf. Appendix 2). Another echo of *FrkT* occurs at 92–3 (cf. *CT* V.984–6).

70   The robbing of the rich is not found in Ha2, but does occur in other versions of the Latin (see Appendix 2), and is confirmed by a detail in the Empress's later speech to her counsellors (114, common to all versions).

79 *flesshly consente*: the analogues do not specify the nature of the sin, though the context makes clear, as does the thrust of the whole story, that an adulterous liaison is being proposed. The Germano-Latin analogues speak at this point of 'amore inordinato' (Oesterley 1872: 649), a phrase later used by the Anglo-Latin analogues in the context of the Empress's repeated subjection to sexual advances (material corresponding to 3.317, 470–3, and cf. 482n., 5.162n.).

80 Here and elsewhere (e.g. 242–4, 521–6) Hoccleve turns reported into direct speech, or creates passages of direct speech (512, 519). By contrast, direct speech appears as indirect at 356–7, 501–4.

93 In having his heroine declare that she is bound to her husband with a tie which overrides natural inclination, Hoccleve anticipates her speech to the second suitor, the earl's steward (321–2); the former detail does not occur in the analogues consulted.

97 *soul*: a most important word here and elsewhere in the *Series* (3.888, 1033, 1039, 5.391, 431), translating 'sola' throughout the tale. Occasionally Hoccleve does not translate the word, as at 338, where the solitude of the Empress makes possible the murder of her charge. At 432 BLSY translate 'sola' correctly against the reading of the holograph: see Introduction p. 23.

115–16 Hoccleve's version makes explicit the Empress's modesty in refusing to name the sin of which she is the proposed object (the analogues simply refer to unspecified greater wrongs proposed). In so emphasizing her silence Hoccleve is drawing on an element of her presentation throughout the story. Elsewhere, her silence is a mark of her need to protect herself; here it refers to her nobility of character.

131–2 Cf. Chauntecleer's dream of the fox in *NPT* (*CT* VII.3697–8).

144–5 The analogues have the brother-in-law entreating the Empress 'propter Christi passionem'. Hoccleve's version places the emphasis on the Empress's own 'hy bontee' and 'grace fre', as a way of suggesting her inadvertent involve-

ment in the coming disaster. Virtue here attracts vice in the way that Virginia does in Chaucer's *Physician's Tale*.

143 *made*: the *H reading 'bad' is probably also authorial, since Hoccleve uses the word regularly in similar contexts (e.g. 112, 457, 501).

162 This moment, probably added by Hoccleve to the source, has regular parallels at other places in the source and in his translation (291, 439).

185 Hoccleve's vivid realization of the calls of the riders-turned-huntsmen ('hay dogge hay') probably develops from the Latin analogue followed (see Appendix 2).

190–6 This and other additions by Hoccleve have the effect, like comparable additions by Chaucer to the sources of *ClT*, of placing the narrative so far away in time and place from the reader ('many a yeer agoon… no swich array… as… this day') as to emphasize its unreality: hence ironic asides about the negatives of female behaviour later in the tale (397–9, 490–7), with clear echoes of *ClT*, which throws in question Hoccleve's acceptance of the terms of his fictional commission. The conventionally pessimistic view of the present here revealed by comparison with an exemplary past also occurs in the narratives of the *Regement* (e.g. 2287–9, 3756–9, 3960–2).

234–5 Cf. 2 Sam. 18.9–10.

246–66 Hoccleve's use of apostrophe in the tale (e.g. 3.433–4, 484–7) has clear parallels with that in Chaucer's *MLT*. Cf. passages of narratorial comment added to the text, another link with *MLT* (e.g. 3.386–99, 488–97).

259 'Hidde' and 'kidde' as variants in this line refer respectively to the intentions and experience of the human protagonists and to the divine purposes underpinning them.

267 *dayes three*: In the analogues closest to Hoccleve the earl gives the Empress three days to leave his territory, whereas Ha2 gives her only a single day (neither version is translated at 416).

269 Hoccleve's phrase 'of a strange contree' follows some of the analogues, though not Ha2 (see Appendix 2) and thus creates a parallel between the earl and the Empress, also a 'strange womman... of fer parties' (280–1). Further parallels include the haste of the earl's arrival at this point and that of the Empress later when she sees a thief in a predicament similar to hers here (in the Latin, both put spurs to their horse; both are moved by pity, cf. 162n.). On the other hand, Hoccleve's realization of the earl's haste, in the phrase 'thidir him hyeth in al þat he may' (276), effects a link with the earlier hunt of the hart (186), so that, where the Latin makes a simple and sustained parallel between the earl and the Empress as active figures and outsiders, Hoccleve complicates the relationship by making the hart and the Empress figures of each other, both hunted by men. Similarly, at 293–7 the earl's negotiations with the Empress before he takes her down from the tree (also in the analogues) make a link of sorts (?unintended) between the earl and the wicked brother-in-law (cf. 217–19).

282–5 On the Empress's secrecy about her origins, material developed by Hoccleve from the source, cf. *MLT* (*CT* II.524–7)

340 *purposid*: the *H variant 'purpose' requires us to read 'malice' adjectivally. OED and MED give few examples, the earliest dated 1447. But since D's reading is repeated, and shared by *H, at 390, *H's reading here is probably scribal.

358 A marginal note in S offers this episode as an exemplum ('nota bene nota exemplum'). Cf. *Series* 2.182n.

389, 393 S highlights these two reasons by marginal 'primo', 'secundo'; D marks the first with a paraph mark.

425 S glosses 'Nota bene nota' (presumably a comment on the sententious quality of the following lines).

447 With this moment, cf. the accord reached between the Empress and the sea-captain (524), the sea-captain and the Empress's servant (576) and between Jonathas and the sea-captain in the second *Gesta* story (5.561). Only the present example has an explicit echo in the analogue ('cum eis convenit').

465–9 the analogues provide the immediate precedent for this passage, but its detail also recalls the portrait of Custance at the start of *MLT*.

482 In this passage, developed from a phrase in the analogues (the suitors speak to her 'de amore inordinato'), Hoccleve refers to Ovid as one of the chief medieval authorities on love. See also VI.191n.

484–97 This passage, pretty certainly added by Hoccleve to his source, contains clear echoes of his own translation of the 'Epistre' of Christine de Pizan (cf. 473), and thus represents a possible response to the terms of his earlier fictional commission to produce a text which would atone for the wrongs done to women in the earlier translation.

529–32 These lines function as an ironic echo of the Emperor's earlier consultation with his wife: he could not conceal his intention from his wife (24); the captain inquires into the servant's ability to keep his plans secret from her (531). The analogues confirm this view by verbal echoes (*karissima/karissime, celari non debet/ consilium meum celaueris*).

541 If 'of my promesse' were read as a phrase dependent on 'gabbe', the two lines would need to be translated, 'if you find I talk idly in respect of what I have promised, then cut my wages'.

544 *aweertee*: MED gives only this example; generally the scribes had difficulties with the word.

621 This line has no parallel in the analogue. Cf. Chaucer's *Troilus* V.1078, *CT* I.4248, V.1480.

659 CD2R mark this speech 'oracio' (D2 adds 'domine imperatoris').

680 E glosses 'marchant'.

701ff. BLSY here indicate the principal antagonists by means of marginal notes: 'the kny3t þat slou3 þe erlis (B emperoures) doughtyr'(701); 'the þeef þat þe emperice saued from þe gallous' (708); 'the shipman' (BLY: S *adds* 'þat bitraied þe emperice') (715).

743–4 These lines ironically echo the earlier moment when the Emperor's wicked brother-in-law, in prison for his attempted seduction of the Empress, learns of his brother's imminent return. They thus indicate that the narrative is about to draw its threads together in a final dénouement. The parallelism is wanting in Ha2 but preserved in other analogues (see Appendix 2), whose wording creates an additional echo of the alleged carrying off of the Empress by a band of men at 244.

776–7 Pearsall 1994: 408 makes the telling point that the prominence of auricular confession as the climax to this and the second *Gesta* story (5.617) acquires significance in the context of contemporary Wycliffite opposition to it, as does the repeated motif of confession elsewhere in Hoccleve's work (e.g. IV.83, VI.66, 2.83, 94), even when treated comically, as in the 'Male Regle'. The other elements of confession— contrition and satisfaction—occur at 2.663–6, 4.478–81.

783 Several MSS here provide the marginal gloss 'humanum est peccare etc.': D2's fuller version adds 'sed diabolicum est perseuerare' and is closer to the wording of *H than D (see apparatus), which may suggest that *H's reading is also authorial (admittedly, the analogues want the material, so it may be that the gloss in D2 is translated from the accompanying English text).

785 S glosses 'the confessioun of the emperours brothir' (cf. following n.).

852ff. CRS divide the narrative with notes about the protagonists: 'the confessioun of the kny3t' (852, R 855); 'the confessioun of þe theef' (883); 'the confessioun of the shipman' (904).

950–2 this material, probably added by Hoccleve to his source, reveals a general indebtedness to its Chaucerian model, *MLT* (cf. II.1132–46, also added to the source), and (so Pryor 1968: 100) serves to prepare for the next item in the collection.

952 A fuller version of the rubric occurs in *H: 'here endiþ a [CBLY my] tale of a good womman which was sometime emperice of Rome and was now sueth a [C the] proloog [BLY add: of the moralisacioun of the same tale].

980 *H rubric: here endith þe prolog and bigynneþ þe moralizing (B moralizacion) [BS add: of þe fornseide (B same) tale].

In the moralization the distinction between the actual narrative and its allegorization is indicated uniquely in S by underlinings of the former. C underlines the Latin quotations in the

present moralization, as does Ha2 among the analogues.

987 *mightes and poweres*: these four powers of the soul ('reson, wil, intellect and conscience') correspond only very loosely to classic medieval formulations of the powers of the soul. Their number probably depends on the number of counsellors in the narrative (101).

995 BCDS gloss 'Maledictus homo qui peccat in spe'.

1034–5 BCD gloss 'munera excecant oculos iudicum etc.' (cf. Deut. 16.19, reading 'munera... sapientum', and Ecclus. 20.31, reading 'xenia et dona... iudicum'). This quotation, and the following, also occur, in reverse order, in a section on penance in the *Fasciculus Morum* (Wenzel 1989: 502).

1035 *equitee or euenehede... torned vpsodoun*. Cf. Is. 59.14.

1040 *etc*. This abbreviation, omitted by BCLY (S has lost a leaf at this point, and its copy resumes at 4.21), has parallels in the moralization to the second *Gesta* narrative (5.721) and at this point in the Latin analogues. Its omission in *H is therefore probably scribal.

1045–7 D glosses 'Ve homini in peccato iacenti etc.' This gloss does not adequately represent the translation, which is better represented by BCR 've homini (C *adds* in) soli peccato iacenti'. Ecclus. 4.10 ('ve soli, quia cum ceciderit, non habet sublevantem se') is the ultimate original of the phrase (cf. *Regement* 205–7), which has been glossed in the analogues so as to make solitude a sign of lying in sin (e.g. Ha2 've soli. id est in peccato iacenti, quia non habet vnde subleuari possit').

1048ff D glosses 'scriptum est, frater qui adiuuatur a fratre etc.' [from Prov. 18.19; BCD2R add 'quasi ciuitas firma [CD2R forma]'. D underlines the English.

1050 *yeueth cold watir*. from Matt. 10.42.

1054–5 D*H gloss 'Ve illis qui dicunt bonum malum et malum bonum etc.' (cf. Is. 5.20).

1057 D glosses 'Ecclesiastes [1.1]: vanitas vanitatum etc.' (C, 'omnia vanitas'). One version of the Latin, Sl, reads 'nauis est mundi uanitas sicut ait Ecclesiastes' [the ship is the vanity of the world as Ecclesiastes says].

1061 *it is impossible*: one MS of the Latin, Sl, makes clear the Biblical origin of this phrase, which conflates several Biblical commonplaces, notably 'you cannot serve God and Mammon'.

1069 *H rubric: 'here endeth þe moralisyng (C amoralisinge) of my tale and begynneth þe moost profitable and holsomest crafte, that is to cunne lerne to dye' (C *for* 'þe moost... to cunne lerne', ' a proces, to lerne').

4. et incipit ars vtillissima sciendi mori. Cum omnes homines naturaliter scire desiderant etc.

[and begins the most useful art of knowing how to die. Since all men naturally desire to know etc.]

'Syn all men naturelly desyre   *since*
To konne, o eterne Sapience,   *know; eternal*
O universel prince, lord and syre,
Auctour of nature, in whos excellence   *author*
5   Been hid all the tresors of science,   *treasures; knowledge*
Makere of al, and þat al seest and woost,   *knowest*
This axe Y thee, thow lord of mightes moost,   *ask*

'Thy tresor of wisdam and the konnynge   *treasury; knowledge*
Of seintes, opne thow to me, Y preye,
10   þat Y therof may haue a knowlechynge.   *understanding*
Enforme eek me and vnto me bywreye,   *also; reveal*
Syn thow of al science berst the keye,   *since; learning; carry; key*
Sotil matires right profownde and greete,   *intricate*
Of whiche Y feruently desire trete.'

15   'O sone myn, sauoure nat so hye,
But dreede, herkne, and Y shal teche thee   *dread; listen*
Thyng þat shal to thy soule fructifie.   *be fruitful*
A chosen yifte shalt thow haue of me.   *special gift*
My lore eternel lyf shal to thee be.   *teaching*
20   The dreede of God which the begynnynge is   *fear*
Of wisdam shalt thow lerne, and it is this.

'Now herkne a doctrine substancial.   *listen to*
First, how lerne dye telle wole Y;   *how to learn to die*
25   The iide, how þat a man lyue shal;   *second*
The iiide, how a man sacramentally   *third (i.e.) in the Eucharist*
Receyue me shal wel and worthyly;
The iiiie, how with an herte cleene and pure   *fourth*
That a man loue me shal and honure.

'Tho thynges iiii, good lord, haue Y euere   *those; four*
30   Desired for to knowe and hem to leere.   *learn*
Vnto myn herte ther is nothyng leuere.   *dearer*
A bettre thyng can Y nat wisshen heer.   *wish*
But tellith me this, this fayn wolde Y heere,
What may profyte the lore of dyynge,   *teaching of death*
35   Syn deeth noon hauynge is but a pryuynge,   *possession; deprivation*

'For shee man reueth of lyf the swetnesse.'   *from man takes*
'Sone, the art to lerne for to dye
Is to the soule an excellent swetnesse,
To which Y rede thow thyn herte applie.   *advise; devote*
40   Ther is noon art þat man can specifie
So profitable ne worthy to be
Preferred artes all as þat is shee.   *before all arts*

'To wite and knowe þat man is mortel   *understand*
It is commune vnto folkes alle.   *common*
45   þat man shal nat lyue ay heer woot he wel.   *knows*
No trust at al may in his herte falle,
That he eschape or flee may dethes galle.   *escape*
But fewe þat can die shalt thow seen.
It is the yifte of God, best þat may been.   *gift*

50   'To lerne for to die is to han ay   *have always*
Bothe herte and soule redy hens to go,
That whan deeth cometh for to cacche hir pray
Man rype be the lyf to twynne fro   *should be ready; depart from*
And hir to take and receyue also
55   As he that the comynge of his felawe   *like one who; friend*
Desirith and is therof glad and fawe.   *pleased*

'But, more harm is, ful many oon shalt thow fynde *many a one*
þat ageyn deeth maken no purueance. *against; provision*
Hem lothen deeth for to haue in hir mynde. *they loathe*
60 þat thoght they holden thoght of encombrance. *burdensome*
Worldly swetnesse sleeth swich remembrance.
And syn to die nat lerned han they, *since*
Fro the world twynne they wolde in no wey. *depart*

'They mochil of hir tyme han despended *much; their; spent*
65 In synne, and forthy whan vnwaarly deeth *therefore; unexpectedly*
Vpon hem fallith, and they nat amendid, *have not repented*
And shal from hem byreue wynd and breeth, *take*
For shee vnreedy fynt hem whan shee sleeth, *finds; unready; strikes*
To hell goon tho soules miserable, *those; wretched*
70 Ther to dwell in peyne perdurable. *everlasting*

'Deeth wolde han ofte a brydil put on thee,
And thee with hir led away shee wolde, *would have*
Nadde the hand of Goddes mercy be. *had not; been (raised)*
Thow art ful mochil vnto þat lord holde *very greatly; obliged*
75 þat, for thow wrappid wer in synnes olde, *for (all that)*
He spared thee. Thy synnes now forsake
And vnto my doctrine thow thee take. *take yourself*

'More to thee profyte shal my lore
Than chosen gold, or the bookes echone *each one*
80 Of philosophres, and, for þat the more
Feruently sholde it stire thy persone
Vndir sensible ensaumple thee to one *sensory example; unite*
To God and thee the bettre for to thewe, *instruct*
The misterie of my lore Y shal thee shewe. *teaching*

85 'Beholde now the liknesse and figure
Of a man dyynge and talkyng with thee.'
The disciple of þat speeche took good cure *paid good heed to that speech*
And in his conceit bysyly soghte he, *mind*
And therwithal considere he gan and see *thereupon*
90 In himself put the figure and liknesse *placed*
Of a yong man of excellent fairnesse

Whom deeth so ny ransakid had and soght   *closely penetrated*
þat he withynne a whyle sholde dye.
And for his soules helthe had he right noght   *nothing at all*
95 Disposid. Al vnreedy hens to hye   *hence; hasten away*
Was he, and therfore he began to crye
With lamentable vois in this maneere,
þat sorwe and pitee greet was it to heere:

'Enuirond han me dethes waymentynges.   *surrounded; lamentations*
100 Sorwes of helle han conpaced me.   *encompassed*
Allas, eternel God, o kyng of kynges,
Wherto was Y born, in this world to be?   *why*
O allas, why in my natiuitee
Nadde I perisshid? O, the begynnynge   *did not I perish*
105 Of my lyf was with sorwe and with weepynge,

'And now myn ende comth. Hens moot Y go   *must*
With sorwe, waylynge and greet heuynesse.
O deeth, thy mynde is ful of bittir wo   *the thought of you*
Vnto an herte wont vnto gladnesse,   *used*
110 And norisshid in delicat swetnesse.
Horrible is thy presence, and ful greeuable,   *hurtful*
To him þat yong is, strong and prosperable.   *prosperous*

'Litil wende Y so soone to han deid.   *thought; died*
O cruel deeth, thy comynge is sodeyn.
115 Ful vnwaar was Y of thy theefly breid.   *unaware; stealthy attack*
Thow haast as in awayt vpon me leyn.   *ambush*
Thy comynge vnto me was vncerteyn.
Thow haast vpon me stolen and me bownde.
Eschape Y may nat now my mortel wownde.   *escape*

120 'Thow me with thee drawist in yren cheynes,
As a man dampned wont is to be drawe   *condemned; drawn*
To his torment. Outrageous been my peynes.
A, now for sorwe and fere of thee and awe,
With handes clight Y crye and wolde fawe   *joined; gladly*
125 Wite the place whidir for to flee.   *know; where*
But swich oon fynde can Y noon, ne see.   *such a one*

'I looke on euery syde bisyly,
But help is noon. Help and confort been dede.   *none*
A vois horrible of deeth sownynge heer Y,   *speaking*
130 þat seith me thus, which encressith my drede: *to me; increases*
"Thow dye shalt. Reson noon ne kynrede,   *family*
Frendshipe, gold ne noon othir richesse
May thee deliure out of dethes duresse.   *hardship*

"'Thyn eende is comen; comen is thyn eende.
135 It is decreed. Ther is no resistence."
Lord God, shal Y now die and hennes weende?   *depart hence*
Whethir nat changed may be this sentence?   *judgement*
O Lord, may it nat put been in suspense?   *be deferred*
Shal Y out of this world so soone go?
140 Allas, wole it noon othir be than so?   *will*

'O deeth, o deeth, greet is thy crueltee.
Thyn office al to sodeynly doost thow.
Is ther no grace? Lakkist thow pitee?
Spare my youthe. Of age rype ynow   *mature enough*
145 To dye am Y nat yit. Spare me now.
How cruel þat thow art, on me nat kythe.   *do not show*
Take me nat out of this world so swythe.'   *quickly*

Whan the disciple this conplaynte had herd,
He thoghte al þat he spak nas but folie,   *was merely*
150 And in this wyse he hath him answerd: *way*
'Thy wordes, freend, withouten any lye
þat thow haast but smal lerned testifie.   *little; witness*
Euene to alle is dethes iugement.   *equal*
Thurghout the world strecchith hir paiement.

155 'Deeth fauorable is to no maner wight.   *no sort of person*
To all hirself shee delith equally.   *shares*
Shee dredith hem nat þat been of greet might,   *fears*
Ne of the olde and yonge hath no mercy.
The ryche and poore folk eek certainly   *also*
160 Shee sesith. Shee sparith right noon estaat.   *seizes; class*
Al þat lyf berith with hir chek is maat.   *bears; check; mated*

'Ful many a wight in youthe takith shee   *person*
And many anothir eek in middil age,   *also*
And some nat til they right olde be.
165 Wendist thow han been at swich auantage   *did you think*
þat shee nat durste han paied thee thy wage,
But oonly han thee spared and forborn,   *tolerated*
And the prophetes deid han heerbeforn?'   *died*

Than spak th'ymage answerynge in this wyse: *way*
170 'Soothly thow art an heuy confortour.
Thow vndirstandist me nat as the wyse.
They þat continued han in hir errour,   *their*
Lyuynge in synne vnto hir dethes hour,
Worthy be dampned for þat they han wroght,   *(are) worthy (to); what*
175 And how ny deeth is they ne dreede noght.   *near*

'Tho men ful blynde been and bestial.   *those*
Of þat shal folwe aftir this lyf present   *what*
Forsighte swiche folk han noon at all.   *such*
I nat bewaille dethes iugement,
180 But this is al the cause of my torment.
The harm of vndisposid deeth Y weepe.   *unprepared*
I am nat reedy in the grownd to creepe.

'I weepe nat þat Y shal hennes twynne,   *hence depart*
But of my dayes I the harm bewaille,
185 Fruytlees past sauf with bittir fruyt of synne.   *save*
I wroghte in hem nothyng þat mighte auaille
To soules helthe. Y dide no trauaille   *took no pains*
To lyue wel, but lened to the staf
Of worldly lustes. To hem Y me yaf.   *pleasures; gave*

190 'The way of trouthe Y lefte and drow to wrong.   *drew*
On me nat shoon the light of rightwisnesse.   *shone*
The sonne of intellect nat in me sprong.   *did not. . . rise*
Y am weery of my wroght wikkidnesse.
Y walkid haue weyes of hardnesse   *difficulty*
195 And of perdicion. Nat kowde Y knowe
The way of God. Wikkid seed haue Y sowe.   *sown*

'Allas, what hath pryde profytid me,
Or what am Y bet for richesse hepynge? *better; heaping up riches*
Alle they as a shadwe passid be, *like*
200 And as a messager faste rennynge, *messenger; running*
And also as a ship þat is sayllynge
In the wawes and floodes of the see, *waves; waters*
Whos kerf nat fownden is whan past is shee. *keel leaves no trace*

'Or as a brid which in the eir þat fleeth, *bird; flies*
205 No preef fownde is of the cours of his flight. *evidence*
No man espie can it, ne it seeth, *sees*
Sauf with his wynges the wynd softe and light *save*
He betith, and cuttith th'eir by the might
Of swich stirynge, and foorth he fleeth his way, *flies*
210 And tookne, aftir þat, no man see ther may. *sign*

'Or as an arwe shot out of a bowe
Twynneth the eir which þat continuelly *divides; air*
Agayn is closid, þat man may nat knowe
Wher þat it paste—no wight the way sy— *person; saw*
215 Right so, syn þat Y born was far haue Y. *since; behaved*
Continuelly Y stynted for to be, *ceased*
And tokne of vertu shewid noon in me. *sign*

'I am consumed in my wikkidnesse.
Myn hope is as it wer a wolle-loke *lock of wool*
220 Which the wynd vp reisith for his lightnesse,
Or smal foom þat desparplid is, and broke *thin foam; scattered; broken*
With tempest, or as with wynd waastith smoke, *wastes*
Or as mynde of an oost þat but a day *memory; host*
Abit, and aftir passith foorth his way. *remains*

225 'For why, my speeche is now in bittirnesse,
And my wordes been ful of sorwe and wo.
Myn herte is plunged deepe in heuynesse.
My yen been al dymme and dirke also. *eyes; dark*
Who may me grante þat Y may be so
230 As I was whan Y beautee hadde and strengthe,
And had beforn me many a dayes lengthe

'In whiche Y the harm mighte han seen beforn,
þat now is on me falle? I yaf no charge   *fallen; gave no care*
Of the good precious tyme. I haue it lorn.   *lost*
235 But as the worldly wynd bleew in my barge   *(the sails of) my ship*
Foorth droof Y therwith, and leet goon at large *free*
Al loos the brydil of concupiscence,
And ageyn vertu made Y resistence.

'My dayes I despente in vanitee.   *spent*
240 Noon heede Y took of hem, but leet hem passe,
Nothyng considerynge hir precioustee,   *not at all; preciousness*
But heeld myself free born as a wylde asse.
Of th'aftirclap insighte had no man lasse.   *unexpected blow; less*
I ouerblynd was. Y nat sy ne dredde   *saw*
245 With what wo deeth wolde haste me to bedde.

'And now, as fisshes been with hookes kaght,   *caught*
And as þat briddes been take in a snare,   *birds; taken*
Deth hath me hent. Eschape may Y naght.   *seized; escape*
This vnwaar woful hour me makith bare   *unexpected*
250 Of my custumed ioie and my welfare.   *accustomed*
The tyme is past. The tyme is goon for ay.
No man reuoke or calle ageyn it may.   *recall*

'So short was nat the tyme þat is goon
But Y of goostly lucres and wynnynges   *spiritual profits*
255 Mighte haue in it purchaced many oon,   *many a one*
Exceedynge in value alle eerthely thynges
Inconparablely, but to his wynges
The tyme hath take him, and no purueance   *provision*
Therin made I my soule to auance.   *better*

260 'Allas, I, caytif, for angwissh and sorwe   *wretch*
My teeres trikelen by my cheekes doun.
No salt watir me needith begge or borwe.
Myn yen flowen now in greet foysoun.   *eyes; abundance*
Allas, this is a sharp conclusioun,
265 Thogh Y the tyme past conpleyne and mourne. *complain*
For al my care wole it nat retourne.

'O my lord God, how laach and negligent   *lax*
Haue Y been. Why haue I put in delay
And taryynge myn amendement?
270 Wherto haue Y dissimuled, welaway?   *dissembled; alas*
Allas, so many a fair and gracious day
Haue Y lost, and arn fro me goon and ronne,   *(they) are; run away*
þat mighte in hem my soules helthe han wonne.   *(I) who*

'Myn hertes woful waymentacions   *lamentations*
275 Who can hem telle? Who can hem expresse?
Now fallen on me accusacions
Wondirly thikke of my wrogt wikkidnesse.   *fearfully frequent*
In flesshly lust and ydil bysynesse   *pleasure; empty*
Leet Y my dayes dryue foorth and slippe,   *let; pass; slip away*
280 And nat was beten with penances whippe.

'Why sette Y so myn herte in vanitee?
O why ne had Y lerned for to die?
Why was Y nat ferd of Goddes maugree?   *displeasure*
What eilid me to bathe in swich folie?
285 Why nadde reson goten the maistrie   *mastery*
Of me? Why? For my spirit was rebel,
And list nat vndirstonde to do wel.   *pleased; (how) to act rightly*

'O alle yee þat heer been present,
Yee þat floure in youthes lusty grennesse,   *pleasant*
290 And seen how deeth his bowe hath for me bent,
And tyme couenable han to redresse   *convenient; make good*
þat your vnruly youthes wantonnesse   *what*
Offendid hath, considereth my miserie.   *done wrong*
The stormy seson folwith dayes merie.

295 'Let me be your ensaumple and your mirour,   *example*
Lest yee slippe into my plyt miserable.   *plight*
With God, despende of your youthe the flour.   *spend; flower*
If yee me folwe, into peril semblable   *similar*
Yee entre shuln. To God yee yow enable.   *make yourselves fit*
300 In holy wirkes your tyme occupie,
And, whyle it tyme is, vices mortifie.   *there is time*

'Allas, o youthe, how art thow fro me slipt.
O God eterne, Y vnto thee conpleyne   *lament*
The wrecchidnesses in whiche Y am clipt.   *embraced*
305 Lost is my youthe. Y smerte in euery veyne   *suffer pain*
The gilt þat wroght hath my synful careyne.   *(for) the guilt; flesh*
O youthe, thy fresshnesse and iolitee   *pleasure*
Hatith thy soothes be told vnto thee.   *truths*

'No lust had Y to doon as Y was taght.   *pleasure; taught*
310 Therof had Y right greet desdeyn and hokir.   *scorn*
Whan men conseillid wel, Y herde it naght.   *counselled; not*
Nat so moche as by an olde boote or cokir   *boot or legging*
Sette Y therby. Into myn hertes lokir   *locker*
Entre mighte noon holsum disciplyne.   *no*
315 No wil had Y to good conseil enclyne.   *to bow*

'Lord God, now in a deep dych am Y falle.   *ditch; fallen*
Into the snare of deeth entred am Y.
Bet had it been than thus had it befalle   *better*
Neuere han be born of my modres body,   *to have been born; mother's*
320 But therin han perisshid vttirly,
For Y despente in pryde and in bobance   *spent; pomp*
The tyme grantid me to do penance.'

To which answerde the disciple tho: *then*
'Lo, we die alle, and as watir we slyde
325 Into the eerthe, which þat neuere mo
Retourne shal, but on a sikir syde   *certain*
We standen alle, for God nat wole hyde
His mercy fro man. Whoso list it craue,   *pleases to*
Be repentant, and mercy axe and haue.   *request*

330 'God haastith nat the gilt of man to wreke,   *hastens; take vengeance for*
But curteisly abydith repentance.   *kindly; waits for*
Heer me now what Y shal to thee speke.
For þat thow haast offendid do penance.   *what; done wrong*
Torne vnto God with hertes obeissance.   *obedience*
335 Axe him mercy þat is al merciable,   *ask; merciful*
And saued shalt thow been; it is no fable.'

Th'ymage of deeth answerde anoon to þat: *at once*
'How spekist thow, man? Shal Y me repente, *what*
Shal Y me torne? O man, ne seest thow nat, *convert*
340 Ne takist thow noon heede ne entente *pay; attention*
Of dethes angwisshes þat me tormente,
And oppressen so greuously and sharpe *sharply*
That Y not what to do or thynke or carpe? *don't know; speak*

'As a partrich þat with the hawk is hent *partridge; seized*
345 And streyned with his clees so is agast *grasped; claws; afraid*
þat his lyf ny from him is goon and went, *almost; passed and gone*
Right so my wit is cleene fro me past, *completely; passed away*
And in my mynde is ther no thoght ne cast *plan*
Othir than serche a way how deeth eschape, *to escape*
350 But Y in veyn theraftir looke and cape. *gape*

'Nat wole it be, for deeth me doun oppressith. *presses*
The twynnynge of my lyf ful bittir is, *separation*
þat hurtith me greuously and distressith.
Ful holsum had it be to me or this *before*
355 Penance han doon for þat Y wroghte amis *to have done; what*
Whyles my tyme was in his rypnesse, *maturity*
For þat had been the way of sikirnesse. *safety*

'But he þat late to penance him takith, *betakes*
Whethir he verraily or feynyngly *truly; dissemblingly*
360 Repente, he noot. Vncertain it him makith. *does not know*
Wo is me þat my lyf so synfully
I ledde, and to correcte it lachid Y. *delayed*
Ageyn my soules helthe haue Y werreied, *against; waged war*
þat for it haue no bettre purueied. *provided*

365 'Allas, to longe hath be the taryynge
And the delay of my correccioun.
A good purpos withoute begynnynge,
Good wil withouten operacioun,
Good promesse and noon execucioun,
370 Foorth dryue amendes fro morwe to morwe *(to) defer; day to day*
And neuere doon—þat causith al my sorwe. *to do (it)*

'O morwe, morwe, thow haast me begilt.   *tomorrow; deceived*

O whethir this miserie nat exceede   *surely this misery exceeds*

Al worldly wrecchidnesse? Allas, my gilt.

375 Wel worthy is it þat myn herte bleede,

And with angwissh and wo me fostre and feede.   *nourish*

See how my dayes alle arn slipt me fro.

xxxti yeer of myn age away been go.   *thirty years*

'Ful wrecchidly, God woot, Y haue hem lost,   *knows*

380 And al myn owne self is it to wyte.   *to blame*

So good a piler was Y neuere, or post,   *support*

Vnto my soule, as o day me delyte   *one; to take pleasure*

In vertu or aght wel to God me qwyte,   *at all; behave*

As þat Y mighte haue doon or oghte.

385 By aght Y woot, Y neuere aftir þat soghte.   *anything; know*

'Lord God, how shamefully stande Y shal

At the doom beforn thee and seintes alle,   *before*

Wher Y shal arted be to rekne of al   *compelled; give account*

That Y doon haue and left. Whom shal Y calle

390 To helpe me? O, how shal it befalle?

My torment and my wo me haaste and hye   *rush*

Hens for to twynne. As blyue shal Y dye.   *hence; depart; quickly*

'O now this hour gretter ioie and gladnesse

I wolde haue of a litil orisoun   *prayer*

395 By me seyd with hertes deuout sadnesse,   *earnestness*

As the angelyk salutacioun,   *(such) as*

Than Y wolde haue of many a milioun

Of gold and siluer. Foule haue Y me born,   *foully; behaved*

And synfully, þat sy nat this beforn.   *saw; before*

400 'Whan Y mighte haue it seen, than wolde Y
      noght.

How many houres haue Y lost þat neuere

Retorne shuln! How mochil haue Y wroght

Ageyn myself! My lust was to perseuere   *pleasure*

In vicious lyf and from it nat disseuere.   *separate*

405 I lefte þat good was, and necessarie,   *what*

Vnto my soule, and dide the contrarie.

'More than was neede or expedient   *needful*
Vnto the help of many anothir wight   *person*
Entendid Y. Y was ful inprudent.   *attended; imprudent*
410 I took noon heede to myself aright.   *paid no attention*
By soules profyt sette Y nat but light.   *little*
Whan tyme was, fynde kowde Y no tyme
Me to correcte of myn offense and cryme.

'But now feele Y þat vnto the gretnesse   *for*
415 Of merites celestial had been bet   *it would have been better*
My wittes han kept with soules clennesse   *to have preserved*
Than, þat left, with herte corruptly set,   *leaving that; on corruption*
And ageyn deedes vertuous ywhet,   *against; stirred up*
Helpe me mighte any mannes preyere,
420 Thogh xxxti yeer he preid had for me heere.   *thirty*

'O herkneth now, herkneth now alle yee
þat heer been and seen my wrecchidnesse.
The tyme, as þat yee seen, now faillith me.
My freendes preide Y þat they sum almesse,   *alms*
425 Of th'abundance of hir goostly richesse   *from; spiritual riches*
And wirkes goode, wolden to me dele   *bestow on me*
In my greet neede for my soules hele,   *salvation*

'And eek in releef and amendement   *also; lessening*
Of my giltes, but hir answer was nay.   *their*
430 They seiden, "Ther to yeuen our assent,   *give*
Wole we nat in no maneere way,   *we will not at all*
Lest it vs and yow nat souffyse may."   *suffice*
On euery part thus am Y destitut.   *side*
Fynde can Y no socour ne refut.   *refuge*

435 'O God benigne, o fadir merciable,   *merciful*
Beholde and reewe vpon thy pacient.   *have mercy; sufferer*
To me, thyn handwerk, be thow socourable.   *handiwork; helpful*
þat Y greetly haue erred and miswent,   *gone astray*
Me wel remembrith this tyme present.   *recalls to mind*
440 Allas, why stood Y in myne owne light
So foule? O lord, me now helpe of thy might.   *foully*

'How grete richesses spirituel
And heuenely tresors, had Y been wys,   *treasures*
Mighte Y han gadered, and nat dide a del.   *nothing at all*
445 O good lord God, o lord of paradys,
Ful leef to me now wer, and of greet prys,   *dear; most precious*
Of satisfaccion the leeste deede.
Right dereworthe wer it in þis neede.   *precious; (time of) need*

'O now the leeste cromes þat ther falle   *crumbs*
450 Fro the lordes bordes and tables doun   *boards*
Refresshe wolden me ful wel withalle,   *moreover*
But noon fynde Y of swich condicion
þat yeue me wole any porcioun.   *give*
Y haue espyd the frendshipe is ful streit   *learned that; narrow/difficult*
455 Of this world. It is mirour of deceit.

'Reewe eek on me, yee alle, and pitee haue,   *have pity; all of you*
And whyles your force and vigour may laste,
And tyme han eek, or yee be ny your graue,   *also; before; near*
Into bernes of heuene gadereth faste   *barns*
460 Tresors celestial, þat at the laste   *treasures*
Yee may receyue, whan þat yee shul twynne   *depart*
From hens, the blisse þat shal neuere blynne.   *here; cease*

'And beeth nat voide of vertu, ne empty,
Whan þat the deeth anothir day to yow
465 Approche shal, as yee may see þat Y
Am voide of deedes vertuous right now.'
'Freend', quod the disciple, 'Y see wel ynow   *enough*
Thy torment and thy greuous passioun,
Of which myn herte hath greet conpassioun,

470 'And by almighty God I thee coniure   *adjure*
þat thow me yeue reed how me to gye,   *give counsel; to conduct myself*
Lest þat heeraftir Y, par auenture,   *by chance*
Into lyk peril haaste may and hye
Of vndisposid sodein deeth, and drye   *unprepared; endure*
475 The wo which Y consider þat thee vexith,   *see*
Wherthurgh myn herte sore agrysid wexith.'   *grows greatly afraid*

Than spak th'ymage, 'The best purueance   *provision*
And wit is, han verray contricioun   *to have true*
In strengthe and hele of the misgouernance   *while strong and in health, for*
480 Of thy lyf, and plener confessioun   *full*
Make of thy gilt, and satisfaccioun
And asseeth do, and all vices leue   *amends*
þat thee mighten the blisse of heuene reue.   *from you; take*

'And so with al thyn herte it is the beste
485 Keepe thee foorth as þat thow this day right,   *continue; as if; very*
Or tomorwe or this wike atte fertheste,
Sholdist departe fro this worldes light,
And therwithal enforce thow thy might,   *therewith; do all you can*
As Y shal seyn, in thyn herte to thynke,
490 And thow shalt it nat reewe ne forthynke.   *be sorry for; repent*

'Caste in thyn herte as now thy soule wer   *reckon; as if*
In purgatorie and hadde pyned be   *tormented*
x. yeer in a fourneys brennynge ther,   *ten; burning*
And this oonly yeer wer grantid thee   *one*
495 For thyn help. So beholde often and see
Thy soule in the flaumbes of fyr brennynge,   *flames*
With a wrecchid vois thus to thee cryynge:

'Of all freendes, thow, the derwortheste,   *dearest*
Do to thy wrecchid soule help and socour,
500 þat is al desolat. Purchace it reste.
See how Y brenne. O, reewe on my langour.   *have pity; disease*
Be for me so freendly a purueyour   *provider*
þat in this hoot prisoun Y no lenger   *hot; longer*
Tormentid be. Lat it nat thus me der.   *harm*

505 'The worldes fauour cleene is fro me went.   *completely; gone*
Forsake Y am. Frendshipe Y can noon fynde.
Ther is no wight þat to the indigent   *person; needy*
Puttith his helply hand. Slipt out of mynde   *helping*
I am. In peynes sharpe Y walwe and wynde,   *twist and turn*
510 And of my wo ther is no wight þat recchith.   *person; cares*
Nat knowe Y frendshipe or to whom it strecchith.

'Men seeken thynges þat to hemself longe,   *belong*
And me leuen in the flaumbes vengeable.   *vengeful*
O good freend, lat me nat thus pyne longe.'   *suffer*
515 To which the disciple, with cheer stable   *settled countenance*
Seide, 'Thy lore were profitable   *teaching*
Whoso it hadde by experience   *to anyone who*
As thow haast. Therto yeue may Y credence.   *give*

'But thogh thy wordes sharpe and stiryng seeme,   *moving*
520 To many a man profyten they but lyte.   *little*
They looke apart and list take no yeeme   *aside; please; heed*
Vnto the ende which mighte hem profyte.
Yen they haan and seen nat worth a myte,   *eyes; nothing of any worth*
And eres han also, and may nat heer.
525 They weenen longe for to lyuen heer.   *think*

'And, for they vndisposid deeth nat dreede,   *unprepared*
Forsighte at al ne haan tho wreches noon   *those; none*
Of the harm which therof moot folwe neede.   *must needs follow*
They deemen stonde as sikir as a stoon.   *think to stand; certain*
530 But weel Y see by thee, so moot Y goon,   *as I hope to thrive*
They shuln haan cause it for to dreede and doute,   *fear*
Or þat hir lyues light be fully oute.   *before*

'Whan dethes messager comth, sharp seeknesse,   *messenger; sickness*
Freendes and felawes hem haaste and hye,   *companions; hurry*
535 The seek man to conforte of his feblesse,   *in his weakness*
And al thyng þat good is they prophecie.   *everything; predict*
They seyn, "Thogh thow seek in thy bed now lye,
Be nat agast. No dethes euel haast thow,   *afraid; mortal evil*
For this thow shalt eschape wel ynow."   *escape; enough*

540 'Thus bodyes freendes been maad enemys   *are made*
To the soule, for, whyl seeknesse greeueth
The man continuelly, yit so vnwys
Is he þat his enformours he wel leeueth.   *informants; believes*
He hopith to been hool and he mischeeueth   *is unfortunate*
545 Wheras he wende han recouered be.   *where*
Vndisposid to dye sterueth he.   *unprepared; dies*

'Right so thyn herkners and thyn auditours,   *hearers*
Tho þat greet trust han in mannes prudence,   *those*
Nat list hir peynes putte, or hir labours,   *do not care. . . to take*
550 To execute thyn holsum sentence.   *opinion*
Thow mightist as wel keepe thy silence.   *keep silent*
They by thy wordes yeuen nat a leek.'   *give*
To which, th'ymage thus answerde and speek: *spoke*

'Forthy, whan they in dethes net been hent,   *therefore; seized*
555 Whan sodein wrecchidnesse hem shal assaille,
Whan deeth, as tempest sharp and violent   *like a; forceful*
With woful trouble hem shal vexe and trauaille,
They shuln crie aftir help and therof faill,
For they in hate sapience hadde,   *wisdom*
560 And despysed my reed and heeld it badde.   *advice; held*

'And right as now ther been but fewe fownde,
þat, of my wordes conpunct, wole hir lyf   *pricked with compunction; their*
Correcte, ne amende in no stownde,   *at any time*
Nat may to hem auaille my motyf,   *proposition*
565 But they hir synnes vsen ay foorth ryf,   *practise; continually; plentiful*
And han no lust fro synnes hem withdrawe,   *desire*
No more than they neuere had herd my sawe.   *than (if); speech*

'Right so, for the malice of tyme and lak   *of (this present) age*
Of goostly loue, and for the iniquitee   *spiritual*
570 Of the world, vertu gooth so faste abak,   *retreats*
þat fewe to the deeth disposid be   *are prepared for death*
So weel þat list this worldes vanitee   *well; (they) please*
Leue, and for desir of lyf þat shal euere   *to leave*
Endur, coueiten hens to disseuere.   *last; desire; depart*

575 'But whan deeth on hem stelith with hir darte,
They vnreedy, wowndid in conscience,
Nat oonly goon hens whan they hens departe,
But they with a manere of violence   *sort*
Been hent away, so þat ful greet prudence   *carried*
580 They wolde han hold it han deid as a man,   *reckoned; died*
And nat as a beest þat no reson can.   *knows*

'If of this commun peril th'encheson   *reason*
Thee lyke knowe, Y wole it now expresse.   *it pleases you*
The desir of honours out of reson,   *beyond measure*
585 The body bathynge in worldly swetnesse,
Eerthely loue, and to greet greedynesse
In mukhepynge, blynden many an herte,   *heaping up muck*
And causen men into tho perils sterte.   *those; to leap*

'If thow desire the perils to flee
590 Of vndisposed deeth, my conseil heer.   *unprepared; hear my advice*
This heuy plyt in which thow seest now me,   *plight*
Reuolue ofte in thy mynde, and by me leere   *learn*
For to be waar. If thow in this maneere   *alert; manner*
Wilt do, it shal be thy greet auantage   *greatly to your profit*
595 And ese thee at thy laste passage.   *departing*

'It shal vnto thee profyte in þat hour
þat nat oonly dye it shal nat thee gaste,   *to die; frighten*
But deeth eek, as eende of worldly labour
And begynnynge of blisse ay þat shal laste,
600 Abyde thow shalt, and desire faste   *await*
With al thyn herte it to take and receyue,
And al worldly lust leye apart and weyue.   *pleasure; forsake*

'Euery day haue of me deep remembrance.
Into thyn herte let my wordes synke.
605 The sorwe and angwissh and greuous penance
Which thow haast seen in me, considere and
   thynke
That of peril tho[w] art ful ny the brynke.   *near*
Remembre on my doom, for swich shal thyn be: *such*
Myn yistirday, and this day vnto thee.

610 'Looke vpon me and thynke on this nyght ay   *always*
Whyles thow lyuest. O how good and blessid
Art thow, Arsenius, which þat alway
This ilke hour haddest in thyn herte impressid.
þat man, as in holy writ is witnessid,
615 Which whan God comth and knokkith at the yate, *gate*
Wakynge him fynt, he blessid is algate.   *finds; without doubt*

'Blessid is he þat thanne fownden is
Reedy to passe, for he blisfully *ready*
Departe shal, and truste right wel this:
620 Thogh deeth assaille and vexe greuously
The rightwys man, or slee him sodeynly, *righteous; attack*
Howso he dye he shal go to þat place *however*
Wheras confort is, refresshynge and grace. *where*

'He shal be pourged cleene and purified *purged*
625 And disposid the glorie of God to see;
Angels shuln keepe him and he shal be gyed *guided*
And led by citeins of the hy contree, *citizens; high*
And to the court of heuene vp taken be,
And of his spirit shal be the issynge *departing*
630 Into eternel blisse the entrynge.

'But allas, wher shal my wrecchid goost *what will become of; spirit*
This nyght become? Whidir shal it go?
What herbergh shal it haue, or in what coost *lodging; region*
Shal it arryue? Who shal receyue it, who?
635 O, what frendshipe shal it haue tho? *then*
O soule abiect, desolat and forsake, *forsaken*
Greet cause haast thow for fere and wo to qwake.

'Wherfore Y, hauynge of myself pitee,
Amonges heuy wordes Y out shede *pour out*
640 Teres in greet habundance and plentee,
But nat auaillith me, it is no drede, *it helps not at all*
Hensfoorth conpleyne, weepe and crye and grede, *(to) complain; wail*
For in no wyse changed it be may. *way*
Al mankyndes fo stoppid hath my way.

645 'In hidles in awayt as a leoun *hiding; ambush; like*
He hath leyn, and my soule led hath he
Into the pit of deeth al deepe adoun.
O my lord God, this sharp aduersitee
To stynte of speeche now conpellith me. *cease*
650 Y may no more hensfoorth speke and bewaille.
My tonge and eek my wit now so me faille.

'Ther is noon othir, Y see wel ynow.   *enough*
The tyme is come. As blyue Y shal be deed.   *forthwith; dead*
See how my face wexith pale now,
655 And my look ful dym and heuy as leed.   *lead*
Myn yen synke eek deepe into myn heed,   *eyes; also*
And torne vpsodoun, and myn hondes two   *upside-down*
Wexen al stif and starke and may nat do.   *rigid; may do nothing*

'Prikkynges of deeth me, wrecche, conpace.   *surround*
660 Stirtemeel gooth my pows and elles naght.   *by starts; goes; pulse; not at all*
Mortel pressures sharply me manace.   *deadly; threaten*
My breeth begynneth faille, and eek the draght   *also; drawing*
Of it fro fer is fet and deepe caght.   *far; fetched; deeply caught*
No lenger Y now see this worldes light.   *longer*
665 Myn yen lost han hir office and might.   *eyes; their*

'But now Y see with myn yen mental   *eyes of my mind*
Th'estat of al anothir world than this.   *condition*
I am ny goon. As faste passe Y shal.   *nearly*
O my lord God, a gastful sighte it is.   *fearful*
670 Now of confort haue Y greet lak and mis.   *privation*
Horrible feendes and innumerable
Awayte vpon my soule miserable.

'The blakefaced Ethiopiens   *black-faced*
Me enuyrone, and aftir it abyde   *surround; wait for it*
675 To hente it whan þat it shal passen hens,   *seize*
If þat parauenture it so betyde   *perchance; happen*
þat the lot therof fall vpon hir syde.   *its allotting;*
Hir viserly faces grim and hydous   *masklike; hideous*
Me putte in thoghtful dreedes encombrous.   *anxious and distressing fears*

680 'O streit and steerne iuge and domesman,   *strict*
Thow weyest moche, in deemynge me, wrecche,   *weighest; judging*
Tho thynges whiche fewe folkes can   *those*
But smal by sette, or of hem charge or recche.   *do other than; little; care for*
Lo, deethes strook haastith me hens to fecche.   *stroke*
685 My membres shee so thirlith and distressith   *limbs; pierces; afflicts*
That nature ouercome is, shee witnessith.   *she herself (i.e. Nature)*

'O gastful is the iust iuges lookynge   *frightening; look*
Vnto me, now present thurgh fere and dreede,   *in fear and trembling*
Which sodeynly shal come, himself sheewynge.   *revealing*
690 Farwel, freendes and felawes, for neede   *fellows; needs*
Moot Y vnclothe me of lyues weede.   *must; garment (i.e. flesh)*
To purgatorie Y shal as streight as lyne,   *shall (go); plummet*
For myn offenses ther to suffre pyne,   *pain*

'And thens twynne Y nat til maad haue Y gree   *depart; satisfaction*
695 Of the leeste ferthyng þat Y men shal,   *for; have in mind*
In whiche place Y beholde and see
Affliccioun and sorwe ynow at al,   *more than enough*
Ther Y no ioie see but wo oueral.   *where; everywhere*
The fyry flaumbes vpon heighte ryse
700 In which the soules brenne in woodly wyse.   *burn; furiously*

'They vp now possid been and now doun throwe,   *pushed; cast*
Right as sparcles of fyr aboute sprede   *sparks; scattered*
Whan þat a greet toun set is on a lowe,   *fire*
And al is fyred bothe in lengthe and brede.   *on fire; breadth*
705 Wo been tho soules in tho brondes rede,   *wretched; those; brands*
For peyne of which torment ful lowde and hye
They in this wyse ful pitously crye: *way; pitifully*

'"Now mercy haue on our captiuitee.
To yow, our freendes, namely we preye.   *especially*
710 Wher is your help now? Wher is your chiertee?   *affection*
Whidir been the promesses goon to pleye
Of yow, our cousins eek? Can yee portreye   *also; depict*
Your wordes so gayly, and effect noon   *no effect*
Folwith, but al as deed is as a stoon?   *follows; dead; stone*

715 "By youre desires inordinat,   *by (following)*
And eek of othir mo, ourself han we   *also those of many others*
Broght into this plyt and wrecchid estat.   *state*
Ioie han we noon, but of wo greet plentee.
Allas, why nat vpon vs reewen yee?   *do you not have pity*
720 We dide al our might to do yow plesance,   *please you*
And yee no routhe han on our sharp greuance.   *pity; pain*

"'Ful euele we rewarded been of yow. *very badly; repaid by*
We brenne, and yee the fyr nat qwenche a deel. *burn; at all*
Allas, we nadden for ourself or now *that we hadn't; before*
725 Ydoon. We wer auysid nothyng weel. *done (good); not at all*
Worldly trust is as slipir as an eel. *slippery*
Al is nat treewe þat the world promettith. *promises*
Ful wys is he þat therby litil settith. *sets little store by it*

"'The leeste torment of this purgatorie
730 þat we souffren excedith in sharpnesse
Tormentes alle of the world transitorie.
Heer of torment more is the bittirnesse
In an hour than the worldes wikkidnesse
May hurte or greeue in an c. yeer. *hundred*
735 Greet is th'affliccioun þat we han heer.

"'But aboue alle kyndes of tormentis,
Of Goddes blissid face the absence
Greeueth moost. þat lak, our moost [wofull *sensation*
  sent is]".
For a memorie leue Y this sentence *memorial; message*
740 To thee, and heer Y die in thy presence.'
Whan the disciple sy þat he was past *saw*
And deed, he tremblid and was sore agast. *dead; sorely afraid*

Aboute he torned him, and thus seide he:
'Wher art thow now, o Sapience eterne? *eternal*
745 O, good lord, haast þou now forsaken me?
Wilt thow thy grace me denye and werne? *refuse*
Thow seidest sapience Y sholde lerne,
And now Y am broght to the deeth almoost,
So troublid is my spirit and my goost. *soul*

750 'This sighte of deeth so sore me astoneth *sorely; astonishes*
þat wite Y can vnnethe, in soothfastnesse, *know; scarcely; truth*
But am in doute wher the soothe woneth— *uncertain; dwells*
That is to meene, if this be in liknesse *that means; a likeness*
Or in deede, swich is my mazidnesse. *reality; bewilderment*
755 But how it be, lord, Y byseeche thee *however it is,*
Be my confort in this perplexitee.

'Neuere the perils of deeth vndisposid   *unprepared*
In my lyf kneew I, as Y do now right.   *knew; duly*
Withyn myn herte been they deepe enclosid,
760   And so sadly therin picchid and pight   *firmly; pitched and made fast*
þat hem foryete lyth nat in my might.   *(to) forget lies not*
That gastful sighte Y hope shal profyte   *fearful*
Vnto my soules helthe nat a lyte.   *greatly*

'Dwellynge place, Y haue espyd and see,   *discovered*
765   Han we noon in this wrecchid world changeable.
For why, vnto þat blisful hy contree   *therefore*
Which nat may varie but is permanable   *permanent*
Shape Y me strecche. O lord God merciable,   *plan; to direct myself*
Y mercy axe. Vpon me, wrecche, reewe.   *ask; have pity*
770   Hensforward wole Y lede a lyf al neewe.

'Now lerne for to die Y me purpose.   *to learn; propose*
Hensfoorth penance wole Y nat delaye.   *postpone*
My lyf to amende wole Y me dispose.
For, syn thoghtes of deeth so me esmaye,   *since; frighten*
775   Wel more, Y am seur, deeth me shal affraye   *terrify*
Whan þat eschue Y shal nat hir presence.   *escape*
O, ther thyn help, eterne sapience.   *there (grant)*

'Now wole Y voide fethirbeddes softe,   *remove*
The pilwes nesshe and esy materas   *soft pillows; mattress*
780   On whiche my careyne hath tymes ofte   *body*
Walwid and leyn. Now stande I in swich cas   *tossed; such*
þat me thynkith al greet folie it was.   *it seems to me*
Of clothynge eek, fy on the precioustee,   *also; extravagance*
And slouthe of sleep also lettynge me.   *hindering*

785   'Syn Y tormentid am so greuously
With thynges smale, how sorwes so grete
Souffre mighte Y, if now die sholde Y,
þat neuere or this my synnes kowde lete?   *before; give up*
O what matire of helle fyr the hete   *matter*
790   Mighte in me thanne fynde. Certes, greet,   *find (to consume); certainly*
For which my body of cold swoot is al weet.   *sweat; wet*

'Now woot I weel what thyng þat may auaille   *know; what may profit*
My soule and it keepe fro perisshynge.
By souffrance of greet labour and trauaille,   *endurance*
795 And excercyse of vertuous lyuynge,
Wole Y it helpe, left al taryynge,   *without any delay*
þat in swich an houres extremitee,   *such*
No peyne but reste fynde may shee.

'O holy and mercyful sauueour,
800 Of so bittir deeth souffre me nat dye.   *permit; to die*
Thogh Y be thikke wrappid in errour,   *thickly*
See, beforn thee plat on the grownd Y lye,   *flat*
Weepynge for myn excessyf folye,
And, curteys lord, of thy benignitee   *kind*
805 This grace vouchesauf to grante me.

'Aftir thy lust be my punysshement   *pleasure*
Whyle Y am heer, and, good lord, nat reserue   *do not*
To othir place the chastisement   *another*
Which þat Y, wrecche, heere in this world disserue.
810 Let me abye it heer or þat Y sterue,   *pay for; before; die*
For in þat place horrible is swich sharpnesse   *such*
Of peyne þat no wight can it expresse.   *person*

'O how vnwys or this haue Y been ay,   *before; always*
Syn þat deeth vndisposid and the peyne   *since; unprepared*
815 Of purgatorie Y kowde by no way
Consider, ne how it kowde distreyne.   *afflict (me)*
Set was myn herte in othir thoghtes veyne,
þat yaf me lettynge and impediment   *gave; hindrance*
To thynke vpon the perils consequent.   *that followed*

820 'But now, thurgh fadirly amonestynge,   *through; admonishing*
My myndes yen þat cloos wer and shit   *eyes; closed; shut*
I opne, and of tho perils am dredynge.'   *those; afraid*
And Sapience answerde anoon to it: *at once*
'My sone, to do so it is greet wit,
825 Whiles thow yong art, and haast strengthe and
    force.
Thy lyf for to correct, thee enforce.   *exert yourself*

'Whan þat deeth cometh which cruel and fel is,   *fierce*
Whom thow nat maist withstonde ne withsitte,   *oppose, standing or sitting*
Help ne refuyt is ther for thee noon ellis   *refuge; no other*
830   But to the mercy of God thee committe.   *(to) commit yourself*
By no way þat nat leue ne ommitte.
My passioun putte eek twixt my doom and thee,   *Crucifixion; judgement*
Lest, more than neede is, adrad thow be.   *needful; afraid*

'My rightwisnesse nat so mochil dreede   *righteousness; much*
835   þat thow fro trust and hope of mercy twynne.   *separate*
Contrytly mercy axe and thow shalt speede.   *ask; prosper*
Now restfuller in thy goost be withynne   *more at peace; spirit*
þat ouer ferd art. Thee pourge of thy synne.   *greatly fearful; purge yourself*
Scourge thyself with repentances rod.
840   Begynnynge of wysdam is dreede of God.   *the fear*

'Scriptures serche, and by hem shalt thow leere   *search the scriptures; learn*
þat vnto man is it greet auantage
Deeth to haue ofte in mynde, in this lyf heere.
If yeeres manye and vnto good age
845   Man lyue, and in all hem glad and sauage   *all of them (is); wild*
Be, good is the dirk hour and dayes wikke   *it is good; dark; wicked*
Remembre or þat he come to the prikke.   *before; point*

'For whan þat tyme is comen, and þat hour,
Repreeued shal be the past vanitee.   *reproved*
850   Remembre therfore on thy creatour
In thy fressh youthe and lusty iolitee,   *pleasant enjoyment*
Or tyme come of sharp aduersitee,   *before (the) time*
And or þat yeeres approche of disese   *before*
In whiche thow wilt seyn they nat thee plese,

855   'And or asshen into hir eerthe also,   *before ashes; their*
Wherof they wer, ageyn hem thidir dresse,   *from which; came; return again*
And thy spirit to God whens it cam fro
Retourne. God with al thyn herte blisse.   *bless*
Thanke him, shewe vnto him thy kyndenesse,
860   For he to thee now opned hath the way
Wherthurgh thow maist be saued, is no nay.   *there is no denying*

'Ful fewe been þat so with hertes ere   *there are; the heart's ear*
Konne apparceyue th'instabilitee   *recognize*
Of the world, and konne of the deeth han fere
865 Which þat alway lyth in awayt pryuee,   *lies; secret ambush*
Ne þat of the ioie and felicitee
Of heuene, which ay shal laste and endure
Take any maner heede at al or cure.   *pay. . . heed or have. . . care*

'Lifte vp thyn yen. Looke aboute and see   *eyes*
870 Diligently, how many folkes blynde
In hir conceites nowadayes be.   *thoughts*
They close and shitte the yen of hir mynde.   *shut; eyes; their*
They nat keepe in hir conceit serche and fynde   *don't care; thought; (to) search*
Vnto what ende needes they shuln drawe,   *needfully; will*
875 And al for lak of dreede of God and awe.   *dread*

'They stoppe hir eres, for they nat ne keepe   *their ears; do not care*
Heer how conuerted be and receyue helthe.   *(to) hear; (to) be converted*
Correccion is noon; they let it sleepe.
They been so dronken of this worldes welthe
880 That deeth, or they be waar, right in a stelthe   *aware; in an act of theft*
Fallith vpon hem, which condicioun
Hem cause shal hastyf perdicioun.   *will cause them speedy*

'The peple now let seen innumerable   *let (us) see*
þat for deeth vndisposid lost han be.   *unprepared*
885 Considere and, if thy wit be therto able,   *sufficient for the purpose*
Noumbre of hir multitude the plentee.   *count; their; abundance*
Eek of hem þat in thy tyme with thee   *also*
Dwelt han, looke how þat they been take away.   *taken*
Thow seest wel, they from hens been past for ay,   *ever*

890 'And as they heer han do, so shuln they haue.   *will*
What multitude in yeeres fewe ago,   *in recent years*
Thee yit lyuynge, han leid been in hir graue—   *in your lifetime*
What brethren, cousins, felawes and mo   *companions; others*
Of thy knowleche. Beholde alle tho.   *known to you; those*
895 Thynke eek, with hem hir olde synne goon is.   *also*
Touche vnto hem, speke and axe hem of this,   *approach them; ask*

'And they with wepynge and with waymentynge   *lamenting*
Shuln to thee seye, and thus ageyn answere,   *will*
Blissid is he þat can see the endynge,
900 And synnes þat the soule hurte and der   *injure*
Eschue can, and hem flee and forber,   *avoid; refrain from*
And þat in my conseil hath good sauour,   *he who; counsel*
Disposynge him alway vnto þat hour.   *preparing*

'And therfore, alle vicious thynges left,   *left (behind)*
905 Weel thee dispose and reedy make thee   *well; ready*
To dye, lest the tyme be thee reft   *taken from you*
Or þat thow be waar, for no certeintee   *before; aware*
Haast thow therof. Thow art nothyng pryuee   *of it; not at all*
Therto. Deeth is nat fer: right atte yate   *to it; afar; at the gate*
910 Shee is. Be reedy for to dye algate.   *always*

'Right as a marchant stondynge in a port   *merchant*
His ship þat charged is with marchandyse
To go to fer parties for confort   *countries*
Of himself lookeþ þat it in sauf wyse   *safely*
915 Passe out, right so, if thow wirke as the wyse,   *depart; follow wise teaching*
See to thy soule so, or thow hens weende,   *before; depart hence*
þat it may han the lyf þat haath noon ende.'
        Amen.

Explicit illa pars per quem sciendum est mori.
[Here ends that part through which you are to learn to die]

De caelesti Jerusalem

The othir iii partes which in this book   *three*
Of the tretice of deeth expressid be,   *are written*
920 Touche Y nat dar. þat labour Y forsook,   *dare*
For so greet thyng to swich a fool as me
Ouer chargeable is, by my leautee,   *too burdensome; faith*
To medle with. Ynow the firste part   *sufficient*
For my smal konnynge is and symple art.   *knowledge*

925 But as the ixe lesson which is rad   *ninth; read*
In holy chirche vpon a[ll] halwen day   *All Saints' Day*

Witnessith, syn it ioieful is and glad   *since*
For hem þat hens shuln wel departe away   *will*
And to the blisse go þat lastith ay,   *forever*
930 Translate wole Y, nat in rym but prose,   *rhyme*
For so it best is, as þat Y suppose.

How greet ioie and blisse is shapen to hem   *prepared for*
þat so shuln passe hens vp to the citee   *thus*
Callid celestial Ierusalem,
935 Aftir our might and possibilitee   *so far as we can*
Let vs considere, althogh it so be
That for to conprehende þat gladnesse
Verraily no wit may, ne tonge, expresse.   *truly; tongue*

Lo, thus is seid of þat citee in a place: therin is no sorwe, heuynesse ne
940 waymentynge [*lamenting*]. What is more blisful than þat lyf is, wher no
dreede is of pouerte [*poverty*], of maladie no feeblenesse? Ther is no wight
[*person*] hurt, no wight wrooth, no wight hath enuye. Ther is no brennynge
[*burning*] or hete of couetyse [*covetousness*], no desir of mete [*food*], noon
ambicioun of honour or of power, no dreede of the feend, noon awaytes
945 [*ambushes*] of deueles, the fer [*fear*] of helle fer [*far*] thens, no deeth of body
ne soule, but ioieful yiftes [*gifts*] and iocounde [*pleasant*] of immortalitee.
Ther shal neuere be discord, stryf ne debat but alle thynges conuenient and
accordynge; no diuision but onhede [*unity*], for ther shal been o [*one*]
concord of alle seintes, o pees and gladnesse continuel, alle thynges peis-
950 ible [*peaceful*], alle in quiete and reste. Ther is an excellent brightnesse and
shynynge, nat this light þat now is, but in so mochil cleerer as it is bettre
and more noble, for, as it is red [*read*], þat citee shal noon neede haue of
the sonnes light, but our lord God almighty shal enlumyne [*illumine*] it.
And the lamb is his lanterne, wheras [*where*] seintes shuln shyne as sterres
955 in perpetuel eternitees, and as the shynynge of the firmament þat spredith
his bemes vpon many men; wherfore in þat place is no nyght, no dirk-
nesses, no concours [*confluence*] of clowdes no [*nor of*] fretynge [*gnawing*]
cold, no sharpnesse, but swich attemperance [*temperance*] of thynges shal
be ther, whiche neither ye [*eye*] of man neuere sy [*saw*] ne ere herde, ne
960 herte can thynke ne conprehende, sauf [*save*] of hem þat been worthy and
han disserued to haue þat blisse, whos names arn writen in the book of lyf
and which wasshid hir stoles [*robes*] in the lambes blood and been beforn
the see [*throne*] of God, and serue him day and nyght. Noon age is ther,
ne miserie or wrecchidnesse of age, whyls [*while*] alle shul been o parfyt

965 [*perfect*] body, o parfyt man, in the mesur of the ful age of Cryst.

And abouen alle thynges is to been associed [*allied*] to the conpaignies
[*companies*] of the trones [*thrones*], dominacions, principatz [*principalities*]
and potestatz, of angels and archangels, and to been in the conpaignie of
alle the celestial and hy vertues, and to beholde the conpaignie of seintes,
970 brighter and yeuynge [*giving*] more light than the sterres [*stars*], shynynge
in the feith of patriarks, gladynge and ioyynge [*rejoicing*] in the hope of
prophetes, deemynge [*judging*] the world of apostles in xii [*twelve*] tribes
of Israel, and to beholde eek [*also*] the shynyng of martirs with purpurat
[*purpled*] corounes [*crowns*] of victorie and to see the conpaignies of virgines
975 werynge brighte gerlandes. [*garlands*]

And for to speke of the kyng þat sittith in the middes [*midst*] of hem, no
vois therto souffisith [*suffices*]; it may nat be told ne expressid. That honour,
þat vertu, þat magnificence and þat glorie excedith and passith all wittes
and intellectes of man, and passynge alle the seintes ioies is to beholde the
980 inestimable brightnesse of þat kyng and to be spred [*overspread*] with the
bemes of his magestee. Let thise thynges sadly [*firmly*] synke into our hertes.
Let vs vndirstande hem with ful feith. Let hem be beloued with alle our
hertes. Let hem be goten by the greetnesse and by the multitude of goode
wirkes and continuel. This thyng is put in [*within*] the might of the wirker,
985 for the kyngdam of heuene souffrith forcible and mighty assautes [*assaults*]
of vertu. O man, this thyng, þat is to seyn, the kyngdam of heuene, seekith
noon othir prys [*price*] but thyn owne self. It is as mochil [*much*] worth as
thow art. Yeeue thee [*give yourself*] and thow shalt haue it. What [*why*]
artow astoned [*astonished*] or adrad [*afraid*] of the prys? Cryst yaf [*gave*]
990 himself to purchace thee the regne to God the fadir. Right so, yeue thow
thyself þat thow maist been his kyngdam and þat no synne regne in thy
mortel and deedly body, but let thy good spirit regne in thee to purchace
thee th'eternel lyf. And therfore, whoso desirith to haue the merites euere-
lastynge, he moot delyte [*must delight*] him to gete hem thurgh goode and
995 vertuous wirkes. That is the path and the streight way to blisse endelees,
the which he vs grante þat boghte vs with his precious blood. Amen, amen.

Now vndirstandith wel and considerith in your hertes þat as mochil ioie as
ther is in that blisful place of heuene, as greet sorwe, angwissh and torment
is in þat othir part in helle. To expresse hem needith nat, for they been the
1000 reuers [*reverse*] and contrarie to the ioies aboue named, wherby euery
persone may resonablely conceyue þat in þat place of torment the peynes

been merueillously sharpe and greuous. And yit for al þat smert, [*pain*] if
any ende sholde sue or folwe, that wolde yeue [*give*] the soules right hy
confort and greetly abregge [*shorten*] and lesne [*lessen*] hir grief, but awayte
1005 [*expect*] nat aftir þat, for it wole nat betyde [*happen*], for right as the seid
ioies been eternel and aylastynge [*everlasting*], so been tho [*those*] peynes
infynyt and endeles. And sikirly [*certainly*], syn [*since*] God of his hy grace
and benigne courtesie hath yeuen [*given*] vs libertee and freedam for to
purchace by our wirkes in this present lyfe þat oon or þat othir, al standith
1010 in [*depends upon*] our choys and eleccioun [*preference*]. To grete fooles been
we but if we cheese [*choose*] the bettre part. Which part God of his infynyt
goodnesse graunte vs alle to cheese. Amen.

Notes

This text, Hoccleve's translation of Suso's *Horologium Sapientiae* II.ii, has formal affinities, in its use of dialogue form, with Boethius—it presents a disciple figure instructed both by Sapientia and, in a vision, by a dying young man whom at first he proposes to instruct: his own *alter ego*—and with Isidore of Seville, whose *Synonyma* furnished a similar dialogue in 'My Compleinte' between a suffering man and Reason. It also echoes Hoccleve's earlier dialogue with Friend; its deliberate confusion of levels of fictional reality (see nn. to 88–90, 134–5, 753–4) has parallels with the confused time scale of 'My Compleinte'. It belongs to a well-established tradition of meditation on the last things—for examples roughly contemporary with the translation, using some of the Biblical texts also found in the *Horologium*, see *The Pricke of Conscience* (comment in Henry and Trottter 1994: 10), a Wycliffite 'Sermon of Dead Men' (Cigman 1989: 207ff.) and 'The Book of the Craft of Dying' (Horstmann 1896 2.406ff.), which includes a quotation from Suso on 2.408, corresponding to 4.43–56; the version of this text in D6 (from the ME *Treatise of the Seven Poyntes*) partners material also from the Suso chapter in a compilation with offered title *Orilogium* [*sic*] *Sapientie*. Hoccleve's translation brings into clearest focus the penitential implications of the *Series* as a whole. On the circulation in England of material excerpted from the *Horologium* see Lovatt 1982, Westlake 1993; on Hoccleve's translation, Westlake 1993: 65–6, and on its relation to the *Series* as a whole, Selman 1998: 186–221, and (especially) von Nolcken 1993. In the following notes, Bible quotations are, for the most part, as identified by *Colloquia Dominiciana* and Künzle 1977.

rubric *H MSS share D's quotation of the opening words from Suso's *Horologium Sapientiae* II.ii, translated 4.1–2.

9 *seintes*: the Latin provides no clear support for this reading; the BLY variant 'sentence' is interesting (it makes for a clearer parallel with the previous phrase, 'tresor of wisdam') and might just refer to the *Sentences* of Peter Lombard, an influential medieval commentator on the Bible.

15 DR gloss 'Sapientia', that is, Wisdom, one of the main speakers of the treatise, also so glossed at 4.37, as also by *H (at 817, anticipating 823) and S (37, 148, 823). The other main figure is 'Discipulus', the disciple, so named by DS (29), H2 (467, 515), *H (323, 515), BSY (467), and S (29, 87, 741). A third figure is the image of a dying man, so named by H2 (477, 553), *H (169) and S (477). SY link the figure of the disciple with the dying man, by way of words spoken by him at 514 (Hoccleve's addition to the source), as 'amicus' (precedent for this role occurs in the disciple's address to the dying man; cf. ll. 151, 467). This last is an important element in the reworking of the chapter in B4 (earlier noted by von Nolcken 1993: 45, n. 15) where the disciple's shifting role is indicated by his change from 'an vnprofitable confortour' (corresponding to l. 323, and marginal 'nota de adulatore') to a 'freend' (corresp. ll. 467, 515 and marginal *nota* to the former 'de consolatore'). The limits of friendship provide a thematic link with earlier and later items in the *Series* (so also von Nolcken 1993).

    sauoure (Lat. 'sapere') is an important element in the work's meaning: it implies not simply theoretical knowledge (cf. 80n.) but an experiential knowledge experienced with the immediacy of sense perception, which the rest of the work will communicate to the disciple.

18 The Latin original of this verse conflates elements from Prov. 4.2 and Wisdom 3.14.

21 D's marginal quotation 'inicium sapiencie timor domini' refers to the ultimate source of the Suso phrase ('a timore domini inchoantes qui inicium est sapiencie') in Ps. 111.10, also used by Richard of St Victor, in his *Twelve Patriarchs*, to mark the first stage of the soul's ascent to God (for a Middle English version, see Hodgson 1982: 131). S cites it when the verse is repeated at 4.840.

22 S marks each stanza from here on with a rubricated 'nota' at the head. Other marginal 'notae' occur at 8 (BLY), 37 (B), 204 (BLY, at head of quotation), 344 (S, against the 'exemplum' of the partridge seized by the hawk), 364 (S, for 372), 438 (BLY), 526, 540 (S). S notes an exemplum at 701. B4 provides a full series of *notae* for its version of the chapter, none paralleled in S.

23–8 Sapientia here summarizes the contents of *Horologium* II.ii-v, though Hoccleve translates only the first chapter, and substitutes other material for the rest (see further below).

34 The various MSS quote Suso here in the margin (D 'ad quid prodest hec doctrina etc.') and elsewhere throughout the work, D much less fully than *H, H2Ha1R only infrequently. D provides glosses for 344–6, 358–60, 507–8, 511–12, 596–8, 614–16, 659, 820–2, not paralleled in *H; *H provides glosses not paralleled in D for 134–5, 141, 144–5, 165–7, 170 (where BS have the correct reading 'honerosus', cf. 170 'heuy', against LY 'meus'), 179–81, 204–9, 229–31, 246–7, 267–72, 281–2, 288–93, 303–8, 372, 386–8, 393–8, 523–4, 638–40, 644–6, 660–4, 673–5, 680–3, 729–31, 850–4. C contains unique marginal citations from Suso; S and B share several (for 43–5, 85–6, 106–12, 123–5, 127–8, 183–5); BCS share one at 78–80; BSY share one at 829–35; S has a few in English (see esp. 673n.) and a number in Latin by another hand (see Appendix 3). D's marginalia are given in full in the notes.

35 *hauynge*, translating 'habitus', refers to a state or condition of being.

38 *swetnesse*: both D and H2 create an instance of *rime riche* here. Hoccleve uses the word elsewhere in the work, which reinforces the metaphor of tasting at 15, often an addition to his source, and often for the sake of rhyme (cf. 36, 61, 110, 585). *H's reading 'richesse' also figures literally and as spiritual metaphor at 132, 198, 425, 442. *Rime riche* is favoured elsewhere by Hoccleve (e.g. I.71/73, 2.212/214, 818–19, 4.512/514), who on occasion repeats a word even without change of function (e.g. VI.359/361, emended by scribes of *H, 4.36/38). Though the scribes generally avoid *rime riche*, their miscopying of Hoccleve's rhymes also occasionally generates examples (see apparatus to 4.535, 773, 889).

52, 54 'deeth' is seen here and commonly elsewhere in the text as feminine ('hir pray', cf. 575, 910) probably because of the feminine gender of 'mors' in Latin. *H reads 'mors' as masculine here; BLY similarly at 575. At 290 Hoccleve himself genders death masculine. A similar variation in the gendering of death occurs in the *Regement* (noted by Batt 1996₂: 65 n. 10).

57 *many oon*: since Suso's text originates in,

and partially addresses, a religious community, this reference in the original applies to both religious and seculars. Unlike the anonymous Middle English translation of the *Horologium*, the *Seven Poyntes* (on which, see Lovatt 1982, Ellis 1982, Westlake 1993), Hoccleve's version suppresses such explicit reference as (presumably) of no relevance to his secular readers. The sense of the few who attend faithfully to their religious observance by contrast with the many who do not (cf. Matt. 20.16), as prominent a feature of Suso's original as of Hoccleve's translation (BLY lose one such reference at 862: see apparatus), overlaps in the *Series* with Hoccleve's initial sense of estrangement from his fellows (e.g. ll. 78–9).

78–9 Suso's original conflates Ecclus. 29.14 and Baruch 3.30 at this point.

80 *philosophres* (Y *philosophies*). In common with much late medieval religious writing (for example, Rolle and the author of *The Cloud of Unknowing*), Suso here opposes the aridity of speculation about God to direct sensuous experience of him.

88–90 The figure of the young man is first presented as an imaginative projection of the disciple: later (cf. 753–4) he will acquire the status almost of a real person (Henry and Trotter 1994: 9 misread the figure as a transformation of Sapientia). This striking exemplification of the unstable boundaries between the real and the fictional, or between acts of meditation and divine revelation, is shared by other Middle English religious writers, notably Langland and Julian of Norwich. Suso presents the imaginative projection more clearly than Hoccleve as a stage in a religious process: preceded by withdrawal of thought from the world of external appearances ('se ab exterioribus colligere'), the act of introspection has an intensity ('diligentissime considerare') which will eventually result in its own transformation. Hoccleve emphasizes the act of recollection by translating 'considerare' twice (87, 89). See also brief comment in Kolve 1984: 69–70.

99 DBS gloss 'Circumdederunt me gemitus mortis etc.' (fuller in BS). Suso is here

quoting from Ps. 17.5–6.

103–4 These lines refer to Job 3.11, and echo lines in 'My Compleinte' (1.327–8), with which this text has many affinities.

129 'sownynge' could also mean 'swooning', in which case it would have referred to the speaker's feelings, but the Latin 'intonantem' establishes the meaning 'speaking' as more likely.

131 *thow dye shalt* translates Suso's 'filius mortis es tu'. Interestingly, a similar phrase was used in the version of the *Gesta* narrative of the virtuous Empress in Ha2 (*var.* 'filius confusionis sum'): there it is spoken by the wicked brother-in-law when he hears of the Emperor's imminent return (translated, 3.154 above, as 'my deeth wole it been and confusion'). Parallels of this sort can suggest some of the many ways in which the different texts of the *Series* interact with one another.

134–5 are in Suso possibly spoken by the young man rather than by death. Hoccleve follows Suso in making capital out of the difficulty of distinguishing the speakers from one another, especially the disciple from his *alter ego*, the fictionalized *imago mortis* (cf. 378n., and 498ff., 708ff. below; cf. also n. to 1.309 above), but, since 'lore' characterizes all these voices (e.g. 19, 78, 516), confusion as to their indentity does not greatly affect the overall meaning of the work. With l. 134, cf. Ezek. 7.2, 6.

141 CRS gloss (S at 155, a quotation not taken from Suso) 'non remuneratur mors diuiciis (C diuicie), non sapiencia (C sapiencie), non moribus (C *adds* non erat etc.)' [death is repaid by neither riches, wisdom nor good behaviour].

161 With this vivid metaphor, an addition by Hoccleve to the text, cf. Chaucer's *Book of the Duchess* 652–71 and n., and Dyboski 1908: 88.12.

168 cf. John 8.53.

190–224 cf. (Old Testament) Wisdom 5.6–15 (verses 8–10 also cited in *Fasciculus Morum*, Wenzel 1989: 558, and source noted, with first words quoted in Latin, in the D6 copy of the chapter from *The Seven Poyntes*). Hoccleve follows Suso in allowing the speaker to individualize and personalize the first person plural and other general reference of the Bible text. Marginal quotations (199, 218, both fuller in *H than in D) are taken from Suso rather than from the Bible (199, 'transierunt omnia illa tanquam vmbra preteriens, et tanquam nuncius cito percurrens [Künzle, praecurrens], et tanquam nauis etc.'; 218 'in malignitate propria consumptus sum, spes mea etc.').

196 With the Biblical metaphor of sowing good or wicked seed, added by Hoccleve to his source, and developing the beautiful added phrase at 185 ('sauf with bitter fruyt of synne'), cf. 2.423 and VI.11, the latter also added by Hoccleve to his source.

201–3 With this metaphor of the sailing ship, cf. a passage in *Fasciculus Morum* (Wenzel 1989: 98).

205 *preef*: Lat. *argumentum*. The H2 reading 'way' is interestingly shared with the prose version in Li which Furnivall thought was based on the same Latin source as Hoccleve was following, but in other instances where D and H2 disagree substantively in rendering the Latin, the Li version agrees with D rather than with H2. So this shared reading is probably accidental. See also 612n. below.

212 Here and at l. 216 D translates Suso's 'continuo' by 'continuelly'; H2 by 'foorthwith redily' and 'anoonrightes'. Either could have been in the original, though since D's version is closer to the letter of the Latin, if not so accurate a translation, it is paradoxically slightly likelier to be the original.

219 *wolle-loke*: trans. *lanugo*. The prose version of this chapter in B4 reads 'þe seed of a þistil' (Westlake 1993).

223 Suso's Latin ('hospitem') shows Hoccleve's 'oost' to mean not an army but a householder.

225–31 Cf. (in sequence) Job 23.2, 6.3, Lam. 5.17 (again plural reference transformed into singular by Suso).

231 D's 'many a dayes lengthe' seems, *prima facie*, not to represent Suso ('et annos plurimos') as well as H2's 'many a yeeres lengthe'. However, immediately before this passage Suso has quoted Micah 7.14, 'Quis michi det ut sim iuxta dies antiquos' [who will give me to be as in former days], so that D's reading may depend on a conflation of the Bible

quotation and Suso's gloss and still be original.

235 Suso here lifts a phrase from Acts 27.15 (the account of the storm which overtook Paul and his followers on the way to Rome) and applies it to his overall moral frame ('datis flatibus navi' [winds having been given to the ship]). Hoccleve's translation makes the link yet more explicit ('the worldly wynd'). Ships figure prominently as narrative properties of both *Gesta* narratives, and equally prominently as carriers of metaphoric meaning (e.g. I.222–3n., II.236–9, 257–8, III.20–2, IV.45n., 4.201–3, 911–15): for comment on the last of these, see Kolve 1984: 349.

242 Pryor offers a parallel with Jer. 2.24, but a closer parallel is with Job 11.12.

243 *th'aftirclap*: with this line, added to the Suso, cf. *Regement* 855, 'Balade to Carpenter' (Furnivall and Gollancz 1970: 63.20).

246–50 Cf. Eccles. 9.12.

263 Cf. Jer. 9.18.

289, 297 The commonplace equation of youth and a flower is in Suso; cf. *Troilus* V.1841. For l. 297 the prose version in Li reads 'spende ȝe ȝoure þouȝte in goddys seruyce', probably because the scribe misread 'ȝouþe' in his exemplar. Marginal *notae* in B4 gloss both lines ('nota de iuuentute', 'nota of ȝouþe') and l. 378 ('nota de tempore male expenso').

313–15 Suso here uses Prov. 5.12–13. Hoccleve's version dramatically increases the local colour of the text, with its reference to the locker of the heart.

319–20 Cf. Job 3.11, used earlier by Suso (at Hoccleve's 103–4).

324–5 D*H gloss 'ecce omnes morimur et quasi aque dilabimur in terram etc.' (2 Sam. 14.14).

333 D*H gloss 'age penitenciam de transactis, et conuertere ad dominum'.

337–8 D*H gloss 'quis est hic sermo quem loqueris, debeo penitere, debeo me conuertere. Nonne vides angustias etc.' (translated 338–41).

344–6 D glosses 'quemadmodum perdrix cum sub vnguibus aucipitris mox discerpenda comprimitur pre angustia mortis, quodammodo exanimis redditur, sic etc.'

358–60 D glosses 'Qui autem tarde penitencie se committit, dubius erit quia nescit vtrum vere vel ficte peniteat'.

365–71 On the insertion of this stanza into a late fifteenth-century copy of Chaucer's *Tale of Melibee*, see Harris 1998: 199.

365–7 D*H gloss 'o longa nimis protractacio (*H protraccio, so Suso) emendacionis mee. Propositum bonum sine inchoacione etc.'

372 *O morwe, morwe*: Künzle offers parallels in Augustine's sermons (*PL* 38. 512, 1095).

378 *xxxti yeer*: presumably a reference to the age of the author, born *c.*1295 and over thirty years old when he produced the German original of his work (Underhill 1911: 464 and Pryor 1968: 87 date the work 1328; Kolve 1984: 400 and Künzle 1977: 27, 1334–5).

389 L adds 'alas' in the margin.

396 that is, the *Ave Maria* (cf. Luke 1.28).

414–16 DH2*H gloss 'vere nunc cognoui quod ad magnitudinem [*H multitudinem] premiorum [H2*H add 'celestium'] plus michi contulisset solicita custodia cordis etc.' Since Hoccleve translated 'celestium' in l. 415 as 'celestial', it is probable that the added word was in Hoccleve's archetype, and inadvertently omitted from the copy in D. *H's reading 'multitudinem', however, is not followed by the translation.

430–2 At this point Suso is citing Matt. 25.9, from the parable of the wise and foolish virgins.

435 *fadir merciable*: cf. 2 Cor. 1.3.

447 Deeds of satisfaction are what the confessor enjoins on the penitent as the public penalty for his sin: cf. below 477–83 on the relation between contrition, confession and satisfaction.

449–51 Cf. Luke 16.21 (from the parable of Dives and Lazarus).

452–3 as these lines appear in *H, they are a nonsense: CR attempt to make sense of them by negating the verb in 453.

459 Suso here conflates Matt. 13.30 and Luke 16.9.

493 *a fourneys*: Künzle offers as source for Suso's 'fornacem ignis ardentis' the furnace into which the Jews were placed by order of Nebuchadnezzar (Dan. 3.11).

498 D*H gloss 'o amicorum omnium

dulcissime [cf. Suso 'dilectissime'] succurre etc.'. *H adds 'misere anime mee/tue': LRS, following Suso, read 'mee', BCY 'tue', the latter shared by the translation at 499, presumably in an attempt to bring the gloss into line with the text and not because Hoccleve's copy of Suso originally read 'tue'. (Alternatively, Hoccleve introduced the error in his marginal gloss, and LRS corrected it against a copy of Suso's Latin.) The reading 'dilectissime' is closer to the translation, though cf. 38n.

507 D glosses 'non est qui fidelitatem ostendat; non est qui manum porrigat egenti etc.'. Cf. Ezek. 16.49, Deut. 15.11, Prov. 31.20.

512–13 D glosses 'Singuli que sua sunt querunt [= Phil. 2.21], et me in vltricibus flammis desolatam derelinquunt etc.'.

521–2 Cf. Ps. 10.11.

523–4 Cf. Jer. 5.21 (Künzle offers Ps. 113.5–6).

533–9 On the deceitful comfort offered the dying man by his friends, cf. 'The Book of the Craft of Dying' (Horstmann 1896: 2.416).

540 S glosses 'and ȝit nota bene nota'.

554 'dethes net' (Suso 'laquei mortis') is a Biblical expression, most closely paralleled in 2 Sam. 22.6 (cf. Ps. 17.6, Prov. 21.6).

554–60 D*H gloss (fuller in *H) 'idcirco, cum laqueo mortis capti fuerint, cum irruerit repentina calamitas et interitus quasi (*H et) tempestas ingruerit etc.' [L for 'etc.' adds 'quando venerit super eos tribulacio et angustia clamabunt et non exaudientur']. Suso is quoting from Prov. 1.27–30.

568–70 The Latin makes clearer than the translation that the 'tyme' spoken of is the present in a world growing old ('senescentis').

575 S glosses 'Nota bene nota Joob [*sic*]', possibly an indication that the scribe saw an echo of material from the Book of Job here (in a passage added to Suso's text).

587 'mukhepynge' is a very distinctive realization of the Latin ('questus rei familiaris'). Cf. 198, *Regement* 1124.

596 D glosses 'ex ea namque proficies vt non solum mori non timeas, verum etiam mortem etc.'.

608–9 Cf. Ecclus. 38.23, also quoted in the

Wycliffite 'Sermon of Dead Men' (Cigman 1989: 208).

612 Arsenius was a thirteenth-century patriarch of Constantinople credited with the composition of part of the ritual of extreme unction (*PG* 140.808): source, Pryor. The ME prose translation in Li omits the name. It shares this omission with the Latin copy of the work in the same MS, as also with the version in *The Seven Poyntes*, though the latter's translation of *Horologium* II.3 includes a reference to Arsenius. Such omissions permit a more general application of the reference to the disciple figure, and show (cf. Westlake 1993: 62–3, 81) that the ME prose translation in Li cannot have been based on the same Latin source as Hoccleve's version, which Furnivall seems to have thought (1970: xlv).

614–16 D glosses 'beatus quem cum venerit dominus et pulsauerit etc.': the passage conflates two Bible texts, Luke 12.37 and Apoc. 3.20. With this image of God at the gate, cf. 909 (death at the gate).

622–3 D*H gloss 'quacumque enim morte etc.' (*H for 'etc.','preoccupatus fuerit iustus, in refrigerio erit'), following Wisdom 4.7. Suso's version wants 'iustus'.

628 *to*: in this line H2's 'of' (meaning 'by') may better translate the Latin 'ab' in a set of parallel phrases ('a sanctis angelis… a supernis civibus … a celesti curia') than D's 'to'.

631 D*H gloss (*H fuller) 'sed heu me miserum etc.'.

640 *H's reading in this line ('full great foyson') has the support of details earlier in the work (263) and of Hoccleve's practice in I.244, but D and H2 both agree in the reading 'greet habundance'. If the *H reading is scribal and not authorial, it suggests a scribe familiar with Hoccleve's favoured turns of phrase.

645 Pryor refers this image to 1 Pet. 5.8 (the devil as a roaring lion), but a likelier source is Lam. 3.10. The 'pit of deeth' (647) is a Biblical commonplace.

659 D glosses 'puncture mortis amarissime me circumdant etc.' H2 adds 'ha me miserum', translated by Hoccleve ('wrecche'), which suggests that the original marginal note is better preserved

in H2 than in D.

659–65 The body's decay at the point of death appears regularly in medieval lyrics (Gray 1972: 194–5) and other writing, e.g. the Wycliffite 'Sermon of Dead Men' (Cigman 1989: 215).

660 D's 'powr' (H2 etc. 'pows') must be a simple error (Lat. 'pulsus') and has been emended accordingly.

662 Both DH2 and *H's readings (respectively, 'breeth' and 'wind') have support from the collocation 'wynd and breeth' (67).

673 S glosses 'þat is to seie, deuellis waiten aftir mannes soule and moost streitly in his dying'.

687–90 D*H (fuller in D) gloss 'o [B *adds* quam] terribilis aspectus iusti iudicis mihi iam presenti [Künzle, presentis] per timorem subito venturus etc [per exhibicionem]; nunc valete socii [*H *adds* amici carissimi] etc.' Either version ('presenti' or 'presentis') makes a distinction between the presence of the judge in the soul in the 'fere and dreede' generated, and that by which he suddenly shows himself to the soul 'per exhibicionem'.

695 'Men' may be a variant form of 'mene' and spelling for either of two distinct words, both of which would just about fit the sense here ('to complain', 'to have in mind'). But since the Latin has 'reddam' (cf. Matt. 5.26) it may be that the text originally read 'owen' and should be emended accordingly (or emended to 'þat Y men payen shal').

709 D*H (fuller in D) gloss (for 706–12) 'pro [Suso pre] dolore cruciatim clamant singule et dicunt [*H *om.* pro… dicunt], Miseremini mei miseremini mei saltem vos amici mei [cf. Job 19.21], vbi est nunc amicorum meorum adiutorium? vbi sunt promissiones bone consanguineorum meorum etc.' [*H *om.* meorum etc.]. *H turns the first person singular references of this passage (deriving from Job 19.21) into plural, and is closer to the translation (709–10) than D with its singular pronominal forms, but since the printed text of Suso agrees with D, the agreement of *H with the translation may be accidental.

730 Suso's Latin makes clear by its choice of relative pronoun ('quod') that it is purgatory itself which is cause of pain;

the *H gloss, by its 'quam', that the individual 'torment' is the cause of pain. Hoccleve's relative pronoun allows for either interpretation.

738 In D this line wants a rhyme. Furnivall supplied 'wofull sent is' from R; the same rhyme is found in all *H MSS except Ha1 ('the cause ys of offence') and accepted here, though it does not make immediate or easy sense, and I think it possible that an original reading, transmitted faithfully in *H, was suppressed in D by Hoccleve in the hope, which he did not realize, of producing a better rhyme. Admittedly, the word occurs elsewhere in the *Series* (the first recorded occurrences of the word according to the MED) in the broadly parallel contexts of the 'wofull man' whose story Hoccleve records, from the *Synonyma* of Isidore of Seville, in 'My Compleinte' (1.325) and of the punishment which the wicked brother of the emperor deserves to undergo for his attempt on the Empress's virtue (3.850). Such usages of the word may imply that the pains of hell are experienced, like their opposite, the Beatific Vision, with the immediacy and totality of sense-experience: parallels exist, for example, in Julian of Norwich (ch. 43 of the Long Version of her *Revelations*, which promises the soul a sight, sound, touch, scent and taste of God).

753–4 The disciple's anxiety about the precise status of the vision he has just experienced has parallels in other visionary literature, where the visionary is regularly presented as anxious about the source and identity of the revelations received, and where, as here (cf. 823ff.), a divine reassurance is sometimes needed.

760 *picchid*: *H's reading 'ficchid' is echoed at 5.501, but in neither passage does the *H reading have the support of the analogues, so it is probably scribal. The present passage is Hoccleve's addition to the text.

764–5 Cf. Hebrews 13.14. *H glosses: 'non habemus hic ciuitatem manentem sed aliam inquirimus', taken not from Suso (who omits the phrase 'sed... inquirimus') but from the Bible, which reads 'futuram' for its 'aliam'.

771 BHa1LSY indicate a new section, BLSY

with a rubricated capital, Ha1 by the phrase 'soli deo honor et gloria', repeated after 917 to mark the end of the work.

799–800 D*H gloss 'o sancte et misericors saluator, tam amari morti ne tradas me'.

820–2 D glosses 'sed nunc paterne admonitus oculos aperio etc.'.

832 Suso at this point makes explicit the identification between Sapience and Christ, to whom wisdom was conventionally appropriated as second member of the Trinity (cf. 1.108n.).

841 Cf. John 5.39.

844–6 D*H (*H fuller) gloss from Eccles. 11.8 'si annis, inquit sapiens, multis vixerit homo et in omnibus hiis letus fuerit, meminisse debet tenebrosi temporis etc.' (*H adds 'et dierum malorum', followed by Hoccleve, where Suso, following the Vulgate, reads 'multorum'; the quotation continues to l. 849).

850–8 Cf. Eccles. 12.1, 7, so glossed by *H, which reads 'in quibus' (Hoccleve's 'in whiche', 854) rather than the Biblical 'de quibus', followed by Suso.

859 Translates 'gratus esto' ('be grateful').

872–7 Cf. Is. 6.10.

895 *olde synne* (*H *old sins*) is a tamer version of Suso's vivid Biblical 'veterem hominem' (i.e. Adam, cf. 1 Cor. 15.47).

904 D glosses 'prepara te ad viam uniuerse carnis ad horam mortis quia pro certo nescis qua hora veniet et quam prope est. Ecce in ianuis est etc.'. By contrast with the other marginal comments, this bears only a loose relation to the material translated in the corresponding lines. The image of death at the gate (Künzle derives 'in ianuis' from Matt. 24.33) echoes the Biblical image of God at the gate earlier (615).

917 rubric: for this rubric *H offers 'here endith lern to die and (C *om.* endith... and) beginneth a prologue on þe ix lesson that is read (C *om.* that is read) on All Hallows Day'. The translation of this 'ix lesson', promised in prose (930), and thus, by implication, functioning as a kind of coda to the Suso chapter parallel to the prose moralizations of the two *Gesta* narratives, in fact begins, as noted by Kurtz 1924, in the last stanza of the prologue. The translation is fluent and for the most part accurate. For a modern printing of the Latin original, with a selection of variants, see Proctor and Wordsworth 1879–96: 3.976–7; the *lectio* is drawn, with cuts, from a sermon on the Feast of All Saints ascribed to St Augustine (*PL* 39.2135–7). Material from the lesson, or its source in ps.-Augustine, also occurs in the sermon on the Transfiguration appended to Mirk's *Festial* by Caxton in his 1491 printing of the work (sig. R3ᵛ, kindly supplied in typescript by Dr Sue Powell) and in the Wycliffite Sermon of Dead Men (Cigman 1989: 235–6).

932–8 BLY gloss this passage with a version of the original Latin (principal variants are given in brackets from Proctor and Wordsworth): 'consideremus vrbem [urbis] illius felicitatem in quantum considerare possibile est. Ut enim vere est comprehendere nullus homo [sermo] sufficit'. BLY 'homo' is not as close to Hoccleve's 'wit… tonge' as the printed version's 'sermo'.

938 BLSY 'here endith þe prolog and begynneth þe lesson'.

939 *in a place*: so also the Latin original and the ps.-Augustinian sermon ('in quodam loco'), where the phrase refers, without specifying it, to the following Bible quotation ('therin… waymentynge', cf. Is. 35.10, 51.11).

941 *of maladie no feeblenesse*: a literal translation of the Latin word order ('non aegritudinis imbecillitas').

945 *fer*. *H's addition 'and gastnes', if authorial, may reflect an awareness that 'fer' was a possible spelling in some dialects (though not with Hoccleve) for 'fire' as well as for 'fear' and hence witness an attempt to remove ambiguity in the context of an account of the terrors of hell. The Latin, 'terror gehennae', confirms the latter reading.

949 *concord*: BLSY use 'corde', probably the aphetic form of *accord* (so CR), a word used regularly through the *Series*, but never in this reduced form, which suggests its use here is scribal rather than authorial.

952 *as it is red*: cf. Apoc. 21.23.

955–6 *spredith his bemes*: the printed text reads 'erudiunt', but a variant 'irradiant', must have been in Hoccleve's source, and is confirmed by his identical translation of the word later in his text ('spred with the bemes of his magestee').

957–8 *fretynge cold no sharpness*: Lat. 'frigoris ardorisve asperitas' [harshness of heat or cold]. Possibly Hoccleve's source omitted 'ardorisve', and Hoccleve translated 'frigoris' as dependent on the previous nominative 'concursus'?

960 'thynke ne conprehende' is Hoccleve's version of 'in cor hominis ascendit', taken, with its partnering phrases, from 1 Cor. 2.9.

961 *names arn writen in the book of lyf*: cf. Luke 10.20, Phil. 4.3, Apoc. 21.27.

962 *which wasshid hir stoles*: cf. Apoc. 7.14.

967–9 Here the *lectio* includes seven of the nine orders of angels: those omitted are cherubim and seraphim.

972–3 *of apostles…Israel*. The literal translation of an awkward expression in the *lectio*, and dependent on Christ's promise to his apostles in Matt. 19.28 that they would sit on twelve thrones and judge the twelve tribes of Israel, this phrase should probably be glossed 'judging the world as the apostles judge the twelve tribes of Israel'.

985 *the kyngdam of heuene souffrith*: cf. Matt. 11.12 (probably a traditional allegorization).

991 *þat no synne regne*: cf. Rom. 6.12.

995–6 *that is the path… precious blood*: probably Hoccleve's addition.

5. Hic additur alia fabula ad instanciam amici mei predilecti assiduam

[Here is added another fable at the earnest request of my dear friend]

This book thus to han endid had Y thoght,
But my freend made me change my cast. *purpose*
Cleene out of þat purpos hath he me broght. *completely*
'Thomas,' he seide, 'at Estren þat was last, *Easter*
5   I redde a tale, which Y am agast *afraid*
To preye thee, for the laboures sake
That thow haast had, for to translate and make,

'And yit ful fayn wolde Y þat it maad wer. *very gladly*
Th'ensaumple of it to yong men mighte auaille,
10 And par cas cause hem riot to forber *perhaps*
The rather, and be bettre of gouernaille. *sooner; behaviour*
Youthe in no wyse wole his thankes faille *way; willingly*
Flessh for to chepe, femel and venal, *buy; female; for sale*
Payyng for it more than worth is al.

15 'þat thyng is deer and ouer deer boght *expensive; too dearly*
That soule sleeth and the body destroieth,
And the purs emptith, leuyng in it noght *empties*
Or smal. Swich chaffar often sythe annoieth, *little; trade; often*
And yong folk encombrith and accloieth, *people; hinders; cloys*
20 Lettynge hem to purchace hem good renoun, *hindering; reputation*
And haastynge hem to hir confusioun. *hastening; destruction*

'For this is þat Y speke, and to this ende:

A sone haue Y xv yeer of age,   *fifteen*

For whom it is, as wisly God m'amende,   *God help me*

25 þat Y desire into our langage

þat tale be translated, for sauage

And wylde is he and likly to foleye   *act foolishly*

In swich cas. Now helpe if thow maist, Y preye. *such*

'Nat fer the tale fro which thow maad haast   *far from the tale*

30 Of th'emperice, this tale is, Y trowe,   *believe*

And is of a womman þat was vnchaast

And deceyuable and sly, as thow shalt knowe   *deceitful*

By þat the lynes thow red haue on rowe.   *in sequence*

Brynge Y shal thee the copie verray   *true*

35 Therof, if thee list. Seye on, yee or nay.' *please*

'Freend, looth me wer nayseye vnto yow,   *I should be loath to say no*

But Y suppose it may noon othir be   *no other (than that I refuse you)*

Lest wommen vnto Magge the good kow   *chough*

Me likne, and thus seye, "O, beholde and see   *liken*

40 The double man; o, yondir, lo, gooth he   *twofaced*

That hony first yaf and now yeueth galle.   *gave; gives*

He fo in herte is vnto wommen alle.

'Til he of wommen oute wordes wikke   *utter; wicked*

He fastynge is, him seemeth, al the day.

45 Out of his mowth lesynges swarmen thikke.   *lies*

On wommen no good word affoorthe he may,   *produce*

And, if he wel speke or wryte, is no nay,   *there's no denying*

He nat meeneth as he spekith or writ.   *writes*

O lewde dotepol, straw for his wit."   *ignorant fool*

50 'This þat yee me now reede is al contrarie   *advise*

Vnto þat yee me red han heerbefore.   *what; advised; before*

Yee seiden, syn Y many an aduersarie

Had of wommen, for Y mis had me bore   *amiss; behaved*

To hem or this, yee redden me therfore   *before; advised*

55 Humble me to hem, and of grace hem preye,

But this reed haldith al anothir weye.   *advice; tends*

'Sholde Y a neewe smoke now vp reyse, *if; much; raised; before*
And Y so mochil rered haue or now?
By your sawe, than wer Y nat to preise.' *account; I should not be*
                   praiseworthy

60 'Thomas, to wikkid wommen wel maist thow
Yeue hir pars, and wryte of hem euele ynow. *give their parts; enough*
To goode wommen shal it be no shame,
Althogh þat thow vnhonest wommen blame. *dishonest*

'For, Thomas, thow shalt vndirstonde this:
65 No womman wole to theeward maligne *rail against you*
But swich oon as hath trode hir shoo amis, *trodden; shoe*
For, who so dooth, ful suspect is the signe. *if anyone; suspicious; sign*
The vertuous womman good and benigne
Noon encheson but good may han to thee *cause (against you); good (will)*
70 For this tale. Wryte on, par charitee. *for charity's sake*

'Nat oonly for my sones tendrenesse *youthfulness*
Coueite Y þat this tale wer makid, *desire; made*
But to rebuke also the wantonnesse
Of lyf of many a womman þat is nakid
75 Of honestee, and with deshonour blakid— *blackened*
Eek to miroure wommen vertuous *show as in a mirror (to)*
What ende takith swich lyf vicious.' *follows such*

'On Goddes half, freend, than let the copie *in God's name*
Of þat tale, whan yow list, be me sent, *please*
80 And with good wil wole Y therto me hye *hasten to it*
Whan Y therof take haue auisament.' *I have considered it*
He glad was therwithal, and wel content. *with that*
The copie on the morwe sente he me,
And thus Y wroot as yee may heer see.

Explicit prologus, et incipit fabula de quadam muliere mala.
[Here ends the prologue, and begins the tale of a certain wicked woman]

85 Whilom an emperour prudent and wys *formerly*
Regned in Rome, and hadde sones three,
Whiche he hadde in greet chiertee and greet prys, *held; tenderness; value*
And whan it shoop so þat th'infirmitee *happened*

Of deeth, which no wight may eschue or flee,   *avoid*
90   Him threew doun in his bed, he leet do call   *had called*
His sones and before him they cam all,

And to the firste he seide in this maneere:
'Al th'eritage which at the dyynge   *inheritance; death*
Of my fadir he me lefte, al in feere   *together*
95   Leue Y thee, and al þat of my byynge   *purchase*
Was with my peny, al my purchacynge,   *money; winnings*
My second sone, byqwethe Y to thee.'
And to the iiide sone thus seide he: *third*

'Vnmeeble good right noon, withouten ooth,   *unmoveable; truly*
100   Thee yeue Y may, but Y to thee dyuyse   *give; assign*
Iewelles iii, a ryng, brooch and a clooth   *three; cloth*
With whiche, and thow be gyed as the wyse,   *if; will be directed; wise (man)*
Thow maist gete al þat oghte thee souffyse.   *to suffice*
Whoso þat the ryng vsith for to were,   *is accustomed*
105   Of alle folk the loue he shal conquere,   *obtain*

'And whoso the brooch berith on his brest,
It is eek of swich vertu and swich kynde   *also; such power; nature*
That thynke vpon what thyng him lykith best   *let him think; pleases*
And he as blyue shal it haue and fynde.   *quickly*
110   My wordes, sone, enprynte wel in mynde.   *imprint*
The clooth eek hath a merueillous nature
Which þat committed shal be to thy cure: *care*

'Whoso sit on it, if he wisshe where   *sits; anywhere*
In al the world to been, he sodeynly
115   Withoute more labour shal be there.
Sone, tho three iewelles byqwethe Y
To thee, vnto this effect, certeynly,   *to this end*
þat to the studie of the vniuersitee   *(house of) studies*
Thow go, and þat Y bidde and charge thee.'

120   Whan he had thus seid, the vexacioun
Of deeth so haastid him þat his spiryt
Anoon forsook his habitacioun   *at once*
In his body. Deeth wolde no respyt

Him yeue at al. He was of his lyf qwyt,   *give; from; released*
125 And biried was with swich solempnitee
As fil to his imperial dignitee.   *befitted*

Of the yongeste sone I telle shal,
And speke no more of his brethren two,
For with hem haue Y nat to do at al.
130 Thus spak the modir Ionathas vnto:
'Syn God his wil hath of thy fadir do,   *since; done*
To thy fadres wil wole Y me confourme,
And trewely his testament parfourme.   *carry out*

'He iii iewelles, as thow knowist weel,   *three; well*
135 A ryng, a brooch and a clooth, thee byqweeth, *bequeathed*
Whos vertues he thee tolde euerydeel,   *powers; every part*
Or þat he paste hens and yald vp the breeth. *before; gave*
O goode God, his departynge, his deeth,
Ful greuously stikith vnto myn herte,   *stabs*
140 But souffred moot been al, how sore it smerte.' *endured; must; (no matter) how; hurt*

In þat cas wommen han swich heuynesse   *case*
þat it nat lyth in my konnynge aright   *lies; ability; properly*
Yow telle of so greet sorwe the excesse,
But wyse wommen konne take it light   *know how to; easily*
145 And in short whyle putte vnto the flight
Al sorwe and wo, and cacche ageyn confort. *take*
Now to my tale make Y my resort.   *repair*

'Thy fadres wil, my sone, as Y seide eer,   *before*
Wole Y parfourme. Haue heer the rynge, and go
150 To studie anoon. And whan þat thow art theer *at once*
As thy fadir thee bad, do euene so,   *bade*
And, as thow wilt, my blessyng haue also.'
Shee vnto him as swythe took the ryng,   *at once*
And bad him keepe it weel, for anythyng.   *guard; whatever happened*

155 He wente vnto the studie general,   *house of general studies*
Wher he gat loue ynow, and aqueyntance   *got; enough*
Right good and freendly, the ryng causynge al,

And on a day to him befil this chance.   *befell*
With a womman, a morsel of plesance,   *pleasure*
160 By the streetes of the vniuersitee,
As he was in his walkynge, mette he,

And right as blyue he with hir had a tale,   *all at once; conversation*
And therwithal sore in hir loue he brente.   *in consequence; burnt*
Gay, fressh and pykid was shee to the sale,   *tricked out; for sale*
165 For to þat ende and to þat entente   *with that intention*
Shee thidir cam, and bothe foorth they wente   *there*
And he a pistle rowned in hir ere,   *a message; whispered*
Nat woot Y what, for Y ne cam nat there.   *know*

Shee was his paramour, shortley to seye.
170 This man to folkes all was so leef   *people; dear*
þat they him yaf habundance of moneye.   *gave*
He feestid folk and stood at hy boncheef.   *great prosperity*
Of the lak of good he felte no greef,
Al whyles þat the ryng he with him hadde,
175 But, faylynge it, his frendshipe gan sadde.   *decline*

His paramour, which þat ycallid was
Fellicula, meruailled right greetly
Of the despenses of this Ionathas,   *expenses*
Syn shee no peny at al with him sy,   *since; saw*
180 And on a nyght, as þat shee lay him by,
In the bed thus shee to him spak and seide,
And this peticion assoille him preyde: *question; answer*

'O reuerent sire, vnto whom,' quod shee,
'Obeye Y wole ay with hertes humblesse,   *humbleness*
185 Syn þat yee han had my virginitee   *since*
Yow Y byseeche, of your hy gentillesse,   *nobleness*
Tellith me whens comth the good and richesse   *riches*
That yee with feesten folk, and han no stoor,   *entertain; money*
By aght Y see can, ne gold ne tresor.'   *for anything*

190 'If Y telle it,' quod he, 'par auenture   *by chance*
Thow wilt deskeuere it and out it publisshe.   *reveal; abroad*
Swich is wommannes inconstant nature,

They can nat keepe conseil worth a risshe.   *to the slightest degree*
Bettre is my tonge keepe than to wisshe   *to hold*
195   þat Y had kept cloos þat is goon at large,   *secret; what; abroad*
And repentance is thyng þat Y moot charge.'   *must; find burdensome*

'Nay, goode sire, haldith me nat suspect.   *do not suspect me*
Doutith nothyng. Y can be right secree.   *fear; completely secret*
Wel worthy wer it me to been abiect   *rejected*
200   From al good conpaignie, if Y,' quod shee,   *company*
'Vnto yow sholde so mistake me.   *misbehave*
Beeth nat adrad your conseil me to shewe.'   *be; afraid*
'Wel,' seide he, 'thus it is, at wordes fewe.   *in short*

'My fadir the ryng, which þat thow maist see
205   On my fyngir, me at his dyyng day
Byqweeth, which this vertu and propretee   *bequeathed; power*
Hath, þat the loue of men he shal haue ay
þat werith it, and ther shal be no nay   *denial*
Of what thyng þat him lykith axe and craue,   *(it) pleases him to ask for*
210   But with good wil he shal as blyue it haue   *at once*

'Thurgh þat rynges vertuous excellence.   *powerful*
Thus am Y ryche, and haue euere ynow.'   *enough*
'Now, sire, yit a word, by your licence,   *consent*
Suffrith me for to seye and speke now.   *permit*
215   Is it wysdam, as þat it seemeth yow,
Wer it on your fyngir continuelly?'   *to wear*
'What woldest thow mene,' quod he, 'therby?   *by this*

'What peril therof mighte ther befalle?'   *from so doing*
'Right greet,' quod shee. 'As yee in conpaignye
220   Walke often, fro your fyngir mighte it falle,
Or plukkid of been in a ragerie,   *off; moment of playfulness*
And so be lost, and þat were folie.   *a foolishness*
Take it me. Let me been of it wardeyn.   *guardian*
For, as my lyf, keepe it wole Y, certeyn.'

225   This Ionathas, this innocent yong man,
Yeuynge vnto hir wordes ful credence,   *giving*
As youthe nat auysed best be can,   *judicious; knows*

The ryng hir took, of his insipience.   *foolishness*
Whan this was doon, the hete and the feruence   *fervency*
230 Of loue, þat he had beforn purchaced,
The was qweynt, and loues knotte was vnlaced.   *quenched*

Men of hir yiftes for to stynte gan.   *their; began to cease*
'A,' thoghte he, 'for the ryng Y nat ne bere,
Faillith my loue. Fecche me, womman',
235 Seide he, 'my ryng. Anoon Y wole it were.'
Shee roos and into chambre dressith here,   *rose; went*
And whan shee therin hadde been a whyle,
'Allas,' quod shee, 'out on falshode and gyle.   *falsehood*

'The chiste is broken and the ryng take out.'   *chest*
240 And whan he herde hir conplaynte and cry,
He was astoned sore and made a shout,   *greatly astonished*
And seide, 'Cursid be þat day þat Y
The mette first, or with myn yen sy.'   *met you; eyes; saw*
She wepte, and shewid outward cheer of wo,   *appearance*
245 But in hir herte was it nothyng so.

The ryng was sauf ynow, and in hir cheste   *safe enough*
It was. Al þat shee seide was lesyng,   *lies*
As sum womman othir whyle atte beste   *on occasion*
Can lye and weepe whan is hir lykyng.   *her pleasure*
250 This man sy hir wo and seide, 'Derlyng,   *saw*
Weepe no more. Goddes help is ny'—
To him vnwist how fals shee was and sly.   *he was ignorant*

He twynned thens, and hoom to his contree   *left*
Vnto his modir the streight way he wente.   *direct*
255 And whan shee sy thidir comen was he,   *saw*
'My sone,' quod shee, 'what was thyn entente   *intention*
Thee fro the scoole now for to absente?   *school*
What causid thee fro scoole hidir to hye?'   *hasten*
'Modir, right this,' seide he, 'nat wole Y lye.

260 'Forsoothe, modir, my ryng is ago.   *gone*
My paramour to keepe Y betook it,   *to my lover; entrusted*
And it is lost, for which Y am ful wo.   *desolate*

Sorwefully vnto myn herte it sit.'   *it grieves my heart*
'Sone, often haue Y warned thee, and yit   *yet*
265 For thy profyt Y warne thee, my sone.
Vnhonest wommen thow heeraftir shone.   *immoral; shun*

'Thy brooch anoonright wole Y to thee fette.'   *at once; fetch*
Shee broghte it him, and charged him ful deepe,   *earnestly*
Whan he it took and on his brest it sette,
270 Bet than he dide his ryng, he sholde it keepe,   *better*
Lest he the los bewaille sholde and weepe.
To the vniuersitee, shortly to seyn,
In what he kowde he haastid him ageyn.   *as fast as; hastened*

And whan he comen was, his paramour
275 Him mette anoon, and vnto hir him took,   *(he) betook himself*
As þat he dide erst, this yong reuelour.   *before*
Hir conpaignie he nat a deel forsook,   *company; at all*
Thogh he cause hadde, but, as with the hook
Of hir sleighte he beforn was caght and hent,   *deceit; caught and taken*
280 Right so he was deceyued eft and blent.   *after; blinded*

And as, thurgh vertu of the ryng before,   *power*
Of good he hadde habundance and plentee,   *goods*
While it was with him, or he hadde it lore,   *before; lost*
Right so, thurgh vertu of the brooch, had he
285 What good him list. Shee thoghte, 'How may   *goods; pleased*
    this be?
Sum pryuee thyng now causith this richesse,   *secret; wealth*
As dide the rynge heerbefore, Y gesse.'   *before*

Wondrynge heeron, shee preide him and besoghte
Bysyly nyght and day þat telle he wolde
290 The cause of this, but he anothir thoghte.   *differently*
He mente it cloos for him it kept be sholde,   *secret; for himself*
And a long tyme it was or he it tolde.   *before*
Shee wepte ay to and to, and seide, 'Allas   *excessively*
The tyme and hour þat euere Y bore was.   *born*

295 'Truste yee nat on me, sire?' she seide.
'Leuer me wer be slayn in this place   *I would rather*

By þat good lord þat for vs alle deide   *died*
Than purpose ageyn yow any fallace.   *plan; against; deceit*
Vnto yow wole Y be, my lyues space,   *while I live*
300 As treewe as any womman in eerthe is
Vnto a man. Doutith nothyng of this.'

Smal may shee do þat can nat wel byheete,   *little; promise*
Thogh nat parfourmed be swich a promesse.
This Ionathas thoghte hir wordes so sweete
305 þat he was dronke of the plesant swetnesse
Of hem, and of his foolissh tendrenesse
Thus vnto hir he spak and seide tho,
'Be of good confort. Why weepist thow so?'

And shee therto answerde thus, sobbynge:
310 'Sire,' quod shee, 'myn heuynesse and dreede
Is this. Y am adrad of the leesynge   *afraid; losing*
Of your brooch, as almighty God forbeede   *forbid*
It happid so.' 'Now, what, so God thee speede,'   *should happen; bless*
Seide he, 'woldist thow in this cas consaille?'   *advise*
315 Quod shee, 'þat Y keepe mighte it, sanz faille.'   *without*

He seide, 'Y haue a feere and dreede algate,   *always*
If Y so dide, thow woldest it leese,   *lose*
As thow lostist my ryng, now goon but late.'   *so recently*
'First, God preye Y,' quod shee, 'þat Y nat cheese   *may not choose*
320 But þat myn herte as the cold frost may freese
Or elles be it brent with wylde fyr.   *burned up*
Nay, seurly it to keepe is my desyr.'   *safely*

To hir wordes credence he yaf pleneer,   *full*
And the brooch took hir, and aftir anoon,   *at once*
325 Wheras he was beforn ful leef and cheer   *very dear; beloved*
To folk and hadde good, al was agoon.   *property; gone*
Good and frendshipe him lakkid. Ther was noon. *goods. . . were wanting*
'Womman, me fecche the brooch,' quod he,   *quickly*
    'swythe.
Into thy chambre for it go. Now hy the.'   *hasten*

330 Shee into chambre wente as þat he bad,

But she nat broghte þat he sente hir fore— *what*
Shee mente it nat—but as shee had be mad, *as if*
Hir clothes hath shee al torent and tore,
And crydc, 'Allas, the brooch away is bore, *has been carried off*
335 For which Y wole anoonright with my knyf *at once*
Myself slee. Y am weery of my lyf.'

This noyse he herde, and blyue he to hir ran, *quickly*
Weenynge shee wolde han doon as shee spak, *thinking*
And the knyf, in al haaste þat he can,
340 From hir took and threew it behynde his bak,
And seide, 'For the los, ne for the lak
Of the brooch, sorwe nat. Y foryeue al. *forgive*
I truste in God, þat yit vs helpe he shal.'

To th'emperice his modir this yong man
345 Ageyn him dressith. He wente hir vnto, *went*
And whan shee sy him shee to wondre gan. *saw*
Shee thoghte, 'Now sumwhat ther is misdo', *has gone amiss*
And seide, 'Y dreede thy iewelles two *fear*
Been lost now, per cas, the brooch with the ryng.' *by chance*
350 'Modir,' he seide, 'yee, by heuene kyng.'

'Sone, thow woost wel no iewel is left
Vnto thee now but the clooth precious,
Which Y thee take shal, thee chargynge eft
The conpaignie of wommen riotous
355 Thow flee, lest it be to thee so greuous
That thow it nat susteene shalt, ne bere. *endure*
Swich conpaignie, on my blessyng, forbere.' *(as you wish for) my blessing*

The clooth shee fette and it hath him take, *fetched*
And of his lady his modir his leeue
360 He took, but first this forward gan he make: *promise*
'Modir,' seide he, 'trustith this weel, and leeue *believe*
þat Y shal seyn, for sooth yee shul it preeue. *what; true; prove*
If Y leese this clooth, neuere Y your face *lose*
Hensfoorth se wole, ne yow preye of grace. *will see; for grace*

365 'With Goddes help Y shal do wel ynow.' *enough*

Hir blessyng he took and to studie is go,   *university; went*
And, as beforn told haue Y vnto yow,   *before*
His paramour, his priuee mortel fo,   *secret deadly*
Was wont for to meete him, right euene so
370 Shee dide thanne, and made him plesant cheere.   *gave; look*
They clippe and kisse and walke homward in   *embrace; together*
     feere.

Whan they wer entred in the hows, he spradde   *spread*
This clooth vpon the ground, and theron sit,   *sat*
And bad his paramour, this womman badde,
375 To sitte also by him adoun on it.
Shee dooth as þat he commandith and bit.   *orders*
Had shee his thoght, and vertu of the clooth,   *power*
Wist, to han sete on it had shee been looth.   *known; sat; loath*

Shee for a whyle was ful sore affesid.   *very frightened*
380 This Ionathas wisshe in his herte gan: *began*
'Wolde God þat Y mighte thus been esid,   *eased*
That, as on this clooth Y and this womman
Sitte her, as fer wer as þat neuere man   *here; far away (we) were; ever*
Or this cam', and vnnethe had he so thoght   *before; came; scarcely*
385 But they with the clooth thidir weren broght

Right to the worldes ende, as þat it wer.
Whan apparceyued had shee this, shee cryde,   *perceived*
As thogh shee thurghgirt had be with a sper,   *pierced; spear*
'Harrow, allas, þat euere shoop this tyde.   *help; happened; time*
390 How cam we hidir?' 'Nay,' he seide, 'abyde.   *came; wait*
Wers is comynge. Heer soul wole Y thee leue.   *worse; alone*
Wylde beestes thee shuln deuour or eue,   *before night*

'For thow my ryng and brooch haast fro me   *held*
     holden.'
'O reuerent sir, haue vpon me pitee,'
395 Quod shee. 'If yee this grace do me wolden,
As me brynge hoom ageyn to the citee
Wheras Y this day was, but if þat yee   *unless*
Hem haue ageyn, of foul deeth do me dye.   *make me die*
Your bontee on me kythe. Y mercy crye.'   *goodness; show*

400 This Ionathas kowde nothyng be waar,   *not at all beware*
    Ne take ensample of the deceites tweyne   *learn from*
    þat shee dide him beforn, but feith him baar,   *before; (she) bore*
    And hir he comanded, on dethes peyne,
    Fro swiche offenses thensfoorth hir restreyne.
405 Shee swoor, and made therto foreward,   *vowed accordingly*
    But herkneth how shee baar hir aftirward.   *behaved*

    Whan shee sy and kneew þat the wratthe and ire   *saw*
    þat he to hir had born was goon and past   *borne*
    And al was wel, shee thoghte him eft to fyre.   *again; enflame*
410 In hir malice ay stood shee stidefast,   *resolute*
    And to enquere of him was nat agast,   *afraid*
    In so short tyme how þat it mighte be
    That they cam thidir out of hir contree.

    'Swich vertu hath this clooth on which we sitte,'   *power*
415 Seide he, 'þat wher in this world vs be list,   *we please to be*
    Sodeynly with the thoght shuln thidir flitte,   *at once; remove*
    And how thidir come vnto vs vnwist,   *(we) came there; unknown*
    As thyng fro fer vnknowen in the mist.'   *far off; hidden*
    And therwith to this womman fraudulent
420 'To sleepe,' he seide, 'haue I good talent.   *strong desire*

    'Let see,' quod he, 'strecche out anoon thy lappe,
    In which wole I myn heed doun leye and reste.'
    So was it doon, and he anoon gan nappe.
    Nappe? Nay, he sleep right wel atte beste.   *slept*
425 What dooth this womman, oon the fikileste   *of the falsest*
    Of wommen alle, but þat clooth þat lay
    Vndir him, shee drow lyte and lyte away.   *drew little*

    Whan shee it had al, 'Wolde God,' quod shee,
    'I wer as I was this day morwenynge.'   *this morning*
430 And therwith this roote of iniquitee
    Had hir wissh, and soul lefte him ther slepynge.   *alone*
    O Ionathas, lyk to thy perisshynge   *likely to die*
    Art thow. Thy paramour maad hath thy berd.   *has deceived you*
    Whan thow wakist, cause hast thow to be ferd,   *afraid*

435 But thow shalt do ful wel. Thow shalt obteene
     Victorie on hir. Thow haast doon sum deede
     Plesant to thy modir, wel can I weene,   *I truly believe*
     For which our lord God qwyte shal thy meede,   *pay; wages*
     And thee deliure out of thy woful dreede.   *free*
440 The chyld whom þat the modir vsith blesse   *is accustomed to*
     Ful oftensythe is esid in distresse.   *often*

     Whan he awook, and neithir he ne fond
     Womman ne clooth, he wepte bittirly,
     And seide, 'Allas, now is ther in no lond
445 Man werse, I trowe, begoon, than am Y.'   *placed*
     On euery syde his look he caste, and sy   *saw*
     Nothyng but briddes in the eir fleynge   *air flying*
     And wylde beestes aboute him rennynge,   *running*

     Of whos sighte he ful sore was agrysid.   *sorely; afraid*
450 He thoghte, 'Al this wel disserued Y haue.
     What eilid me to be so euel auysid,   *ailed; unreflecting*
     That my conseil kowde I nat keepe and saue?
     Who can fool pleye, who can madde or raue,   *play the fool; grow mad*
     But he þat to a womman his secree
455 Deskeuereth? The smert cleueth now on me.'   *reveals; hurt; sticks*

     He thens departed, as God wolde, harmlees,   *unharmed*
     And foorth of auenture his way is went,   *by chance; took his way*
     But whidirward he drow he conceitlees   *where; went; without idea*
     Was. He nat kneew to what place he was bent.
460 He paste a watir which was so feruent   *passed; hot*
     þat flessh vpon his feet lefte it him noon.
     Al cleene was departid fro the boon.   *was completely taken; bone*

     It shoop so þat he had a lytil glas,   *happened*
     Which with þat watir anoon filled he,   *at once*
465 And whan he ferther in his way goon was,   *had gone*
     Before him he beheeld and sy a tree   *saw*
     þat fair fruyt baar, and þat in greet plentee.   *bore*
     He eet therof—the taast him lykid wel —   *ate; pleased*
     But he therthurgh becam a foul mesel,   *leper*

470 For which vnto the ground for sorwe and wo
He fil, and seide, 'Cursid be þat day   *fell*
þat I was born, and tyme and hour also
þat my modir conceyued me for ay.   *ever*
Now am I lost, allas and weleaway!'   *woe*
475 And whan sumdel slakid his heuynesse,   *somewhat slackened*
He roos and on his way he gan him dresse.   *betook himself*

Anothir watir before him he sy   *(body of) water; saw*
Which for to comen in he was adrad,   *afraid*
But, nathelees, syn therby othir way   *nevertheless; since near it*
480 Ne aboute it ther kowde noon been had,
He thoghte, 'So streytly am I bystad   *placed in such dire straits*
þat, thogh it sore me affese or gaste,   *terrify; frighten*
Assaye it wole I,' and thurgh it he paste.   *attempt*

And right as the firste watir his flessh
485 Departed from his feet, so the secownde   *removed*
Restored it, and made al hool and fressh.   *whole*
And glad was he and ioieful þat stownde,   *time*
Whan he felte his fete hoole wer and sownde.
A viole of the watir of þat brook   *phial*
490 He filde, and fruyt of the tree with him took.

Foorth his iourneye this Ionathas heeld,
And, as þat he his look aboute him caste,
Anothir tree from afer he byheeld,   *afar off; beheld*
To which he haastid and him hyed faste.
495 Hungry he was, and of the fruyt he thraste   *(some) of; thrust*
Into his mowth and eet of it sadly,   *fully*
And of the leepre he pourged was therby.   *leprosy; cured*

Of þat fruyt more he raghte and thens is goon,   *took; departed*
And a fair castel from afer sy he,   *afar; saw*
500 In compas of which heedes many oon   *circuit; many heads*
Of men ther heeng as he mighte wel see,   *hung*
But nat for þat he shone nolde or flee.   *shrink back*
He thidirward him dressith the streight way   *took the direct way*
In al þat euere þat he can or may.   *as quickly as*

505 Walkynge so, two men cam him ageyn   *towards*
     And seiden thus, 'Deer freend, we yow preye
     What man be yee?' 'Sires,' quod he, 'certeyn,
     A leeche I am, and, thogh myself it seye,   *doctor*
     Can for the helthe of seek folk wel purueye.'   *sick; provide*
510 They seide him, 'Of yondir castel the kyng
     A leepre is, and can hool be for nothyng.   *leper; healed; under no*
                                                                   circumstances

     'With him ther hath been many a sundry leeche
     þat vndirtook him for to cure and hele
     On peyne of hir heedes, but al to seeche   *of (losing) their heads; in vain*
515 Hir art was. Waar þat thow nat with him dele,   *beware*
     But if thow canst the chartre of helthe ensele,   *unless; know how to; ensure*
     Lest þat thow thyn heed leese as diden they.   *lose*
     But thow be wys, thow fynde it shalt no pley.'   *unless; game*

     'Sires,' seide he, 'yow thanke I of your reed,   *advice*
520 For gentilly yee han yow to me qwit,   *generously; conducted*
     But I nat dreede to leese myn heed.   *lose*
     By Goddes help ful sauf keepe I wole it.   *safe*
     God of his grace swich konnynge and wit   *learning*
     Hath lent me þat I hope I shal him cure.   *believe*
525 Ful wel dar I me putte in auenture.'   *to the trial*

     They to the kynges presence han him lad,
     And him of the fruyt of the second tree
     He yaf to ete, and bad him to be glad,   *gave*
     And seide, 'Anoon your helthe han shul yee.'
530 Eek of the second watir him yaf he
     To drynke, and whan he tho two had receyued,   *those*
     His leepre from him voided was and weyued.   *leprosy; removed; healed*

     The kyng, as vnto his hy dignitee
     Conuenient was, yaf him largely,   *fitting; gave; generously*
535 And to him seide, 'If þat it lyke thee   *please*
     Abyden heer, I more habundantly
     Thee yeue wole.' 'My lord, sikirly,'   *give; certainly*
     Quod he, 'fayn wolde I your pleisir fulfille,   *pleasure*
     And in your hy presence abyde stille,   *remain*

540 'But I no whyle may with yow abyde,
    So mochil haue I to doone elleswhere.'   *much; do*
    Ionathas euery day to the see-syde,
    Which was ny, wente to looke and enquere   *ask*
    If any ship drawynge thidir were
545 Which him hoom to his contree lede mighte,
    And on a day of shippes had he sighte.

    Wel a xxxti toward the castel drawe,   *about thirty; drew*
    And atte tyme of euensong they alle
    Arryueden, of which he was ful fawe,   *very glad*
550 And to the shipmen crie he gan and calle,
    And seide, 'If it so happe mighte and falle   *befall*
    þat some of yow me hoom to my contree
    Me brynge wolde, wel qwit sholde he be',   *rewarded*

    And tolde hem whidir þat they sholden go.
555 Oon of the shipmen foorth stirte atte laste   *came; at the last*
    And to him seide, 'My ship, and no mo
    Of hem þat heer been, hem shape and caste   *prepare and plan*
    Thidir to weende. Let see, tell on faste,'   *journey*
    Quod the shipman, 'þat thow for my trauaille   *what; labour*
560 Me yeue wilt if þat I thidir saille.'   *give*

    They wer accorded. Ionathas foorth gooth   *agreed*
    Vnto the kyng, to axe of him licence   *ask; permission*
    To twynne thens, to which the kyng was looth,   *depart; reluctant*
    And nathelees, with his beneuolence,   *nevertheless; good will*
565 This Ionathas from his magnificence
    Departed is, and foorth to the shipman
    His way he takith as swythe as he can.   *quickly*

    Into the ship he entrith, and, as blyue   *as soon*
    As wynd and wedir good shoop for to be,   *were in prospect*
570 Thidir as he purposid him arryue   *where; proposed*
    They saillid foorth and cam to the citee
    In which this serpentyn womman was shee
    That had him torned with false deceitis—   *turned*
    But wher no remedie folwith, streit is.   *follows; it is difficult*

575 Tornes been qwit, al be they goode or badde,   *repaid, whether*
    Sumtyme thogh they put been in delay.   *put off*
    But to my purpos. Shee deemed he hadde   *thought*
    Been deuoured with beestes many a day
    Goon. Shee thoghte he deliured was for ay.   *past; removed*
580 Folke of the citee kneew nat Ionathas,
    So many a yeer was past þat he ther was.   *since*

    Mislykynge and thoght changed eek his face.   *unhappiness; also*
    Abouten he gooth, and for his dwellynge   *about*
    In the citee he hyred him a place,
585 And therin excercysid his konnynge   *skill*
    Of phisyk, to whom weren repeirynge   *medicine; coming*
    Many a seek wight, and all wer helid.   *sick person; healed*
    Wel was the seek man þat with him hath delid.   *happy; dealt*

    Now shoop it thus, þat this Fellicula—   *happened*
590 The welle of deceyuable doublenesse,   *deceitful*
    Folwer of the steppes of Dalida—   *in the footsteps of Delila*
    Was thanne exaltat vnto hy richesse,   *raised up; riches*
    But shee was fallen into greet seeknesse,
    And herde seyn, for nat mighte it been hid,
595 How maistreful a leche he had him kid.   *doctor; shown himself*

    Messages solempne to him shee sente
    Preyynge him to do so mochil labour   *much*
    As come and seen hir, and he thidir wente.
    Whan he hir sy, þat shee his paramour   *saw*
600 Had been, he wel kneew and, for þat dettour
    To hir he was, hir he thoghte to qwyte   *repay*
    Or he wente, and no lenger it respyte,   *before; defer*

    But what þat he was, shee ne wiste nat.   *knew*
    He sy hir vryne and eek felte hir pous,   *saw; urine; also; pulse*
605 And seide, 'The soothe is this, pleyn and plat.   *bare*
    A seeknesse han yee strange and merueillous,
    Which for to voide is wondir dangerous.   *remove; very difficult*
    To hele yow ther is no way but oon.
    Leche in this world othir can fynde noon.   *doctor; no other*

610 'Auysith yow whethir yow list it take *consider; please*
Or nat, for Y told haue yow my wit.'
'A, sir,' seide shee, 'for Goddes sake,
þat way me shewe and Y shal folwen it,
Whateuere it be, for this seeknesse sit *sits*
615 So ny myn herte þat Y woot nat how *near*
Me to demene. Telle on, preye Y yow.' *to conduct myself*

'Lady, yee muste openly yow confesse, *make confession*
And, if ageyn good conscience and right *against*
Any good han yee take, more or lesse, *property; taken*
620 Beforn this hour of any maner wight, *before; from anyone at all*
Yilde it anoon, elles nat in the might *return; at once; or*
Of man is it to yeue a medecyne *give*
þat yow may hele of your seeknesse and pyne. *pain*

'If any swich thyng be, telle out, Y rede, *advise*
625 And yee shul been al hool, Y yow byheete, *whole; promise*
Elles myn art is naght, withouten drede.' *otherwise; useless; doubt*
'O lord,' shee thoghte, 'helthe is a thyng ful sweete.
Therwith desir Y souerainly to meete. *with it (i.e. health)*
Syn Y it by confessioun may rekeuere, *regain*
630 A fool am I but I my gilt deskeuere.' *unless; reveal*

How falsly to the sone of th'emperour,
Ionathas, had shee doon, before hem alle,
As yee han herd aboue, al þat errour
Bykneew shee. O Fellicula, thee calle *confessed*
635 Wel may Y so, for of the bittir galle
Thow takist the begynnynge of thy name,
Thow roote of malice and mirour of shame.

Than seide Ionathas, 'Wher arn tho three *those*
Iewelles þat yee fro the clerk withdrow?' *removed*
640 'Sir, in a cofre at my beddes feet yee
Shul fynde hem. Opne it and see, preye Y yow.'
He thoghte nat to make it qweynte and tow, *make difficulties*
And seye nay and streyne courtesie, *insist too much*
But with right good wil thidir he gan hye. *thither; hastened*

645 The cofre he opned and hem ther fond.   *found*
     Who was a glad man but Ionathas, who?
     The ryng vpon a fyngir of his hond
     He putte, and the brooch on his brest also.
     The clooth eek vndir his arm heeld he tho   *also; held; then*
650 And to hir him dressith to doon his cure,   *takes himself; perform*
     Cure mortel, way to hir sepulture.   *fatal; tomb*

     He thoghte reewe shee sholde, and forthynke   *repent; be sorry*
     þat shee hir hadde vnto him misbore,   *misbehaved*
     And of þat watir hir he yaf to drynke   *gave*
655 Which þat his flessh from his bones before
     Had twynned, wherthurgh he was almoost lore   *separated; lost*
     Nad he releeued been, as yee aboue   *had he not been delivered*
     Han herd, and this he dide eek for hir loue.   *also*

     Of the fruyt of the tree he yaf hir ete   *gave*
660 Which þat him made into the leepre sterte,   *develop leprosy*
     And as blyue in hir wombe gan they frete   *at once; gnaw*
     And gnawe so þat change gan hir herte.
     Now herkneth how it hir made smerte.   *suffer*
     Hir wombe opned and out fil eche entraille   *fell; organ*
665 That in hir was. Thus seith the book sanz faill.   *in truth*

     Thus wrecchidly, lo, this gyle [wom]man dyde.   *deceiving*
     And Ionathas with tho iewelles three   *those*
     No lenger ther thoghte to abyde   *longer; remain*
     But hoom to th'emperice his modir hastith he,
670 Wheras in ioie and in prosperitee
     His lyf ledde he to his dyynge day.
     And so God vs graunte þat we do may.
        Amen

Th'emperour þat Y spak of aboue is our lord God, þat hath iii sones. By
the firste sone, we shul vndirstonde angels, to whiche God yaf swich confir-
675 macion [*whom God so confirmed*] þat they may nat synne, for aftir þat the
wikkid angels fillen [*fell*], the goode angels so sadly [*firmly*] weren adherent
[*attached*] to God, and by him so confermed þat they mighten nat synne.
By the second sone, we shul vndirstonde patriarks and prophetes, to whiche
God yaf and bytook [*entrusted*] the olde lawe (þat is to seye, the lawe of

680 Moyses), which was meuable [*moveable*], for it changid by the comynge of
Cryst.

To the iiide [*third*] sone this emperour yaf the iewelles, þat is to seyn the
ryng, the brooch and the clooth. By the ryng þat is rownd we shul vndirstande feith which is rownd withouten obliquitee or crookidnesse, and
685 whoso hath the ryng of verray [*true*] feith he shal haue the loue of God and
of his angels. Wherof our sauueour spekith and seith thus: 'If yee haue as
mochil feith as is the greyn of senefee [*mustard*], yee shuln mowe [*be able
to*] seye to this hil, "Passe and go", and it shal passe'. And therfore he þat
hath the ryng of verray feith, he shal haue al thyng at his lust and plesance.
690 [*desire and pleasure*] God yaf [*gave*] also to the Cristen man a brooch (þat
is to seyn, the holy goost), and seyde, 'I shal sende to yow the holy goost
and he shal telle and informe yow of al þat Y seye.' And if we haue the holy
goost in our hertes, withouten doute we shul han alle goodes þat profyten
to the helthe of soule. Also God yaf to the Cristen man the iiide [*third*]
695 iewel, þat is to seyn, the precious clooth. This clooth is parfyt charitee
[*perfect love*], which God shewid [*showed*] vs in the crois [*Cross*]. He loued
vs so mochil þat he deide [*died*] for vs to brynge vs to eternel blisse. Therfore
whoso sittith vpon parfyt charitee, doutelees he shal be translated out of
this world vnto perpetuel reste.

700 The seid Ionathas may be clept [*called*] a Cristen man which is sliden or
fallen into synne. His paramour (þat is to seyn, his wrecchid flessh) cometh
to him and meetith him, stirynge him to synne, and so he leesith [*loses*] the
ryng of feith which he receyued and took in his bapteme. Also the brooch
(þat is to seyn, the holy goost) fleeth from hym by cause of his synne. The
705 clooth eek [*also*] is withdrawen from him (þat is to seye, parfyt charitee)
as often as he consentith to synne, and thus the wrecchid man dwellith or
abydith withouten help among beestes (þat is to seyn, with the feend, the
world and the flessh).

Do therfore as dide Ionathas. Ryse vp fro thy synne, ryse vp, for al to longe
710 haast thow slept in the lappe of carnalitee or flesshlyhede [*fleshliness*], as it
is writen: 'Aryse vp, thow þat sleepist, and Y shal enlumyne [*enlighten*]
thee.' Right so Sampson slepte in the lappe of Dalida, and loste his
strengthe. Ionathas roos and entred into the watir of penance, which twynneth and disseuerith [*divides and removes*] the flessh (þat is to seyn, flesshly
715 affeccions). Aftirward he eet of the fruyt of sharpnesse which changed his
cheer [*appearance*] into the manere of a leepre, as it is red of Cryst: 'We sy

[*saw*] him as hauynge no chiere or contenance.'[*human expression*] Right
so of the soule, which is in bittirnesse for the wroght offense and synne,
wherof it is seid in the figure and liknesse of the soule, 'Blak Y am, but Y
720 am fair', þat is to seyn, blak in body, and fair in soule.

Ionathas entred the second watir which restored al etc. This watir is the
holy communioun aftir penitence, wherof spak our sauueour,'I am the
welle. Whoso drynkith of þat watir, he shal nat thriste ageyn.' Aftir, this
Ionathas eet of the fruyt of the second tree, which restored al þat was lost
725 (þat is to seyn, whan man is glorified in eternel lyf), and helith the kyng
(þat is to seyn, resoun), and so he entrith the ship of the chirche and to his
paramour (þat is to seyn, his flessh) he purueieth [*provides*] watir of contricioun and fruyt of penance and sharpnesse, for which the flessh (þat is to
seyn, carnel or flesshly affeccioun), sterueth [*dies*] and dieth, and the man
730 purchaceth and getith by penitence the goodes þat wer lost, and so he gooth
into his contree (þat is to seyn, the regne [*kingdom*] of heuene), to which
God of his grace brynge vs alle. Amen.

Go, smal book, to the noble excellence
Of my lady of Westmerland, and seye
735 Hir humble seruant with al reuerence
Him recommandith vnto hir nobleye   *recommends; nobility*
And byseeche hir on my behalue and preye   *behalf*
Thee to receyue for hir owne right,
And looke thow in al manere weye   *every way*
740 To plese hir wommanhede do thy might.   *womanliness; all you can*

Humble seruant to your gracious noblesse   *ladyship*
    T. Hoccleue.

Notes

For general comment on the genre of this tale, see headnote to 3. No easily accessible modern edition exists of any of the analogues other than those in Middle English, for which see Herrtage. The version in Ha2 was edited by Mitchell in his dissertation (full reference, Mitchell 1968: 46). The tale's distinctive sexual interest has a parallel of sorts in the last section of the *Fasciculus Morum*, on lechery: for example, its ch. 14, which links the prodigal son of Luke 15 and the whore of Prov. 29.3 (Wenzel 1989: 692).

rubric *H offers: [B this book, *ruled through*] here bigynneþ þe prologe of the tale [B *om*. of the tale] of Jonathas [LS Jonatas].

21   *haastynge*: haste is important as both narrative element and moral comment in the tale of Jonathas: cf. 121, 153, 258, 273, 328–9, 335, 338, 494, 558, 567–8. This material is often without parallel in the analogues (though at 258 'hye' parallels Ha2 'cito'; at 324, 'anoon' renders 'cito'). It also figures prominently in the other tales, where it links figures as disparate as the repentant sinner (5.709) and Hoccleve himself (3.976): cf. 1.137–8, 148, 375, 2.12, 247, 249, 3.41–2, 75, 276, 415, 438, 462, 616, 637, 738, 741, 894, 4.95, 200, 330, 392, 459, 473, 534, 570, 668, 684. Haste is a shifting moral figure: disapproved of at 2.646, 655 by contrast with mature deliberation, it is also approved of at 5.709 in the context of securing the soul's salvation.

29   In the text cited by Mitchell 1968 and Seymour as closest to the source of Hoccleve's two translations from the *Gesta* (i.e. Ha2), some 30 folios separate the two tales. Other copies of the *Gesta* consulted have a similar gap, the Jonathas story occurring in the middle and the Ierelaus story near the very end, which may explain why there are fewer instances of variation between the analogues to this story than between the corresponding analogues to the Ierelaus

story. (As with the Ierelaus story, though, the instances of variation noted here generally favour other MSS than Ha2 as closest to Hoccleve's source.)

38   Pryor suggests a parallel with *ProlWBT* (*CT* III.232): the implication is that Hoccleve has turned chatterer?

65   All MSS so read this line, and MED glosses 'malign' in the sense given in the sidenote, but the usage is sufficiently uncommon to suggest emendation to 'to theeward be maligne'.

84   BCS have the rubric: 'here endith the prolog and bygynneth the tale.'

88–9   'th'infirmitee/Of deeth which no wight may eschue or flee/Him threew doun in his bed' is a fuller version of what occurs in the analogues (cf. Ha2 'in extremis iacuisset'); similarly at 120–1 'the vexacioun/ Of deeth so haastid him' (Ha2 'vertit se ad parietem') makes death active and the father passive, by contrast with the analogues. The opening may therefore evoke echoes of Hoccleve's Suso translation (4.47, 351, 391, 473, 475, 534, 557, 620, 684, 701, 776).

90   'threew doun': did Hoccleve read 'iacuisset' of Ha2 (ME analogues 'laye') as 'iecisset' ('had thrown')? Or did his source contain the latter reading?

127–9   Hoccleve's addition? The analogues briefly describe how the two sons took what had been left to them.

131–2   This probable addition, repeated at 148–9 (also an addition), presents a figure of obedience not unlike that in *ClT* ('how sore it smerte', 140). Since Hoccleve doesn't elaborate upon or otherwise modify the moralization at the end, he denies himself the possibility of reading the mother (as Chaucer's source for *ClT*, Petrarch, reads Griselda) as emblematic of obedience, the obverse of Fellicula. Fellicula pretends obedience at 184, where Hoccleve is following the Latin.

138–47 Again, a probable addition by Hoccleve. The Latin analogues are not characterized by extensive narratorial comment of this sort, reserving their comment for the concluding *moralizacio*. The heightening of the emotional temperature has reminiscences of Chaucer's practice in *MLT* (similarly based on a fairly bloodless semi-allegorical narrative); Hoccleve's added authorial comments about 'wyse wommen' (an echo of *ProlWBT*?) throw in question the sufferings previously described by the Empress and at first endorsed by the narrator.

155 *studie general* translates literally 'studium generale'.

156–7 The analogues want this material, though Hoccleve may have been translating Ha2's 'miro modo proficiebat' (Herrtage 'he lerned in a mervelous maner'). Hoccleve's version, that is, sets Jonathas up from the start as a youthful prodigal, who engages in 'ragerie' (221) and is ill-advised and foolish (226–7), phrases with no equivalents in the analogues. The focus on his activity continues with his meeting the prostitute (see also following nn.). Against the view of Jonathas as prodigal (cf. 276 'yong reuelour') whose 'foolissh tendrenesse' (306) contributes to his own downfall, we also have the view of him as an innocent abroad (225, not in the analogues). Similarly, his repentance (262–3), his trust in God (343, 365, 523, derived from an earlier expression of trust, 251), and his unspecified good deed for his mother (436–7), most of these wanting in the analogues, point forward to God's care of him (456) and his moral recovery (cf. Seymour's n. to l. 251), and help to make the moral line, as opposed to the allegorical reading

offered by the moralization, clearer from the start.

159 Cf. previous n. Fellicula is described from the outset as a prostitute (159, 164–6), and worse, his 'priuee mortel foo' (368), 'oon the fikileste of wommen alle' (425–6), 'roote of iniquitee' (430: cf. *MLT*, *CT* II.358), 'serpentyn womman' (572: cf. *CT* II.360) so as to accommodate her as well to the cautionary frame requested by Friend in the prologue (and cf. below 177); by contrast, in the analogues, which want this added material, she is merely a fair woman, and the Empress warns Jonathas against women in general and not specifically against 'vnhonest wommen' (266) and 'wommen riotous' (354). A vague parallel exists with Hoccleve's modifications to his source's reference to women in the 'Epistre' (cf. VI.10n.).

161 The analogues have the prostitute meeting him here, as she will do on his later returns (275, 369) and as the two men do when he is on his way back from his desert experience (505), possibly as a way of suggesting that evil and good impulses come from outside a person. With the former, cf. Prov. 7.10, also cited in *Fasciculus Morum* (Wenzel 1989: 704).

162 Cf. 167, the latter with a clear echo of *WBT* (*CT* II.1021). Ha2 wants the latter phrase, and its nearest approximation in the other analogues is 'et cum ea statim de amore inordinato loquebatur' (so D4D5Ha3, followed by the ME prose versions): this phrase is used again for illicit love in the *Gesta* narrative of Ierelaus (cf. 3.79n.).

175 *sadde*: MED gives the sense 'grow wearied of/grow sated with' for 'sadde'. The sense offered in the gloss is recorded by the OED but not until the seventeenth century.

189 The two main readings of D and *H have equal support from the analogues: Ha2 reads 'pecunias', D4D5 'denarium nec thesaurum', Oxford Bodley MS Douce 101 'aurum vel pecuniam'. Parallels with the Middle English analogues may favour *H's reading: Ad2 reads 'peny', Ha5 'mony'.

194 On holding one's tongue: this speech, which expands on the analogues, strengthens the parallels between Fellicula and Delila (see further 591n.).

207 *of men*: *H's reading 'of alle folk' may also be authorial because it echoes the earlier words of the dying Emperor (105): cf. Introduction n.111. The analogues provide support for both readings: D4Ha2 hominum, D5 omnium.

241 'was astoned sore' corresponds to the ME analogues; at this point the Latin analogues all offer the much stronger 'commota sunt omnia viscera eius', a phrase also generally applied, though not in Ha2, to characters in the other *Gesta* narrative at points corresponding to Hoccleve's 3.364–5, 621. The present narrative ends (664–5) with a literalization of the Latin.

242 An echo of Job 3.3, repeated at 471–3, and found both times in the analogues, best in Ha2 and Ad1, which makes for connections with 'My Compleinte' and the Suso, in both of which material from the book of Job is prominent (cf. 1.400, 4.103–4, 318–19).

246–9, 252 Without parallel in the analogues, this material makes clear, as Hoccleve did earlier when he made her a prostitute, Fellicula's moral state. In leaving an uncertainty, however slight, over the character of the prostitute at this point, the analogues dramatize rather more directly than Hoccleve the deceitful appearances of the 'wrecchid flessh'. Hoccleve, within the terms of the fictional commission, is at pains to leave his teenage reader in no doubts about his protagonists' moral states. (On suspense in Hoccleve's version, cf. 377n.)

254 *the streight way* (repeated at 503): Hoccleve maybe adds 'streight' for its moral implication. Alternatively, since haste characterizes so many of the actions in the *Series* (see 21n. above), he simply uses the word to impart speed to his narrative.

285 The characters' private thoughts (cf. 346–7, 481–3, 627–30) are generally not found in the analogues (an exception is 380–4, of Jonathas). Private thoughts are slightly more in evidence in the first *Gesta* narrative (3.136, 346–8). It may be significant that morally undesirable characters generally have the monopoly

of such thoughts: we should contrast these with the private thoughts of Hoccleve in 'My Compleinte' (1.33n.).

307 In the analogues Jonathas explains the virtue of the brooch to his lover at this point, and she weeps again (as in the following lines) for fear it might be lost.

372–3 Comparable material is wanting in Ha2, which has only 'dixit amasie ut secum super pannum sederet', but provided by D4D5: 'cumque hospicium intrabat, pannum sub se extendebat et dixit amasie ut secum super pannum sederet'.

377 Hoccleve generates suspense at this point in the narrative, in a passage growing out of a phrase in the analogues (Ha2 'ipse vero dissimulabat'), when he has Jonathas conceal his real motive for asking his mistress to join him on the magic carpet. The moment develops his earlier refusal to share the secret of the brooch with her (291–2).

381 *wolde God*: repeated at 428 when Fellicula leaves Jonathas alone. In the first instance D4D5 offer 'ut vellet Deus' against Ha2's 'utinam', but the similarity to Hoccleve's version may be accidental, and at 428 all the analogues share Ha2's 'vtinam'.

402 D's reading 'feith him baar', in ironic anticipation of 406, may mean '(she) promised faith to him' on the analogy of 'swear/promise faith' (neither MED nor OED offers this sense of the phrase). Of the alternatives, that of *H, 'fayr him baar' could just carry a sense like 'made him a fair promise', while the emendation of Seymour and Furnivall, 'feith hir baar', with the support of one MS (Y), continues the sense of 400–1 (the credulity of Jonathas) and is the easiest of the three. It receives the support of the analogues (e.g. Ha2 'Jonathas vero adhi[b]ebat fidem dictis suis').

420 The *H reading is possibly closer to the analogues: Ha2D4 'ultra quam credi potest', Douce 101 'oculi mei vero tam sunt gravati quod libenter vellem dormire'.

422 Cf. Judges 16.19 (Samson and Delilah) and 591n.

429 *this day morwenynge*: the analogues variously offer 'hodie' (Ha2) or 'mane' (D4D5). Since there have been no time references prior to this moment, Hoccleve's 'morwenynge' may be translating the latter.

432–41 An apostrophe without parallel in the analogues, which reinforces Hoccleve's bending of the allegory in the direction of a moral lesson relevant to the first fictional reader.

448 *rennynge*: Ha2 'ambulantes', D4D5 'currentes', where the latter is probably closer to Hoccleve's version.

447–8 Here and later in the story (580–82) the situation of Jonathas has interesting parallels with that of the Middle English romance *Sir Orfeo* (for a recent edition see Burrow 1977): with the later material, cf. Arcite in Chaucer's *Knight's Tale*.

455 A metaphoric anticipation of his future punishments (460–2).

463 This 'glas' was prepared for in Ad1 as part of the food Jonathas took with him when first he sat upon the carpet. Here, its unexpected appearance reinforces the romance feel of the narrative.

482 Fear ('affese', 'gaste') characterizes other actions in the later part of the story (379, 411) and makes for clear verbal links with the Suso (4.345, 597, 669, 687, 742, 762; cf. 2.474, 3.50).

496 'sad' is a recurring word, usually applied to firmness of purpose in the *Series* (1.126, 255, 2.366, 558, 3.485, 4.395, 760); in the moralization to this and the Suso it is a property of heaven. Only rarely does it carry a negative meaning (3.402, 5.175n.). So, though it may here mean only 'to satiety', it may also carry an implicit moral charge.

501 *men*: Hoccleve does not follow the analogues here, most of which explain that the heads belonged to unsuccessful doctors. A note in a nineteenth-century hand (that of Douce?) against this moment in D5 notes that it is 'not in the other Gesta. The incident of the heads is used by Occleve'. All the Anglo-Latin analogues consulted do contain this episode, but it is missing from the Germano-Latin tradition, as represented by Oesterley (1872: 468).

512 The unsuccessful doctors recall, earlier in the *Series*, the doctors who could not effect Hoccleve's cure from mental illness (2.85ff.), by contrast with the heavenly 'leeche' who did (1.236). The

figure of the foreign doctor who heals the sick when local doctors could not has a parallel in Ross 1940: 126.22–30.

546–7 At 546 *H's reading is possibly also authorial, and has a parallel in Ad1 ('at the laste'); that in Ha5 ('at the laste, in a certeyne day') has elements of both *H and D. At 547, by contrast, D shares the reading of the analogues (*exc.* Ha3 xxxi) against *H.

552 D's 'me' is probably an accidental error of anticipation of the pronoun at the head of the next line; *H omits it.

558–60 This speech in which the shipman negotiates a price for the voyage with Jonathas has a parallel in Ha2 ('convenit cum eis') and Ad1 ('made a covenaunt with him'). Its development by Hoccleve may echo the episode in the earlier *Gesta* narrative when the Empress negotiates with the hangmen for the life of the thief (3.442–8, paralleled in the analogues).

568–71 The haste of Jonathas' departure suggests a speedy return to the place where his troubles began (so Ha5, but not Ha2 'post multos dies' or Ad1 'after that many dayes').

573 *torned*: Furnivall reads 'terned' and glosses 'cheated' (from Fr. *terner*, 'to throw a three with a dice').

591 This figure has informed many of the narrative moments previously, notably that where Jonathas lays his head in Fellicula's lap to sleep (cf. 422n.).

634–6 The analogues consulted all call this prostitute Felicia, with the exception of the ME version in Ad1 which reads 'amasia' [lover] as the proper name of the prostitute. (Dr Diane Speed informs me that some copies of the Anglo-Latin *Gesta* do so name her, however.) 'Felicia' makes possible a pun of sorts on *felix/felicitas* and reinforces the story's point about the dangers of false appearances: the felicity which Felicia represents is as false as that offered to Chaucer's Criseyde (*Troilus* III.814) and condemned by Boethius, who makes a prostitute a figure of false appearances in *Consolatio* Bk. III pr.8 (cf. Wenzel 1989: 650). In both D and *H she appears as Fellicula, which gives Hoccleve the chance to pun on the first element of her name (*fel* meaning venom), so as to blacken her character still more, as here.

666 *dyde*: 'did' (so BCLY) or 'died' (so S), though the rhyme requires the latter meaning (though he also uses 'deide' as a spelling of 'died', Hoccleve uses 'y' forms, as here, only for 'died', cf. 2.751, 3.367, never for 'did'). That being so, the emendation of D's 'man' to *H's 'womman' is required, and is supported by the analogues (Ha2 'spiritum tradidit').

673 *H MSS have a rubric: 'here endiþ þe [LY my] tale of Jonathas and of [L om. of] a wickid woman and bigynneth [B begynnyng] þe moralizing [B moralite] therof [LY om. therof]'.

679 *yaf and bytook*: *H 'gave and committed'. Both phrases have a partial parallel in the moralization to the first *Gesta* story: 'committed and bytook'.

682 *the iewelles* is an obvious error in D for 'thre iewelles' (so *H) and is confirmed by the reading of the analogues ('tria iocalia').

686ff D glosses 'Si habueritis fidem sicut granum synapis etc.' (quoting from Matt. 17.20). BCLY include the quotation in the body of the text (all but C om. sicut) and preface it by 'dicit christus'.

691–2 D glosses 'Mittam vobis paraclitum etc.' (cf. John 14.26); *H adds 'suggerit [L suggeret] vobis omnia [BLY gratiam]', from the same verse.

696–7 *loued vs so mochil*: perhaps *H's reading is also authorial, since it echoes a phrase at the beginning of the story (l. 87) and establishes a further link between Jonathas's father and God/Christ.

702 *stirynge*: again, the *H variant 'stirring and exciting' may also be authorial, since it echoes phrases earlier in the *Series* (2.234, 437, 3. moralisatio 985,

1028).

711 D glosses 'Surge qui dormis et illuminabo te etc.' (from Eph. 5.14). *H prefaces by 'dicit [C dixit] Dominus'); BCL end with 'thus seith criste' (BL om. thus). One Latin analogue offers 'surge a sompno id est a peccato'.

712 *in the lappe of Dalida*: cf. above 591n.

716–17 D glosses 'Vidimus eum tamquam vultum non habentem etc.' (*H precedes by 'legitur de Christo'). Cf. Is. 53.2.

719–20 D glosses (*H adds 'in figura anime dicitur') 'Nigra sum set formosa etc.' Cf. Cantic. 1.4.

722 *communioun*: this term could be understood as referring to reception of the Eucharist, though the term is not used before Hoccleve in this sense (the earliest dated example in MED is 1440). In conjunction with penitence, though, it reinforces orthodox teaching, which may have been a subsidiary aim in the production of the narrative. (On Hoccleve's view as heretical of Wycliffite hostility to both 'confessioun auriculeer' and the Eucharist, see his poem against Oldcastle, Furnivall and Gollancz 1970: 11, 18). The alternative reading 'conversation', meaning 'manner of life', and not authorial, figures prominently in the Rule of St Benedict as one of the vows the monk takes.

722–3 D glosses 'Ego sum fons. Qui biberit etc.' (cf. John 4.13–14, represented more fully in *H and preceded by 'ait saluator').

732 *Amen*. Variants: C 'etc. explicit'; S 'amen amen'.

733–40 Omitted in the *H MSS: for comment on the dedicatee, see Burrow 1994: 216 [28].

Appendix 1

The stanzas added to the 'Conpleynte paramont' in the Middle English *Pilgrimage of the Soul*: text from Eg.

My dere childe, my fruyt þat on [me] growed,
Myn lusty appil, blisful faire and sweet,
Now deth hath him beclapped with his clowde,
That him perced vnto the herte rote.
Go to, thow man, þere thu myght haue thi bote.
Go suke the iuce. The is no thing so sweet.
Go take thin part. I rede the not forgete.

Go nere, and see how þat he is forbete,
And alle forpersed sore and pietously.
See how there renne fyve stremes grete,
That yelde owt the iuce habundauntly.
Go sowke therof. I say you faithfully,
In good tyme was he bore, þat hath þat grace,
In tho woundes to make his duellyng place.

O aduersari, [t]how cruel drye tree,
To the speke I, nowe hast þu thi entent.
My sweet fruyt þu hast bereved me
Ageyn my will, nothing of myn assent.
I se how al toraced and torent
On the he hongith: is this weel idoo?
I bare him monethis nyne, but no thing so.

O cruel tree, sith thu hast thi desire,
Whi wilt þu not to my fruyt be fauorabill,
To saue it hool? But feruenter than the fier

He findeth, and nothing agreable.
It is to me but alle discounfortable
To se myn herte attached the vpon,
For he and I, oure hert is but one.

Now with my fruyt art þu here openly,
That alle the world it may beholde and see
Restored, which I sey the sekerly
Is more of vertue and of dignyte
Than was the fruyt þat spoyled was from the.
Thu hast thi will. Thin honoure schal suffise
To the. Yelde me my fruyt in goodly wise.

---

1 me] Eg *om.*   15 thow] Eg how   26 discounfortable] Eg discountfortable

Appendix 2

2A. A comparison of the version of Hoccleve's first *Gesta* narrative with selected Latin and Middle English analogues

This appendix aims to provide fuller substantiation of the claim advanced in the Introduction (pp. 13–14) that the version of this narrative preserved in Ha2 is regularly inferior, as witness to Hoccleve's source, to the versions in D4, D5, Ha4 and Sl. Admittedly, no one manuscript consulted shared all Hoccleve's distinctive readings, and sometimes the translation makes use of words with correspondences in more than one Anglo-Latin version. Thus, for example, in the moralization, where Hoccleve writes of the Empress as 'the soule þat is wel beloued of God, and vnto Cryst weddid and oned' (3.1009–10), that final phrase corresponds to the wording of both Ha2 ('anima deo dilecta et christo nupta') and Sl and Ha4 ('anima deo dilecta et christo unita'). Whether we should conclude from this that Hoccleve was working from two versions of the Anglo-Latin *Gesta*, or rather, and more probably, that he was working from a copy which contained both variants, there is at present no determining. Of course, a third possibility exists, of what we might call a 'doublet translation': that is, the translator, unsure of the reading of the word in his original, translated two possible readings of the word (see discussion of this practice in Brook 1991:121). Nor is it certain but that passages of Hoccleve's text without parallel in any of the manuscripts of the Latin studied may eventually turn out to have derived from Hoccleve's source text (though cf. comments p. 36 above on features of the translated text which I agree with Mitchell 1968 are likely to originate with Hoccleve himself).

In the following list of variants, Hoccleve's version of the *Gesta* narrative is cited by line number alone. Not every variant is recorded, nor is every variant recorded significant. I have asterisked readings closest to Hoccleve's.

3 Ha2 Menelaus] D4D5Ha4 Gerelaus, *Sl Ierelaus.

7 Ha2 pulcra] *D4D5Ha4Sl et oculis hominum (D4 omnium) graciosa.

21 Ha2 ait imperatrici] *D5Ha4Sl imperatrici et fratri suo dixit.

22 Ha2D5 carissima] Ha4Sl karissima domina.

23 Ha2 quod meum propositum est] *D4D5Ha4Sl quod stabilitum est in corde meo.

24–5 Ha2 celari non debet] D4D5Ha4Sl (celare) non possum nec volo.

29–35 *Ha4Sl ut specialem curam de populis meis (Sl populo meo) et terris meis habeas et subtus te frater meus senescallus tocius populi ad ordinandum quod mihi et populo utile fuerit secundum tuum consilium et assensum] Ha2 *om.*, D5 *omits all but last five words.*

50–2 Ha2 quia spero cum sanitate domum venietis] *D5Ha4Sl quia ut (D5 *om.*) spero terram sanctam in uita non (D5 *om.*) exibis, D5 quin terram sanctam visitabis.

65–6 Ha2 eleuauit (D4D5Ha4Sl *add* ultra quam credi posset) cor suum.

70 *D4D5Ha4Sl et diuites spoliauit] Ha2 *om.*

96 Ha2 quando] *Ha4Sl *add* semper.

98 Ha2 ad peccatum] Sl *om.*

111 Ha2 sine consilio meo] *D4D5Sl *add* et assensu.

118 Ha2 precipio vobis] *D4D5Ha4Sl *add* ex parte domini.

124–30 *D4D5Ha4Sl sed in hoc facto oportet vos pro nobis stare coram imperatorem. At illa, in nullo timeatis quia si dominus meus sciret ea in quibus sum experta eum morte turpissima condempnaret] Ha2 *om.*

136 Sl heu mihi] Ha2 *om.*

138 *Ha2 hac de causa] Ha4 *om.*

139–40 Ha2 et tunc pro perpetuo gratiam fratris mei et forte vitam meam amittam] Ha4 (*for* perpetuo) ea nullam, (*after* mei) inveniam; Sl dolor erit mihi meo perpetuo uel uitam amittam.

141 *D4D5Ha4Sl non fiet (Sl erit) ita] Ha2 *om.*

151 *Sl humiliter] D5Ha2Ha4 *om.*

152 Ha2 o bona (D5Ha4Sl *om.* bona) domina.

154 Ha2D5 filius mortis (Ha4Sl confusionis) sum ego (*both possible*).

163–4 Ha2 si scirem, quod … honestum (D4D5Ha4Sl bonum hominem) ammodo (Ha4 *om.*, D4 in amando) inuenirem.

182 Ha2 at ille presto sum] D4Ha4Sl *add* per omnia voluntati tue subici (Sl obedire, D4 me subicere).

185 Ha2 cum cornibus] *D4D5Ha4Sl canibus.

197 Ha2 cum hoc ille vidisset] *D5Ha4Sl *add* quod sola esset.

200 D5Ha2Ha4 domina] Sl o bona domina.

206–7 Ha2 perpetuam (*D4Ha2Sl propter tuam) correccionem promisisti (*D4Ha4Sl *om.* promisisti).

236 Ha2 ligauit] *D5Ha4Sl stantem dimisit, D4 ligauit et dimisit.

244 Ha2 multitudo populi (D4D5Ha4Sl *add* eis obuiauit et) ab eo imperatrici rapuerat.

268 *Ha2 venatus] Ha4 equitatus, Sl equitaturus.

269 Ha2 comes] *D4D5Ha4Sl *add* extraneus.

275 Cf. Ha2 admirabatur eo quod pulcra erat] D4D5Ha4Sl *add* et oculis hominum graciosa (*repeating* 7 above).

279–80 Ha2 at illa per miraculum Dei uiua fuit] D4D5Ha4Sl *om.*

281–2 Ha2 quomodo huc veni nescio (Sl noui, D5Ha4 *om.*) deus scit (D5Ha4Sl nouit).

290 Ha2 o domina bona, appares generosa] Ha4Sl *om.* appares.

310 Ha2 et comitissa] *D4D5Ha4Sl cum comite et comitissa.

316 Ha2 senescallus qui] D4D5Ha4Sl *add* ultra quam credi potest (*repeating* 65–6 *above*, *phrase later repeated when the Shipman is planning to abduct the Empress, but not translated there*).

319   Ha2 votum] D4D5Ha4Sl *add* solenne.

332–4   Ha2 de nocte] *D4D5Ha4Sl *add* cameram intrauit, *needed for the sense.*

342   Ha2 longum (Sl *om.*) cultellum.

345   Ha2 ipsa nesciente] *Sl dormientis et ignorantis.

349   D4D5Sl unde totum quod cogitauit impleuit] Ha2 *om.*

361–4   Ha2 turbatus est] D4D5Sl commota sunt omnia viscera eius (*a phrase also used of the Empress in Sl at 3.621 and in the second Gesta story of Jonathas in Ha2 at 5.241*).

369   Ha2 expergefacta] D4D5Sl a somno excitata (D5 excitare).

379–80   Sl o domine mi (Ha2 *om.*) interficiatur ista domina diabolica.

448   *Ha2 hominis] D4D5 latronis.

460–4   Ha2 illic vero sic fecit, et in ciuitate moram per aliquos dies traxit] Sl in quo per aliquot dies moram possimus trahere. Qui sicut imperatrix preceperat precessit et hospicium vtile recepit, vbi aliquot dies commorati sunt; D4 et hospicium pro me accipere. Perrexit honestum hospicium pro domina accepit. Cum domina per dies aliquot moram ibidem traxisset.

470   Ha2 homines… (Sl *adds* multi) de amore inordinato ei loquebantur.

522   D4 de pannis presiosis] Ha2 *om.* presiosis.

529   *D4D5Sl karissime] Ha2 *om.*

534   *D4D5Sl et mihi auxilium prebueris] Ha2 *om.*

563   Ha2 extendere] D4D5Sl ostendere (*shown as correct by rep. at 590, though Hoccleve translates neither closely*).

634–6   Ha2 in medio maris *twice*; D4D5Sl in mari *for the second.*

643   Ha2 in medio (*D4D5Sl fine) nauis.

666   Ha2 facta] D4D5 finita.

673   *D4D5 ad terram eam saluam (Ha2 *om.* saluam) duxit.

704–5   *D4D5 et paralisi percussus] Sl et paraliticus, Ha2 *om.*

708–9   Ha2 famulus qui decepit] *D4D5Sl latro qui prodidit (prodidit *confirmed by reading at 900*).

713–14   *D4D5Sl et potagrus (D5 *adds* magnus) plenus et diuersis aliis infirmitatibus percussus] Ha2 *om.*

743–5   *D4D5Sl moniales uero cum de aduentu imperatoris audissent processionaliter ei obuiam processerunt (D4 perrexerunt)] Ha2 *om.*

752   Ha2 talis (D4 *adds* sancta) domina.

801–12   *D4Ha2 at ille: Etiam, domine, magnam offensionem contra vos feci et (D4 nimis graue et ideo) et misericordiam peto, antequam delictum meum pandam. Imperator vero de imperatrice non cogitabat, eo quod credidit eam a multis temporibus esse defunctam, et ait ei: dic mihi, quid contra me deliquisti, quia sine dubio totum tibi remitto] Sl *retains only last five words.*

815   Sl coram omnibus] Ha2 *om.*

884   Ha2 vel quo iuit] Sl vel vbi deuenerit, D4 iuit.

901   Ha2 eam secum duxit] Sl *om.*

904   Ha2 pulcram dominam ac generosam] Sl *om.* ac generosam (cf. apparatus: *H agrees with Ha2, H with Sl).

935–6   Ha2 pre gaudio fleuit] D4Sl *adds* amare (D4 *ruled through*).

Moralization from Ha2, ff. 82r–v

Moraliter. Karissimi, iste imperator est dominus noster Jesus Christus, vxor anima, frater imperatoris est homo cui Deus tradidit curam imperii, scil-icet corporis, tamen principaliter anime. Sed misera caro sepius instigat animam ad peccatum. Sed anima que totaliter Deum pre ceteris amat
5   semper peccato resistit, et accipit suas potencias, scilicet racionem, volun-tatem et intellectum, et talem carnem spiritui non obedientem facit incarcerari carcere penitencie donec racioni in omnibus obediat. Imperator est venturus, scilicet Christus ad peccatorem. Tamen graciam petendo clamat caro et quociens misericordiam habet spem habet, et propter miseri-
10   cordiam cicius vult delinquere. Contra tales loquitur scriptura dicens, Maledictus homo qui peccat in spe. Vnde sepe imperator dimittit carnem a carcere penitencie exire. Lauat eam a peccati sordibus, induit eam bonis virtutibus et facit eam dextrarium caritatis ascendere et in bonis virtutibus equitare vt dominus occurrat in die pasche. Sed prochdolor sepe peccator
15   per viam sacro tempore deliquit. Ceruus fugit, scilicet delectacio peccati, omnes sensus per peccatum currunt et canes, scilicet praue cogitaciones, semper latrant et instigant, sic quod homo, scilicet caro et anima, simul in hac vita derelicta est sine aliqua virtute. Caro hoc percipiens audacter animam Christi nobilem sponsam ad peccatum sollicitat. Tamen anima
20   Deo dilecta et Christo nupta non vult deserere nec ad peccatum concedere [de concedere, de *cancelled*]. Vnde misera caro sepe spoliat animam vesti-mentis, id est bonis operibus et virtutibus, et eam tunc super quercum, id est super delectacionem mundanam, suspendit per crines, id est per malas concupiscencias, donec comes, id est predicator vel discretus confessor,
25   foresta huius mundi venetur sermonizando in piis [*orig.* impiis] operibus consulendo et latrando per verba sacre scripture pronunciando, et sic dominam, scilicet animam, ducit ad domum ecclesie vt nutriat puellam, id est saluet conscienciam in operibus misericordie. Comes autem iuxta lectum habet lampadem; id est, confessor discretus aut predicator semper habet
30   oculum [oculum, osculum *cancelled*] cordis lampadem sacre scripture in qua videt anime noticiam virtutibus in seruiendo. Seneschalus qui eam solic-itauit certe est superbia vite, que est seneschalus mundi, per quam multi decipiuntur, sed anima Deo dilecta non vult superbie consentire, sed aliquando aufert homini bursam plenam auri vel argenti, et proicit eam ante
35   oculos, et sic puellam, id est conscienciam, interficit. Vnde scriptum est, Munera excecant oculos iudicum et peruertunt sapientes quod veritas siue equitas non potuit ingredi et iudicium conuersum est retrorsum. Tales sunt expulsi et expulendi [*sic*] de gremio ecclesie. Anima vero sola equitabat,

vidensque hominem vnum etc. Homo potest duci ad mortem per peccatum
40   mortale. Faciamus nos sicut fecit domina. Percusit [*sic*] equum cum
calcaribus. Sic et nos debemus carnem cum calgaribus [*sic*] penitencie stim-
ulare per proximum sublevare in necessitate, non tantum in temporalibus
sed etiam in spiritualibus. Vnde Salomon, Ve soli, id est in peccato iacenti,
quia non habet vnde subleuari possit. Festina ergo et suscita proximum
45   tuum. Vnde idem, Quicumque dederit potum aque tantum non perdet
mercedem suam. Sed multi sunt ingrati sicut ille latro qui postquam domina
eum saluauit eam decepit, sicut aliqui pro bono reddunt malum. Vnde
Ysaias dicit, Ve illis qui dicunt bonum malum et malum bonum. Magister
nauis est mundus. Iste per quem multi sunt deducti [*corr. to* seducti] in mari,
50   id est in mundo. Nauis frangitur quociens aliquis paupertatem voluntariam
eligit et prelato suo propter deum obedit. Tunc mundum odit et concupi-
scienciam eius, quia inpossibile est mundo placere et Deo. Domina perrexit
ad cenobium. Sic anima ad vitam sanctam propter mundanas vanitates se
diuertit vnde omnes sensus per quos anima erat tribulata interficiuntur
55   diuersis infirmitatibus sicut per oculos per concupiscenciam, auditus per
detraccionem, et sic de ceteris. Vnde anima non potest aperte videri a sponso
suo Christo donec omnes oculi aperti sunt et sic ad gaudium sine dubio
poterit duci. Ad quod nos perducat Christus dominus noster. Amen.

1   Ha2 *dominus noster Jhesus Cristus] Ha4Sl pater celestis.
2   anima] D5 domina sancta.
2–3   Ha2 *scilicet, corporis, tamen (Ha4 sui)] Sl *om.*; Ha2 *sepius] Sl *om.*, D4 semper.
4   Ha2 pre ceteris] Sl *om.*, *D4 pre cunctis, D5 pre cunctis aliis.
5   Ha2 *peccato (Sl carnem) resistit.
5–6   Ha2 rationem, voluntatem (Ha4 *trsp.*) et intellectum (Sl conscienciam), D4 rationem et
         potestatem, intellectum et conscienciam; *D5 rationem, voluntatem, intellectum et
         conscienciam.
8   Ha2 *gratiam petendo] Ha4Sl infundendo, D4 inferendo.
9   Ha2 *quociens misericordiam] D4Ha4Sl, *for* misericordiam, propter (D4 *om.* nimiam)
         habet spem (Ha4Sl *add* misericordie) habet et propter misericordiam (Ha4 *om.* et …
         misericordiam) cicius vult delinquere.
10   Ha2 scriptura] Ha4Sl *add* sacra.
11   Ha2 sepe imperator] *Ha4Sl unde anima eius sepe inclinatur (D4 ei inclinatus).
13   Ha2 *ascendere] Sl sedere; Ha2 in bonis virtutibus] *Ha4Sl operibus.
14   Ha2 in die pasche] *D4D5Ha4 *add* sancto (D5 sancti); Ha2 prochdolor] *D4D5Ha4Sl
         heu et prochdolor.
15   Ha2 per viam (D4D5 *add* carnis) *sacro tempore (Sl, Ha4 sacre scripture); Ha2 fugit
         (D4D5Ha4Sl *surgit) sc. delectacio (Sl dilacio).
16   Ha2 omnes sensus per (*D4D5 post) peccatum currunt] Sl *om.*; Ha2 praue (D4D5
         viles, Ha4 male et pessime, Sl male) *cogitaciones (Sl delectaciones).
19   Ha2 *Christi nobilem] D4 deo dilecta sponsam et nobilissimam.
20   Ha2 et Christo nupta] Ha4Sl unita: *both readings required*; Ha2 deserere] D4Ha4Sl
         dominum (D4 deum) spernere.
21–2 Ha2 bonis operibus et virtutibus] *D4Sl bonis virtutibus.

22   Ha2 delecationem *mundanam] H4Sl *om.* mundanam.

24   Ha2 *predicator vel discretus confessor] Ha4 discretus confessor vel verbi dei predicator.

26   Ha2 sacre (Ha4Sl dei, D5 de) scripture (D5 *om.*) pronunciando et (Sl *om.* scripture… et); Ha2 dominam *scilicet animam] Sl dominam.

27   Ha2 saluet] *Sl Ia4 sanet, D4 lauct, D5 lauat.

28   Ha2 autem iuxta lectum] *D4Ha4Sl ante lectum.

29   Ha2 confessor discretus aut (*D4D5Ha4Sl *add* prelatus uel) confessor; Ha2 oculum] D4D5Ha4Sl oculos.

30–1 Ha2 anime noticiam virtutibus] *D4Ha4Sl nociua et proficua anime, virtutes inserendo et vicia extirpando.

31   Ha2 solicitauit] *Ha4 *adds* ad peccatum.

32   Ha2 *multi (Sl mundani) decipiuntur] *D5Ha4 *add* et seducuntur, D4 seducuntur.

33   Ha2 sed aliquando aufert (D4D5 offert)] *Ha4Sl Quid facit ergo superbia mundana? Certe accipit cultellum auaricie quando offert

34   Ha2 auri vel argenti] D4D5Ha4Sl denariis; Ha2 *ante oculos] D4D5Ha4Sl *add* iusti (Ha4 iustos).

35   Ha2 conscientiam] D4D5Sl *add* sanam, Ha4 *adds* suam.

36   Ha2 *veritas siue equitas] D4D5Ha4Sl equitas.

37   Ha2 et (D4 *adds* vidit quasi retrorsum iudicium); iudicium] *D4D5Ha4Sl sed stetit a longe et iudicium (D5 convertit retrorsum).

37–8 Ha2 *tales sunt… equitabat] Ha4Sl *om.*; *expulsi et] D5 *om.*

38   Ha2 anima] D4D5 *domina.

39   Ha2D4D5 *etc.] Ha4Sl ad patibulum ductum.

40–1 Ha2 *sic et nos… cum calgaribus] Sl *om.*

43–4 Ha2 subleuari possit (Ha4 subleuamentum)] *D4D5 *add* id est auxiliari. Ha4Sl *add* *cum dicitur, frater qui adiuuatur a fratre quasi ciuitas firma.

44   Quicumque] D4Ha2 cum dicitur, Quicumque.

45   Ha2 aque] *D4Ha4Sl *add* frigide.

46   Ha2 decepit] *D4D5Ha4Sl prodidit.

49   Ha2 deducti] *D4D5Sl seducti; Ha2 nauis] Sl nauis est mundi vanitas sicut ait Ecclesiastes, sed; D4 nam omnia vanitas; *D5 nam omnia vanitas ut dicitur Ecclesiastes.

50–1 Ha2 propter deum] D4D5Sl *add* *in omnibus.

53   Ha2 vanitates] D5Sl *tribulaciones.

54   Ha2 interficiuntur] D4D5Sl *inficiuntur.

55   Ha2 sicut per oculos] Sl oculos, *D4D5 sicut oculus; Ha2 per concupiscentiam] *D4D5Sl *add* oculorum.

57   Ha2 omnes oculi (*D4D5 sensus) aperti sunt (*Sl *adds* confessi). Ha2 gaudium] *Sl *adds* paradisi.

2B. The source of Hoccleve's 'Balade… translatee au commandement de… Robert Chichele.'

One full copy survives of the French text of this poem, in R2, used by Stokes and collated with a copy in Ad5, which begins at l. 25 of the copies in R2 and Ca, and omits their ll. 73–80. The Ca copy, edited by Sandison, ends at l. 120 of the copy in the other two manuscripts. The R2 copy appears as prose, with occasional indications of stanza breaks—notably, at ll. 85 and 128, where illuminated capitals have been used. Substantive variants between the manuscripts, printed below, confirm Stokes's view of two distinct textual traditions, represented by Ca and Ad5–R2 respectively. Asterisks indicate close links of particular readings with Hoccleve's version; the ordering of ll. 17–18, 69–70 in Ad5–R2 is especially close to Hoccleve's version, though, as with the *Gesta* versions above, Hoccleve's 'source' may have contained elements of both textual traditions. Sandison's edition should probably be emended at ll. 96 (Si vous pri[ez] me fferrez certain) and 107 (que malme espie).

2   Ca pensant R2 pensif H(occleve) in an heuy musynge.
6   Ca point R2 pright H stang.
10   Ca paynte R2 dedepaint H depeynted.
15   Ca en ihesu crist dounque me, R2 en dieu de tout me cf. H l. 17 on God to thynke.
16   Ca criant Ad2 priant cf. H l. 15 I preyde God mercy.
17–18   Ca De faire bien de mal retrere/ Mes de ceo metter en long respit, *R2 *precedes l. 17 by* De dieu penser donne delit, *and follows with* de fare le bien (*later added*: du mal retrere/ mes le bien) mettre en respit H l.17 On god to thynke it yeueth a delyt/ Wel for to doon and fro synne withdrawe.
29   Ca et verray penaunce si parfere, *?Ad5R2 penaunce et vertue a moi atrere, H l. 30 grante me grace to vertu me take.
32   Ca en cuer et alme estre home parfit Ad5R2 *om.*
41   Ca souerayn jhesu, *Ad5R2 souerain refu, H l. 41 oure souereyn refuyt.
48   Ca de fel enemy, Ad5R2 dil enemy.
49   Ca desire, Ad5R2 et dire, H l. 49 hyly holde I am.
51   *Ca suffrist si grant martire, Ad5R2 a gref maniere, H l. 51 swich a martirdam.
52   Ca soy digne, Ad5R2 deigna.
54   Ca pour mon prie touz iours, Ad5R2 pour amour tou3 maus.
63   Ca que puisse touz malz, *?Ad5R2 que puisse le tiraunt, H l. 63 so þat the feend.
68   Ca teint, Ad5 depeint, R2 teint, H l. 68 died.
69   Ca ceo que iay mepris countre ma foy, *Ad5R2 Allas aallas pieche purqoi, H l.69 Allas, why haue I me to synne applied.
70   Ca par vertu de vous sire soit esteint, *Ad5R2 Malmes aues si dure estraint, H l. 70 why is my soule encombird so with synne.
After 70, *Ad5R2 *add* l. 69, H l. 71 Lord in al þat I haue me misgyed.
78–80   *Ca come faucement ay ma foy enfraint/Et amendre lcz faitz dc moy/De touz que iay foruey plus meint, R2, Des cin3 plaies dont ele fu teint, H l. 79 Of þat forueyed haue I.
85   Ca peyne, R2 pendu.
89–90   Ca saphire/Vaillant de noble engrain, Ad5R2 (R2 la) renomee/ saphir de noble grain.
93   *Ca la seurte de ta pite, *Ad5 la surse de piete, R2 la porte de piete, H 92 Thy welle of pitee, 95 for my seurtee to keepe me fro blame.
97   Ca biens, *Ad5R2 vertuz, H l. 97 vertu.
103   Ca de amendre ma folie vie, Ad5R2 (R2 de) redrescer ma folie.
118   Ca voillez, *Ad5R2 voil, H l. 118 I purpose.

For variants from Ad5 and R2 after l. 120, where the copy in Ca stops, see Stokes 1995. It isn't possible to decide on the superiority of these variants.

Appendix 3

The glosses to 'Ars vtillissima sciendi mori' in S and D

The Introduction argued for the importance of Hoccleve's Suso translation for an under-standing of the whole *Series*. This can be readily demonstrated by a consideration of the glosses to the copies of the text in S (fifteenth century) and D (sixteenth century). Those in S, given in full below, are extremely traditional. Those that occur on the same leaf as the illumination may as well have been generated as a response to that as to the text itself, and their relevance to the text is of a very general kind. The glosses to ll. 155 and 372, by contrast, seem to have been directly inspired by Hoccleve's words. The glosses in D operate an interestingly different (Renaissance) frame of reference, advocating moral living, self-knowledge, and stoic acceptance of the mean, and citing Diogenes, Socrates, and other classical authors. Since these latter are readily available in Furnivall's edition, they are not reprinted here, though the versified comments of one sixteenth-century reader, Thomas Carter, are noteworthy (e.g., alongside l. 98, 'before thou pretend any evill in thyn harte/Remember the end when thow shalt departe').

Glosses in S:

Against ll. 78–98

vos modo viuentes et mundi vana tenentes
estis qui fragiles est[ot]e mei memores
[*You now living and holding the vain pleasures of the world,
you who are fragile, be mindful of me*]

sunt tria que faciunt miserum me sepe dolere.
Est primum durum quia scio me moriturum.
Est magis addendo moriar sed nescio quando.
Inde magis flebo quia nescio quo remanebo
[*there are three things that make me, wretch, often weep.*

The first is hard because I know that I shall die.
the second is more, adding I shall die but I do not know when.
Thence I shall weep still more because I do not know where I shall remain]
For other instances of this commonplace verse, cf. Woolf 1968:349, n. 1, Herrtage 1879:304, Horstmann 1896:2.65, Dyboski 1908:141.

est homo res fragilis durans solum tempore paruo.
Nunc est nunc non est, quasi flos qui crescit in agro
[*Man is a fragile thing lasting but a short time.*
Now he is and now he is not, like the flower that grows in the field]
For other instances of this verse, see Horstmann 1896:2.65 and the preaching notes (1372) of John of Grimestone (Wilson 1973:26).

Est nostre sortis transire per hostia mortis.
Est graue transire quia transitus absque redire
[*It is our fate to pass through the gates of death.*
It is hard to pass through because that passage has no return]

Iudicii memor esto mei viuens homo laute. Namque meum nunc crasque tuum forsan erit arte (repeated below alongside l. 603)
[*be mindful of the judgement upon me, o man living in splendour. For what is now mine will be yours perhaps tomorrow, and it will be hard*]
Cf. Ecclus. 38.23–4, cited in the Wycliffite 'Sermon on Dead Men' (Cigman 1989:208.46).

Vestis pulcra, genus, honor et dominacio mundi a penis animam non saluant corpore raptam
[*Splendid clothing, rank, honour and lordship of the world do not save from pains the soul snatched from the body*]

mors tua, iudicium, mors cristi, gaudia celi et dolor inferni sunt meditanda tibi
[*your death, judgement, the death of Christ, the joys of heaven and the pain of hell: you should meditate upon these things*]

per cras cras caveas differre tuas homo metas
Nam per cras cras cras omnis consumitur etas
[*be wary of postponing your measures to tomorrow, tomorrow, man,*
For by tomorrow and tomorrow every age is consumed]
A version of this quotation is given in Wenzel 1989:452.

amplius in rebus noli sperare caducis
sed cupiat tua mens eterne gaudia lucis
[*do not trust further in unstable things,*
but let your mind desire the joys of the eternal light]
Source: the ps.-Bernardine 'Carmen Paraeneticum', *PL* 184.1308.

At the head of folios beginning ll. 155, 183 (top lines difficult to read because of cropping of leaves):

est commune mors...
occidit iuuenes diuites atque senes
[*death is common...*
it kills young, rich and old]
Cf. Suso: equum est iudicium mortis. Personam non accipit, nec alicui parcit... nec iuvenis aut senis miseretur... divitem ut pauperem similiter perdit [the judgement of death is equal. She accepts no person nor spares any... she pities neither young nor old... she destroys the rich like the poor]

Alongside l. 195:

Vnde superbimus? Quid ego, tu nisi limus?
Limus homo primus. Sortem mutare nequimus
[*Why are we proud. What am I, what are you, but clay?*
The first man was clay; we cannot change our fate]

Alongside l. 197:

diues diuicias non congregat absque labore non tenet absque metu non deserit absque dolore
[*the rich man does not assemble riches without labour or hold them without fear or leave them without pain*]
Also cited in *Fasciculus Morum* (Wenzel 1989:314) and *Dives and Pauper* (Barnum 1980:274).

o diues dives non omni tempore viues. Fac bene dum viuis, post mortem viuere si vis
[*O rich man, rich man, you will not live for ever. Do well while you are alive, if you wish to live after death*]
The first sentence, and the first element of the second, have parallels in a collection of proverbs by Richard Hill (Dyboski 1908:130, 135).

Near l. 372:

nota versum per cras cras
[*note the verse about tomorrow and tomorrow*]

Near l. 713:

subiaceo lapide corrosus vermibus ecce
qui viuens quondam talis ut estis eram
Si quis sentiret quo tendet et vnde veniret
numquam gauderet sed in omni tempore fleret
[*Lo I lie beneath a stone eaten by worms, I who was once living such as you are. If anyone could really experience where he was going and whence he came he would never rejoice but would always weep*]

Appendix 4

Additional notes on the textual relations of the non-holograph copies of the 'Conpleynte paramont', 'L'epistre de Cupide' and the *Series*.

I. 'Conpleynte paramont'

For general comment on textual relations of copies of the *Pilgrimage*, see Burrow 1994: 240–1 [52–3] and McGerr 1990: c–cv. Copies of the *Pilgrimage* are: MSS London British Library Additional 34193 (Ad3), Egerton 615 (Eg); Cambridge Gonville and Caius College 124/61 (G), University Library Kk.i.7 (U2); Hatfield House MS Cecil 270 (H); Melbourne, Victoria State Library 096/G94 (M); New York, Public Library MS Spencer 19 (N); Oxford Bodleian Library Bodley 770 (B3), Corpus Christi College 237 (Co), University College 181 (Un).

Two main subgroups exist of this text, as noted by McGerr: they are EgGMNU2 and Ad3B3CoHUn.

The extent of the variations within individual manuscripts—proportionately greater than for any of the other texts here edited—may suggest not only the popularity of the text, a popularity owed in some measure to the text from which it came and to which, in translation, it was returned, but also the challenges with which Hoccleve's translation presented the scribes.

The first six stanzas, missing from H1, are edited from the copy in Eg, though Eg is in error at I.18 (shared with GMNU2) and I.37 (shared with MN).

VI. 'L'epistre de Cupide'

Non-holograph copies are: MSS Cambridge Trinity College R.3.20 (Tr1) and University Library Ff.i.6 (U); Durham, University Library Cosin V.ii.13 (D3); Edinburgh National Library of Scotland, Advocates' MS 1.1.6 (Ba); Oxford Bodleian Library Bodley 638 (B2), Digby 181 (D1), Fairfax 16 (F), Selden B.24 (S2), and Tanner 346 (T).

The MSS divide into one main subgroup, B2D1D3FTU, and three other copies, Tr1 (by Shirley) and the sixteenth-century copies BaS2 and 1532 edition of Chaucer's works by Thynne (Th).

The main subgroup is established by its reordering of Hoccleve's text, as noted above p. 15. Doyle earlier noted this feature in the, as yet unpublished, catalogue entry (revised by A.J. Piper) for D3. B2D3T and the incomplete copies in D1U arrange the poem in large blocks as follows: stanzas 1–19, 30–9, 50–9, 20–9, 40–9, 60–8 (D1 wants stanzas 1–10, U stanzas 29, 40–9, 60–8), which suggests that their archetype had ten stanzas per leaf, with a blank final leaf, and swapped the third and fourth bifolia of the quire of eight leaves on which the text was copied (the fourth bifolium must have been reversed). F distorts the order still more, but since it shares with the other MSS their combinations of 17–19 and 30–6, 57–9 and 20–6, 37–9 and 50–6, 27–9 and 40–9, it can also be seen as deriving from the archetype of B2D1D3TU, and not, as I earlier thought (1996: 43), an exercise of independent editorial function by the scribe. The break in the sense between stanzas 59 and 60 in all MSS of this group establishes that this order cannot be authorial: see further Boffey and Thompson 1989: 281.

The copies which depend directly on Hoccleve's original, because they share the ordering of the stanzas in the holograph, introduce numerous erroneous readings, and individually represent worse witnesses to the original than the MSS of the previously-noted group. S2 suppresses the sowing metaphor of VI.10–11, swaps 'deynous or proud' (VI.150) with 'sly, qweynte and fals' (VI.152), and reads 'but ȝit þe fend that ageyn stoden wold' for VI.357. Tr1 reads 'who þat hem trusteþe, ofte gyled shal he be' for VI.111. Ba omits VI.397, and reads 'bewar wemen of thair fikilnesse', 'is blissit of God to quhon sone belongith', and 'thou luver trew thow madin mansueit' for VI.327, 412, 423. Fox and Ringler 1980: xxxvii, xli claim that Ba depends on the Thynne edition; since Ba does not always follow Thynne into error (e.g. VI.440 H2Ba perdee] Th proued) it is likely that both descend independently from a common original in which the errors first appeared. Th appears to have closest links with B2D1FT, though it cannot have been based on any of them.

The archetype of the main subgroup of MSS must also have swapped stanzas 61–2 and 63–4. All but one of the six MSS of the subgroup share this rearrangement: the relevant material is missing in the sixth MS, U. This change makes for an easier chronological progression from the Virgin Mary (60, 63–4) to St Margaret (61–2). On the face of it, and given the major reordering of Hoccleve's text found in these MSS, one might have supposed that this reordering of the text originated with the scribe of the common ancestor of the group. Now, Ba and the linked Thynne edition, which in all other respects follow the arrangement of the stanzas in H2, also contain this distinctive ordering of the stanzas (i.e. 60, 63–4, 61–2). Possibly therefore Hoccleve himself was responsible for the rearrangement: in which case the version in H2 would represent an accidental miscopying by Hoccleve of his own text, or an instance of Hoccleve having second thoughts about its ordering. Since, however, Ba/Th share a number of other variants with MSS in this group (see apparatus), their witness is possibly compromised, and their agreement over the rearranged stanzas would not then signify for the establishment of Hoccleve's original version.

VII. The *Series*

Non-holograph manuscript copies of the *Series* are as follows: of the complete work, Coventry City Record Office 325 (C); Oxford Bodleian Library Bodley 221 (B), Laud Misc. 735 (L), Selden Supra 53 (S); New Haven Yale University 493 (Y); of the *Gesta* narratives, London British Library Royal 17 D vi (R) and Oxford Bodleian Library Digby 185 (D2) and Eng.poet.d.4 (E); and of the Suso, R and London British Library Harley 172 (Ha1).

Two principal subgroups exist: BLY (links between B and L were noted by Seymour 1981: 132, cf. Burrow 1999: xxii–xxiii, who notes that LY were copied by the same scribe) and CD2R. Burrow 1999 argues for three independent witnesses to what I have called *H: S, C and the ancestor of BLY.

BLY are linked by their mangling of VII.4.117–18 and 815–16, omission of VII.4.848–54, and shared errors at VII.2.81 (see n.) and VII.3.544; they also share the reading 'nuncio [S responsio] ymaginis' in their marginal note to VII.4.337. Each has unique readings which mean it cannot have served as exemplar for either of the others. B has several unique readings: it rewrites VII.3.461–2, VII.4.561/3, VII.587–8 to produce new rhymes (right/wight, fynde/kynde, man/se non can), and loses the rhyme at VII.3.699 by transposing 'a whyle' and 'abyde'. L has errors of haplography in the moralization to the first *Gesta* narrative. Y loses VII.1.326.

CD2R are similarly linked in error at VII.3.88–91, VII.3.432 (see above p. 23), VII.5.305–6, and (CR only) VII.4.302/304, 363–4, 377, 408, 417, 678, 831. CD2R share readings with D at VII.3.182, 432, the latter an error, and CR with D at VII.3.565, VII.4.194, but if their common ancestor were copied from D, which is possible, it must have been a poor copy. Additionally, C mistransposes VII.4.661–2, and R wants VII.4.564, with a space for correction. Ha2 rewrites the first words of VII.4.211 ('take heede by an arowe'), and offers 'blynde' for 'blyue' at VII.4.392.

S belongs to neither of these principal subgroups, and has fewer errors, though these include errors of haplography in the prose moralisations of the

Gesta narratives. It also shares a few distinctive marginal readings with B against LY in the Suso translation. Seymour's view of the superiority of S may be correct so far as the 'Compleinte' is concerned: elsewhere in the *Series*, where comparison with the Latin is possible, S regularly agrees with the other MSS against D, which hardly argues for its greater superiority, though at VII.5.552 it shares with D against the other *H MSS a pleonastic 'me'.

Subdivisions of the texts occur at VII.3.400 (*H), 498 (BELSY), 680 (ES), 694 (BLSY), 841 (ES: BL could not so divide their text because they had misdivided the stanzas at this point), VII.4.771 (BLSY), VII.5.344 (E), and, with rubrics, VII.3.852, 883, 904 (CRS), VII.3.939 (E): see the relevant notes for these last. Interestingly, L has a number '6' in the margin against VII.3.694, and a '7' in the margin against what it calls the prologue to the next item (VII.3.953). This numbering suggests a continuous numbering of the sections of the *Gesta* story, so that in L the contents of the MS were to be divided into very uneven 'chapters': 1, prologue and complaint; 2, dialogue; 3–6, the *Gesta* story; 7, the prologue to the moralization. No numbering occurs later in the MS, so it seems as if the attempt to divide the MS into sections was not carried through. It seems very unlikely that this numbering is Hoccleve's own.

Appendix 5

Selected variants from the non-holograph manuscript copies of the texts here edited

I. 'Conpleynte paramont'

> Copies: (holograph) H1 (wanting stanzas 1–6, supplied here, following Furnivall, from Eg); for other copies, see Appendix 4. Modern editions: Smalley 1953, Seymour 1981. Title from rubric to l. 245.

15 alle] B3GHUnU2 a, Ad3 *om.*; 16 woful] Ad3B3CoHUn hevy; 18 hey] Ad3B3CoHUn thy, Fr. ta; 19 thi] *so also* M; *other MSS om.*; 21 agasted] *so also* MN; *other MSS* abashed; 24 O] Ad3CoU2Un *om.*; 25 me as weel] B3 *om.*, Ad3CoUn me; 29 aplace] Ad3 on place, Co apace, U2 in place; 32 thu] *so also* M; *other MSS add* tho; 37 wordes] EgMN word; 46 which on hy] *H the (Ad3Un *om.*) which that; 49 wombe] Ad3B3CoHU herte, EgGMNU2 body, Fr. ventre; 52 soule] *H *adds* eke; 56 hurt] Ad3B3CoGHUU2 hert (U2 *corr. from* hurt), Fr. la plaie; 58 and] *H *adds* thou; 59 or²] EgGMN of, Un and; 60 broghten.... foorth] *H engendered ye me, Fr. engendrastes; 65 syn] B3MU2 swich; 66 me make] *H (*exc.* Eg) to make, EgMN to hauen; 72 oonly] *H singularly; 76 Eek] H1 eek; 79 wrongful] MN wronge; 80 thynke] *H thou (Ad3B3 þe); 84 shamely] *H shamefully; a] B3EgMNU2 this, Ad3CoH þe; 87 folk] Eg men, Ad3B3CoHUn þe world; 88 largeliche] EgGMN *add* lo; opned] Ad3B3CoHUn *add* now; 89 syn] EgGMNUnU2 þat sith; I] B3HUn it, Co I it; nat may] *H *trsp.*; it] Ad3EgMN *om.*; 91 put art also] *H art also now put (EgGMN now *after* put, Ad3 *before* also); sone] EgGMN *om.*; 92 thow] CoGHNUnU2 þough; wer.... and] *H my son had been (Ad3 *om.* ben) a, Fr. comme fusses; 93 perauenture] *H *adds* eke (Eg also, Ad3B3 *om.*); 94 thy] Ad3B3CoH his; 99 þat] Ad3EgMN *om.*; 102 fadir] *H *adds* here; 107 pleyne] *H weep; 108 þat] *H now; thow] G *adds* now; 112 hoolly] *H all wholly (U2 al hol); 116 sone the] *H this ransom or; 119 thow wilt] EgN *om.*, Ad3EgNU2 *add* þat it; me] Ad3 I itte, U thu, EgN the, M me it; 123 that] *H that thus; thurgh thy] *H with; 127 thow] *H the; 128 from] *H now from; 132 as²] *H as ever; 137 the] *H this; 140 nakid] *H (*exc.* Ad3) *adds* so; 142 come of] *H let see; 145 sparcle] *H drop; 148 thow] *H (*exc.* Ad3H) *adds* so; 151 þat thow werist] *H thou (MN þat þou) on wearest (Ad3 werist on); 153 qwake] *H now quake (EgMN *add* þou); 154 restore] *H restore thou; 158 by taast] EgMN be tasted, B3U been taast; of swich] B3 *om.*; dewynge] U2 deluynge; 159 clothe] N clepe, Eg calle; 160–1 art namely/ Holden] *H art holden namely/ So; so] *H perdee (M *om.*); 162 deeth] *H *adds* now; 166 he.... maiden] *H so be that he a virgin, Fr. comment que soit vierge; 167 and thogh.... thow] *H if (Ad3 ȝitte) thou... wouldest; 169 and] *H *om.*; a] EgGMU2 his; 175 twixt] *H of; for ay] Ad3Co *om.*; 176 womman] *H *exc.* B3 but woman; 177 and] *H and all; 181 talke] EgMN take; 182 from, I] EgMN *om.*; doon] B3GUn doun, U2 am don; away]

GUn alwey; is] B3 am, U2 as; nowe] G newe; 183 clepe] calle EgM; calle] *H name; 186 I which is Ihesus] B3 swete Ihesus, Ad3 I se þat is iesu, EgMN he the which is (M *om.* is, N *om.* the) called Jhesus; 187 al] EgMN and, *other MSS* o; 188 syn.... which] B3HUnU2 whiche þat (U2 *om.* þat), Ad3 siþ þat I was, EgMN sith he (N *adds* the) whilk; 189 of] *H lo (H so) of; bynome] *H bereft; 192 othir] Ad3 harte, M honour; 196 ful careful] *H o careful now (M, *for* now, may); 200 restreyne] *H (*exc.* EgH) refrain; 201 othir] EgMN *add* but; 203 heere] *H right here; 205 wrong] EgMNU2 *add* for; 207 dethes] *H the death's; 210 ful] *H most; hem] CoEgMNUn of hem; 212 strong] *H full strong, Fr. trop fort; 214 the taast I feele and] *H I taste (B3 finde) and feel (B3 tast); 215 feele I] *H *after* deeth[3]; 217 is] *H (*exc.* EgGMN) is al, EgGMN is now; 223 steerelees] Ad3B3Co stormeles, EgGHNU sterneles (G sterernelesse); 224 woful] B3Un sory; 226 clept be by] *H (*exc.* EgGMN) avaunt of, Eg be called; thy] *H (*exc.* M) that; 230 hangith] *H lo hangeth; al] *H *om.*; 237 and amendes] Ad3B3CoHU and ful amendes, EgGMN and amendith; right] *H (*exc.* EgGMN) *om.*; 240 sy men] *H saw ye, Fr. veistes; 241 þat shee] EgMN *om.*; 242 as] *H and (*exc.* B3 of); 244 and hath] Ad3B3CoHU and al, EgGMN (M he) hath of (M *om.* of); despent] B3CoHUn isched, Ad3 he blede, EgGMN spyld; 246 it was] *H is lo (Eg his lo, H is so).

II. 'Male regle'

Copy: (holograph) H1. Modern editions: Hammond 1927, O'Donoghue 1982, Seymour 1981.

227 deceyuours] H1 deceyuous; 380 an] H1 *om.*; 424 spirit] H1 spirt

III. 'Balade et chaunceon'

Copy: (holograph) H1. Modern editions: Hammond 1927, O'Donoghue 1982, Seymour 1981.

18 suppoialle] Furnivall supportaille

V. 'Item de beata Virgine'

Copies: (holograph) H2; Ch (in a copy of CT, and there assigned to the Ploughman), Tr2. Modern editions: Beatty 1902, Boyd 1964.

2 needful] ChTr2 holsom; 10 seur] ChTr2 *om.*; 13 eternel peyne] ChTr2 peyne ay duryng; 35 goddes] ChTr2 cristys; the flour] ChTr2 myrroure; 63 thow] ChTr2 ryght; 69 receyue] ChTr2 conceyue; 80 meene] ChTr2 neuen; 87 Aue Maria he] ChTr2 suyng (Tr2 aftyr) her psalter he; 89 suynge] ChTr2 folwyng; 92 seide] ChTr2 seide she; 93 fressh] ChTr2 good; 105 in] ChTr2 of; 114 vp[1]] ChTr2 *om.*; 116 tolde him] ChTr2 *trsp.*; 126 Ch *adds* Amen

VI. 'L'epistre de Cupide'

Copies: (holograph) H2; for other copies, see Appendix 4. Modern editions: Fenster and Erler 1991 (Erler for the Hoccleve, Fenster for Christine).

4 the] *H all; 7 greetynges] *H *adds* heartly; 14 hir] B2BaFTThU this, Tr1 þe; 15 yle] litell yle D3FTThTr1U; 28 moot] BaB2D3FTU *om*.; 30 shewe] *H as (Ba I, S2 3e) do (Ba haif); 32 humble] *H (exc. D3) *adds* and low; euery] *H each; 33 secree] BaFTThU as secree; 34 as þat yourseluen lykith] *H right as (U as þat) yourself list; 39 sholde.... reson] B2BaFTTh by resoun semyd euery wight to; 42 betrayed] *H deceived; 43 meeued] B2BaFTTh movith; of] B2BaFTh oft; 46 they] B2BaD3FTTh þat men; 50 pot] D3FTThU pan; 51 of hir hath] *H is in his; 55 foule] B2BaD3FTTr1U euyll; 56 ooth] B2BaD3FTTr1U othis; 70 greet repreef] *H great (S2 get a) slander (Ba disklandir); 72 pitee] *H virtue (exc. Tr1 good); 75 shame] *H slander; 79 ignorant] BaB2D1D3FTTh innocent, Fr ignorant; 83 al] B2BaD1D3FT *om*.; 85 remes] B2BaD1D3FTTh citees, Fr royaumes; 87 false and hid] B2BaD1D3FTTh falsly, Tr1U falsly hid, S2 *om*. and; 88 castes] B2BaD1D3FTTh craftes; 89 whos.... reedy] S2 þat is qhuo redy ay; wil] B2BaD1D3FTTh witte; 90 hy] B2BaD1D3FTTh *om*.; 92 the] *H these (exc. Ba thay, S2 othre); 97 qwytith] *H guerdoneth; 98 smal] *H little; 99 to] *H unto; anothir wrecche] *H *trsp. before* to his felawe; 107 shee] *H for she; 108 can] *H will; 109 qwikly] *H smartly; 110 the[1]] *H these; 115 *H he speaks her reproof and villainy; 116 labbyng] D1D3Tr1Th blabbyng, B2F babbyng, Ba bakbytting, U lablyng; 117 sundry] *H (exc. Ba) diverse; 123 his lady] *H her plainly; 131 he] *above line*, H *trsp. after* but (S2 *om*.); 140 therto] *H his (Tr1 mans) great; 141 vice] B2D1D3FU thyng, TTr1 *om*.; 143 man] T hem, B2D3FU men; 145 sueth] Ba schewin, S2 schewit, Th is shewed; 152 vnthrift] B2Ba vntrust, S2 vnthrist; 155 the hy] D1D3 *before* angels; 158 men] *H all men; 171 his] TTr1 her; 185 it] *H he; 186 wont is] *H useth; 189 hem list] BaD1D3FTr1ThU they woll; 190 ladyes] *H these (Th the) ladies; 192 lakken] *H despise; 197 wikkid] *H sorry; 202–3 *H the world (T worde) their malice (B2 *adds* it) may not comprehend, as (S2 and) that the (F thise, D1D3 *om*., Ba *om*. that the) clerks say, (Ba *adds* for) it hath no end; 216 trappid] BaB2D1D3FTTh wrappi(d); 218 the] *H these; 219 we] *H I (*cf.* 221, 225 etc.); 223 clerkes] *H *adds* these; outrageous] *H cruel (D1 *adds* grete); 241 mennis] *H folks; 244 sharpe.... sore] *H sharp piercing, *om*. sore; 254 kneewen] BaB2D1D3Tr1U knowen; 258 venym] D1D3 womman; 260 ne] *H nor these; 261 nat they] *H none of those; 266 honur] *H worship; 273 oon] *H a wight, *exc.* Tr1 folkes, Ba ane; 278 restreyne] BaB2D1D3FTTh refreyn, S2 withseyn; 299 feyne] BaTTr1 seyn; 303 in the] D1D3 in the greet; 307 falsen] D1D3T faylen; 310 man] *H wretch; 312 greeues] *H smarts (S2 hertis); 313 gentillesse] BaD1D3S2T gentilnesse; 319 repreef ne of shame] *H reprovable shame; 320 conceites trewe arn dede] *H truth hath (Tr1 *adds* now) no stead; 322 is hir vice] *H namely it is (Tr1 is þis); 327 yee strah] *H no force, BaTh bewar (BaTh *cont.* 'wemen of thair fikilnesse'); 333 duchees] B2BaD1 duchesses, D3 duchesse; 335 folk enpoysone] *H *trsp*.; 342 discreet] D1D3S2 swete; 350 nothyng] *H not; 355 ete] B2BaD3FTThTr1U tasten; 357 feend] *H devil; 361 welthe] *H health *exc.* Th; 375 þat gilt] *H this (D1Th his) harm (U arme); 389 on] *H me; 393 þat] B2BaD1FS2TTr1U this; 396 mankynde of the] BaTh man of his; 397 Ba *om*., Th *trsp. before* 396; 400 fro] *H to; 407 hepid] D1D3 happy, S2 hicht; 408 weyk] *H lean (Ba leif, S2 lowe); 410 laude] *H praising; 411 we witen] *H I say; 414 wight] *H man; 416 it is to taken] *H take now (S2 takith here, ThTr1 *trsp*. take now) right (S2Tr1 *om*. right) good; 430 nat] D1D3FTh neuir; 432 leeueth wel yee] *H moveth (S2 commend) me; 434 of] *space in H2 for extra word*; B2D1D3FS2T my; 446 it may preeued be] *H I may prove well; 447 al the] *H stable (S2 alway); 448 al] BaB2D3FS2T the, D1TrU *om*.; 451 is nat told] *H told (S2 writt) I, Fr. ne l'ay fait; 455 enhaunce] D1Th avaunce; 457 noble.... worthy] *H *trsp*. (*H, for* worthy, digne); 458 shee] BaB2D1D3FT he; 459 shee] BaB2D1D3FS2T he; of] BaB2D1FT of his, S2 of hir; 460 shee *both times*] *H he; 466 vntreewe] *H false (F *om*.); 472 th'eir] *om*. BaD1D3Th

VII.1 'My compleinte'

Copies: see Appendix 4 (and fragments in MS formerly Phillips 8267). Modern editions: Pryor 1968, Burrow 1977 (ll. 1–308), 1999, O'Donoghue 1982, Seymour 1981, Wogan-Browne et al. 1999 (ll. 1–35, 197–224).

2 broun] CD brome: *see Burrow's n. on D's reading*; 24 on] D *om.*; 27 spirite] D wite; 28 no] S *above line*; 29 sore] BCDLY *om.*, S *added above line*; 32 kepe it] D *trsp.*; 37 folke] D folks; 49 my] D *om.*; 53 his²] BCDLY *om.*; 54 for] D *om.*; 55 at] BCDLY was at; 57 euere] D every; 62 sith] S *over erasure*; BCDLY *om.*; 71 wich] SBLY with; *cf. Burrow's n.*; 87 as] S be as, be *erased*; 97–8] D *trsp.*; 100 hertis] BD mannes; 113 but] D *om.*; 126 can] BS (S *above line*) he; 127 my] S me; 136 me] DY *om.*; 137 that] D *om.*; 142 þat] D *om.*; 148 euere] BCDLY *om.*, Y *adds* þene; ful] CD *om.*; 153 ynow] S *above line*; 155 þat] CD *om.*; 159 othir] D *om.*; 160 not had] BCDLY *trsp.*; 167 it] DLY *om.*; 172 same] D *om.*; 174 in] D at; 192 wole] D wele; 199 not] S *above line*; 232 þat] D *om.*; 234 deuoided] S *final* d *above line*, BCDLY voided; the] D this; 238 greuous] CD *om.*; pine] DY peyne; 245 prefe] D prese; 248 alþou3] S as þou3; þat] D *om.*; 282 a] D *om.*; 291 or] D nor, Y ne; 294 ay] CD they; 298 yuel] D yll; 308 deeme] D drem; 327 I] BCDLY it; 333 verre] D wery; 342 heuynesse] D heuynesses; 343 duresse] SY duresses; 352 men] *so* D; 358 seest] D seyst; 364 if] S *above line*; 378 wel þerof] BCDLY wherof; 412 and¹] BCDLY for

VII.2 'A dialoge'

Copies: (holograph, after l. 252; before, hand of Stowe) D; other copies, see Appendix 4. Modern editions: Pryor 1968, O'Donoghue 1982 (omits 134–96, 211–38, 323–64, 428–90, 512–693, 799–826), Seymour 1981 (omits all but 526–714), Burrow 1999.

ll. 1–252
4 thinketh] Y *extra minim*; it] BCDLY *om.*; 9 he] Y *above line*; 10 telle] Y *adds* me; 14 C went in streit; 15 to²] CBLY *om.*; it] B *om.*; 25 war] BCLY *om.*; 27 reherse] Y wherse; it²] LY it not; 30 it²] Y *above line*; 31 kepe] B *orig.* slepe, *ruled through*; 32 þat] C it; 33 as] C so; 37 han seide.... seien] C *trsp.*; of] LY on; 38 as 3it] C *om.*; 42 it] C þat; but] BLY *om.*; 49 vnto] CL to; 52 mynge or touche] C touche or meve; 53 answere thus] C *trsp.*; 55 or] Y no mann or, no mann *subpuncted*; 61 were] CBL where; wich] C þat; 63 hath me] C *trsp.*; 66 coin] D comon; 67 werriour] B? merrure; 69 þou3] C 3yff *over corr.*; 70 had] D have; 71 for] CLY *om.*; 73 3oue hath] C *trsp.*; 74 for] BLY *om.*; no] C woo; 78 sothly] BCLY trewly; 81 it] BLY to tell it; 82 if] Y of; 83 I thenke] D *om.*; 86 and] BLY of; 87, 89] B *trsp.*; 90 his] B *above line*; 93 me] B *om.*; þe] D *om.*; 100 oone] Y, *above*, none, *subpuncted*; dar I] C dar I wel; 102 feble] BLY felle, D feole; 103 þei] BY þe, L if þe; 104 not] L þat; 105 þei] Y 3e; wole] L with; 109 it²] BCLY *om.*; and] BDLY and in; 110 is] D in; than] D that; sholde] B holde; 112 ful sore] B forsoith; 118 smal] BLY *add* þat; is] BLY coyn is; 120 if] C and, D if he, he *cancelled*; 123 smal] C so smale; 125 leese] C moche leese; 127 ben haue] CBLY *trsp.*; 129 coyne] C þe coyne; 130 þe] D a; 132 so] Y *om.*; 134 men] B a man, D me; 135 thei] BS *orig.* the; 136 made] D *om.*; þat] BCDLY *om.*; 137 charged nowe] C *trsp.* BLY *om.* nowe; 140 that] C *om.* al] C *om.*; 142 countirfete] B confrete; 143 copir, clothe] BLY *trsp.*; 149 to] B vnto; 151 a] DY *om.*; 154 that] C *om.*; 156 wiþ] L þat; 157 be] BD to be; 161 a day] BLY days; 164 foule and] C *om.*; 166 one] BLY men; 167 al] C *om.*; 168 foule] C grete; 169 is] C it is; 170 and] C *om.*; 172 into] BLY into þis; 174 3e¹,²] BLY the; 175 outereris]

B entrers, C actores, D outeris, LY outrers; 178 noon] C nowe; falle shal] B *trsp.*; 178–9 B *added in marg.*; 179 trewe] C *om.*; enditement] S *over corr.*, CD entendement; 181 shal hid be] B hid be shall, C hidde shal be; 182 waisshe] D vanysshe; 188 meenes] B meneys, D mens, L menes; 195 therwiþ] B with þer; adoun] C doun; 199 the] C ʒou; 204 BCDLY þat shall I as blyue yow tell (CD yow telle as blyue), ywys; 205 C haue I sene a smal tretice in latyn or this; 206 callid] C calles; 208 þat] C *om.*; 209 he] Y *om.*; thanne] BLY tane; 210 war] B whare; for] BLY and, C whan; 211 haue I purposid] C purpos I; 212 God his] C godis; list] C luste; 213 helþe] Y his helþe, C helpe; 214 for] L and; all lene] C is al clene; 215 foule] D and foule; 222 this] CDY his; or] D and; 223 and freissh.... vigour] B wit helth and vigour; 224 not] B not to; vnto] B to; 225 þis] C þe; 228 til] B to; 229 offensis] BLY offence; 230 and] B and a; 234 the] C *om.*; mocioun] D monicioun; 236 wole I] B *trsp.*, C wole; 237 reed] C reed and; 240 after] C *om.*; 247 now] C *om.*, BLY *before* fast; 249 faste and] C *trsp.*; 252 sentement] C discent

ll. 253–826

256 now] *later hand adds* ther *or* then; 258 al²] *H *om.*; 263 nat] BLY neuer; 273 *later hand adds* be, to *before* gynneth, dye; *H *om.* to; 274 and] *H and all; 282 lent] BLY *add* vs; 289 hir] BSLY here hir; ofte] *added above line*; 291 good] *H God; 326 trouble] *H *adds* now; 337 made] *H *adds* have; 342 ny] BLY so ny; 349 dooth] C do and, Y do þus; 350 bond] *H knot, *cf.* 338; 364 and dul and] BLY and ful, C ful dul and, S and ful dul and; 365 and] BLY full; 371 thow] SC thow nowe, BLY thow not; 373 al] *H at all; 380 now] *H *adds* thou, *om.* (*exc.* L) now; 385 ouersore] B euermore, LY euer sore; 394 wol] *H well; B *wants ll. 400–551 inclusive*; 406 it] *H *om.*; 407 more] *H more but that; 413 al as] Y as, L as *corr. to* als; 426 it] D is, *H it; 432 smal] BLY litil; 445 serche] D serchee; 450 weyue] C swyth, L wyiue; 466 euene] *H ever; 480 lyth] *H is; 495 hem] *H it; 502 lightly nat] *H *trsp.*; cacche may] *H *trsp.*; 517 now] CSY þou, L ʒow; 530 tyme] *orig.* thine?; 540 yee] CLS *om.*, Y *after* sikir; ful] LY ʒe, CS ʒe ful; 548 with] *H therewith; 550 God] *H him; 553 it] *H *om.*; 557 swich] BLY seth; ful] BC *om.*; 561 Vegece] C *om.*, S *added later*; 577 hy] CS by; 581 prince] *H *adds* and that is; 583 wroot] BLY wroght; 584 a place elles] *H another place; 586 expresse] *so* *H. D? yepresse; 595 worthynesse] *H prowess (B proves); 631 þat] LY þerto, BLS *add* to; 648 wel¹] BLY *om.*; 654 out] BLY *om.*; 659 tyme] *H while; 660 aftir þat] *H (*exc.* L) afterward, D þat *above line*; 663 man] *H wight; 675 misberynge] CS mysheering; 680 bewar] *H be wise; 694 auctrice] BC auctorite, LY auctorice; 722 with] *H through; 727 now] *H O; of] *H on; 731 thogh] *H that; 756 swart] *H black; 757 ther] *H *om.*; 759 þat] BLY *add* cas; 762 as] BLY and as, CS and þat; 776 may] L *adds* he, BSY *add* þei, C *adds* þere; 782 in] D *above line*; 787 thee] BLY ther; 808 the] *H his

VII.3 'Fabula de quadam imperatrice Romana'

Copies: (holograph) D; other copies, see Appendix 4. Modern edition, Pryor 1968.

1 actes] CD2R jestys; 3 Iereslaus] *H Gerelaus, Lat. (Sl) Ierelaus (D5H4) Gerelaus; 14 fer] *H for; 24 ne concele] B ne councell, C my counsele; 46 take] *H take it; 51 your] BLY *om.*; 54 kiste] CR lefte; seide] *H *adds* now (*cf.* 130, 166, 181, 219, 220, 224, 381); 55 nat dreedith] *H *trsp.*; 61 out] BLY to; 72 thoghte] BLY in thoghte; 86 to þat synne] C to none othir, D2R to no (D2 noon) synne; 88 CD2R *displace to end stanza, and rewrite* for he right feithful trust in you hath he; 92 dye] CD2R so dye; 98 vicious] CD2R ful vicious; 100 nat wolde he stynte] *H and that he not (C ne) stint would ; 111 vnhad] *H not had; 117 vpon] B anone, LY vnon; 125 allowe] BCLRY avowe; 127 doutith] *H dreadeth; 130 yow] BLY now; 143 made] *H bade; go] *H anon go; 155 yow] BLY it, C it yow; 166 thee] BCLY thee nowe; 180 now] *H good, Lat. bone;

181 and] *H and now (B and no); *H *exc.* CD2R *om.* foorth; 183 in the hy way] *H in the way, cf. Lat. in via; 203 be] CD2R I; 216 for] BLSY it, C *om.*; 217 way] *D above line*; me] D2R *om.*, C nowe; 219 wilt] *H wilt now; 220 right] *H now; 224 noon] *D above line*; *H *adds* other; at al] BLSY now, C *om.*; 233 left al] *H without more; 234 heeng hir] *H *trsp.*; 235 ook] CSY hook; 245 amen] D *om.*, CD2RS amen, BLY men; 246 O] *H O thou; 250 the] *H and worthy; 251 O] *H O foul (Y o full); 253 feendly] CY frendly; 255 and] *D above line*; 259 seur] *H *adds* then (CS *after* trouthe), hid] CD2R kidde (*followed by Pryor*); 265 wole] *H will I again; 270 whos] BY was, L *om.*; 271 it] *H it full; blyue] L blithe; folewynge] BLY blowinge; 289 mighte] *H *adds* then (C *before* mighte); 298 on] BLSY of; thee to be] C the; 301 wel wole] B wole, LY wel; 307 the¹] *H this; 326 do] BC *om.*; 327 quod] BLY *om.*; 330 fro thensfoorth] *H busily; 338 the²] BLSY þis; 340 purposid] *H purpose (D2R *add* and); 342 he out] *H *trsp.*; 351 aftir, of hir slepe] *H after her sleep, Lat. cito.... a sompno; 352 to] *H and to; 376 spak] BLY *after* contesse; 380 slee] *H *after* feend; 381 on] *H now on (*followed by Furnivall*); 383 flayn] BCD2LRY slayn; 386 cas] BLY *om.*; vengeable] B veniall, Y veniable; 393 as] *H is as; 404 wolde] *H will; 414 on] BCSY *om.*, L *after* foorth; 422 spoken had] *H had said; 424 yseyd] *H ispoke; 427 been had] BLY *trsp.*; 432 so] BLSY soul, Lat. sola; 435 right] *H left, Lat. sinistra; 441 right] *H *om.*; 489 fee] CD2RS to flee; 494 hurte mighte] *H *trsp.*; 499 this] *H the (*exc.* R that); 503 hoom] *H *om.*; 510 to] *H unto (*followed by Furnivall*); 515 hir, do] *H to her, to do; 519 in come] *H *trsp.*; 535 wilt so] D2R wilt now; 542 labbe] BL lable; 544 be] BLY bewrey; aweertee] CD2RS weerte, BLY vterte; 556 so] *om.* BLY; 558 to] RS vnto, BCLY wele (vn)to; owne] *H *om.*; 564 lust] BD2LSY list (cf. 565); 565 list] CR lust; ful] BLSY riȝt, C *om.*; 567 euene thvs vnto] *H in this wise to; 570 thow] *H right; 572 þat thow doost] *H thy labour; 576 this] BCLY þe; 586 deuel] *H fiend; 590 clothes] *H his clothes; his] *H the; 592 muste] CD2R mighte; 604 bysyly] *H full busily; 609 this] *H thus; 616 hir] *H *after* ship; the] S *om.*; ship] R shipman; 618 at] *H to (C vnto); 626 maad] *H *after* I; 627 *H that never man there (S þus) shall (R ther shal neuer man) do so (S so do) to (LY with) me; 628 for] *H for no; outake] *H save; 632 wel] *H this; 635 conforme] *H *adds* thee; 643 the²] CD2R your; 658 shal rehercen] *H *trsp.*; 664 deitee] CD2R dignitee ; 671 of] *D above line*; 675 fil wondirly] *H shoop wonderfully; 677 þat] *D above line*; 680 this] BCLY þe; 682 by] *H *adds* thither; 684 and] *D above line*; 687 tymes] BLY tyme and; 718 ful²] *H *om.*; 721 qwitte] *H quitteth; 722 yee] BY the; 724 yee] BY þei; 726 yow shal] *H *trsp.*; 727 yow] *H be your; 728 it] CD2R it ful; 738 go] *H and go; 741 they] *H and they; hem] *H *om.*; 755 dwellynge is] *H *trsp.*; 757 *H the abbess her (L *orig.* he) made approach his high presence; 758 hir face hid] *H covered her face; 768 by] *H fast by; 769 tho] BLY þe; 774 empryse] BLY emperyce; 777 dirke] CD2R grete; 778 this] *H the; 782 cured be] *H *trsp.*; out] CD2R on; 784 longe lye] *H persevere; 785 forme] *H the form; 792 whan þat] *H but when; 795 maad haath] *H *trsp.*; 798 telle out] *H say on; 803 mercy] *H *before* I; 811 what] BLY what more, CD2R whatsoeuere; 814 al] *H and; 817 vnpayed] *H delayed; 832 mis] *H lack, 835 þat him to him] CRY þat he to him (C *trsp.* he, to him); 837 oghte] *H must; 838 ful] *H right; 841 purpos] *H tale; 843 thow²] *H and; 849 ther] BLY therto; 863 the charge bytook to hir] *H betook her the charge; cure] *H the cure; 864 a] *H his; 866 misauenture] *H wicked aventure; 868 al] *H yet; 872 euere] *H ay; 875 ful] *H right; 881 suppose] *H think; how] *H *om.*; but] *H else but; 884 nat] *H *before* am; 887 a lady] *H a fair lady; 888 cam] *H was; 893 of] *H for; 894 hath] *H fast; 895 be] *H have be; 896 lyf] *H guilt; 897 as] CD2RS was; 901 him shoop lede] *H shoop him to lead; 904 fair lady] *H fair gentle lady, Lat. pulcram dominam et generosam; certein] *H *om.*; 906 haue hir] *H *trsp.*; 913 bolne] CD2R below; 916 euerychone] BLY nye euerychone; 917 knowe Y] *H I wot; 923 on hy.... seide] *H on courteous height (C heih) right; 925 haue of me] *H take; 927 seeknesse] *H disease; his] *H their; 929 shewid] *H *before* hir; 934 and kiste] *H kissing; 939 wrecche] *H man; 945 han him] BLSY *trsp.*; harmynge] CD2R hinderyng; 946 I now thus] *H is at an; 948 weende] *H with him gan; 949 lyueden] *H led their life; 955 almoost] *H well nigh; 957 my tale anoon] *H this tale to him; 960 wel] *H sumdel; 981 this emperour] *H the; aboue] *H before; 992 he hath mercy] BLY *continues* the rather and the

sooner woll he synne; 993 the rather wole he] *H the rather and the sooner will he; 997 the flessh of] D2R *om.*; 998 makynge] *H make; 1005–6 the flessh and the.... vertu and] S *om.*; 1007–9 spowse vnto synne.... vnto Cryst] L *marg.*; 1017 berkynge] CD2R werkyng; 1019 þat is to meene] BY þat is to sey (Y *corr. to* meene); 1020 teche and norisshe] *H nourish; 1020–2 þat is to seyn (CD2R þe).... the laumpe] B *om.*, L *marg.*; 1032 castynge] *H and casteth, Lat. et proicit; 1036 vpsodoun] *H backward (S *om.*), Lat. retrorsum; 1037 swiche] BLY wiche; þat been] BLY þat been put out; oghte] L anyght; 1040 etc.] BLY *om.*; 1042–3 so sholde we.... the spores] L *om.*; 1049–51 whoso.... but manye] *underlined*; 1056 feend] *H world, Lat. mundus; 1062 fro (worldly)] *H for, Lat. propter; 1064 infect] CD2R effect; ye by the] BLY by the; 1067 wittes] BLY vices

VII.4 'Ars vtillissima sciendi mori'

Copies: (holographs) DH2 (the latter to l. 672); other copies, see Appendix 4. Modern edition: Pryor 1968.

2 konne] BCR knowe; 9 seintes] BLY sentens (L *adds* þe); 15 so] H2 to; 16 teche] BLY tell, Lat. docebo; 20–1 the dreede.... wisdam] D *underlined*; 21 lerne] H2*H lere; 33 this fayn] *H hereof; 38 swetnesse] *H richesse; 45 heer woot he] *H wot he full; 52 hir]*H his; 54 hir]*H him; 56 is therof] H2 *trsp.*; 63 fro] BLY for, Lat. a (mundo); 69 tho] H2*H the; 74 ful] H2 right; 78 H2*H gretter (Y grette) profit shall to þe be (C be to þe) my lore; 85 now] H2 inward (Lat. nunc); 87 good] *H great; 98 greet] CR *om.*; 106 myn ende comth] *H nigheth mine end; 117 comynge] H2 hour; was] H2 *trsp. before* vnto; vncerteyn] H2 ful vncerteyn; 117–18 BLY thy commyng vnto me stole and me bounde (LY *marg.* defect., dele); 125 whidir] *H *adds* now; 127 bisyly] *H now full busily; 132 ne noon othir] *H cattle nouþir; 139 this] H2BLY þe, Lat. hoc; 145 now] D *marg. adds* ynow; 150 him] H2 vnto him; 155 no] H2 *om.*; 161 check is] CR *trsp.*; 163 anothir eek] H2 oon also; 164 right] *H *om.*; 165 been] *H stond; 170 soothly] l *of* soothly *added above*; 176 bestial] BLY *add* ouer; 193 am weery] H2*H *trsp.*; 194 hardnesse] BLSY hardinesse, Lat. difficiles; 205 preef] H2 way, Lat. argumentum; 209 swich stirynge and] *H which stirring; 212 þat continuelly] H2*H foorthwith redily, Lat. continuo; 214 sy] CR se(e)th, R *adds* verrily; 216 continuelly] H2*H anoonrightes. Lat. continuo; 220 which.... vp reisith] H2*H with (*H by).... blowe away, Lat. tollitur; 225 now] *H all, Lat. nunc; 231 dayes] H2 yeeres, Lat. annos (*but see Introduction* n. 51); 260 angwissh] CR wo; 276 accusacions] *H *adds* many foul (C *om.* foul); 279 leet Y] H2 *H *trsp.*; 280 beten] H2 scourgid; 297 youthe] H2 dayes, Lat. iuventutis; 301 it] H2*H *om.*; vices] H2*H your vices; 302, 304 slipt, clipt] CR slept, crept; 304 wrecchidnesses] H2*H wrecchidnesse, Lat. miseriam; 308 be told] *H that told be; 310 right] H2 ful; 311 conseillid] *H *adds* me; 318 thus had it] H2 it had thus, *H it thus had; 322 grantid] H2 lent to, Lat. concessum; 329 be repentant] BCLY by repentance; 332 to thee] H2 seye and; 335 þat] BLY *om.*; 348 mynde] *H heart; 349 serche] BRY sech, CL such; 355 penance] D *corr. to* repentance; 359 verraily] i *of this word added above*; 363 haue Y] CR *after* werreied; 364 haue.... purueied] CR no bettre purueied haue Y; 371 al] H2 now; 376 me] H2*H him; 377 alle] H2 ny; slipt] CR spilte; 379 Y haue] H2 *trsp.*; 387 and] *H and thy; 393 hour gretter] H2 day more, Lat. hora; 399 synfully] H2*H folyly; 408 help] CR helth; 417 left] B lest (*or* left), CR life; 430 therto] *H thereto to; 435 fadir] CR God; 445 good, lord[2]] *H my, God, cf. Lat. deus meus; 448 neede] *H great need; 451 ful] H2*H right; 452 noon fynde Y] *H now find I folk, cf. Lat. nemo; 453 yeue me wole] CR me ne yeue wole; 458 tyme han eek] H2 han eek tyme; be ny] *H to; 460 tresors] H2 tresor, Lat. thesauros; 472 heeraftir Y] H2 *trsp.*; 473 may] CR me; 480 lyf] *H self; 483] mighten] *H *after* heuene; H2Ha1 that heuenes blisse myghten thee byreue; 492 hadde] BLY *om.*; 493 x yeer] CR than; 498 thow] CR than; 502 me] *H *adds* now; 513 me leuen] H2 *trsp.*; 516 were] *H *add* now (C

before thy); 519 stirynge] C sterne, Y streng; 520 profyten] H2*H auaill; 524 and¹, han] H2 *om.*; heer] H2 with hem heer; 527 ne] H2*H *om.*; noon] H2 right noon; 529 stonde] *H they stand; 535 feblesse] *H sickness; 552 yeuen] *H set; 570 gooth so faste] H2 is so dryue; 575 hir] BLY his; 583 lyke] H2*H list to; now] BLY not; 588 men] H2*H folke, Ha1 pepull; 597 nat] *D above line*, H2*H *om.*; it shal] H2*H *trsp.*; 598 eek as eende] *H is end eke; 607 thow] D thogh; 610 vpon me] *H on me well; 621 rightwys man] C rightfull man, H2 good lyuer; 622 howso] *H or how; shal go] H2 gooth vp; 623 wheras confort is] *H where is comfort of; 627 the hy] CR that; 628 to] H2*H of, cf. Lat. a (curia); the court] CR the (R that) contree; 635 haue] *H find; 637 cause haast thow] *H is thy cause; and wo] LSY *om.*; 640 greet habundance] *H full great foyson; 642 conpleyne, weepe] H2*H *trsp.*; 651 now so] H2B *trsp.*, Y now *after* me; 655 my look ful dym and] H2*H dim my look and as; 662 breeth] *H wind (*exc.* Y mynde); 667 of al] H2*H *trsp.*; 671 feendes] H2 freendes; 672 H2 *ends after this line*; 678 viserly] CR grislie; 680 iuge] BLY *add* riʒtwise; 681 weyest] CR *add* me; 685 shee] CR eke; 688 thurgh] *H for, Lat. per; 692 streight as] CR right as (C *adds* a); 695 men] CR man, Ha1 mene; 701 been] BLY me (B *orig.* be); 708 haue] *H *adds* ye (C þou); our] CS ʒour, Y *corr. to* our; 716 and eek of othir] *H and other folks; 738 wofull sent is] *om.* D, *supplied from* *H; 756 this] BLY my; 758 lyf] *H self, Lat. vita; 760 picchid] *H ficched; 764 dwellynge] *H no dwelling; 765 noon] *H here; 766 for why] B forþi, CR without; 767 permanable] CR perdurable; 768 strecche] B stright, Y streght; merciable] *H miserable; 773 dispose] BLY purpose; 778 now wole Y voide] *H O fy upon the, Lat. tolle tolle a me; 787 Y¹] *D above line*; 790 certes] *H certainly full; 800 souffre] *H let; 805 to] BLSY now to; 807 t *of* nat *above line*; 815–16 of purgatorie.... distreyne] BLY of purgatorie I cowde distreyne, *and* (LY) *marg.* defec[it]; 819 vp *of* vpon *above line*; 831 ne ommitte] BLS vnmyte, Y vamytte, CR *om.*; 835 trust and] CR *om.*; of] CR and; 838 ouer] BL euery, Y euere; 848–54] BLY *om.*; 858 retourne] CR *add* to; 861 is] *H this (C it) is (S is, *above line*); 862 fewe] BLY well; 877 how] *H how men, cf. Lat. ne.... convertantur; 889 for ay] LY away, B and away; 902 conseil] CR conceite; 907 waar] BL raft, Y past; 921 swich a] CR touche a (C as); 923 the firste] *H this first (BLY *om* first); 925 as] *H with; 926 all] D an; 927 witnessith] *H this (C thus) end I; 928 hem þat.... hens] B wel þat hens, CS hem þat wel, LY wel þat hem; 934 celestial] *H *adds* high; 943 (or) hete] BL hert; 945 fer of helle] *H the fear and gastnes of; 947 conuenient and] *H *om.*, Lat. convenientia; 948–9 o concord] BLSY one corde, CR oon accorde; 950 peisible alle] *H restful (C rest at ful, R in reste all full); and reste] *H *om.*, Lat. tranquilla sunt omnia et quieta; 954 lamb (is his)] C laumpe; 956 bemes] *H brightness; 980 inestimable] B stabill, C instabilite, LY instable, R *om.*, S instellable; 984 might (of the)] BLY mynde; 985–6 souffrith.... this thyng] B for wele of man; 990 to (God the fadir)] *H of, Lat. Deo patri; so] *above line*; 992 and deedly] CR *om.*; 994 to gete] CR to haue and to gete; 996 Amen amen] *H amen; 1004 lesne] CR ease, BLSY lesse; 1007 (syn) God] *H our lord God; of his hy.... courtesie] *H *om.*; 1009 present] *H *om.*; standith] *H is; 1010 and eleccioun] *H *om.*; 1012 of his.... goodnesse] *H *om.*; cheese] *H *add* through his merciable grace

VII.5 'Fabula de quadam muliere mala'

Copies: (holograph) D; other copies, see Appendix 4. Only BCDLSY have the framing introduction. Modern editions Pryor 1968, Seymour 1981 (ll. 85–455).

9 men] *H folk; 27 foleye] BY folye, Y *above line*; 29 fer] BLY for; 33 lynes] B leves, C lifes (Furnivall *reads* lyues); 35 seye] *H speak; 47 wryte] BCLY wit (Y *adds* it); 50 me] BLY may; reede] *second* e *above*; 51 me red han] *H have counselled me; 61 euele] BLY wel; 65 wole] BLY wole not; 81 auisament] *H mine avisement; 85 whilom] *H sometime; 87 greet²] *H *om.*; 96 al]

*H and; 99 withouten ooth] B with ough, L withouten oght; 108 thynke] CD2R *om.*; 110 in] *H
in thy; mynde] B hert; 121 of] *D above line*; 133 testament] *H intent; 134 he] CR here, D2 the;
136 he] BLY bene; 138 his²] BCY is, R and; 140 it] *H I; 145 while] CR wise; 182 this] *H a,
cf. Lat. unam peticionem; 184 ay] BLY *om.*; 189 ne gold ne] *H ne coin in; 192 swich] *H which;
205 dyyng] CD2R endyng (cf. 671); 207 men] *H all folk, cf. Lat. omnium; 210 but....good]
*H and.... right good, CD2 *om.* as blyue; 217 *H what would ye my love quoth he mean thereby;
228 his] *H her; 231 qweynt] BLY went; loues knotte] *H the knot of love; 249 whan is hir] *H
at her own; 254 way] BLY *om.*; 258 scoole] *H (CD2R the) study; 260 forsoothe.... ryng] *H
the ring that ye me (BLY to me) took; 263 sorwefully] *H right grievously; 271 he the los] *H
for the (Y his) loss he; 289–90 þat telle.... of this] CD2R þat.... hir telle; 291 for him] *H from
her; 292 it was or he] *H he not to her; 294 Y] CD2R she; 296 slayn] CD2R dede; 305 CD2R
to (C of) hym, and of his foolish (C foles) tendirnesse; 306 D2R: Why makest thou all this wo
and hevynesse (C *reads as l. 307, and precedes by a new* 306: thus vnto hir he spak and said thus);
313 thee] BLY me; 318 now] *H not; 320 myn herte] LY myght, B night; 325 cheer] *H dear;
328–9 quod he, swythe.... hy the] *H he said, now.... tarry not thou; 339 in al haaste þat] *H as
hastily as; 348 thy] *H the; 353 take] *H take eke; 363 Y²] CD2R Y in; 368 priuee] CD2R *om.*;
377 his] BLY this; 380 wisshe in his herte] *H thinking wish; 381 Y mighte thus been] *H my
heart thus were; 388 thogh] *H that; thurghgirt] L thurth hert; 391 soul] CD2R alone; 402 feith]
*H fair (C *over corr.*) him] *H her; Seymour *accepts* Furnivall's *queried emendation* hir, cf. Lat.
Jonathas adhibebat fidem dictis suis; 417 and] *H *om.*; come] *H to come is; 420 good] *H full
great, *cf. note in commentary*; 424 right wel] *H strong, Lat. fortiter; 431 soul] CD2R ther; 442
he¹] *H Jonathas; he ne] *H *om.*; 446 look] *H eye, cf. 492; 447 eir] CD2RY see, Lat. aere; 458
he¹] *H it; 459 he²] *H it; 462 al] BCY as; 479 therby] CD2R ther was noon; 480 ther] *H nigh;
486 al] *H it; 491 this Ionathas] *H and his way he (B *om.* he); 499 from afer] *H far from him;
501 heeng as] *H ficched were; 509 helthe] *H cure; 510 they seide him] *H well, quod they;
515 hir art] BL her hert, L *orig.* hert; 516 helthe] CD2R lyfe; 522 ful sauf] BLS all safe, Y ai safe,
CD2R as faste; 524 I²] *H *om.*; 525 ful] *H right; 539 in] BLY *om.*; 546 on a day] *H at (the)
last, Lat. tandem post longum tempus (*var.* post plures annos) quadam die; 547 xxxti] *H twenty,
Lat. triginta; 552 me] BCLRY *om.*; 567 swythe] *H blive; 568 and] BLSY and þan, CR and þat;
569 good] *H God; 573 torned] *D poss.* terned, *H tormented; 574 is] *H it is; 575 or] BLY be
þei; 596 messages solempne] *H solemn messengers; 606 strange] *H strong; 622 y *of* yeue *orig.*
s-; 635 Y so] *H men; 643 streyne courtesie] CD2R strive curteysly; 645 fond] *later hand adds*
leyynge; 646 who²] CD2R tho; 657 nad he] BL nad had, Y and had; 659 yaf] *H made; 660 him]
CD2R her; 666 woman] D man, *H woman (*om.* E); dyde] BCLY did; 667 tho] BLY the; 669
th'emperice] *H *om.*; 671 dyynge] CR endyng; 672 amen] BCLY *om.*; 673 th'emperour] CSY
this emperour; þat Y spak of] *H above expressed; iii] C iiii; 677 confermed] *H strongly
confirmed; 679 bytook] *H committed; 682 this emperour] *H the emperor; the iewelles] *H
three jewels; 683–4 we shul.... is rownd] CD2R *om.*; 684 crookidnesse] R *adds* is vnderstond
feith; 686 spekith and] *H *om.*; 688 this hil] *H the (S þi) hill (C hillis), Lat. huic monti; 691–2
and seyde.... holy goost] CD2R *om.*; telle and] *H *om.*; Y seye] *H ever I say; 693 alle goodes
þat profyten] *H all that good and profitable is (B *om.* all, CD2R is *before* and), Lat. omnia....
que prosunt ad salutem anime; 696–7 loued vs so mochil] *H had us in so fervent love and charity;
698 sittith vpon] CD2R deyeth in; 699 this (world)] *H this laborious and unrestful; reste] *H
ease and rest; 702 to him] *H *om.*; stirynge] *H exciting and stirring; leesith] *H loseth and
forgoeth; 704–5 by cause.... from him] S *om.*; 705–7 parfyt charitee.... beestes, þat is to seyn] C
copies three times (ending with is left); dwellith or abydith] *H is left; 711–12 enlumyne thee] *H
adds seith (C thus seith) Criste; 717–18 right so of the soule] *H *om.*; wroght offense and synne]
*H sin or offence done; 719 and liknesse] *H *om.*; 722 communioun] *H conuersation, Lat.
communio; penitence] BC penaunce; 724 eet] *H ate also; 725 man] *H he; helith] CL helthe;
728 the flessh] CD2R *after* þat is to seyn; 729 steruyeth and dieth] *H dieth (C deth); 732 God
of his grace] B he, RS God, CLY *om.*

Bibliography

(For a fuller bibliography specifically devoted to Hoccleve, consult Burrow 1994.)

Editions of texts or selections

Bale, J. (1559) *Scriptorium Illustrium Maioris Brytannie* (Basle)

Barnum, P.H. (1976, 1980) *Dives et Pauper*, vols 1–2, EETS 275, 280 (London, Oxford: Oxford University Press)

Barr, H. (1993) *The Piers Plowman Tradition* (London: J.M. Dent)

Beatty, A. (1902) *A New Ploughman's Tale*, Chaucer Society 2,34 (London: Kegan Paul, Trench, Trübner and Co.)

Benson, L. et al. (1988) *The Riverside Chaucer*, 3rd ed. (Oxford; Oxford University Press)

Blamires, A., Marx, C.W., and Pratt, K. (1992) *Woman Defamed and Woman Defended: an Anthology of Medieval Texts* (Oxford: Clarendon Press)

Boyd, B. (1964) *The Middle English Miracles of the Virgin* (San Marino, Ca.: The Huntington Library)

Brown, C. (1939) *Religious Lyrics of the XVth Century* (Oxford: Clarendon Press)

Burrow, J. (1977) *English Verse 1300–1500* (London and New York: Longman)

— (1999) *Thomas Hoccleve's Complaint and Dialogue*, EETS 313 (Oxford: Oxford University Press)

Cigman, G. (1989) *Lollard Sermons*, EETS 294 (Oxford: Oxford University Press)

Colloquia Dominiciana (1923) [no editor] Bibliotheca Mystica Sanctorum Ordinis Predicatorum Patrum (Im Selbstverlag des Verfassers)

Davies, R.T. (1963) *Medieval English Lyrics* (London: Faber and Faber)

Dickins, B., and Wilson, R.M. (1951) *Early Middle English Texts* (London: Bowes and Bowes)

Dyboski, R. (1907) *Songs, Carols and Other Miscellaneous Poems*, EETS ES 101 (London: Kegan Paul, Trench, Trübner and Co.)

Fenster, T.S., and Erler, M.C. (1990) *Poems of Cupid, God of Love* (Leiden etc.: E.J. Brill)

Fox, D., and Ringler, W.A. (1980) *The Bannatyne MS, National Library of Scotland Advocates MS 1.1.6* (London: Scolar)

Furnivall, F.J. (1897) *Hoccleve's Works III, The Regement of Princes*, EETS ES 72 (London: Kegan Paul, Trench Trübner and Co.)

— (1901) *The Minor Poems of the Vernon Manuscript* II, EETS OS 117 (London: Kegan Paul, Tench, Trübner and Co.)

— and Gollancz, I. (1970) *Hoccleve's Works: the Minor Poems*, EETS ES 61 and 73 (orig. 1892, 1925: revised J. Mitchell and A.I. Doyle, printed in one volume, London etc.: Oxford University Press)

Hammond, E.P. (1927) *English Verse Between Chaucer and Surrey* (Durham, Nth. Carolina: Duke

University Press)

Henry, A. (1985) *The Pilgrimage of the Lyfe of the Manhode*, EETS 288 (London etc.: Oxford University Press)

— and Trotter, D. (1994) *De Quatuordecim Partibus Beatitudinis, Medium Ævum* Monographs NS 17 (Oxford: Basil Blackwell)

Herrtage, S.J.H. (1879) *The Early English Versions of the Gesta Romanorum*, EETS ES 33 (London: Humphrey Milford)

Hodgson, P. (1982) *The Cloud of Unknowing and Related Treatises*, Analecta Cartusiana 3 (Exeter: Catholic Records Press)

Hogg, J. (1973–4) *The Speculum Devotorum of an Anonymous Carthusian of Sheen*, Analecta Cartusiana 13: 2–3 (Salzburg: Institut für Englische Sprache und Literatur)

Horstmann, C. (1896) *Yorkshire Writers: Richard Rolle of Hampole and his Followers* (London: Swan Sonnenschein and New York: Macmillan)

Künzle, P. (1977) *Heinrich Seuse Orologium Sapientiae* (Freiburg: Universitätsverlag)

McGerr, R.P. (1990) *The Pilgrimage of the Soul, A Critical Edition of the Middle English Dream Vision*, vol. 1 (New York and London: Garland)

Miller, R.P. (1977) trans. *Chaucer Sources and Backgrounds* (Oxford: Oxford University Press)

Muir, K. (1944–7) 'Unpublished Poems in the Devonshire MS', *Proceedings of the Leeds Philosophical and Literary Society*, 6, 253–82

O'Donoghue, B. (1982) *Thomas Hoccleve Selected Poems* (Carcanet: Manchester)

Oesterley, H. (1872) *Gesta Romanorum* (Berlin: Weidmannsche Buchhandlung)

Poole, R.L. and Bateson, M. (eds) (1902) *Index Britanniae Scriptorum* (Oxford: Clarendon Press)

Proctor, E., and Wordsworth, C. (1879–86) *Breviarum ad Usum Insignis Ecclesiae Sarum*, 3 vols. (Cambridge: Cambridge University Press)

Pryor, M.A. (1968) 'The Series' (Los Angeles: University of California Ph.D. thesis)

Robinson, P. (1980) (intro.) *Manuscript Tanner 346: A Facsimile* (Norman: Pilgrim Books)

Ross, W.O. (1940) *Middle English Sermons*, EETS OS 209 (London: Oxford University Press)

Sandison, H.E. (1923) '"En mon deduit a moys de May": the original of Hoccleve's "Balade to the Virgin and Christ"', *Vassar Medieval Studies*, ed. C.F. Fiske, 233–45.

Sargent, M.G. (1992) *Nicholas Love's Mirror of the Blessed Life of Jesus Christ*, Garland Medieval Texts (New York and London: Garland)

Seymour, M.C. (1981) *Selections from Hoccleve* (Oxford: Clarendon Press)

Skeat, W.W. (1898) *Chaucerian and Other Pieces (Supplement to the Works of Geoffrey Chaucer)* (Oxford: Clarendon Press)

Smalley, J. (1953) 'Poems of the Middle English Pilgrimage of the Soul' (University of Liverpool: M.A. thesis)

Stürzinger, J.J. (1895) *Le Pèlerinage de l'âme* (London: Roxburghe Club)

Wallensköld, A. (1907), 'Le conte de la femme chaste convoitée par son beau-frère', *Acta Societatis Scientiarum Fennicae* 34,1 (Helsingfors)

Wenzel, S. (1989) *Fasciculus Morum: A Fourteenth-Century Preacher's Handbook* (University Park and London: Pennsylvania State University Press)

Whiting, B.J. (1968) *Proverbs, Sentences and Proverbial Phrases from English Writings Mainly Before 1500* (Cambridge, Mass: Harvard University Press, London: Oxford University Press)

Wilson, F.P. (1970) *The Oxford Dictionary of English Proverbs*, 3rd ed. revised (Oxford: Clarendon Press)

Windeatt, B.A. (1984) *Geoffrey Chaucer: Troilus and Criseyde* (London and New York: Longman)

Secondary literature

Arn, M.-J. (1994) 'Charles d'Orléans: Translator?', in Ellis and Evans pp. 125–35

Bassnett, S. (1991) *Translation Studies* (rev. 1st ed., 1980, London and New York: Methuen)

Batt, C. (1996₁) ed. *Essays on Thomas Hoccleve*, Westfield Publications in Medieval Studies 10 (London: Centre for Medieval and Renaissance Studies, Queen Mary and Westfield College/Brepols)

— (1996₂) 'Hoccleve and…. Feminism? Negotiating Meaning in *The Regiment of Princes*', in Batt 1996₁ pp. 55–84

Beaty, N.L. (1970) *The Craft of Dying: The Literary Tradition of the 'Ars Moriendi' in England* (New Haven: Yale University Press)

Beer, J. (1991) 'Julius Caesar and *Li Fet des Romains*', in Ellis 1991 pp. 89–97

Bornstein, D. (1977) 'French Influence on Fifteenth-century English Prose as Exemplified by the Translation of Christine de Pisan's *Livre du corps de policie*', *Medieval Studies* 39, 369–86

— (1981) 'Anti-feminism in Thomas Hoccleve's Translation of Christine de Pizan's *Epistre au dieu d'amours*', *English Language Notes* 19, 7–14

Boffey, J., and Thompson, J.J. (1989) 'Anthologies and Miscellanies: Production and Choice of Texts', in Griffiths and Pearsall pp. 279–315

Bowers, J.M. (1989) 'Hoccleve's Two Copies of "Lerne to Dye": Implications for Textual Critics', *Papers of the Bibliographical Society of America* 83, 437–72

Boyd, B. (1956) 'Hoccleve's Miracle of the Virgin', *Texas Studies in English* 35, 116–22

Brook, L.C. (1991) 'The Translator and His Reader', in Ellis 1991 pp. 99–122

Burnley, J.D. (1983) *A Guide to Chaucer's Language* (Houndmills and London: Macmillan)

— (1986) 'Curial Prose in English', *Speculum* 61, 593–614

Burrow, C. (1999) 'Literature and Politics under Henry VII and Henry VIII', in Wallace pp. 793–820

Burrow, J. (1981) 'The Poet as Petitioner', *SAC* 3, 61–75

— (1982) 'Autobiographical Poetry in the Middle Ages: the Case of Thomas Hoccleve', *Proceedings of the British Academy* 68, 389–412

— (1984) 'Hoccleve's *Series*: Experience and Books', in Yeager pp. 259–73

— (1994) *Thomas Hoccleve*, Authors of the Middle Ages, English Writers of the Late Middle Ages, ed. M.C. Seymour, I:4 (Aldershot, Hants.: Variorum) [originally issued as a single volume, the latter cited in Seymour, and in this volume, by page numbers in square brackets]

— (1995) 'Thomas Hoccleve: Some Redatings', *Review of English Studies* NS 46, 366–72

— (1997) 'Hoccleve and the Middle French Poets', in *The Long Fifteenth Century* (full reference, Cooper and Mapstone) pp. 35–49.

— (1998) 'Hoccleve's *Complaint* and Isidore of Seville Again', *Speculum* 73, 424–8

Catto, J. (1985) 'Religious Change Under Henry V', in *Henry V; The Practice of Kingship*, ed. G.L. Harriss (Oxford: Oxford University Press), pp. 97–115

Classen, A. (1990) 'Love and Marriage in Late Medieval Verse: Oswald von Wolkenstein, Thomas Hoccleve and Michael Beheim', *Studia Neophilologica* 62, 163–88

— (1991) 'The Autobiographical Voice of Thomas Hoccleve', *Archiv* 228, 299–310

Connolly, M. (1996) '"Your Humble Suget and Seruytoure": John Shirley, Transcriber and Translator', in Ellis and Tixier pp. 419–31

Cooper, H. (1989) *Chaucer's Canterbury Tales*, Oxford Guides to Chaucer (Oxford: Clarendon Press)

— and Mapstone, S. (eds) (1997) *The Long Fifteenth Century: Essays for Douglas Gray* (Oxford: Clarendon Press)

Copeland, R. (1991) *Rhetoric, Hermeneutics and Translation in the Middle Ages* (Cambridge: Cambridge University Press)

— (ed.) (1996) *Criticism and Dissent in the Middle Ages* (Cambridge: Cambridge University Press)

Cummings, B. (1999) 'Reformed Literature and Literature Reformed', in Wallace pp. 821–51

Doob, P.B.R. (1974) *Nebuchadnezzar's Children: Conventions of Madness in Middle English Literature* (New Haven, Conn.: Yale University Press)

Doyle, A.I., and Pace, G.B. (1968) 'A New Chaucer MS', *PMLA* 83, 22–34

— and Parkes, M.B. (1978) 'The Production of Copies of the *Canterbury Tales* and the *Confessio Amantis* in the Early Fifteenth Century', *Medieval Scribes, Manuscripts and Libraries: Essays Presented to N.R. Ker* (London: Scolar Press), pp. 163–210

Eagleton, T. (1977) 'Translation and Transformation', *Stand* 19(3), 72–7.

Edwards, A.S.G. (ed.) (1984) *Middle English Prose: A Critical Guide to Major Authors and Genres* (New Brunswick, NJ: Rutgers University Press)

Ellis, R. (1982) 'The Choices of the Translator in the Late Middle English Period', in Glasscoe 1982 pp. 19–49

—— (1984) *Syon Abbey: the Spirituality of the English Bridgettines*. Analecta Cartusiana 68,2 (Salzburg: Institut für Anglistik und Amerikanistik)

— (1986) *Patterns of Religious Narrative in the Canterbury Tales* (London: Croom Helm)

— (ed.) (1991) *The Medieval Translator*, Westfield Publications in Medieval Studies XX (London: Centre for Medieval and Renaissance Studies, Queen Mary and Westfield College)

— (1994) 'Second Thoughts on the Authorship of *[þ]e Tretyse of [þ]e Stodye of Wysdome*', *Neuphilologische Mitteilungen* XCV, 307–17

— (1996) 'Chaucer, Christine de Pisan, and Hoccleve: the "Letter of Cupid"', in Batt 1996i pp. 29–54

— and Evans, R. (eds) (1994) *The Medieval Translator* 4 (Exeter: University of Exeter Press)

— and Tixier, R. (eds) (1996) *The Medieval Translator* 5 (Turnhout: Brepols)

— and Wogan-Browne, J., Medcalf, S., and Meredith, P. (eds) (1989) *The Medieval Translator* (Cambridge: D.S. Brewer)

Ferster, J. (1996) *Fictions of Advice: the Literature and Politics of Counsel in Late Medieval England* (Philadelphia: University of Pennsylvania Press)

Field, R. (1989) '*Ipomedon* to *Ipomedon A*: Two Views of Courtliness', in Ellis, Wogan-Browne et al. pp. 135–41

Fleming, J.V. (1971) 'Hoccleve's "Letter of Cupid" and the "Quarrel" over the *Roman de la rose*', *MÆv* XL, 21–40

Frantzen, A.J. (1990) *Desire for Origins: New Language, Old English and Teaching the Tradition* (New Brunswick and London: Rutgers University Press)

Glasscoe, M. (ed.) (1982) *The Medieval Mystical Tradition in England* (Exeter: Exeter University Press)

— (ed.) (1984) *The Medieval Mystical Tradition in England. Exeter Symposium III* (Cambridge: D.S. Brewer)

Gray, D. (1972) *Themes and Images in the Medieval English Religious Lyric* (London: Routledge and Kegan Paul)

Green, R.F. (1980) *Poets and Princepleasers: Literature and the English Court in the Late Middle Ages* (Toronto, Buffalo, London: University of Toronto Press)

Greetham, D.C. (1987) 'Challenges of Theory and Practice in the Editing of Hoccleve's *Regement of Princes*', in *Manuscripts and Texts: Editorial Problems in Later Middle English Literature*, ed. D. Pearsall (Cambridge: D.S. Brewer), pp. 60–86

— (1989) 'Self-Referential Artefacts: The Hoccleve Persona as a Literary Device', *Modern Philology* 86, 242–51

Griffiths, J., and Pearsall, D. (eds) (1989) *Book Production and Publishing in Britain 1375–1475* (Cambridge: Cambridge University Press)

Haines, R.M. (1971) '"Wilde Wittes and Wilfulnes": John Swetstock's Attack on those "Poyswunmongeres", the Lollards', *SCH* 8, 143–53

— (1975) 'Church, Society and Politics in the Early Fifteenth Century as Viewed from an English Pulpit', *SCH* 12, 143–57

Harris, K. (1998) 'Unnoticed Extracts from Chaucer and Hoccleve: Huntington MS HM 144, Trinity College, Oxford MS D 29 and *The Canterbury Tales*,' *SAC* 20, 167–99

Hasler, A. (1990) 'Hoccleve's Unregimented Body', *Paragraph* 13(2), 164–83

Hines, J. (1993) *The Fabliau in English* (London: Longman)

Hudson, A. (1975) 'The Debate on Bible Translation, Oxford 1401', *English Historical Review* 90, 1–18 (repr. in Hudson, A. (1985) *Lollards and Their Books*, London: Hambledon)

— (1988) *The Premature Reformation* (Oxford: Clarendon Press)

— (1997) '*Visio Baleii*: an Early Literary Historian', in *The Long Fifteenth Century* (full reference, Cooper and Mapstone), pp. 313–329.

Jacob, E.F. (1961) *The Fifteenth Century* (Oxford: Clarendon Press)

Johnson, I.R. (1989) 'Prologue and Practice: Middle English Lives of Christ' in Ellis, Wogan-Browne et al. pp. 69–85

Keiser, G. (1985) 'The Middle English *Planctus Mariae* and the Rhetoric of Pathos', in *The Popular Literature of Medieval England*, ed. T.J. Heffernan, Tennessee Studies in Literature 28 (Knoxville: University of Tennessee Press), pp. 167–93

Kerby-Fulton, K. (1997) 'Langland and the Bibliographic Ego', in *Written Work: Langland, Labor and Authorship*, eds. S. Justice and K. Kerby-Fulton (Philadelphia: University of Pennsylvania Press), pp. 67–143

— (1999) '*Piers Plowman*,' in Wallace pp. 513–38

Kolve, V.A. (1984) *Chaucer and the Imagery of Narrative* (London: Edward Arnold)

Kurtz, B.P. (1924) 'The Prose of Occleve's *Lerne to Dye*', *Modern Language Notes* 39, 56–7

— (1925) 'The Relation of Occleve's *Lerne to Dye* to its Latin Source', *PMLA* 40, 252–75

Lawton, D. (1985) *Chaucer's Narrators*, Chaucer Studies xiii (Cambridge: D.S. Brewer)

Lefevere, A. (1992) *Translation and the Manipulation of Literary Fame* (London: Routledge)

Lovatt, R. (1982) 'Henry Suso and the Medieval Mystical Tradition in England', in Glasscoe 1982 pp. 47–62

Machan, T.W. (1985) *Techniques of Translation: Chaucer's Boece* (Norman, Oklahoma: Pilgrim Books)

— (1989) 'Chaucer as Translator', in Ellis, Wogan-Browne et al. pp. 55–67

Medcalf, S. (ed.) (1981) *The Later Middle Ages* (London: Longman)

Mills, D. (1996) 'The Voices of Thomas Hoccleve', in Batt 1996₁ pp. 85–107

Minnis, A.J. (1984) *Medieval Theory of Authorship: Scholastic Literary Attitudes in the Later Middle Ages* (London: Scolar Press, rev. ed. 1988)

Mitchell, J. (1968) *Thomas Hoccleve: A Study in Early Fifteenth-Century English Poetic* (Urbana, Chicago, London: University of Illinois Press)

— (1984) 'Hoccleve Studies, 1965–81', in Yeager pp. 49–63

— (1983) 'Hoccleve's *Minor Poems*: Addenda and Corrigenda', *Edinburgh Bibliographical Society Transactions* 5(3), 9–16

Moyes, M. (1984) 'The Manuscripts and Early Printed Editions of Richard Rolle's *Expositio Super novem Lectiones Mortuorum*', in Glasscoe 1984 pp. 81–103

Muscatine, C. (1986) *The Old French Fabliaux* (New Haven, Conn., and London: Yale University Press)

Olson, G. (1999) 'Geoffrey Chaucer', in Wallace pp. 566–88

Pearsall, D. (1977) *Old English and Middle English Poetry* (London: Routledge and Kegan Paul)

— (1989) 'Gower's Latin in the *Confessio Amantis*', in *Latin and Vernacular: Studies in Late-Medieval Texts and Manuscripts*, ed. A.J. Minnis (Cambridge: D.S. Brewer) pp. 13–25

— (1992) *The Life of Geoffrey Chaucer: a Critical Biography* (Oxford: Basil Blackwell)

— (1994) 'Hoccleve's *Regement of Princes*: the Poetics of Royal Self-Presentation', *Speculum* 69, 386–410

Phillips, H. (1994) '*The Complaint of Venus*: Chaucer and de Graunson', in Ellis and Evans pp. 86–103

Quinn, W.A. (1986) 'Hoccleve's "Epistle of Cupid"', *Explicator* 45, 7–10

Richardson, M. (1985–6) 'Hoccleve in his Social Context', *Chaucer Review* 20, 313–22

Rigg, A.G. (1970) 'Hoccleve's *Complaint* and Isidore of Seville', *Speculum* 45, 564–74

Robinson, D. (1991) *The Translator's Turn* (Baltimore and London: Johns Hopkins University Press)

Savage, A. (1994) 'The Translation of the Feminine: Untranslatable Dimensions of the Anchoritic Works', in Ellis and Evans pp. 181–99

Scattergood, V.J. (1971) *Politics and Poetry in the Fifteenth Century* (London: Blandford Press)

Schulz, H.C. (1937) 'Thomas Hoccleve Scribe', *Speculum* 12, 71–81

Selman, R. (1998) 'Voices and Wisdom: a Study of Henry Suso's *Horologium Sapientiae* in Some Late Medieval English Religious Texts' (Exeter: University of Exeter Ph.D. thesis)

Shepherd, G. (1959) *Ancrene Wisse Parts 6 and 7* (London: Nelson, reissued Exeter: University of Exeter Press, 1986)

Silvia, D.S. (1974) 'Some Fifteenth-Century Manuscripts of the *Canterbury Tales*', in *Chaucer and Middle English Studies in Honour of Rossell Hope Robbins*, ed. B. Rowland (London: George Allen and Unwin) pp. 153–63

Simpson, J. (1991) 'Madness and Texts: Hoccleve's *Series*', in *Chaucer and Fifteenth-Century Poetry*, eds J. Boffey and J. Cowen, King's College London Medieval Studies V (London: King's College London Centre for Late Antique and Medieval Studies) pp. 15–29

— (1995) 'Nobody's Man: Thomas Hoccleve's *Regement of Princes*', *London and Europe in the Later Middle Ages*, eds J. Boffey and P. King, Westfield Publications in Medieval Studies 9 (London: Centre for Medieval and Renaissance Studies, Queen Mary and Westfield College) pp. 149–80

Smith, L. Toulmin (1882) 'A Ballad by Thomas Occleve Addressed to Sir John Oldcastle', *Anglia* V, 9–42

Staley, L. (1994) *Margery Kempe's Dissenting Fictions* (University Park, Pa.: Pennsylvania State University)

Steiner, G. (1975) *After Babel: Aspects of Language and Translation* (Oxford: Oxford University Press)

Stokes, C.S. (1995), 'Thomas Hoccleve's *Mother of God* and *Balade to the Virgin and Christ*: Latin and Anglo-Norman Sources', *MÆv* LXIV, 74–84

Strohm, P. (1992) *Hochon's Arrow: The Social Imagination of Fourteenth-Century Texts* (Princeton, NJ.: Princeton University Press)

— (1998) *England's Empty Throne: Usurpation and the Language of Legitimation, 1399–1422* (New Haven and London: Yale University Press)

— (1999) 'Hoccleve, Lydgate and the Lancastrian Court', in Wallace pp. 640–61

Thornley, E. (1967) 'The Middle English Penitential Lyric and Hoccleve's Autobiographical Poetry', *Neuphilologische Mitteilungen* LXVIII, 295–321

Torti, A. (1991) *The Glass of Form: Mirroring Structures from Chaucer to Skelton* (Cambridge: D.S. Brewer)

Underhill, E. (1911) *Mysticism* (London: Methuen and Co., paperback edition 1960)

Venuti, L. (1995) *The Translator's Invisibility: a History of Translation* (London and New York: Routledge)

Von Nolcken, C. (1993) '"O why ne had I lerned for to die?": *Lerne for to Dye* and the Author's Death in Thomas Hoccleve's *Series*', *Essays in Medieval Studies* 10, 27–51

Wallace, D. (ed.) (1999) *The Cambridge History of Medieval English Literature* (Cambridge: Cambridge University Press)

Ward, H.D.L. and Herbert, J.A. (1883–1910) *Catalogue of Romances in the British Museum* 3 vols. (London: Trustees of the British Museum)

Watson, N. (1995) 'Censorship and Cultural Change in Late-Medieval England: Vernacular Theology, the Oxford Translation Debate, and Arundel's Constitutions of 1409', *Speculum* 70, 822–64

Weitemeier, B. (1996) 'Latin Adaptation and German Translation: the Late Medieval German D-Translation of the *Visiones Georgii* and its Source Text', in Ellis and Tixier pp. 99–119

Westlake, E. (1993) 'Learn to Live and Learn to Die: Suso's *Scite Mori* in Fifteenth-Century England' (Birmingham: Birmingham University Ph.D. thesis)

Wilson, E. (1973) *A Descriptive Index of the English Lyrics in John of Grimestone's Preaching Book*, *Medium Aevum* Monographs (Oxford: Basil Blackwell)

Windeatt, B. (1979) 'The Scribes as Chaucer's Early Critics', *SAC* 1, 119–41.

Wogan-Browne, J., Watson, N., Taylor, A., and Evans, R. (eds) (1999) *The Idea of the Vernacular: An Anthology of Middle English Literary Theory 1280–1520*. Exeter Medieval Texts and Studies. Exeter: University of Exeter Press (co-published with Pennsylvania State University Press).

Woods, M. Currie, and Copeland, R. (1999) 'Classroom and Confession', in Wallace pp. 376–406

Woolf, R. (1968) *The English Religious Lyric in the Middle Ages* (Oxford: Clarendon Press)

Yeager, R.F. (ed.) (1984) *Fifteenth Century Studies* (Hamden, Conn.: Archon Books)